Lecture Notes in Computer Science   7385

Commenced Publication in 1973
Founding and Former Series Editors:
Gerhard Goos, Juris Hartmanis, and Jan van Leeuwen

T0280336

Alastair Donaldson   David Parker (Eds.)

Model Checking Software

19th International Workshop, SPIN 2012
Oxford, UK, July 23-24, 2012
Proceedings

 Springer

Volume Editors

Alastair Donaldson
Imperial College London
Department of Computing
180 Queen's Gate
London SW7 2BZ, UK
E-mail: alastair.donaldson@imperial.ac.uk

David Parker
University of Birmingham
School of Computer Science
Edgbaston
Birmingham B15 2TT, UK
E-mail: d.a.parker@cs.bham.ac.uk

ISSN 0302-9743   e-ISSN 1611-3349
ISBN 978-3-642-31758-3   e-ISBN 978-3-642-31759-0
DOI 10.1007/978-3-642-31759-0
Springer Heidelberg Dordrecht London New York

Library of Congress Control Number: 2012941285

CR Subject Classification (1998): D.2.4-5, D.3, F.3

LNCS Sublibrary: SL 1 – Theoretical Computer Science and General Issues

Typesetting: Camera-ready by author, data conversion by Scientific Publishing Services, Chennai, India

Printed on acid-free paper

Springer is part of Springer Science+Business Media (www.springer.com)

Preface

This volume contains the proceedings of the 19th International SPIN Workshop on Model Checking of Software, held at the University of Oxford, during 23–24 July, 2012. The SPIN workshop series is an annual forum for researchers and practitioners interested in verification of software systems. The traditional focus of SPIN has been on explicit-state model checking techniques, as implemented in SPIN and other tools. While such techniques are still of key interest to the workshop, its scope has broadened over recent years to cover techniques for verification and formal testing of software systems in general.

SPIN 2012 features three invited talks, from Tom Ball, Andrey Rybalchenko and Andreas Zeller. Tom Ball (Microsoft Research) is one of the pioneers of practical software verification, especially through his work on the SLAM project. His talk and associated invited paper (co-authored with colleagues at Microsoft Research) provide an overview of recent advances in SMT solving at Microsoft Research related to fixed points, interpolants, automata and polynomials. Andrey Rybalchenko (TU Munich) is an expert in theories, algorithms and tools for improving the quality of software. One of his major interests, and the topic of his SPIN talk, is automatic synthesis of software verification tools. Andreas Zeller (Saarland University) is well known for his work on analysis of large software systems and their development process, particularly through repository mining techniques. His talk at SPIN was on the challenge of modular verification for legacy systems, using mining to discover specifications automatically.

The workshop also featured an invited tutorial from Cristian Cadar (Imperial College London): "How to Crash Your Code Using Dynamic Symbolic Execution." Cristian is an expert on software testing and bug-finding using dynamic symbolic execution and related techniques, and is one of the authors of the widely used KLEE system. In addition to the tutorial, Cristian contributed an invited paper, "High-Coverage Symbolic Patch Testing," co-authored with Paul Marinescu.

SPIN 2012 received 30 submissions, from which the the Program Committee accepted 11 regular papers and 5 tool demonstration papers. All papers received at least three reviews, with the majority receiving at least four. Program Committee members with conflicts of interest were excluded from all discussions of relevant submissions. The reviewers discussed papers with neither overwhelmingly positive or negative reviews until a consensus was reached. In some of these cases, papers were accepted subject to a shepherding process in which the Chairs ensured that authors revised their papers to incorporate particular changes recommended by reviewers. In all such instances, the authors obliged and the papers were accepted. The editors are extremely grateful to the members of the Program Committee and their subreviewers for working under a tight deadline, and to the authors of the accepted papers for the quick turnaround in producing camera-ready copies.

We are indebted to the members of the SPIN Steering Committee, especially Gerard Holzmann and Stefan Leue, and the Chairs of SPIN 2011, Alex Groce and Madanlal Musuvathi, for their advice related to the organization of this workshop. Thanks also to Gerard Holzmann for designing this year's workshop poster. We are also very grateful to Elizabeth Walsh at the University of Oxford for invaluable assistance with local organization. The submission, review and revision processes, as well as the collation of the workshop proceedings, were all supported by the EasyChair conference management system; we are extremely grateful to the authors and maintainers of EasyChair for this free service. Finally, we offer our sincere thanks to ARM, Codeplay, Microsoft Research and Monoidics, who generously provided financial support to SPIN 2012.

July 2012   Alastair Donaldson
David Parker

Organization

Steering Committee

Dragan Bošnački	Eindhoven University of Technology, The Netherlands
Susanne Graf	CNRS/VERIMAG, France
Gerard Holzmann	NASA/JPL, USA
Stefan Leue	University of Konstanz, Germany
Willem Visser	University of Stellenbosch, South Africa

Program Chairs

Alastair Donaldson	Imperial College London, UK
David Parker	University of Birmingham, UK

Local Organization

Michael Tautschnig	University of Oxford, UK

Program Committee

Christel Baier	University of Dresden, Germany
Dirk Beyer	University of Passau, Germany
Dragan Bošnački	Eindhoven University of Technology, The Netherlands
Alastair Donaldson	Imperial College London, UK
Stefan Edelkamp	TZI University Bremen, Germany
Alex Groce	Oregon State University, USA
Gerard Holzmann	NASA/JPL, USA
Radu Iosif	VERIMAG, CNRS, France
Stefan Leue	University of Konstanz, Germany
Eric Mercer	Brigham Young University, USA
Alice Miller	University of Glasgow, UK
Madanlal Musuvathi	Microsoft Research, Redmond, USA
David Parker	University of Birmingham, UK
Corina Pasareanu	NASA Ames, USA
Doron Peled	Bar Ilan University, Israel
Jaco van de Pol	University of Twente, The Netherlands
Kees Pronk	Delft University of Technology, The Netherlands
Shaz Qadeer	Microsoft Research, Redmond, USA

Alastair Reid   ARM, UK
Tayssir Touili   LIAFA, CNRS, France
Helmut Veith   Vienna University of Technology, Austria
Thomas Wahl   Northeastern University, USA

Subreviewers

Amin Alipour	Florian Leitner-Fischer	Mitra Tabaei Befrouei
Adrian Beer	Carl Leonardsson	Mark Timmer
Axel Belinfante	Stefan Löwe	Oksana Tkachuk
Annu John	Hugo Daniel Macedo	Philipp Wendler
Gijs Kant	Kristin Yvonne Rozier	Anton Wijs
Filip Konecny	Philipp Ruemmer	Chaoqiang Zhang
Igor Konnov	Jiri Simacek	Florian Zuleger
Alfons Laarman	Fu Song	

Sponsors

ARM Ltd.   Codeplay Software Ltd.
Microsoft Research   Monoidics Ltd.

Table of Contents

Beyond First-Order Satisfaction: Fixed Points, Interpolants, Automata and Polynomials

Thomas Ball, Nikolaj Bjørner, Leonardo de Moura,
Kenneth L. McMillan, and Margus Veanes

Microsoft Research, One Microsoft Way, Redmond, WA, 98074, USA
{tball,nbjorner,leonardo,kenmcmil,margus}@microsoft.com

Abstract. In the last decade, advances in satisfiability-modulo-theories (SMT) solvers have powered a new generation of software tools for verification and testing. These tools transform various program analysis problems into the problem of satisfiability of formulas in propositional or first-order logic, where they are discharged by SMT solvers, such as Z3 from Microsoft Research. This paper briefly summarizes four initiatives from Microsoft Research that build upon Z3 and move beyond first-order satisfaction: *Fixed points*—μZ is a scalable, efficient engine for discharging fixed point queries over recursive predicates with logical constraints, integrated in Z3; *Interpolants*—Interpolating Z3 uses Z3's proof generation capability to generate Craig interpolants in the first-order theory of uninterpreted functions, arrays and linear arithmetic; *Automata*—The symbolic automata toolkit lifts classical automata analyses to work modulo symbolic constraints on alphabets; *Polynomials*—a new decision procedure for the existential theory of the reals allows efficient solving of systems of non-linear arithmetic constraints.

1 Introduction

Automated reasoning about logical formulas has a long and rich history. Starting with propositional logic, we have seen great advances in data structures and algorithms such as binary decision diagrams [5] and satisfiability solvers [23], which have powered finite-state symbolic model checking [20], bounded model checking [1], and symbolic execution [6]. Satisfiability-modulo theories (SMT) solvers [25], such as Z3 from Microsoft Research (MSR) [10], extend the power of SAT solvers to a variety of first-order theories, such as linear arithmetic, algebraic data types, arrays, and quantifiers. Z3 powers many software tools, ranging from tools for formal design (FORMULA [17]) and program verification (Boogie [4], Daphny [19], VCC [11], F* [27]), to program analysis (HAVOC [2], SLAM [3], Yogi [26]) and program testing (Pex, SAGE [12]).

So, what's beyond first-order satisfiability and SMT solvers such as Z3?

First, there are queries other than satisfiability that programmers of software tools would like help with:

A. Donaldson and D. Parker (Eds.): SPIN 2012, LNCS 7385, pp. 1–6, 2012.

- *Fixpoints.* μZ is a new engine for computing fixed points over recursive predicates with logical constraints, integrated with Z3 [14]. Developers of program analysis tools can query μZ programmatically or via a Datalog input format to establish facts that hold along all possible program execution paths. (See Section 2).
- *Interpolants.* The automated computation of interpolants has numerous applications, including abstraction refinement and invariant generation. Interpolating Z3 extends Z3 to enable the generation of interpolants for various theories [22]. (See Section 3).

Second, we can consider theories that would be useful to many users but that are traditionally outside the realm of SMT solvers:

- *Automata.* The symbolic automata toolkit lifts classical automata analyses to work modulo symbolic constraints on alphabets, using Z3, enabling the precise analysis of programs that manipulate strings [29]. A distinguishing feature of the toolkit is its use of and operations over symbolic constraints, unlike representations based on classical automata theory that assume a concrete finite alphabet. (See Section 4).
- *Polynomials.* A new decision procedure for the existential theory of the reals allows Z3 to efficiently solve systems of non-linear arithmetic constraints [18]. The applications of this algorithm are many, ranging from hybrid systems to virtual reality environments. (See Section 5).

2   Fixed Points and μZ

In the realm of program analysis and many other domains, the computation of a fixed point, a (least or greatest) solution to a set of mutually recursive equations, is a basic need [8].

How do we get from programs to such equations? In program analysis, we wish to compute a set of facts that holds along all paths from the start of a program to a designated statement (or set of statements). Generally, the facts that hold after execution of a statement s are a function of the facts that hold before execution of s, and can be expressed by a transfer function (or transition relation) f_s. Loops and recursive procedures in programs naturally gives rise to a set of mutually recursive transfer functions.

Additionally, a key part of any analysis framework is the definition of the abstract domain(s) over which the fixed point solution ranges [9]. The representation of the abstract domain and operations on it must be carefully designed for efficiency. Furthermore, there are many domain-independent transformations and optimizations that can be applied to the recursive set of equations to convert them into a form that is more efficiently evaluable. All these requirements can add up to a massive design and engineering challenge for the creators of program analysis tools.

μZ is a scalable, efficient engine for discharging fixed point queries over recursive predicates with logical constraints expressed as rules (Horn clauses), integrated in Z3 [14]. The μZ engine contains numerous optimizations specific to the computation of fixed points and is extensible with new abstract domains. The engine transforms the rules to avoid large intermediate results, applies the classical magic sets transformation to specialize the rules with respect to a query, and carefully plans the order of join operations to minimize time/space overhead.

3   Interpolants

Given a valid implication $P \to Q$, an *interpolant* I is a formula, expressed using the common vocabulary of formulas P and Q, such that $P \to I$ and $I \to Q$.

Interpolants are very useful for the automated refinement of abstractions via counterexamples [13] and generation of invariants [21]. Consider formulas P and Q such that $P \wedge \neg Q$ is unsatisfiable (equivalently, $P \to Q$ is valid). In the context of counterexample-guided abstraction refinement, P represents an underapproximation of the set of states reachable from the initial state of a program C, and formula Q represents a set of good states (that we wish to prove that all executions of C stay inside).

Using an SMT solver, if can show that $P \wedge \neg Q$ is unsatisfiable, then the set of states P does not contain a bad state (a state outside of Q). An interpolating SMT solver allows us to take the proof of unsatisfiability of $P \wedge \neg Q$ and learn from it facts that could help prove the correctness of program C in general (all reachable states of program C are in Q). An interpolant I is weaker than P (since $P \to I$), and so represents more states than P (abstracting P), while staying within the set of good states (since $I \to Q$).

Stated another way, interpolation is a way to derive a generalization about the unbounded behaviors of a system from an analysis of its bounded behaviors, with the goal of finding and inductive invariant that is strong enough to prove a property of the system.

A major difficulty in extracting interpolants from SMT solvers lies in the fact that the proofs generated by efficient solvers such as Z3 may not contain sufficient detail to produce an interpolant. Rather than attempt to directly interpolate the proofs from Z3, *interpolating Z3* uses the proofs as a guide for a secondary and much simpler interpolating prover [22]. The Z3 proofs are translated into a proof calculus that admits interpolation but in which the proofs may contain "gaps" that must be discharged by the secondary interpolating prover. Furthermore, because of the translation, the second prover need not implement all the theories supported by Z3.

4   Symbolic Automata

Finite-state automata (FSA) have many uses in software. FSA are the basis of lexical analysis for compilers, regular expression matching for data processing, string sanitization for web pages, among other uses. Classical algorithms for manipulating and analyzing FSA based on explicit representations can break down as the size of the FSA increases. For example, if the alphabet over which an FSA is defined is very large then the FSA itself may be very large, with a huge number of transitions leaving each state. In such cases, a symbolic representation of the alphabet and transitions can yield substantial reductions in the size of the automata, as transitions can be labelled with symbolic constraints over the alphabet.

The symbolic automata toolkit [29] lifts classical automata analyses to work modulo symbolic constraints on alphabets (using Z3). In practice, these symbolic algorithms outperform classical algorithms, often by orders of magnitude, when alphabets are large [16]. Additionally, symbolic automata can work with infinite alphabets, leveraging Z3 theories such as arithmetic, algebraic data-types, and arrays. Symbolic automata have been used in concolic testing of applications that make use of regular expression matching in predicates [24].

The toolkit also allows the definition of symbolic finite-state transducers, a form of input/output automata [30]. Such transducers are very useful for analyzing and synthesizing string manipulating functions, with applications to the correctness of string sanitization routines [15].

5   Polynomials

When Tarski showed that the theory of real closed fields admits elimination of quantifiers, it became clear that a general decision procedure for solving polynomial constraints was possible [28]. Unfortunately, Tarski's procedure has non-elementary complexity, making it totally impractical. The first relatively effective method of quantifier elimination over the reals, cylindrical algebraic decomposition (CAD) [7], has a doubly-exponential worst-case behavior that remains a serious impediment to its use.

A new decision procedure for the existential theory of the reals (R) [18] performs a backtracking search for a model in R, where the backtracking is powered by a novel conflict resolution procedure. The approach takes advantage of the fact that each conflict encountered during the search is based on the current assignment and generally involves only a few constraints, a conflicting core. When in conflict, the new algorithm algorithm projects only the polynomials from the conflicting core (using CAD) and explains the conflict in terms of the current model.

A new solver called *nlsat*, incorporated in Z3, has been experimentally compared to three classes of solvers that perform reasonably well on fragments of nonlinear arithmetic: (1) the SMT solvers Z3, CVC3, and MiniSmt; (2) the quantifier elimination based solvers Mathematica 8.0, QEPCAD, Redlog-CAD and Redlog-VTS; (3) the interval based iSAT solver. The main take away from these experiments is that nlsat is consistently one of the best solvers for a variety of sets of benchmarks: nlsat manages to solve the most problems and in much faster time.

References

1. Biere, A., Cimatti, A., Clarke, E., Zhu, Y.: Symbolic Model Checking without BDDs. In: TACAS 1999. LNCS, vol. 1579, pp. 193–207. Springer, Heidelberg (1999)
2. Ball, T., Hackett, B., Lahiri, S.K., Qadeer, S., Vanegue, J.: Towards Scalable Modular Checking of User-Defined Properties. In: Leavens, G.T., O'Hearn, P., Rajamani, S.K. (eds.) VSTTE 2010. LNCS, vol. 6217, pp. 1–24. Springer, Heidelberg (2010)
3. Ball, T., Levin, V., Rajamani, S.K.: A decade of software model checking with SLAM. Commun. ACM 54(7), 68–76 (2011)
4. Barnett, M., Chang, B.-Y.E., DeLine, R., Jacobs, B., Leino, K.R.M.: Boogie: A Modular Reusable Verifier for Object-Oriented Programs. In: de Boer, F.S., Bonsangue, M.M., Graf, S., de Roever, W.-P. (eds.) FMCO 2005. LNCS, vol. 4111, pp. 364–387. Springer, Heidelberg (2006)
5. Bryant, R.E.: Graph-based algorithms for boolean function manipulation. IEEE Transactions on Computers C-35(8), 677–691 (1986)
6. Cadar, C., Ganesh, V., Pawlowski, P.M., Dill, D.L., Engler, D.R.: EXE: automatically generating inputs of death. In: ACM Conference on Computer and Communications Security, pp. 322–335 (2006)
7. Collins, G.E.: Quantifier Elimination for Real Closed Fields by Cylindrical Algebraic Decomposition. In: Brakhage, H. (ed.) GI-Fachtagung 1975. LNCS, vol. 33, pp. 134–183. Springer, Heidelberg (1975)
8. Cousot, P., Cousot, R.: Abstract interpretation: a unified lattice model for the static analysis of programs by construction or approximation of fixpoints. In: POPL 1977: Principles of Programming Languages, pp. 238–252. ACM (1977)
9. Cousot, P., Halbwachs, N.: Automatic discovery of linear restraints among variables of a program. In: POPL 1978: Principles of Programming Languages, pp. 84–96. ACM (1978)
10. de Moura, L., Bjørner, N.: Z3: An Efficient SMT Solver. In: Ramakrishnan, C.R., Rehof, J. (eds.) TACAS 2008. LNCS, vol. 4963, pp. 337–340. Springer, Heidelberg (2008)
11. Cohen, E., Dahlweid, M., Hillebrand, M., Leinenbach, D., Moskal, M., Santen, T., Schulte, W., Tobies, S.: VCC: A Practical System for Verifying Concurrent C. In: Berghofer, S., Nipkow, T., Urban, C., Wenzel, M. (eds.) TPHOLs 2009. LNCS, vol. 5674, pp. 23–42. Springer, Heidelberg (2009)
12. Godefroid, P., de Halleux, J., Nori, A.V., Rajamani, S.K., Schulte, W., Tillmann, N., Levin, M.Y.: Automating Software Testing Using Program Analysis. IEEE Software 25(5), 30–37 (2008)
13. Henzinger, T.A., Jhala, R., Majumdar, R., McMillan, K.L.: Abstractions from proofs. In: POPL, pp. 232–244 (2004)
14. Hoder, K., Bjørner, N., de Moura, L.: μZ– An Efficient Engine for Fixed Points with Constraints. In: Gopalakrishnan, G., Qadeer, S. (eds.) CAV 2011. LNCS, vol. 6806, pp. 457–462. Springer, Heidelberg (2011)
15. Hooimeijer, P., Livshits, B., Molnar, D., Saxena, P., Veanes, M.: Fast and precise sanitizer analysis with BEK. In: USENIX Security Symposium (2011)
16. Hooimeijer, P., Veanes, M.: An Evaluation of Automata Algorithms for String Analysis. In: Jhala, R., Schmidt, D. (eds.) VMCAI 2011. LNCS, vol. 6538, pp. 248–262. Springer, Heidelberg (2011)
17. Jackson, E.K., Schulte, W.: Model Generation for Horn Logic with Stratified Negation. In: Suzuki, K., Higashino, T., Yasumoto, K., El-Fakih, K. (eds.) FORTE 2008. LNCS, vol. 5048, pp. 1–20. Springer, Heidelberg (2008)

18. Jovanovic, D., de Moura, L.: Solving Non-Linear Arithmetic. In: IJCAR (to appear, 2012)
19. Leino, K.R.M.: Dafny: An Automatic Program Verifier for Functional Correctness. In: Clarke, E.M., Voronkov, A. (eds.) LPAR-16 2010. LNCS, vol. 6355, pp. 348–370. Springer, Heidelberg (2010)
20. McMillan, K.L.: Symbolic Model Checking: An Approach to the State-Explosion Problem. Kluwer Academic Publishers (1993)
21. McMillan, K.L.: Quantified Invariant Generation Using an Interpolating Saturation Prover. In: Ramakrishnan, C.R., Rehof, J. (eds.) TACAS 2008. LNCS, vol. 4963, pp. 413–427. Springer, Heidelberg (2008)
22. McMillan, K.L.: Interpolants from Z3 proofs. In: FMCAD, pp. 19–27 (2011)
23. Moskewicz, M.W., Madigan, C.F., Zhao, Y., Zhang, L., Malik, S.: Chaff: Engineering an efficient SAT solver. In: DAC, pp. 530–535. ACM (2001)
24. Veanes, M., de Halleux, P., Tillmann, N.: Rex: Symbolic regular expression explorer. In: ICST, pp. 498–507. IEEE Computer Society (2010)
25. Nieuwenhuis, R., Oliveras, A., Tinelli, C.: Solving SAT and SAT Modulo Theories: From an abstract Davis–Putnam–Logemann–Loveland procedure to DPLL(T). J. ACM 53(6) (2006)
26. Nori, A.V., Rajamani, S.K., Tetali, S., Thakur, A.V.: The YOGI Project: Software Property Checking via Static Analysis and Testing. In: Kowalewski, S., Philippou, A. (eds.) TACAS 2009. LNCS, vol. 5505, pp. 178–181. Springer, Heidelberg (2009)
27. Strub, P.-Y., Swamy, N., Fournet, C., Chen, J.: Self-certification: bootstrapping certified typecheckers in F* with coq. In: POPL, pp. 571–584 (2012)
28. Tarski, A.: A decision method for elementary algebra and geometry. Technical Report R-109, Rand Corporation (1951)
29. Veanes, M., Bjørner, N.: Symbolic Automata: The Toolkit. In: Flanagan, C., König, B. (eds.) TACAS 2012. LNCS, vol. 7214, pp. 472–477. Springer, Heidelberg (2012)
30. Veanes, M., Hooimeijer, P., Livshits, B., Molnar, D., Bjørner, N.: Symbolic finite state transducers: algorithms and applications. In: POPL, pp. 137–150 (2012)

High-Coverage Symbolic Patch Testing

Paul Dan Marinescu and Cristian Cadar

Department of Computing, Imperial College London
London, United Kingdom
{p.marinescu,c.cadar}@imperial.ac.uk

Abstract. Software patches are often poorly tested, with many of them containing faults that affect the correct operation of the software. In this paper, we propose an automatic technique based on symbolic execution, that aims to increase the quality of patches by providing developers with an automated mechanism for generating a set of comprehensive test cases covering all or most of the statements in a software patch.

Our preliminary evaluation of this technique has shown promising results on several real patches from the `lighttpd` web server.

1 Introduction

Writing correct software patches is a difficult task because developers have to ensure that new code not only executes correctly in itself but also interoperates flawlessly with already existing code, often written by other developers. That is, patches have to produce the expected behavioral changes without interfering with existing correct behavior, which is difficult to accomplish without thoroughly testing the patch. As a result, patches have a high rate of introducing failures [20,31,33]; for example, a recent study of software updates in commercial and open-source operating systems has shown that at least 14.8% to 25% of fixes are incorrect and have affected end-users [31].

Poor testing of patch code is therefore one of the main reasons for the high number of incorrect software updates. Most projects contain large amounts of untested code, and even those that come with regressions suites achieving relatively high patch coverage only test each statement on a limited number of paths and input values.

In this paper, we propose a practical technique that aims to improve the quality of software updates by providing an automatic way to generate test suites that achieve high coverage of software patches. Our approach is based on dynamic symbolic execution, a technique that has gathered a lot of attention recently, due to its ability to automatically generate complex test cases and find deep errors in the code under test.

In our approach, we enhance symbolic execution with the ability to focus on the lines of code affected by a patch. This is accomplished in two ways: first, we implement a new exploration strategy that prioritizes execution paths based on their distance from the patch, and has the ability to revert to an early state

A. Donaldson and D. Parker (Eds.): SPIN 2012, LNCS 7385, pp. 7–21, 2012.

when the patch cannot be reached under the current path condition. Second, we make use of existing concrete runs in order to quickly find program paths that reach, or are close to reaching, the patch. This latter enhancement is based on the observation that software developers sometimes accompany submitted patches with a test case that partially exercises the new code, and this test case could be easily used as a starting point for the symbolic exploration.

We envision a system in which program patches are comprehensively tested at the press of a button. For example, our approach could be embedded into a continuous integration system so that each update would trigger the generation of a set of test cases covering all or most of the statements in the patch being submitted.

The rest of the paper is structured as follows: Section 2 gives a high-level overview of our approach, while Section 3 presents our technique in more detail. Then, Section 4 discusses the most important implementation choices that we made, and Section 5 presents our preliminary results. Finally, we conclude with a discussion on related work in Section 6 and future work in Section 7.

2   Overview

The standard approach for ensuring that software updates do not introduce bugs is to enhance the program's regression suite with tests that cover the newly added code. The tests are either added in the same revision with, or shortly after, the patch; or, following agile development methods, before the patch is even written [2]. The technique is powerful because the tests encode developer knowledge about the program structure and past bugs, but requires discipline and manual effort to write the tests.

Symbolic execution-based testing, on the other hand, is an automatic technique that can systematically explore paths through a program, enabling high coverage test generation without manual effort. However, the technique inherently suffers from *path explosion*, the roughly exponential increase in number of execution paths through a program relative to the program size.

In this paper, we propose an approach that adapts symbolic execution to perform high-coverage regression testing. Our approach is motivated by the following two insights:

1. Testing patches requires exhaustive exploration of patch code but not of the entire program. The fact that patches are most of the time orders of magnitude smaller than the entire code base can be exploited to significantly improve testing scalability.
2. Developer regression tests usually execute the patch partially but do not cover all statements and corner cases. Therefore, we can effectively use them as a starting point for symbolic exploration, which then drives program execution towards uncovered code.

Our approach relies on prioritizing paths based on their distance from the patch code and on their compatibility with the patch context requirements, i.e. the conditions which have to hold in order for execution to flow towards the patch code. In addition, the approach leverages existing regressions tests to *seed* symbolic execution. The main contributions of our approach are:

1. A novel dynamic technique for guiding symbolic execution towards instructions of interest;
2. A prototype implementation of our technique based on the KLEE symbolic execution engine [6] and the ZESTI testing tool [19];
3. A case study of the application of our technique to real patches from the lighttpd[1] web server.

3 Design

The main goal of our technique is to construct program inputs that execute the uncovered parts of a patch. For the purpose of this presentation, we use line coverage as the coverage metric, but the technique can be easily adapted to other metrics as well. For simplicity of presentation, we consider that inputs are constructed for one instruction—*the target*—at a time. One can then simply apply the algorithm in turn to each uncovered instruction to cover the entire patch.

Synthesizing inputs which cover a target is an essential problem in automated test generation and debugging [1, 16, 27, 29, 30, 32]. While we borrow ideas from the state of the art in these areas, and combine symbolic execution, static analysis and various heuristics, our approach differs by treating the task as an optimization problem with the goal of exploring paths that minimize the estimated distance to the target. Given a suitable distance metric (which we discuss at the end of this section), a solution is found when minimizing the distance to zero.

Our patch discovery technique uses an iterative process, starting from an existing program input—*the seed*—obtained from the program test suite, standard symbolic execution, or a random input. For best results, this input should exercise instructions near the target. Intuitively, the approach attempts to steer execution off the path exercised by the seed input towards the target, guided by the estimated distance to it.

We begin by executing the program on the seed input, and remembering all branch points that depend on symbolic input, together with the symbolic path condition collected up to that point.[2] We refer to these branch points as *symbolic branch points*.

Then, at each iteration, we select the symbolic branch point whose unexplored side S is closest to the target (according to the estimated distance) and attempt to explore this side. If the current path condition allows S to be reached, we eagerly explore it, in what we call a *greedy exploration step*. Otherwise, if S is

---

[1] http://www.lighttpd.net/

[2] More details on how this process works can be found in [19].

```
1   void log(char input) {
2       int file = open("access.log", O_WRONLY|O_APPEND);
3       if (input >= ' ' && input <= '~') { // printable characters
4           write(file, &input, 1);
5       } else {
6           char escinput = escape(input);
7           write(file, &escinput, 1);
8       }
9       close(file);
10  }
```

Fig. 1. Example showcasing the greedy exploration step. Lines 5–8 represent the patch. Error handling code ommited for brevity.

```
1   if (0 == strcmp(requestVerb, "GET")) { ... }
2       . . .
3   for (char* p = requestVerb; *p; p++) {
4       log(*p);
```

Fig. 2. Example showcasing the execution regeneration step. As in Figure 1, the patch is on lines 5–8 of the log function.

infeasible under the current path condition, we enter the *informed path regeneration* mode, in which we travel back to the last symbolic branch point that made S unreachable and take there the other side of the branch. At this point, our current strategy is to explore the program path that preserves as much as possible from the initial path condition, in an attempt to quickly reach the desired branch side S. However, in future work, we plan to improve our technique by exploring multiple paths to S.

To illustrate our algorithm, we use the code snippet in Figure 1, which is based on a patch introduced in revision 2660 of lighttpd. The log function takes a single character as input and writes it into a text file. The function was initially always writing the character unmodified, but was patched in order to escape sensitive characters that could corrupt the log file. However, the program was tested only with printable character inputs and thus the patch was never executed. After seeding the analysis with such an input containing only printable characters, our technique determines that the else side of the symbolic branch point at line 3 is the unexplored branch side closest to the patch (in fact, it is part of the patch), and goes on to explore it (in a *greedy exploration step*) by negating the condition on line 3.

To understand when *informed path regeneration* is necessary, consider the example in Figure 2, in which the log function of Figure 1 is called for each character of the requestVerb string. Assuming that the seed request contains the GET verb, the comparison at line 1 constrains this input to the value GET for the remainder of the execution. Changing any of the characters in the requestVerb is impossible after this point because it would create an inconsistent execution, and thus on this path we cannot follow the `else` side of the branch in the `log` function.

Instead, our *informed path regeneration* step travels back just before the execution of the symbolic branch point that introduced the constraint that makes the patch unreachable, and then explores the other side of that branch point. In our example, that symbolic branch point is the one at which `requestVerb[2]` was constrained to be 'T', and thus our technique takes here the other side of the branch, in which `requestVerb[2]` is constrained to be different from 'T'. With this updated path condition, execution reaches again line 3 of the `log` function, where execution is allowed to take the `else` path and thus cover the patch.

We end this section with a discussion of our distance estimation function for the interested reader.

Our technique uses a context-sensitive, path-insensitive static analysis [21] to compute an approximation of the actual distance between two instructions. The distance is then further refined at runtime using callstack information. This analysis is used by KLEE itself to implement the search heuristic that minimizes the distance to an uncovered instruction, and works as follows. At the intra-procedural level, we define the distance between two instructions A and B contained in basic blocks BB_A, respectively BB_B as the minimum distance between BB_A and BB_B in the program control flow graph (CFG). Extending this definition to the inter-procedural level is not immediate; while edges can be introduced for function call instructions in the inter-procedural CFG, matching them statically with return edges is not trivial.

The solution to this problem involves two steps. First, we statically introduce two edges for each call instruction: one pointing to the called function with an associated weight of zero and another pointing to the instruction immediately following the call with a weight equal to the shortest path from the beginning to the end of the called function. These edges are modelling the two possible situations that can be encountered: the target is found before returning from the call or after. We call the resulting graph the *statically augmented CFG* and the shortest path between two of its nodes, their *static distance*.

Second, we add at runtime the return edges corresponding to the current call stack. While the resulting graph could be used directly to determine the minimum distance using a standard shortest path algorithm, this would add a significant overhead. Instead, we avoid running the full algorithm at runtime by observing that the target can be reached either by taking the shortest path in the statically augmented CFG or by returning from the current function and continuing on the shortest path. The minimum distance to the target is therefore the minimum between these two alternatives: the static distance to the target and the sum between the static distance to the closest return statement plus the distance from the associated call site to the target.

More formally, given the set of program instructions I, a callstack represented as an instruction vector $[I_1, I_2, \ldots, I_n] \in I^n$, the static distance from an instruction to the target $D : I \to \mathbb{N}$, and the static distance from an instruction to the closest return instruction $R : I \to \mathbb{N}$, the context-sensitive minimum distance to the target is recursively defined as:

$$CSD([]) = \infty$$
$$CSD([I_1, I_2, \ldots, I_n]) = min(D(I_n), R(I_n) + CSD([I_1, \ldots, I_{n-1}]))$$

Because functions D and R do not depend on the context, our analysis computes them once per program. The CSD is computed at each iteration of our algorithm for each candidate state, but note that the computation is independent of program size, depending linearly only on the size of the state's callstack.

4   Implementation

Our prototype implementation is built on top of the KLEE symbolic execution engine [6] and inherits the code responsible for combining concrete inputs with symbolic program exploration from ZESTI [19]. The LLVM infrastructure [17] is used to enable integration with KLEE and facilitate the static and dynamic analyses.

Compared to KLEE and ZESTI, our prototype implementation maintains only the last path explored instead of a tree containing all paths explored so far. While this simplifies the implementation, it makes our prototype miss targets which can only be reached via paths in which the distance to the target does not monotonically decrease, e.g., a target that is accessible only after a few iterations through a loop. We did not find such cases in the lighttpd revisions considered, but intend to handle this case in future work.

We also decided to execute at each iteration through our algorithm a batch of instructions, instead of a single one. This offers the advantage of generating more states from which to choose at the next iteration, with only a small time penalty, effectively providing a form of look-ahead. In certain scenarios, this compensates for the underestimation of the distance between two instructions, by permitting the execution of *longer* paths than dictated by the static estimation. Our implementation currently uses batches of 10,000 instructions during both the greedy exploration and the informed path regeneration steps.

5   Experimental Evaluation

We evaluated our protype implementation on the lighttpd web server, an efficient lightweight open-source server used by services such as YouTube and SourceForge. lighttpd is a mature system consisting at revision 2631—the earliest used in our experiments—of 37,517 effective lines of code, as reported by the CLOC[3] line counting tool, and containing a good test suite achieving 64.1% line coverage. We examined in detail three revisions from the last two years, period in which the number of lines of code and the coverage were largely unchanged. We ran all tests on a 64bit Ubuntu 10.04 i5-650 machine with 8GB of RAM.

---

[3] http://cloc.sourceforge.net/

Table 1. Patches examined in our evaluation; total effective lines of code (ELOC), ELOC covered by the regression suite, and ELOC covered by our tool. Revision 2660 contains 6 ELOC of dead code and 3 ELOC inaccessible in the test configuration.

Revision	ELOC	Covered ELOC	
		Regression test	Our tool
2631	20	15 (75%)	20 (100%)
2660	33	9 (27%)	24 (72%)
2747	10	4 (40%)	10 (100%)

In the following, we present three case studies in which we analyze the patches associated with `lighttpd` revisions 2631, 2660 and 2747. Our tool was able to cover all patch code accessible in the server test configuration. In the process, we found dead code in one of the patches, which turned out to be a bug. We reported the bug to the `lighttpd` developers, who promptly fixed it.[4]

The starting input for the analysis was manually chosen; we used the test case added with the patch for revision 2631 and a generic HTTP request from the `core-request.t` tests for the other two revisions, where no specific test existed.

Table 1 presents an overview of the three revisions, along with the number of new or modified effective lines of code (ELOC column). The lines are further placed into two categories: lines covered by the test suite and lines covered by our tool. It can be seen that for revision 2660, nine lines of code are not covered by our tool. Upon manual analysis, we discovered that six are dead code and three are unreachable in the server test configuration. Table 2 presents a summary of the additional code covered by our technique in each of the three revisions, with lines grouped by basic block. For each basic block, we report the number of iterations and the time needed to generate an input which covers it. We generate a total of 13 new inputs which added to the regression suite leave its execution time virtually unchanged at 6.6 seconds.

Revision 2631

Revision 2631 introduced the ability to handle requests for absolute URLs, e.g.:

```
GET http://www.example.com/ HTTP/1.0
```

The patch contains code which handles separately HTTP and HTTPS URLs but none of the existing regression tests contains absolute URLs. Furthermore, the test added with the patch only contains an HTTP request. Our tool successfully derives from it a new request for an HTTPS resource, exercising the previously uncovered code. We reproduce in Figure 3 the relevant part of the code.[5]

---

[4] See `http://redmine.lighttpd.net/issues/1551` for more details.

[5] The patch contains an additional, unrelated line of code not covered by the regression tests—line 566. This line was covered in our experiments by virtue of the modified order in which we sent requests to the server.

Table 2. Number of greedy and path regeneration iterations and time in seconds needed by our tool to generate inputs covering the lines of code not executed by lighttpd's test suite. Lines are grouped by basic block.

Location (line numbers)	Greedy iterations	Path regeneration iterations	Time (seconds)
Revision 2631			
461	3	2	329
462,463,465	3	2	329
566	0	0	131
Revision 2660			
168	1	1	68
176,177	2	1	68
179,180	2	1	68
185,186	2	1	68
188,189	2	1	68
192-197	1	0	55
Revision 2747			
172	1	1	82
173	1	1	82
175,177	1	1	82
202,204	1	1	81

The target code is between lines 461 and 465—the other lines are already covered by the regression tests. We consider line 462 to show how our technique derives an input to cover new code from an existing test suite input. Table 3 presents the five derivation steps performed to transform the seed input http://zzz.example.com/ into https://zz.example.com/, which covers the newly added code. We briefly explain how these steps relate to our algorithm.

(1) Our technique attempts to reach the else statement at line 460 and sets the 7th input character to an arbitrary value different from '/'. The string comparison on line 454 no longer returns 0 and the else branch is reached.
(2) Our technique attempts to satisfy the first part of the condition at line 460 and detects that the 5th input character must be 's'. However, it cannot directly set it to this value because it would create an inconsistent path; the strncmp function call at line 454 already compared this character to ':' and witnessed equality. Therefore, our technique travels just before this comparison and sets the 5th character to 's'.
(3) We continue to modify the input to satisfy the first part of the condition at line 460 and directly sets the 6th input character to ':'.
(4) We continue to modify the input to satisfy the first part of the condition at line 460 and directly sets the 7th input character to '/'.
(5) We continue to modify the input to satisfy the first part of the condition at line 460 and directly sets the 8th input character to '/'.

```
454    if (0 == strncmp(uri, "http://", 7) &&
455        NULL != (nuri = strchr(uri + 7, '/'))) {
456            reqline_host = uri + 7;
457            reqline_hostlen = nuri - reqline_host;
458
459            buffer_copy_string_len(con->request.uri, nuri, proto - nuri - 1);
460    } else if (0 == strncmp(uri, "https://", 8) &&
461        NULL != (nuri = strchr(uri + 8, '/'))) {
462            reqline_host = uri + 8;
463            reqline_hostlen = nuri - reqline_host;
464
465            buffer_copy_string_len(con->request.uri, nuri, proto - nuri - 1);
466    } else {
```

Fig. 3. Part of `lighttpd` revision 2631, which handles absolute request URLs. The patch is represented by lines 456, 457 and 460–465.

Table 3. Input derivation chain for covering the basic block containing target line 462 in `lighttpd` revision 2631. ↻ represents a path regeneration iteration and → represents a greedy iteration.

Step	Input	Type	Condition
	`http://zzz.example.com/`		
(1)	`http:/?zzz.example.com/`	↻	`url[6] != '/'`
(2)	`https/?zzz.example.com/`	↻	`url[4] == 's'`
(3)	`https:?zzz.example.com/`	→	`url[5] == ':'`
(4)	`https:/zzz.example.com/`	→	`url[6] == '/'`
(5)	`https://zz.example.com/`	→	`url[7] == '/'`

The input obtained after step 5 exercises the target line (462) and the algorithm terminates. As it can be seen, the newly found input is similar to the original, and not a pathological case, which we believe developers would prefer to incorporate into the regression suite.

Revision 2660

Revision 2660 was responsible for fixing a bug in the `accesslog` module. This module is responsible for logging all the requests made to the server so that they can be later viewed or processed by web analytics software. The log is maintained as text records, with space-separated fields. Remotely-provided data is quoted to allow automatic parsing of the file; this requires in turn special treatment of all quote (") characters. For example, a request with the referrer set to `foo" "bar"` would create the record:

```
127.0.0.1 - - [18/Apr/2012:02:14:44 +0100] "GET /index.html HTTP/1.0" 200
4348 "foo" "bar" "-"
```

```
165    if (str−>ptr[i] >= '␣' && str−>ptr[i] <= '~') {
166        /* printable chars */
167        buffer_append_string_len(dest, &str−>ptr[i], 1);
168    } else switch (str−>ptr[i]) {
169    case '"':
170        BUFFER_APPEND_STRING_CONST(dest, "\\\"");
171        break;
```

Fig. 4. Part of `lighttpd` revision 2660, which escapes senstive characters before logging them. The patch includes all of the lines shown.

The unpatched code detects a record with ten fields, the last three being `foo`, `bar` and -, while the correct interpretation is a record with nine fields, the last two being `foo" "bar` and -. The fix attempts to treat separately the quote and other control characters by escaping them. Figure 4 shows the relevant part of the patch. Printable characters are handled on line 167, on the `then` branch, while special characters are handled on the `else` branch. However, the `else` branch was not tested because no special characters were used in the regression tests. It turned out that the patch was incorrect because lines 170 and 171 are dead code; the quote character always satisfies the `if` condition on line 165 causing it to be always treated as a regular character. Another piece of dead code was handling the carriage return character, which cannot exist in the input because the request parsing code strips these caracters when breaking the request into lines.

Our tool covered all code accessible in the test server configuration, by generating appropriate HTTP requests. The rest of the code could have been reached by allowing our technique to change the server configuration file.

Revision 2747

Revision 2747 optimizes the `accesslog` module by introducing output buffering; instead of writing characters one by one, they are accumulated in an internal buffer and flushed when one of two events are encountered: a control character is logged or the end of the input is reached. Figure 5 shows the relevant code. As in the previous case, none of the regression tests contains control characters in the logged fields and the code associated with this event is never executed. Our tool successfully synthesizes the inputs needed to cover this code.

6   Related Work

Our technique fits within the paradigms of longitudinal and differential program analysis [22, 28], in which the testing effort is directed toward the parts of a program that have changed from one version to the next, i.e. software patches. In particular, differential symbolic execution [23] introduces a general framework

```
167    for (ptr = start = str->ptr, end = str->ptr + str->used - 1; ptr <
              end; ptr++) {
168         if (*ptr >= '␣' && *ptr <= '~') {
169            /* nothing to change, add later as one block */
170         } else {
171            /* copy previous part */
172            if (start < ptr) {
173                buffer_append_string_len(dest, start, ptr - start);
174            }
175            start = ptr + 1;
176
177            switch (*ptr) {
```

Fig. 5. Part of `lighttpd` revision 2747, which introduces output buffering for the access log. The patch includes all of the lines shown.

for using symbolic execution to compute the behavioral characterization of a program change, and discusses several applications, including regression test generation.

Xu and Rothermel [30] introduced directed test suite augmentation, in which existing test suites are combined with dynamic symbolic execution to execute uncovered branches in a patch. Given an uncovered branch $s_i \to d_i$ and a test case that reaches s_i, the technique uses dynamic symbolic execution to try to generate a test case that executes the branch, and then repeats this process until no more branches can be covered. The technique depends on the availability of tests that reach the source node of an uncovered branch and do not constrain the input to take only the already covered branch, while our approach tries to actively steer execution toward the patch by combining the greedy exploration and the informed path regeneration techniques.

eXpress [27] improves on directed test suite augmentation by pruning CFG branches which provably do not lead to the patch. While eXpress does not depend on having existing test cases that reach the source node of an uncovered branch and its algorithm allows it to prune significant parts of the search space, it does not actively try to steer execution toward the patched code. Statically-directed test generation [1] addresses this issue by guiding symbolic execution using a heuristic which includes the static instruction distance to the target and the size of the target's backward slice reachable from the current point. This heuristic roughly corresponds to our greedy exploration stage, but our approach is more robust due to its path regeneration component.

In addition to dynamic symbolic execution techniques to improve regression testing, the problem of generating inputs that reach a specific program point or execution path has been addressed through various other techniques and in different application scenarios. In the context of answering programmer queries regarding reachability, Ferguson and Korel [11] employ data dependence analysis to find test cases that reach a specified statement. They start with an initial random guess, and then iteratively refine the guess to discover a path likely to hit the desired statement. Gupta et al. [14] use a combination of static analysis and generated test cases to hit a specified path. They define a loss function consisting of "predicate residuals" which roughly measures by "how much" the branch conditions for that path were not satisfied and then use a numerical solver to find test case values that can trigger the given path.

Research on automatic generation of filters based on vulnerability signatures [4, 5, 8, 9] addresses the problem of executing a specific target from a different angle. Given an existing input which exploits a program vulnerability, the goal is to infer the entire class of inputs which have the same behavior. Similarly, generating inputs with the same effect as a crashing input but which do not leak sensitive data, is used in bug reporting to preserve user privacy [7]. In the context of automated debugging, execution synthesis [32] and path optimization [16] attempt to solve a similar problem: generating an input or a path starting from a set of 'waypoints' through which execution has to pass.

While orthogonal to our approach, the software engineering community studied extensively test suite prioritization and selection techniques, e.g. [3,10,18,24]. These techniques are particularly useful for very large projects where running the entire test suite at each change of the system is infeasible (for example in the Windows operating system testing infrastructure [26]). Our approach is different in that it attempts to discover new test inputs but can leverage these techniques to choose the initial seeds.

Also orthogonal to our work, research on test suite augmentation requirements has used the differences between two program versions to derive requirements that test suites have to meet in order to ensure proper patch testing [15, 25]. While we currently only use simple coverage metrics to guide our analysis, it should be possible to combine our approach with such requirements.

A different approach for covering specific program points is to use genetic algorithms [12,29]. Such algorithms usually encode program paths as binary strings, each bit representing the outcome of a branch condition evaluation, and then define a fitness function and crossover and mutation operators operating on this encoding. While such algorithms proved effective when testing several protocols, it is unclear whether this approach yields good results on larger systems. The main concern is that the solution encoding does not naturally lend itself to effective crossover; in particular, given two paths which get close to the target (high fitness), alternating branch decisions from the first path with decisions from the second, does not generally yield a better path. Subsequent experiments [13] directly comparing genetic algorithms with directed search found that the latter generally performs better for this problem.

7   Discussion and Future Work

Motivated by the large number of buggy software patches, we have designed a new technique for patch testing, which successfully synthesized inputs to cover all accessible patch code in three case studies from the lighttpd web server. We defined the code-covering challenge as an optimization problem for which we employed a novel heuristic based on two complementary components: a greedy path exploration, and an informed regeneration stage. The key aspect of our approach is the informed path regeneration stage, a technique that when the greedy exploration stage gets stuck, can derive a modified path which allows the greedy search to make progress.

Given the promising results obtained on our `lighttpd` case study, we plan to validate the algorithm by applying it to more patches across multiple systems. For best results, we also intend to remove all limitations discussed in the paper, in particular the ability to deal with the case when the static distance to the target must temporarily increase in order to reach the patch code.

Another aspect which we wish to address is automation. While our technique currently requires the manual specification of a seed input for each basic block in the patch, it would be desirable to automatically select the most promising input from the set of regression tests. This would be valuable for large patches, especially those touching multiple code areas. To this purpose, we envision leveraging test selection techniques [24]. Furthermore, we plan to improve our prototype by allowing it to automatically infer the patch location from a `diff` file.

Finally, we intend to evaluate the effectiveness of our technique in exercising uncovered program code. While we designed our approach for patch testing, one can immediately apply it to a standalone system version by considering all code not covered by the regression tests to be "patch".

Acknowledgments. We would like to thank the SPIN program committee chairs, Alastair Donaldson and David Parker, for their invitation to write this paper. We would further like to thank Alastair for his valuable comments on the text. This research has been supported by EPSRC through a DTA studentship and the grant EP/J00636X/1.

References

1. Babić, D., Martignoni, L., McCamant, S., Song, D.: Statically-directed dynamic automated test generation. In: Proc. of the International Symposium on Software Testing and Analysis, ISSTA 2011 (July 2011)
2. Beck, K.: Extreme Programming Explained: Embrace Change. Addison Wesley (1999)
3. Binkley, D.: Semantics guided regression test cost reduction. IEEE Transactions on Software Engineering (TSE) 23(8) (1997)
4. Brumley, D., Newsome, J., Song, D., Wang, H., Jha, S.: Towards automatic generation of vulnerability-based signatures. In: Proc. of the IEEE Symposium on Security and Privacy, IEEE S&P 2006 (May 2006)
5. Brumley, D., Wang, H., Jha, S., Song, D.: Creating vulnerability signatures using weakest preconditions. In: Proceedings of the 20th IEEE Computer Security Foundations Symposium, CSF 2007 (July 2007)

6. Cadar, C., Dunbar, D., Engler, D.: KLEE: Unassisted and automatic generation of high-coverage tests for complex systems programs. In: Proc. of the 8th USENIX Symposium on Operating Systems Design and Implementation, OSDI 2008 (December 2008)
7. Castro, M., Costa, M., Martin, J.P.: Better bug reporting with better privacy. In: Proc. of the 14th International Conference on Architectural Support for Programming Languages and Operating Systems, ASPLOS 2009 (March 2009)
8. Costa, M., Castro, M., Zhou, L., Zhang, L., Peinado, M.: Bouncer: securing software by blocking bad input. In: Proc. of the 21st ACM Symposium on Operating Systems Principles, SOSP 2007 (October 2007)
9. Costa, M., Crowcroft, J., Castro, M., Rowstron, A., Zhou, L., Zhang, L., Barham, P.: Vigilante: end-to-end containment of Internet worms. In: Proc. of the 20th ACM Symposium on Operating Systems Principles, SOSP 2005 (October 2005)
10. Elbaum, S., Kallakuri, P., Malishevsky, A.G., Rothermel, G., Kanduri, S.: Understanding the effects of changes on the cost-effectiveness of regression testing techniques. Software Testing Verification and Reliability 12 (2003)
11. Ferguson, R., Korel, B.: The chaining approach for software test data generation. ACM Transactions on Software Engineering Methodology (TOSEM) 5(1), 63–86 (1996)
12. Godefroid, P., Khurshid, S.: Exploring very large state spaces using genetic algorithms. Int. J. Softw. Tools Technol. Transf. 6(2), 117–127 (2004)
13. Godefroid, P., Klarlund, N., Sen, K.: DART: Directed automated random testing. In: Proc. of the Conference on Programing Language Design and Implementation, PLDI 2005 (June 2005)
14. Gupta, N., Mathur, A.P., Soffa, M.L.: Automated test data generation using an iterative relaxation method. In: Proc. of the ACM Symposium on the Foundations of Software Engineering, FSE 1998 (November 1998)
15. Gupta, R., Jean, M., Mary, H., Soffa, L.: Program slicing-based regression testing techniques. Software Testing Verification and Reliability 6, 83–112 (1996)
16. Lal, A., Lim, J., Polishchuk, M., Liblit, B.: Path Optimization in Programs and Its Application to Debugging. In: Sestoft, P. (ed.) ESOP 2006. LNCS, vol. 3924, pp. 246–263. Springer, Heidelberg (2006)
17. Lattner, C., Adve, V.: LLVM: A compilation framework for lifelong program analysis & transformation. In: Proc. of the International Symposium on Code Generation and Optimization, CGO 2004 (March 2004)
18. Li, Z., Harman, M., Hierons, R.M.: Search algorithms for regression test case prioritization. IEEE Transactions on Software Engineering (TSE) 33(4) (2007)
19. Marinescu, P.D., Cadar, C.: make test-zesti: A symbolic execution solution for improving regression testing. In: Proc. of the 34th International Conference on Software Engineering, ICSE 2012 (June 2012)
20. Mockus, A., Weiss, D.M.: Predicting risk of software changes. Bell Labs Technical Journal 5(2), 169–180 (2000)
21. Nielson, F., Nielson, H.R., Hankin, C.: Principles of Program Analysis. Springer Publishing Company, Incorporated (2010)
22. Notkin, D.: Longitudinal program analysis. In: Proceedings of the ACM Workshop on Program Analysis for Software Tools and Engineering, PASTE 2002 (November 2002)
23. Person, S., Dwyer, M.B., Elbaum, S., Păsăreanu, C.S.: Differential symbolic execution. In: Proc. of the ACM Symposium on the Foundations of Software Engineering, FSE 2008 (November 2008)

24. Rothermel, G., Harrold, M.J.: Analyzing regression test selection techniques. IEEE Transactions on Software Engineering (TSE) 22 (1996)
25. Santelices, R., Chittimalli, P.K., Apiwattanapong, T., Orso, A., Harrold, M.J.: Test-suite augmentation for evolving software. In: Proc. of the 23rd IEEE International Conference on Automated Software Engineering, ASE 2008 (September 2008)
26. Srivastava, A., Thiagarajan, J.: Effectively prioritizing tests in development environment. In: Proc. of the International Symposium on Software Testing and Analysis, ISSTA 2002 (July 2002)
27. Taneja, K., Xie, T., Tillmann, N., de Halleux, J.: eXpress: guided path exploration for efficient regression test generation. In: Proc. of the International Symposium on Software Testing and Analysis, ISSTA 2011 (July 2011)
28. Winstead, J., Evans, D.: Towards differential program analysis. In: Workshop on Dynamic Analysis, WODA 2003 (May 2003)
29. Xu, Z., Cohen, M.B., Rothermel, G.: Factors affecting the use of genetic algorithms in test suite augmentation. In: Proc. of the 12th Annual Conference on Genetic and Evolutionary Computation, GECCO 2010 (July 2010)
30. Xu, Z., Rothermel, G.: Directed test suite augmentation. In: Proc. of the 16th Asia-Pacific Software Engineering Conference, ASPEC 2009 (December 2009)
31. Yin, Z., Yuan, D., Zhou, Y., Pasupathy, S., Bairavasundaram, L.: How do fixes become bugs? In: Proc. of the Joint Meeting of the European Software Engineering Conference and the ACM Symposium on the Foundations of Software Engineering, ESEC/FSE 2011 (September 2011)
32. Zamfir, C., Candea, G.: Execution synthesis: A technique for automated software debugging. In: Proc. of the 5th European Conference on Computer Systems, EuroSys 2010 (April 2010)
33. Zeller, A., Hildebrandt, R.: Simplifying and isolating failure-inducing input. IEEE Transactions on Software Engineering (TSE) 28(2), 183–200 (2002)

Towards Automatic Synthesis of Software Verification Tools

Andrey Rybalchenko

Technische Universität München

Software complexity is growing, so is the demand for software verification. Soon, perhaps within a decade, wide deployment of software verification tools will be indispensable or even mandatory to ensure software reliability in a large number of application domains, including but not restricted to safety and security critical systems. To adequately respond to the demand we need to eliminate tedious aspects of software verifier development, while providing support for the accomplishment of creative aspects.

We believe that the next generation of software verifiers will be constructed from logical specifications designed by quality/verification engineers with expertise in the application domain. Given a specification describing a verification method, a corresponding software verifier will be obtained by implementing a frontend that translates software source code into constraints according to the specification and then coupling the frontend with a highly-tuned general-purpose constraint solver, thus eliminating the need for algorithmic implementation efforts from the ground up. I will discuss the necessary methodology, solving algorithms, and tools for building verifiers of the future [1,2].

Joint work with Sergey Grebenshchikov, Nuno Lopes, and Corneliu Popeea.

References

1. Grebenshchikov, S., Gupta, A., Lopes, N.P., Popeea, C., Rybalchenko, A.: HSF(C): A Software Verifier Based on Horn Clauses - (Competition Contribution). In: Flanagan, C., König, B. (eds.) TACAS 2012. LNCS, vol. 7214, pp. 549–551. Springer, Heidelberg (2012)
2. Grebenshchikov, S., Lopes, N.P., Popeea, C., Rybalchenko, A.: Synthesizing software verifiers from proof rules. In: PLDI (2012)

A. Donaldson and D. Parker (Eds.): SPIN 2012, LNCS 7385, p. 22, 2012.
© Springer-Verlag Berlin Heidelberg 2012

Mining Models

Andreas Zeller

Saarland University – Computer Science, Saarbrücken, Germany
zeller@cs.uni-saarland.de

Abstract. Modern Model Checking techniques can easily verify advanced properties in complex software systems. Specifying these models and properties is as hard as ever, though. I present techniques to extract models from legacy systems—models that are precise and complete enough to serve as specifications, and which open the door to modular verification.

Automated validation of software systems has made tremendous progress over the past decade. But all validation, be it static, dynamic, or manual, depends on a *specification* to be validated against. Where shall we get these specifications from? It is easy to specify that a pointer be not null, that a buffer shall not overflow, or that a number may stay within a specific range (and it is hard enough to validate such claims!). But if we want to validate more complex patterns of behavior, we will have to deal with *specifying* these patterns first. This is not so much a technical challenge, but a *social* challenge: We can easily incorporate our validation knowledge into automatic verifiers, which can then be used as black boxes even by laymen. But how shall we teach programmers how to specify behavior—at a time when entire domains like the Web have programming languages designed by amateurs and programs written by amateurs? Our only luck so far is that the exploits are written by amateurs as well.

One attempt to improve the situation is to *mine models* from existing systems—models that are precise and concise enough that they can serve as *specifications* for building, validating, or even synthesizing new systems. This is motivated by two key observation: First, it is easier to read (and possibly extend) a given specification rather than develop one from scratch. Second, the past 40 years of programming have encoded lots of knowledge into existing programs that is in daily usage, and possibly a more trustworthy source than any specification I can write from scratch.

Specification mining is hard, however. First, we need *accurate* approaches: Static approaches suffer from *overapproximation:* they encode more behavior than is actually possible. Dynamic approaches suffer from *underapproximation,* as they can learn only from a finite number of executions. Second, the *language* by which we express specifications needs to be *general,* such that it can be easily understood, yet *specific* for the project at hand, such that we can exploit the abstractions of the domain. Third, there is an unlimited number of properties one can mine; and we need to find out which of these are *relevant* for the functionality—and for the programmer. In this SPIN 2012 invited keynote, I present some solutions for these challenges and highlight the potential of model mining, up to a vision of seamless integration of specification and programming.

Reference

1. Zeller, A.: Specifications for Free. In: Bobaru, M., Havelund, K., Holzmann, G.J., Joshi, R. (eds.) NFM 2011. LNCS, vol. 6617, pp. 2–12. Springer, Heidelberg (2011)

A. Donaldson and D. Parker (Eds.): SPIN 2012, LNCS 7385, p. 23, 2012.
© Springer-Verlag Berlin Heidelberg 2012

Counterexample Explanation by Anomaly Detection

Stefan Leue and Mitra Tabaei Befrouei

Department of Computer and Information Science
University of Konstanz
D-78457 Konstanz, Germany
{Stefan.Leue,Mitra.Tabaei}@uni-konstanz.de

Abstract. Since counterexamples generated by model checking tools are only symptoms of faults in the model, a significant amount of manual work is required in order to locate the fault that is the root cause for the presence of counterexamples in the model. In this paper, we propose an automated method for explaining counterexamples that are symptoms of the occurrence of deadlocks in concurrent systems. Our method is based on an analysis of a set of counterexamples that can be generated by a model checking tool such as SPIN. By comparing the set of counterexamples with the set of correct traces that never deadlock, a number of sequences of actions are extracted that aid the model designer in locating the cause of the occurrence of a deadlock. We first argue that the obvious approach to extract such sequences which is by sequential pattern mining and by contrasting patterns that are typical for the deadlocking counterexample traces but not typical for non-deadlocking traces, fails due to the inherent complexity of the problem. We then propose to extract substrings of specific length that only occur in the set of counterexamples for explaining the occurrence of deadlocks. We use a number of case studies to show the effectiveness of our approach and to compare it with an alternative approach to the counterexample explanation problem.

Keywords: model checking, deadlocks, counterexample explanation, anomaly detection, concurrency bugs.

1 Introduction

Model checking is an established technique for the automated analysis of hardware and software systems. A model checker systematically checks whether a formal model M of the system satisfies a formalized property P [2]. If M contains a fault so that M does not satisfy P, as a symptom of the fault in the model, the model checker generates a counterexample to the satisfaction of P. Given that counterexamples are only symptoms of faults in the model, a significant amount of manual analysis is required in order to locate a fault that constitutes a root cause for the presence of the counterexample in the model. Model designers need to inspect lengthy counterexamples of sometimes up to thousands of events in order to understand the cause of the violation of P by M.

A. Donaldson and D. Parker (Eds.): SPIN 2012, LNCS 7385, pp. 24–42, 2012.

Since this manual inspection is time consuming and error prone, an automatic method for explaining counterexamples that assist model designers in localizing faults in their models is highly desirable.

In this paper we aim at developing an automated method for explaining counterexamples indicating the occurrence of deadlocks in concurrent systems. Our method is based on an analysis of a set of counterexamples that can be generated by a model checking tool such as SPIN [14]. When SPIN explores exhaustively the state space of a model in order to locate all property violating states, it can generate a set of counterexamples. We refer to the set of counterexamples that show how the model violates a property, as the *bad dataset*. With the aid of SPIN, it is also possible to produce a set of execution traces that do not violate the property. We refer to this set of non-violating traces as the *good dataset*.

By examining the differences in the traces of the good and bad datasets, we extract a number of sequences of actions that aid the model designer in locating the cause of the occurrence of a deadlock. Since the extracted sequences of actions are those that are common in the bad dataset but not common in the good dataset, we refer to them as anomalies. In fact, examining the differences between faulty and successful runs is a widely used approach for locating faults in program codes [26]. Lewis' theory of causality and counterfactual reasoning provides justification for this type of fault localization approaches [16].

A widely adopted paradigm for the semantics of concurrent systems is that of an *interleaving*, which gives rise to a nondeterministic choice between activities of the concurrently executing processes [2]. In fact, the interleaving semantics determines in which order the actions of the processes that run concurrently in the system are executed. System designers tend to think sequentially when designing the model of a system. In concurrent systems it is therefore highly probable that they have not foreseen some interleavings that their model encompasses. As a consequence, one of the main sources of failure in concurrent systems is unforeseen interleavings resulting in undesired behavior or unexpected results [2]. The anomalies produced by our method, which are given in the form of sequences of actions, can reveal to the model designer unforeseen interleavings that lead the system to a deadlock state. Deadlocks occur in a concurrent system when processes wait in a circular, non-preemptive fashion for each other and cannot make progress [13]. Proving the absence of deadlocks is one of the first sanity checks undertaken in the analysis of concurrent systems.

Although, in this work we only apply our method on the deadlocking counterexamples, we maintain that it can easily be extended to other types of reachability properties [2]. Our method is not complete which means that it may not be able to hint at some causes for the occurrence of a deadlock. It can mainly explain an occurrence of a deadlock which is due to an unexpected order of execution of actions.

Related Work. There are a number of works on automatically explaining counterexamples using different technical approaches and having different objectives. The work documented in [5] using the notion of *causality* introduced by Halpern and Pearl [12] formally defines a set of causes for the failure of a property on a given counterexample trace. For the explanation of a counterexample, this method deals with what values on the counterexample cause it to falsify the property. In [22] Wang et al. focus on explaining the class of assertion violation failures. Their method uses an efficient weakest precondition algorithm which is executed on a single concrete counterexample in order to extract a minimal set of contradicting word-level predicates. Groce et al. [10] developed a tool called *explain*, which extends the CBMC model checker [15], for assisting users in understanding and isolating errors in ANSI C programs based on Lewis' counterfactual causality reasoning. Given a counterexample, *explain* finds the most similar successful execution based on a *distance metric* on execution traces. The differences (Δ s) between the most successful execution and the counterexample, after being refined by a slicing step, is given to the programmer as an explanation. The distance between executions a and b is measured based on the number of the variables to which a and b assign different values. In contrast to the three methods cited above, our counterexample analysis method does not consider any values that are assigned to variables, instead only the order of execution of actions inside execution traces are taken into account. Therefore, we are able to give explanations to counterexamples in which the violation of a property is due to a specific *order* of execution of actions. Moreover, the other methods are based on an analysis of one single counterexample while in our method for extracting commonalities we use non-singleton sets of counterexamples.

The work by Ball et al. [3] compares a counterexample with a set of similar correct traces in order to extract single program statements that are only executed in the counterexample. These program statements are reported to the user as the suspicious parts of the program code that are likely to be the cause of the violation of the property. In this method, if a counterexample violates a property at some control location c of the program code, then the execution traces that reach to c without violating the property are considered as similar correct traces. The method has been implemented in the context of the *SLAM* project in which a software model checker that automatically verifies temporal safety properties of C programs has been developed [4]. Since this method only considers single program statements, it cannot express counterexamples in which the violation of a property is due to a specific *order* of execution of actions. The criteria they use for finding similar correct traces are similar to those used by the method in [11]. In fact, the method in [11] is most closely related to ours, so we provide a detailed comparison of this method with ours in Sect. 6.

There are a few fault localization techniques based on testing which are analogous to ours and consider the actual order of execution of the statements in the program in order to locate the fault in the program code [18] [6]. The work of [6] had an important influence on our method.

Structure of the Paper. Section 2 presents a detailed example to show how an unforeseen interleaving can cause a deadlock to occur in the model of a concurrent system. Section 3 argues that a sequential pattern mining based approach for extracting sequences that can explain the occurrence of a deadlock will fail due to the inherent complexity of the problem. Section 4 describes our proposed method based on an extraction of substrings of a specific length that only occur in the set of counterexamples for explaining the occurrence of deadlocks. We then present the experimental results in Section 5, followed by a detailed comparison of our method with the work by Groce and Visser [11] in Section 6. Finally Section 7 concludes with a note on future work.

2   A Motivating Example

In this section, using an example case study we illustrate how a deadlock can occur due to the specific order of execution of a set of actions in the model of a concurrent system. The model we use in this example is taken from the BEnchmarks for Explicit Model checkers (BEEM) [20]. It is a Real-time Ethernet protocol named Rether. This protocol is a contention-free token bus protocol for the data-link layer of the ISO protocol stack. Its purpose is to provide guaranteed bandwidth, deterministic and periodic network access to multimedia applications over commodity Ethernet hardware. In order to make the original model taken from [20] smaller and simpler, we have reduced the values of its parameters as follows:

$N = 2$ Number of the nodes
Slots $= 3$ Number of slots (a bandwidth)
RT_slots $= 1$ Maximum number of slots for real-time transmission
                (should be smaller than Slots)

The Promela code of this model consists of three proctypes:

1. The *Bandwidth* proctype, which manages the access of the nodes to the real-time transmission. It allocates and frees the real-time transmission slots upon receiving *reserve* and *release* messages from the nodes.
2. The *Token* proctype, which guarantees deterministic and periodic access to the bandwidth by handing in a token to the nodes in turn.
3. The *Node* proctype, which corresponds to a node in the protocol. It communicates with the *Token* and *Bandwidth* proctypes in order to access the bandwidth slots. In our example, only two instances of this proctype, which are named *Node_0* and *Node_1*, are created at run time.

In Fig. 1, the last 32 events of a counterexample with 72 events which shows how the Rether model goes to a deadlock state are given. The events in this figure are displayed along with the name of the proctypes to which they belong. The events are, in fact, Promela statements [14]. The name of the events are separated by a "." from the name of the proctype to which they belong.

By manual inspection and using knowledge of the functioning of the model we can identify a subsequence of 10 events of the counterexample that can explain the occurrence of the deadlock. These 10 events are highlighted by arrows on the left hand side of the trace in Fig. 1. In order to understand how this subsequence leads the system into a deadlock state we need to inspect the parts of the Promela code of the model which include the statements corresponding to the 10 events identified above. These parts are given in Fig. 2 in which the

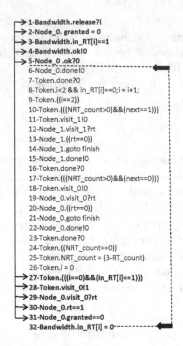

Fig. 1. The last 32 events of a counterexample in the Rether model

statements corresponding to the spotted 10 events are displayed in bold font. The numbers inside parenthesis in front of these statements show the number of the corresponding event from Fig. 1. When events 4 and 5 in Fig. 1, which correspond to line 7 of the *Bandwidth* and line 20 of the *Node_0* proctypes, are executed, line 8 of the *Bandwidth* and line 17 of the *Node_0* proctypes become enabled simultaneously. In the trace from Fig. 1, line 17 of the *Node_0* proctype, which corresponds to event 6 in this figure is chosen for execution. Following the execution of event 30 in Fig. 1, corresponding to line 7 of the *Node_0* proctype, control is transfered to line 10 of this proctype which is an *if* statement. Lines 11 and 12 of this *if* statement are enabled simultaneously since line 12 is a *goto* statement and the guard of line 11, *granted == 0*, is true. The value of *granted* is set to zero at event 2 in Fig. 1 and remains unchanged up to event 30. As Fig. 1 shows, if line 11, which corresponds to event 31 in this figure, is executed, then a deadlock will occur.

One interesting characteristic of the identified subsequence in Fig. 1 is that the 10 events belonging to it do not occur adjacently inside the counterexample. While the first and the last five events occur next to each other, between these two groups of events there is a gap of 21 events. This is due to the non-deterministic scheduling of concurrent events due to the interleaving semantics implemented in SPIN. As we have seen above, although line 8 of the *Bandwidth*

```
proctype Node_0:                              proctype Token:

1    byte rt=0;                               1    byte i=0;
2    byte granted=0;
                                              2    start: if
3    idle: if                                 3    :: i = 0; goto RT_phase;
4    :: visit_0?rt; goto start;  (29)         4    fi;
5    fi;
                                              5    RT_phase: if
6    start: if                                6    :: d_step {i<2 && in_RT[i]==0;i = i+1;} goto RT_phase;
7    :: rt==1; goto RT_action;  (30)          7    :: atomic {i==0 && in_RT[i]==1; (27)
8    :: rt==0; goto NRT_action;               8    visit_0!1;} goto RT_wait;  (28)
9    fi;                                       9    :: atomic {i==1 && in_RT[i]==1;visit_1!1;} goto RT_wait;
                                              10    :: i==2; goto NRT_phase;
10   RT_action: if                           11    fi;
11   :: granted==0; goto error_st; (31)
12   :: goto finish;
13   :: atomic {release!0;
14   granted = 0;} goto wait_ok;  (2)         proctype Bandwidth:
15   fi;
                                              1    idle: if
16   finish: if                               2    :: reserve?i; goto res;
17   :: done!0; goto idle;  (6)               3    :: release?i; goto rel;  (1)
18   fi;                                      4    fi;

19   wait_ok: if                              5    rel: if
20   :: ok?0; goto finish;  (5)               6    :: atomic {in_RT[i]==1;  (3)
21   fi;                                      7    ok!0;  (4)
                                              8    in_RT[i] = 0; (32)
22   error_st:                               9    RT_count = RT_count-1;} goto idle;
23   false;
```

Fig. 2. Parts of the Promela code of the Rether model

proctype was enabled after event 5, due to the non-deterministic execution of concurrent actions its execution is deferred to step 32. Dashed lines and thick arrows on the right hand side of the Fig. 1 illustrate the gap between the position in the trace in which the statement $Bandwidth.in\_RT[i]=0$ becomes enabled, and the position in which it is actually executed.

The identified subsequence in Fig. 1 explaining the deadlock is an example of an unforeseen interleaving. The presumed intention of the model designer is that event 5 and 32 be executed in an atomic step, which means they could not be interleaved with the actions of other proctypes. However, the proctype was implemented in a faulty way, so that its concurrent execution with other proctypes allowed the two mentioned events to be executed as a non-atomic sequence of events, and hence a deadlock occurred.

3   Mining Sequential Patterns for Counterexample Explanation

As we have seen above, in an interleaved trace of concurrent events, the events belonging to a sequence which reveals an unforeseen interleaving do not necessarily occur next to each other. To the contrary, they can occur at an arbitrary, unbounded distance from each other. It therefore seems an obvious choice to use sequence or sequential pattern mining algorithms [1] [8] in order to devise error explaining subsequences of concurrent system executions. However, as we will argue in this section, this at first sight promising tool fails due to the inherent complexity of the problem.

3.1 Sequential Pattern Mining

We first define a subsequence relationship amongst sequences.

Definition 1. *A sequence $\eta = \langle a_0, a_1, a_2, ..., a_m \rangle$ is a subsequence of another sequence $\rho = \langle \alpha_0, \alpha_1, \alpha_2, ..., \alpha_n \rangle$, which is denoted by $\eta \sqsubseteq \rho$, if there exist integers $0 \leq i_0 < i_1 < i_2 < i_3... < i_m \leq n$ where $a_0 = \alpha_{i_0}, a_1 = \alpha_{i_1}, ..., a_m = \alpha_{i_m}$ [17].*

When applying a sequential pattern mining algorithm we consider a dataset of sequences, S, and a user defined threshold to decide whether a subsequence is frequent or not. The support of a sequence α is defined as the number of the sequences of S that α is a subsequence of:

Definition 2. $support_s(\alpha) = |\{s|s \in S \wedge \alpha \sqsubseteq s\}|.$

The sequence α is considered a sequential pattern or a frequent subsequence if its support is above a user defined threshold: $support_s(\alpha) \geq threshold$.

By contrasting the sequential patterns of the bad and the good datasets, we can extract patterns that are only frequent in the bad dataset. These patterns that are only frequent or common in the bad dataset, reveal anomalies, and hence can be indicative to the cause of the occurrence of deadlock,

$$anomalies = sequential\ patterns\ \text{of the bad dataset} \backslash$$
$$sequential\ patterns\ \text{of the good dataset}$$

$$(1)$$

3.2 Challenges in Applying Sequential Pattern Mining Algorithms

In general, it can be shown that the problem of mining sequential patterns from a dataset of sequences is NP-hard. The complete proof is given in [24], [25]. The proof uses the following essential premises and lemmas:

1. In order to show that the *sequential pattern mining* problem is NP-hard, it is sufficient to prove that the *frequent itemsets mining* problem [9], which is the problem of mining frequent *itemsets* from a dataset of *transactions*, is NP-hard. This is because the latter problem can be reduced to the former one. In the frequent itemsets mining problem, transactions are sets of items. An *itemset*, which is also a set of items, is frequent if the number of the transactions of which the itemset is a subset is above a user defined threshold.
2. In the frequent itemsets mining problem, the dataset of transactions can be represented as a *bipartite graph* $G = (U, V, E)$. U and V, which are the two distinct vertex sets of G, correspond to the set of items and the set of transactions, respectively. The edge set $E = \{(u,v)|u \in U \text{ and } v \in V\}$ of G represents all the (item, transaction) pairs.

3. The problem of enumerating all maximal frequent itemsets from a dataset of transactions corresponds to the task of enumerating all maximal *bipartite cliques* in a bipartite graph. A bipartite clique is a complete bipartite subgraph of a bipartite graph.
4. Determining the number of maximal bipartite cliques in a bipartite graph is a *#P-complete* problem [21]. #P-completeness is used to capture the notion of the hardest counting problems, just as the concept of NP-completeness characterizes the hardest decision problems.

The above complexity arguments are based on worst-case complexity considerations [24]. A number of sequential pattern mining algorithms have been developed that have proven to be efficient in practice with respect to various test datasets [1], [23], [19]. However, the datasets that these algorithms have been evaluated on are sparse, with an average sequence length of less than 100. The densest dataset that an efficient sequential pattern mining algorithm, BIDE, can mine with a high support threshold of 90% has an average sequence length of 258 [23].

The characteristics of the bad and the good datasets of a number of Promela modeling case studies of concurrent systems are given in Table 1. In this table, the first four case studies are taken from [20]. The POTS model was developed by us as a sample model with numerous deadlock problems. This model is a non-trivial example of a telephony switch which comprises four concurrently executing proctypes corresponding to two users and two phone handlers. Each user in this model talks to a phone handler for making calls. The phone handlers are communicating with each other in order to switch and route user calls. In Table 1, the column "#seq." gives the number of the sequences in the bad and the good datasets and the columns "avg. seq. len." and "max seq. len." represent average and maximum sequence lengths in these datasets, respectively.

It can be inferred from Table 1 that the bad and the good datasets are highly dense with the average sequence length of more than 1000. We conclude that mining sequential patterns from the dataset of counterexamples generated from typical concurrent system models is intractable due to lengthy sequences and dense datasets.

Table 1. Dataset characteristics

Model	#seq.		avg. seq. len.		max seq. len.	
	bad ds.	good ds.	bad ds.	good ds.	bad ds.	good ds.
Brp	660	25671	5985	10539	5580	10501
Rether	1061	26249	73263	134629	63201	134629
lann	989	20838	5737	12612	6369	12617
gear	614	10174	1994	4512	3837	4547
POTS	4109	11316	2995	7977	6134	6736

4   Counterexample Explanation Method

To address the complexity challenges we encountered in mining sequential patterns from the bad and the good datasets, we abandon the feature of arbitrary distance between the events of a subsequence that we consider to reveal anomalies pointing at the causes for the occurrence of a deadlock. As an approximation we extract sequences that consist of consecutive events. These sequences are, in fact, substrings of the execution traces contained in the good and bad datasets. Even though, as we have seen in the example of Sect. 2, a sequence that explains how a deadlock occurs is not necessarily the substring of a counterexample, it may contain portions which actually occur as substrings of a counterexample. In the example of Sect. 2, the sequences $\langle 1, 2, 3, 4, 5 \rangle$ and $\langle 27, 28, 29, 30, 31 \rangle$, which are portions of the identified subsequence for explaining the occurrence of a deadlock, are substrings of the counterexample. As we will explain in this Section, by extracting substrings from the counterexamples we can reveal parts of the sequences that give hints at why a deadlock occurs.

The basis of our method is that we extract the common substrings of length l from the bad dataset and contrast them with those of the good dataset in order to reveal anomalies that explain the occurrence of deadlocks,

$$anomalies = substrings\ of\ length\ l\ of\ the\ bad\ dataset \backslash$$
$$substrings\ of\ length\ l\ of\ the\ good\ dataset$$

$$(2)$$

The length of the substrings, l, which is the parameter of the method, can take various values. Since substrings of length l can be extracted from a sequence of length n in $O(n)$ time, we avoid scalability problems. As we will see when presenting the experimental evaluation, the small value of $l = 2$ is adequate for explaining counterexamples using a fairly large set of case studies. To further justify this point, consider how a relatively short substring of length two can be indicative for the cause of a deadlock occurrence. In Fig. 3, the counterexample of Fig. 1 is given along with a non-failing trace on the right hand side. The given traces in this figure only differ in the last two events. The events above the horizontal black line are the same both in the counterexample and in the non-failing trace, and only the two events below the line are different. Therefore, the small substring $\langle 30, 31 \rangle$ only occurs in the counterexample. Although $\langle 30, 31 \rangle$ is only a small part of the spotted sequence which explains the occurrence of deadlock, $\langle 1, 2, 3, 4, 5, 27, 28, 29, 30, 31 \rangle$, it can greatly help the model designer by using the knowledge about the functioning of the model to identify the other eight events of this anomalous subsequence in the counterexample. In particular, the substring $\langle 30, 31 \rangle$ shows that the variables *Node_0.rt* and *Node_0.granted* have the values 1 and 0, respectively. The statements which affect the values of these two variables, can be easily found in the counterexample. The value of the variable *Node_0.granted* becomes 0 at step 2 and remains unchanged until the end of the trace. The value 1 of the variable *Node_0.rt* is due to the value 1 of

Fig. 3. Part of a counterexample on the left, its corresponding part from a good trace on the right

the variable $in\_RT[0]$ while the value of this variable should be changed to 0 at the same step that the variable $Node\_0.granted$ gets the value 0.

Mainly based on what we have seen above, we assume that the substrings that only occur in the bad dataset, such as $\langle 30, 31 \rangle$ in the above example, can aid the model designer to find the cause of the deadlock occurrence. The following subsections describe in detail the steps of our method.

4.1   Generation of the Good and the Bad Datasets

For generating the good and the bad datasets, we use the explicit state SPIN model checking tool [14]. The default search algorithm that SPIN uses for the exhaustive exploration of the state space is depth first search. When SPIN locates the first violating state, it stops the search and reports the path from the initial state to the violating state as a counterexample. The presence of one counterexample is sufficient to show that the model does not comply with the specification.

There is also an option in SPIN to not stop the search after locating the first violating state [14]. With this option, SPIN continues the search up to a given depth limit or until all states have been reached in order to locate all property violating states. Our current strategy for generating the bad dataset is to use this option of SPIN in order to explore the complete state space of the model and to detect all the violating states and their corresponding counterexamples. Since the default depth limit in SPIN is 10,000, we increase the depth limit until we can be certain that the complete state space has been explored. Since DFS is used by SPIN for exploring the state space, each violating state is visited once and so only one counterexample per violating state is generated.

Since the bad dataset contains the traces that violate some ϕ, the good dataset should include the traces that satisfy ϕ. Such traces can be generated by producing counterexamples to $\neg\phi$ because a counterexample that shows the violation of the negation of a property actually satisfies that property. This is justified by the following lemma:

Lemma 1. *For an execution π, if π satisfies φ, which is denoted as $\pi \models \varphi$, then it holds that $\pi \models \varphi \Leftrightarrow \pi \not\models \neg\varphi$ [2].*

Since the reachability property we consider in this paper is deadlock-freedom, we need to find a way to formalize the negation of that property in SPIN. Notice that while the absence of deadlock is a safety property, its negation, which claims the presence of deadlocks, is a liveness property. As a consequence, the counterexamples to the presence of deadlocks are *lasso-shaped* infinite traces [14].

We specify the presence of deadlock property in Promela, the modelling language of the SPIN model checker, by using a special state predicate named *timeout*. It becomes true when the system blocks, i.e., when no statement in the model is executed. We then specify the presence of deadlock property as *always eventually there will be a deadlock*, which can be expressed as requiring that always eventually the timeout predicate will become true. SPIN tries to generate a counterexample for this property. The resultant counterexample will be a lasso-shaped infinite trace that never deadlocks. For the generation of the good dataset we also use the SPIN option to not stop the search after generating the first counterexample for this property.

4.2   Contrasting Sequence Sets

Substrings of length l can be extracted from an execution trace by sliding a window of size l over it. Fig. 4 shows the nine possible substrings of length two that can be extracted from a trace of length 10 by sliding a window of size two over it. This set of substrings of length two, in fact, shows which two events occur next to each other in an execution trace.

Definition 3. *Sequence sets can be formally defined as follows: Let $execution(S) = \langle \alpha_1, ..., \alpha_n \rangle$, if the window is l actions wide, the set $P(S, l)$ of observed windows are the substrings of length l of S:*
$P(S, l) = \{w | w \text{ is a substring of } S \wedge |w| = l\}$ [6].

As an example, consider $S = \langle abcabcdc \rangle$ and a window of size $l = 2$ slid over S. The resulting set of sequences of length two, P(S,2), will be: $P(S, 2) = \{ab, bc, ca, cd, dc\}$ [6].

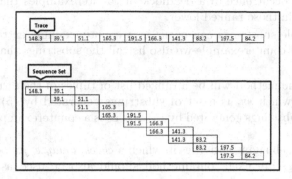

Fig. 4. Original trace with nine extracted short sequences of length two

The two following formulas define how to extract common substrings of length l from the bad and good datasets, respectively.

$$seq\_sets(bad, l) = \bigcup_{1 \leq i \leq n} \{P_i(S_i, l)|S_i \in bad, n = |bad|\} \qquad (3)$$

$$seq\_sets(good, l) = \bigcup_{1 \leq i \leq m} \{P_i(S_i, l)|S_i \in good, m = |good|\} \qquad (4)$$

The result set of the method, which is the set of substrings of length l that only occur in the bad dataset, is generated as follows:

$$anomalies = seq\_sets(bad, l) - seq\_sets(good, l) \qquad (5)$$

The length of the short substrings, l, is the only parameter in computing the result set. We shall discuss the impact of choosing different values for l in the experimental results section.

After generating anomalies by using (5), we take the following steps to facilitate the interpretation of the resulting anomalies for the user.

1. Since each substring can occur in multiple counterexamples, we extract for each substring the counterexample in which it occurs earlier than in other counterexamples. Each substring is only a portion of a sequence that explains the occurrence of a deadlock, so the model designer needs to identify other events of that anomalous sequence in the counterexample in order to understand how a deadlock occurs and consequently to localize the faulty part of the model. Intuitively, we assume that the substrings that occur earlier are closer to the beginning of such anomalous sequences in the counterexamples, and hence the user needs to inspect less events in order to identify them.
2. We rank the substrings based on their location in the extracted counterexamples in the previous step. Those that occur earlier in a counterexample will be ranked higher. It will be easier for the user to locate the sequence that

explains the occurrence of a deadlock in counterexamples that are ranked higher than in those ranked lower.

3. Since multiple substrings can occur in a counterexample extracted in step one, for each counterexample we also list all the substrings that occur in it.

The output of the method will be a ranked list of tuples of the form $\langle\{ss_i|0 \le i \le max\}, ce\rangle$ in which ss_i is a set of substrings generated by (5), max is the number of the substrings generated by (5) and ce is a counterexample containing the ss_is.

Like all other debugging activities in which a *check, analyze, fix* loop is iterated until all the bugs are fixed, our method should also be used as an iterative process.

Evaluation Score. To evaluate the quality of the outputs generated by our method we propose a quantitative measure that enables us to compare different outputs. We define a score based on the amount of the effort that is required for locating a sequence that explains a deadlock occurrence in a counterexample by using the output of our method. Since these sequences directly allow the user to identify the faulty part of the model, as we assumed above, the computed score also reflects the amount of manual effort required for locating the faulty part of the model.

The output of our method consists of a number of substrings, so we first define a score for individual substrings. The score of the output will then be the score of the substring which is ranked first in the output. The score of a substring is defined based on the distance in terms of the number of the events between the location of the substring in a counterexample and the first event of a sequence that explains the occurrence of a deadlock in the same counterexample. This number, in fact, represents the maximum number of events that the user needs to inspect in the counterexample in order to find a sequence that explains the occurrence of a deadlock. Referring to the example of Sect. 2, the identification of such deadlock explaining sequences and their beginnings in the counterexamples is done manually by the user. Therefore, the score of a substring depends on the manually determined beginning of the deadlock explaining sequence. We normalize this distance with respect to the counterexample length.

The following formulas define how a score is computed for an output of the method. In these formulas, *explanatory sequence* refers to a manually determined sequence that explains the occurrence of a deadlock. If $Loc_{ce}(substring)$ and $Loc_{ce}(explanatory\ sequence)$ represent the location of a substring and the location of the start event of an explanatory sequence in a counterexample, respectively, and $|counterexample|$ shows the length of the counterexample, the score of a substring will be:

$$distance = Loc_{ce}(substring) - Loc_{ce}(explanatory\ sequence)$$
$$score_{substring} = 1 - \frac{distance}{|counterexample|} \tag{6}$$

For the substring $\langle 30, 31 \rangle$ in the example of Sect. 2, the score will be $\frac{30}{72}$, where 30 is the number of the events between the location of $\langle 30, 31 \rangle$ and the start of the spotted sequence in the counterexample, and 72 is the length of the counterexample. If substring$_1$ shows the first ranked substring in the output, we define the score of the output as:

$$score_{output} = score_{substring_1} \tag{7}$$

5   Experimental Results

In this section, we present a number of experiments in which we apply our counterexample explanation method to the Promela models of a number of concurrent systems which we took from [20]. The experiments were performed on a 2.67 GHz PC with 8 GB RAM and Windows 7 64-bit operating system. In fact, the experimental results illustrate how the outputs of our method can aid the user to identify the sequences of events in the counterexamples that explain the occurrence of a deadlock. We assume that the identified sequences directly allow the user to identify the faulty part of the model. This assumption is true for all case studies that we used as well as for the example presented in Sect. 2.

In Table 2, the results of applying our method to six case studies when $l = 2$ are given along with the corresponding scores. The name of the corresponding Promela file is given inside parentheses in front of the name of the model. The average running time of the method for these case studies is 52.44 sec. In this table, the last column shows the number of the root causes that can be detected by the model designer with the aid of the generated substrings of length two. As the numbers in this column show, with this method it is possible to detect multiple causes for the occurrence of deadlocks at the same time. Referring to the method of the generation of the bad dataset in Sect. 4.1, the counterexamples in the bad dataset may represent different causes for the occurrence of a deadlock. Therefore, the substrings generated by our method may hint at several causes for the occurrence of a deadlock. For example, as Table 2 shows for the Brp model, the model designer with the aid of the extracted 6 substrings can detect 3 different causes for the occurrence of a deadlock. It is, in fact, up to the user to realize whether the extracted substrings refer to the same fault or multiple faults.

Table 2. Summary of the results of the method

Model	#$l = 2$ substrings	Score	#causes
Brp(brp.3.pm)	6	1	3
Modified Brp	6	1	2
Rether(rether.4.pm)	24	0.27	15
lann(lann.1.pm)	8	0.97	2
gear(gear.1.pm)	21	0.66	14
train-gate(train-gate.1.pm)	27	0.78	9

By increasing the value of parameter l, the number of the generated substrings will also be increased. Consequently, the model designer needs more effort for examining them. In Table 3, the numbers of the generated substrings for $l = 2$ and $l = 3$ for five case studies are given in the columns "#substrings $l = 2$" and "#substrings $l = 3$", respectively. The last column in this table shows the percentage of increase in the number of the generated substrings. We can see in this table that for the last three case studies, the number of the generated substrings of length three is significantly larger than those with length two. Therefore, the substrings of length three increase the amount of manual effort required for inspecting them. From Table 3 we can infer that substrings of length two impose less inspection effort on the model designer when analyzing the counterexamples. As a consequence, the generation of substrings of length three is only done when no substrings of length two can be generated by (5).

Table 3. Comparison of the number of the substrings with $l = 2$ and $l = 3$

Model	#substrings		rel. increase
	$l = 2$	$l = 3$	
Brp(brp.3.pm)	6	6	%0
Rether(rether.4.pm)	24	24	%0
lann(lann.1.pm)	8	29	%262.5
gear(gear.1.pm)	21	35	%66
train-gate(train-gate.1.pm)	29	62	%113.8

In Table 2, the Brp model has the highest score of 1 which means that the first ranked substring in the output coincides with the start of a sequence that explains a deadlock occurrence. Notice that we use the proposed method as part of an iterative debugging process. After each run of the method, aided by the generated substrings, the user will try to remove as many causes of deadlock as possible. In case the model still contains a deadlock after being modified, the user will apply the method again. This procedure can be iterated until all deadlocks in the model have been removed. As an example, after the first iteration on the Brp model the total number of counterexamples was reduced from 660 to 182 due to the removal of the root cause of some deadlock. The results achieved by applying the method to the modified version of the Brp model in the second iteration are given in the second row of Table 2.

6   Comparison with the Work by Groce and Visser

The most closely related work to ours is that of Groce and Visser [11]. It extends Java PathFinder with error explanation facilities. Given a counterexample, their method generates a set of *negatives*, which are multiple variations of that counterexample in which the error occurs, and a set of *positives*, which are variations in which the error does not occur. They analyze the common features of each set and the differences between the sets in order to provide an explanation for the counterexample. The focus of their work is on finite counterexamples demonstrating the violation of safety properties such as assertion violation and deadlock.

To compare our work with theirs, we implemented the algorithm proposed in [11] for the generation of a set of positives for a given counterexample inside the Spinja [7] toolset. The main problem we encountered in applying this algorithm to our case studies was that we could not always generate a non-empty set of positives. This occurred, for instance, in our experiments with the Brp model. Notice that the potential emptiness of the positive set is also mentioned as a potential difficulty in practice in [11]. In our method, on the other hand, we consider the complete set of good traces that can be generated with the aid of SPIN, and hence we cannot encounter the problem of an empty positive set for any case study that does at all reveal a "good" behavior.

The work in [11] proposes three different analyses for explaining counterexamples, namely *transition* analysis, *invariant* analysis and minimal *transformation* analysis between negatives and positives. Among these three analyses, only the third one, which takes the order of execution of actions into account, is similar to our method and can be used for revealing concurrency problems such as unforeseen interleavings. In this analysis, the authors of [11] compare a negative and a positive in order to determine the divergent sections of what they refer to as a state-action path. These divergent sections along with the associated positive and negative form a *transformation*. In Fig. 5, a negative with 64 events along with a positive with 473 events derived for the Rether case study [20], are given. Due to space limitations, only the first 20 events and the last 15 events of these traces are shown in this figure. The first 19 events are identical both in the positive and in the negative, thus the divergent sections start from event 20 in both traces. These divergent sections last until the end of the positive and the negative since they do not share a common portion at the end of their traces. Therefore, the transformation generated by [11] will consist of two traces with 45 and 454 events. However, in our method two substrings of length two, $\langle 369.9, 375.9 \rangle$ and $\langle 375.9, 9.0 \rangle$, as well as the negative itself with 64 events are given to the model designer for further analysis. We conclude that while with the transformation analysis of [11] the model designer needs to inspect traces of 45 and 454 events, in our method the model designer needs to inspect at most 48 events in order to understand how a deadlock occurs. 48 is, in fact, the number of events between the location of $\langle 369.9, 375.9 \rangle$ and the event "2.1" which is the beginning of the sequence that explains the occurrence of the deadlock in the trace. These two locations in the trace are 62 and 15, respectively, and in Fig. 5 they are connected by arrows and straight lines. In conclusion, our method appears, at least for the case study we considered here, to require less effort on behalf of the model designer in order to understand the reason for the occurrence of a deadlock than the equivalent analysis according to the work in [11].

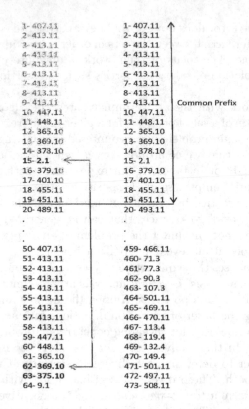

1- 407.11	1- 407.11
2- 413.11	2- 413.11
3- 413.11	3- 413.11
4- 413.11	4- 413.11
5- 413.11	5- 413.11
6- 413.11	6- 413.11
7- 413.11	7- 413.11
8- 413.11	8- 413.11
9- 413.11	9- 413.11 Common Prefix
10- 447.11	10- 447.11
11- 448.11	11- 448.11
12- 365.10	12- 365.10
13- 369.10	13- 369.10
14- 378.10	14- 378.10
15- 2.1	15- 2.1
16- 379.10	16- 379.10
17- 401.10	17- 401.10
18- 455.11	18- 455.11
19- 451.11	19- 451.11
20- 489.11	20- 493.11
.	.
.	.
.	.
50- 407.11	459- 466.11
51- 413.11	460- 71.3
52- 413.11	461- 77.3
53- 413.11	462- 90.3
54- 413.11	463- 107.3
55- 413.11	464- 501.11
56- 413.11	465- 469.11
57- 413.11	466- 470.11
58- 413.11	467- 113.4
59- 447.11	468- 119.4
60- 448.11	469- 132.4
61- 365.10	470- 149.4
62- 369.10	471- 501.11
63- 375.10	472- 497.11
64- 9.1	473- 508.11

Fig. 5. A negative and a positive in the Rether case study

7   Conclusion

We have presented an automated method for the explanation of model checking counterexamples demonstrating the occurrence of deadlocks in concurrent
system models. In particular, we have focussed on deadlock detection using the
SPIN model checker. By comparing a set of counterexamples with a set of correct traces that never deadlock, we extract a number of ordered sequences of
actions that prove to point to the root cause of the deadlock occurrence in the
model. Experimental results showed the effectiveness of our method and discussed measures to reduce the effort of the model designer when localizing the
root cause for the occurrence of a deadlock in the model. We also compared
our work extensively to related work, in particular the approach by Groce and
Visser.

In future work we plan to reduce the computational effort that our method
entails by generating subsets of good and bad traces based on some similarity
measure. We also plan to extend our method to safety properties other than
deadlock.

Finally, we plan to investigate how to apply the proposed method to large models where a complete state space exploration is impossible.

Acknowledgements. The authors wish to acknowledge inspiring discussions on the subject of this paper held with Alberto Lluch Lafuente, Chao Liu and David Lo.

References

1. Agrawal, R., Srikant, R.: Mining sequential patterns. In: 11th International Conference on Data Engineering, ICDE 1995 (1995)
2. Baier, C., Katoen, J.-P.: Principles of Model Checking. The MIT Press, Cambridge (2008)
3. Ball, T., Naik, M., Rajamani, S.K.: From symptom to cause: Localizing errors in counterexample traces. In: Proceedings of the 30th ACM SIGPLAN-SIGACT Symposium on Principles of Programming Languages (2003)
4. Ball, T., Rajamani, S.K.: The SLAM project: Debugging system software via static analysis. In: POPL 2002: Principles of Programming Languages. ACM (2002)
5. Beer, I., Ben-David, S., Chockler, H., Orni, A., Trefler, R.: Explaining Counterexamples Using Causality. In: Bouajjani, A., Maler, O. (eds.) CAV 2009. LNCS, vol. 5643, pp. 94–108. Springer, Heidelberg (2009)
6. Dallmeier, V., Lindig, C., Zeller, A.: Lightweight Defect Localization for Java. In: Gao, X.-X. (ed.) ECOOP 2005. LNCS, vol. 3586, pp. 528–550. Springer, Heidelberg (2005)
7. de Jonge, M., Ruys, T.C.: The SPINJA Model Checker. In: van de Pol, J., Weber, M. (eds.) SPIN 2010. LNCS, vol. 6349, pp. 124–128. Springer, Heidelberg (2010)
8. Dong, G., Pei, J.: Sequence Data Mining. Springer (2007)
9. Goethals, B.: Survey on frequent pattern mining (2003) (manuscript)
10. Groce, A., Chaki, S., Kroening, D., Strichman, O.: Error explanation with distance metrics. In: International Journal on Software Tools for Technology Transfer, STTT (2006)
11. Groce, A., Visser, W.: What Went Wrong: Explaining Counterexamples. In: Ball, T., Rajamani, S.K. (eds.) SPIN 2003. LNCS, vol. 2648, pp. 121–135. Springer, Heidelberg (2003)
12. Halpern, J., Pearl, J.: Causes and explanations: A structural-model approach. part I: Causes. The British Journal for the Philosophy of Science (2005)
13. Holt, R.C.: Some deadlock properties of computer systems. In: ACM Computing Surveys, CSUR (1972)
14. Holzmann, G.J.: The SPIN Model Checker: Primer and Reference Manual. Addision-Wesley (2003)
15. Clarke, E., Kroning, D., Lerda, F.: A Tool for Checking ANSI-C Programs. In: Jensen, K., Podelski, A. (eds.) TACAS 2004. LNCS, vol. 2988, pp. 168–176. Springer, Heidelberg (2004)
16. Lewis, D.: Counterfactuals. Wiley-Blackwell (2001)
17. Lo, D., Khoo, S., Liu, C.: Efficient mining of iterative patterns for software specification discovery. In: Proceedings of the 13th ACM SIGKDD International Conference on Knowledge Discovery and Data Mining (2007)

18. Nessa, S., Abedin, M., Wong, W.E., Khan, L., Qi, Y.: Software Fault Localization Using *N*-gram Analysis. In: Li, Y., Huynh, D.T., Das, S.K., Du, D.-Z. (eds.) WASA 2008. LNCS, vol. 5258, pp. 548–559. Springer, Heidelberg (2008)
19. Pei, J., Han, J., Mortazavi-Asl, B., Pinto, H., Chen, Q., Dayal, U., Hsu, M.: Prefixspan: Mining sequential patterns efficiently by prefix-projected pattern growth. In: 17th International Conference on Data Engineering, ICDE 2001 (2001)
20. Pelanek, R.: Benchmarks for explicit model checkers (2006), http://anna.fi.muni.cz/models
21. Valiant, L.: The Complexity of Computing the Permanent. Theoretical Computer Science (1979)
22. Wang, C., Yang, Z.-J., Ivančić, F., Gupta, A.: Whodunit? Causal Analysis for Counterexamples. In: Graf, S., Zhang, W. (eds.) ATVA 2006. LNCS, vol. 4218, pp. 82–95. Springer, Heidelberg (2006)
23. Wang, J., Han, J.: Bide: Efficient mining of frequent closed sequences. In: 20th International Conference on Data Engineering, ICDE 2004 (2004)
24. Yang, G.: The complexity of mining maximal frequent itemsets and maximal frequent patterns. In: Proceedings of the Tenth ACM SIGKDD International Conference on Knowledge Discovery and Data Mining (2004)
25. Yang, G.: Computational aspects of mining maximal frequent patterns. Theoretical Computer Science 362(1-3), 63–85 (2006)
26. Zeller, A.: Why Programs Fail: A Guide to Systematic Debugging. Morgan Kaufmann, Burlington (2009)

Combining the Sweep-Line Method with the Use of an External-Memory Priority Queue*

Sami Evangelista[1] and Lars Michael Kristensen[2]

[1] LIPN — Laboratoire d'Informatique de l'Université Paris Nord
99, av. J-B Clément, 93430 Villetaneuse, France
sami.evangelista@lipn.univ-paris13.fr
[2] Department of Computer Engineering, Bergen University College, Norway
Lars.Michael.Kristensen@hib.no

Abstract. The sweep-line method is an explicit-state model checking technique that uses a notion of progress to delete states from internal memory during state space exploration and thereby reduce peak memory usage. The sweep-line algorithm relies on the use of a priority queue where the progress value assigned to a state determines the priority of the state. In earlier implementations of the sweep-line method the progress priority queue is kept in internal memory together with the current layer of states being explored. In this paper we investigate a scheme where the current layer is stored in internal memory while the priority queue is stored in external memory. From the perspective of the sweep-line method, we show that this combination can yield a significant reduction in peak memory usage compared to a pure internal memory implementation. On an average of 60 example instances, this combination reduced peak memory usage by a factor of 25 at the cost of an increase in execution time by a factor of 2.5. From the perspective of external memory state space exploration, we demonstrate experimentally that the state deletion performed by the sweep-line method may reduce the I/O overhead induced by duplicate detection compared to a pure external memory state space exploration method.

Keywords: Algorithms and storage methods for explicit-state model checking, Engineering and implementation of software verification tools, External-memory algorithms, Sweep-line method.

1 Introduction

A large collection of explicit state space-based methods for software verification has been developed relying on various paradigms to make the approach feasible in presence of the inherent state explosion problem. Of particular relevance in the context of this paper are methods that delete states from internal memory to free storage resources during state space exploration, and methods that use external memory to increase the storage resources available.

* This work has been supported by an Yggdrasil mobility grant from the Research Council of Norway (RCN) and RCN project 194521 (FORMGRID).

A. Donaldson and D. Parker (Eds.): SPIN 2012, LNCS 7385, pp. 43–61, 2012.

Deleting states from memory during state space exploration to free storage resources is the paradigm underlying state caching [20], the to-store-or-not-store method [6], and the sweep-line method [9]. The basic idea of the sweep-line method is to exploit a notion of *progress* exhibited by many systems. Exploiting progress makes it possible to explore all reachable states while storing only small fragments of the state space in internal memory at a time. This means that the peak memory usage is reduced. Progress in a system can originate from, e.g., phases in a transaction protocol, sequence numbers, control flow, and retransmission counters. The foundation of the sweep-line method has been developed in several papers [9,17,23] and the method has been implemented in the ASAP verification platform [30] and the LoLA tool [27]. The sweep-line method has been applied for the software verification, in particular in the domain of protocols [18,19,21,28]. Algorithms based on *directed model checking* [12] are also related to the sweep-line method in that a value is associated with each state to determine the search order. In the case of directed model checking, this value is used to obtain a heuristic for how close a state is to goal (error) state.

Increasing the resources available for storing the set of visited states is the paradigm underlying external memory model checking algorithms. Checking whether a newly encountered state has already been explored (i.e., performing duplicate detection) then ultimately involves costly I/O operations. Most external memory algorithms are based on the idea of *delayed duplicate detection*: duplicate detections are not interleaved with state explorations but instead grouped together to reduce I/O overhead. From an I/O perspective this replaces multiple "random" accesses by a single file scan. Breadth-first search [10] is a typical exploration algorithm that can be efficiently coupled with that strategy. Another approach to reducing the I/O overhead of duplicate detection is to use partitioning [3] and store the set of currently visited states (and unprocessed states) in a set of files (e.g., one file for each partition). A single partition is then loaded into memory at a time. When no more processing is possible for the currently loaded partition, it is moved to external-memory and another partition is loaded into memory for processing. Both the breadth-first and partitioning approaches will be compared to our new algorithm in this paper. We discuss further the relationship to external-memory directed model checking when presenting the implementation of the new sweep-line algorithm.

The primary contribution of this paper is the idea of combining the sweep-line method with the use of external memory, and to conduct an extensive experimental evaluation based on an implementation in the ASAP platform [30]. Our experimental results show that our approach can be viewed as both an improvement of the sweep-line method (reducing peak memory usage) and of external memory algorithms (reducing I/O overhead). A secondary contribution is the identification and experimental evaluation of an external memory priority queue [7] in the context of explicit state model checking. Our algorithm can also be viewed as a state space partitioning algorithm that uses the progress notion of the sweep-line method to partition the state space, but this partitioning is used internally in the external memory priority queue in contrast to the explicit partitioning approach of [3]. We thus do not have to deal with it explicitly in contrast to other external memory model checking algorithms.

Outline. In Sect. 2, we introduce the required background on the sweep-line method and external memory algorithms, and we present some initial experimental results that made us pursue the combination of the sweep-line method with the use of an external memory priority queue. In Sect. 3 we present the sweep-line algorithm that uses external memory, the data structure used to realise the priority queue in external memory, and we give a theoretical analysis of the I/O complexity of the algorithm. Section 4 presents the results from the experimental evaluation of our algorithm. Finally, in Sect. 5, we sum up the conclusions and discuss future work. The reader is assumed to be familiar with the basic ideas of explicit state space exploration methods.

2   The Sweep-Line Method and Motivation

For the presentation, we assume a universe of system states $\mathcal{S}$, an initial state $s_0 \in \mathcal{S}$, and a successor function $succ : \mathcal{S} \to 2^{\mathcal{S}}$. We want to explore the state space implied by these parameters, i.e., the triple (R, E, s_0) such that $R \subseteq \mathcal{S}$ is the set of *reachable states* and $E \subseteq R \times R$ is the set of *edges* defined by:

$$R = \{s_0\} \cup \{ s \in \mathcal{S} \mid \exists s_1, \ldots, s_n \in \mathcal{S} \text{ with } s = s_n \land \\ \forall i \in \{0, \ldots, n-1\} : s_{i+1} \in succ(s_i)\}$$
$$E = \{(s, s') \in R \times R \mid s' \in succ(s)\}$$

The progress exploited by the sweep-line method is formalised by providing a *progress measure* as defined below.

Definition 1 (Progress Measure). *A **progress measure** is a tuple $\mathcal{P} = (O, \sqsubseteq, \psi)$ such that O is a set of **progress values**, $\sqsubseteq$ is a total order on O, and $\psi : \mathcal{S} \to O$ is a **progress mapping**. $\mathcal{P}$ is **monotonic** if $\forall (s, s') \in E : \psi(s) \sqsubseteq \psi(s')$. Otherwise, P is **non-monotonic*** □

A progress mapping implies a partition of edges upon *progress edges* marking a system step that increase the progress value (i.e., edges (s, s') with $\psi(s) \sqsubset \psi(s')$); *stationary edges* connecting states having the same progress value; and *regress edges* that decrease the progress value (i.e., edges (s, s') with $\psi(s') \sqsubset \psi(s)$).

The progress measure used by the sweep-line method can either be obtained based on a structural analysis of the model or it can be provided by the user/analyst based on knowledge about the modelled system. It is important to note that the sweep-line method can use any mapping from states to progress values. In particular, there is no proof obligation associated with a provided progress measure for the sweep-line method to work.

The operation of the sweep-line method is illustrated in Fig. 1 which depicts a generic snapshot during state space exploration. The progress mapping partitions the state space into *layers* where all states in a given layer shares the same progress values. State space exploration starts from the initial state s_0 and states

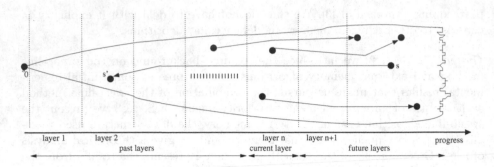

Fig. 1. Snapshot illustrating basic principle of sweep-line state space exploration

are *processed* (i.e., successor states calculated) in a least-progress first-order using a *priority queue* to store states that are still to be processed. At any given moment, the state space being explored is divided into three regions: *past layers* (where all states have been processed), *current layer*, and *future layers*. The heuristic assumption underlying the sweep-line method is that the system makes progress which means that no states in future layers have edges going back to states in the current or past layers. This means that once all states in the current layer n have been processed, then these can be deleted from memory, and the states in layer $n + 1$ can now be processed. This heuristic assumption is indeed valid if the progress measure used is monotonic (which can be checked on-the-fly during the state space exploration). If the progress measure is non-monotonic, i.e., there exists regress edges leading from a state s to a state s' such that the progress value of s is larger than the progress value of s', then the sweep-line method marks s' as *persistent* which means that it can never be deleted again. The sweep-line method then uses multiple explorations (called *sweeps*) of the state space where new persistent states added in the current sweep are used as roots in the subsequent sweep. In case of non-monotonic progress measures, the sweep-line method may therefore explore parts of the state space multiple times. As proved in [23], complete state space coverage and termination is guaranteed.

Peak memory usage is reduced with the sweep-line method compared to conventional state space exploration due to the fact that states in past layers are not stored in memory. The actual peak experienced with the use of the sweep-line method is influenced by the number of states in each layer, the number of states generated in future layers, and the number of persistent states. A heuristic for getting a low peak memory usage is to keep the layers small and also ensure locality so that not too many states are pushed into future layers as these also need to be stored in memory. The initial hypothesis underlying the work presented in this paper was that in many cases the individual layers contains few states, but a substantial number of the states stored in memory are states in future layers that will not be processed until much later in the state space exploration. It would therefore be potentially useful to store the states in future layers in external memory instead of internal memory.

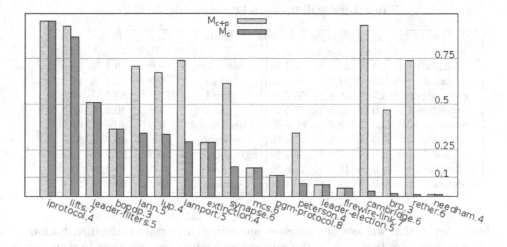

Fig. 2. Measuring memory usage of the sweep-line algorithm

As an initial investigation of this hypothesis, we report below on some statistics we collected using the ASAP [30] verification tool. We ran the sweep-line algorithm on a number of models from the BEEM database [25] and recorded for each run:

- M_{c+p+f} — The peak memory usage during the state space exploration[1].
- M_{c+p} — The peak memory usage when not counting states in future layers.
- M_c — The peak memory usage when not counting states in future layers and persistent states in past layers.

Hence, M_{c+p} is insensitive to the quantity of states in future layers while M_c is also insensitive to the quantity of persistent states found so far. Obviously it holds that $M_{c+p+f} > M_{c+p} > M_c$.

We have plotted in Fig. 2, the values M_{c+p} and M_c for a number of models. Both values are expressed relatively to M_{c+p+f} which is given a value of 1. For instance, for model pgm_protocol.8, we have $M_{c+p} \approx M_c \approx 0.11 \cdot M_{c+p+f}$. Table 1 also gives, for each of these models, the proportion of regress (Reg.), forward (Fwd.) and stationary (Sta.) edges. Figure 2 shows that there is indeed some room for improvement. For example, the state space of model needham.4 has $6,525,019$ states. The progress measure used is very successful in clustering the state space as attested by the fact that the largest layer only contains 420 states. However, the peak memory usage of the algorithm still reaches $1,339,178$ states and since the state space does not have any regress edges, this means that a huge proportion of states memorised by the algorithm are states belonging to

---

[1] Throughout this paper, we use as a memory usage measure the number of states present in memory at a given step rather than actual memory sizes. This is due to implementation issues that prevent us from easily measuring memory usage during a run. Moreover, this measure has the advantage of being implementation independent.

Table 1. Edge distribution for the models of Fig 2

Model	Edges			Model	Edges		
	Reg.	Fwd.	Sta.		Reg.	Fwd.	Sta.
bopdp.3	0.0 %	27.6 %	72.4 %	leader_filters.5	0.0 %	9.1 %	90.9 %
brp.3	3.3 %	38.6 %	58.1 %	lifts.7	0.5 %	2.4 %	97.1 %
cambridge.6	3.5 %	39.8 %	56.7 %	lup.4	17.3 %	82.7 %	0.0 %
extinction.4	0.0 %	22.5 %	77.5 %	mcs.6	0.0 %	40.2 %	59.8 %
firewire_link.7	0.0 %	13.4 %	86.6 %	needham.4	0.0 %	30.5 %	69.5 %
iprotocol.4	0.0 %	2.4 %	97.6 %	peterson.4	1.8 %	46.7 %	51.5 %
lann.5	2.0 %	17.3 %	80.7 %	pgm_protocol.8	0.0 %	27.9 %	72.1 %
lamport.5	2.9 %	19.4 %	77.6 %	rether.6	5.5 %	47.4 %	47.1 %
leader_election.5	0.0 %	29.9 %	70.1 %	synapse.6	14.7 %	60.7 %	24.6 %

future layers that will not be processed immediately. Moreover, the distribution
of edges indicates that even in the extreme case where we only keep in memory
the states of the current layer (i.e., with a peak memory usage of 420 states),
only 30.5% of the edges will generate an I/O since 69.5% of edges connects states
within the same layer and that should be simultaneously present in memory.
Note that this distribution is somehow surprising since we would expect from
the small layer sizes to instead have a large majority of forward edges.

The initial investigations reported above indicated that states stored in future layers can be a main determining factor in terms of peak memory usage
and that storing future layers instead in external memory would be beneficial
(Fig. 2). Furthermore, compared to a pure external memory state space exploration algorithm, the deletion of states in the past layers would potentially be
able to reduce the I/O overhead as there would be fewer states for which duplicate detection needs to be performed (Table 1). The latter is certainly the case
when the progress measure is monotonic, and in case of non-monotonic progress
measure the I/O overhead may be reduced in cases where there are not too many
states being re-explored.

3   Using an External Memory Priority Queue

We introduce in this section a new algorithm that combines the sweep-line
method with the use of external memory. Details are also given on the external
priority queue data structure we use, as this represents a central component of
our algorithm. Moreover, the description of this data structure is required to
have a better insight on the I/O complexity of our algorithm which is examined
in the last part of this section.

3.1   Description of the Algorithm

Algorithm 1 presents a sweep-line algorithm that uses an external priority queue
Q to store future layers and persistent states. The algorithm maintains the following data structures:

- The disk files $\mathcal{AP}$, $\mathcal{P}$, and $\mathcal{NP}$ contain, respectively, the set of All Persistent states found so far; the set of Persistent states discovered by the current sweep; and the set of New Persistent states obtained by as the difference of the two first ones.
- An internal memory hash table $\mathcal{H}$ contains, during a sweep, states of the currently processed layer and a set $\mathcal{U} \subseteq \mathcal{H}$ contains states to be processed by the algorithm. Both are present in internal memory.
- An external memory priority queue $\mathcal{Q}$ stores, during a sweep, states in future layers. This structure also has some internal memory part as described later in this section.

The main procedure alternates between sweeps exploring the state space and detection of new persistent states. A sweep may indeed find new persistent states through the exploration of regress edges and the purpose of procedure *detectNewPersistent* is to determine whether these are actually new or have already been found during previous sweep(s). This set of new persistent states, $\mathcal{NP}$, is computed by removing all persistent states found during previous sweeps ($\mathcal{AP}$) from the set of persistent states discovered during the last sweep ($\mathcal{P}$). It is then inserted into $\mathcal{AP}$ and all its elements put in the priority queue $\mathcal{Q}$ to serve as root states during the next sweep. The difference of the two sets can be efficiently implemented by first loading $\mathcal{P}$ into $\mathcal{H}$, and then reading states from $\mathcal{AP}$ one by one to remove them from the table. If $\mathcal{P}$ is too large to fit in memory an alternative is to first sort the states in $\mathcal{P}$ which can be done efficiently in $\mathcal{O}(N \cdot log_2 N)$ I/O operations [1] and then merge the two files.

An iteration of procedure *sweep* first loads in an internal memory hash table $\mathcal{H}$ all states of $\mathcal{Q}$ sharing the same minimal progress value. These states are also added to $\mathcal{U}$ to be processed by procedure *expandLayer*. Once this procedure has finished, *sweep* can terminate if the priority queue has been emptied or otherwise move to the next layer. Procedure *expandLayer* works as a basic exploration algorithm operating on a queue of unprocessed states $\mathcal{U}$ and storing visited in an hash table $\mathcal{H}$. The only difference is that when a state s' has a different progress value than the one of the state s it is generated from, s' is put in the priority queue $\mathcal{Q}$ if it belongs to a future layer or in the set of persistent set $\mathcal{P}$ if it belongs to a past layer.

3.2   External Priority Queue Data Structure

A priority queue is a data structure that must support two operations: an *insert* operation; and a *deleteMin* operation that removes and returns from a queue the smallest state (i.e., with the smallest progress measure in our case). We use an external-memory data structure called *external array heaps* [7]. Our choice is mainly motivated by the simplicity of this data structure and the fact that it achieves a nearly optimal I/O complexity. External-memory directed model checking also relies on the use of a priority queue, and an external-memory priority queue designed for this context was presented in [22]. The data structure of [22] was not considered appropriate for our purposes as it may store all states

Algorithm 1. A sweep-line algorithm designed for external memory priority queues

1: **procedure** *externalSweep* **is**	19: **procedure** *detectNewPersistent* **is**
2: $\mathcal{AP} := \emptyset$	20: $\mathcal{NP} := \mathcal{P} \setminus \mathcal{AP}$
3: $\mathcal{Q} := \{s_0\}$	21: $\mathcal{AP} := \mathcal{AP} \cup \mathcal{NP}$
4: **while** $\mathcal{Q} \neq \emptyset$ **do**	22: $\mathcal{Q} := \emptyset$
5: *sweep* ()	23: **for** $s \in \mathcal{NP}$ **do**
6: *detectNewPersistent* ()	24: $\mathcal{Q} := \mathcal{Q} \cup \{s\}$
7: **procedure** *sweep* **is**	25: **procedure** *expandLayer* **is**
8: $\mathcal{P} := \emptyset$	26: **while** $\mathcal{U} \neq \emptyset$ **do**
9: **while** $\mathcal{Q} \neq \emptyset$ **do**	27: **pick and delete** s **from** $\mathcal{U}$
10: $\mathcal{H} := \emptyset$	28: **for** $s' \in succ(s)$ **do**
11: $\mathcal{U} := \emptyset$	29: **if** $\psi(s') = \psi(s)$ **then**
12: $\phi := minProgress\,(\mathcal{Q})$	30: **if** $s' \notin \mathcal{H}$ **then**
13: **while** $\phi = minProgress\,(\mathcal{Q})$ **do**	31: $\mathcal{H} := \mathcal{H} \cup \{s'\}$
14: $s := deleteMin\,(\mathcal{Q})$	32: $\mathcal{U} := \mathcal{U} \cup \{s'\}$
15: **if** $s \notin \mathcal{H}$ **then**	33: **else if** $\psi(s') \sqsubset \psi(s)$ **then**
16: $\mathcal{H} := \mathcal{H} \cup \{s'\}$	34: $\mathcal{P} := \mathcal{P} \cup \{s'\}$
17: $\mathcal{U} := \mathcal{U} \cup \{s'\}$	35: **else**
18: *expandLayer* ()	36: $\mathcal{Q} := \mathcal{Q} \cup \{s'\}$

with the same heuristic value (i.e., the progress measure in our case) in a single file. Since the ideal progress measure clusters the state space into many small progress layers, storing each layer in a single file is not desirable.

The external array heaps structure [7] is a two level data structure with smallest states being kept in internal memory and others in external memory. Figure 3 is a graphical representation of its organisation. The internal part can be implemented with any data structure that efficiently supports *insert*, *deleteMin* and *deleteMax* operations. For instance, a balanced binary tree matches these requirements and we will assume this choice hereafter. The internal memory part is split in two parts: one balanced tree $\mathcal{T}_{ins}$ storing states put in the queue via the *insert* operation and one balanced tree $\mathcal{T}_{del}$ used as a buffer to store the last states read from external memory and filled in by the *deleteMin* operation. It is an invariant property that a state stored in external memory cannot be smaller than a state stored in internal memory (in $\mathcal{T}_{ins}$ or $\mathcal{T}_{del}$).

The *insert* operation puts the new state in $\mathcal{T}_{ins}$. If the size of $\mathcal{T}_{ins}$ exceeds a specified threshold denoted T, we remove the B largest states from this tree and write them into a new disk file as described below. The *deleteMin* operation removes and returns the smallest state kept in internal memory in one of the two balanced trees $\mathcal{T}_{ins}$ or $\mathcal{T}_{del}$. If the state is taken from $\mathcal{T}_{del}$ the deletion can then trigger disk accesses as described below.

Let us now describe the organisation of the external memory part of this data structure. It consists of an array of disk files. Each disk file is a sorted list of states, the smallest state first. This array is organised in levels. Each level consists of μ disk files: level 0 contains files $0, \ldots, \mu - 1$, level 1 contains files $\mu, \ldots, 2 \cdot \mu - 1$ and so on. Following an *insert* operation, we may have to write B

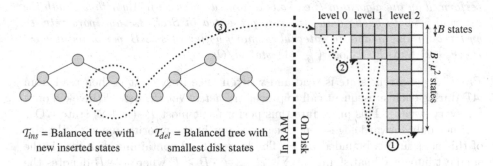

Fig. 3. Organisation of the external memory priority queue with $\mu = 3$. Dashed arrows indicate operations triggered when tree $\mathcal{T}_{ins}$ reaches the bound of T states: merging of the 3 files of level 1 in an available slot of level 2 (op. 1), same operation for level 0 merged into a newly available slot of level 1 (op. 2), and writing of the B largest states of $\mathcal{T}_{ins}$ in the first slot of level 0 (op. 3).

sorted states to a disk file of level 0. If there is no free slot at this level, all files of level 0 are merged resulting in a new sorted list that is written to a disk file of level 1. If level 1 is also full, we first have to merge level 1 into a new disk file of level 2 and so on. Hence, a disk file of level $l \geq 0$ always contains at most $B \cdot \mu^l$ states. The next unprocessed K states (i.e., to be removed from the queue via the *deleteMin* operation) of every file are kept in internal memory in the binary tree $\mathcal{T}_{del}$. If, following a *deleteMin* operation, $\mathcal{T}_{del}$ does not contain anymore any state of a specific disk file, the K next states of this file are read and inserted in $\mathcal{T}_{del}$. The correctness of *deleteMin* stems from the fact that (1) files are sorted and (2) all the smallest unprocessed states stored in external memory are in $\mathcal{T}_{del}$.

The dashed arrow of Fig. 3 describes the operation sequence performed after a state insertion. If the memory tree become full, i.e., contains T states after the insertion, the largest B states must be sorted and written in a disk file associated with slot of level 0. Since this level is full, we first have to merge its slots in a slot of level 1, which for the same reason implies to merge the slots of level 1 in the last slot of level 2 which is free (arrow 1). We can then merge level 0 in the first slot freed by the previous operation (arrow 2) and finally write the B largest states of $\mathcal{T}_{ins}$ in the first slot of level 0 (arrow 3).

This data structure occupies at most $T + K \cdot f$ states in internal memory where f is the maximal number of disk files simultaneously in use (T for $\mathcal{T}_{ins}$ and $K \cdot f$ for $\mathcal{T}_{del}$). Although f is theoretically unbounded, it grows logarithmically, hence it is not a problem in practice.

3.3 I/O complexity

We now examine the I/O complexity of our algorithm.

Theorem 1. *Let F be the number of forward edges, P be the number of persistent states computed by Alg. 1 (i.e., set $\mathcal{AP}$) and w be the number of sweeps* *performed by the algorithm (i.e., calls to procedure sweep). Algorithm 1 with the external priority queue data structure presented in Sect. 3.2 and parametrised by levels of size μ and an internal memory buffer of size B performs at most $P \cdot (w + 2) + w \cdot F \cdot 2 \cdot \log_\mu \left(\frac{F}{B} + 1 \right)$ state I/Os.*

Proof. A persistent state is read and written once in $\mathcal{NP}$. It is then read from $\mathcal{AP}$ during each subsequent call to procedure *detectNewPersistent* (invoked once for every sweep). This procedure thus performs at most $P \cdot (w + 2)$ state I/Os.

Since only forward edges generate states put in the priority queue $\mathcal{Q}$, the size of this structure is bounded by F. The largest level containing disk files is the smallest integer l^m satisfying: $\mu \cdot \sum_{i \in [0..l^m]} \mu^i \cdot B \geq F$ where $\mu^i \cdot B$ denotes the number of states stored in each disk file of level i. Since $\sum_{i \in [0..l^m]} \mu^i = \frac{\mu^{l^m+1}-1}{\mu-1}$, it follows that $\mu \cdot \frac{\mu^{l^m+1}-1}{\mu-1} \geq \frac{F}{B}$ and that $l^m \geq \log_\mu \left(\frac{F}{B} \cdot \frac{\mu-1}{\mu} + 1 \right) - 1$. Now let $l = \log_\mu \left(\frac{F}{B} + 1 \right) - 1 > l^m$. The destination state of a forward edge is written once in a file of level 0 and then due to level merging, it can be moved l times from any level $i \in \{0, \ldots, l-1\}$ to level $i+1$. This implies at most $2 \cdot (l+1)$ I/Os per state. Since each sweep performed by the algorithm can explore all the F forward edges, it follows that the overall number of state I/Os performed to maintain the priority queue is bounded by $w \cdot F \cdot 2 \cdot \log_\mu \left(\frac{F}{B} + 1 \right)$. □

For the sake of comparison, we give in Table 2 the I/O complexity of two other external memory algorithms: BFS^{ext}, the external memory breadth-first search from [10] and PART, a state space partitioning based algorithm from [3]. Using BFS^{ext}, a state will be written once in external memory when first met, and then read once during each of the subsequent duplicate detections. Since the algorithm performs exactly one duplicate detection per BFS level, a state s will be read at most h times where h is the height of the graph, i.e., the number of BFS levels.

An important parameter for the I/O complexity of PART is the number of cross edges implied by the partitioning function mapping states to partitions. A cross edge is an edge linking to states belonging to different partitions. To give a better insight of its complexity we recall that the principle of algorithm PART is to cluster the state space using a partition function and to store each partition in a single disk file. During the exploration, only one partition is loaded in memory

Table 2. Comparison of I/Os bound of three external memory algorithms

Algorithm	Source	State I/Os bound
BFS^{ext}	[10]	$S \cdot (1 + h)$
PART	[3]	$S \cdot (1 + C^{max})$
SL^{ext}	This work	$P \cdot (w + 2) + w \cdot F \cdot 2 \cdot \log_\mu \left(\frac{F}{B} + 1 \right)$

S = states in the graph C^m = max. over all partitions p of cross edges
                                         with a destination in p
F = forward edges P = persistent states computed by Alg. 1
h = height of the graph w = sweeps performed by Alg. 1

at a time. Any cross edge (s, s') visited by the algorithm is eventually followed by the reading of the disk file associated with the partition of s' to check whether s' is a new state or not. With this algorithm, a state will be written once in external memory when first met and then read again each time the partition it is stored in is loaded in memory, hence at most C^m times where C^m is the maximum over all partitions p of cross edges with a destination in p.

In the case of BFS^{ext}, the bound given is usually close to the number of I/Os actually performed while the practical I/O complexity of PART is in general much smaller than the theoretical bound we give here. The proportion of cross edges has nevertheless a large impact on its performance. Similarly, the bound of Algorithm 1 may seem high at first sight since the number of sweeps performed by the algorithm is bounded by the number of regress edges. However, in practice, w is usually low, typically less than 10. This is precisely why the sweep-line method works well in practice for a wide range of models. First because the progress measure provided usually generates few regress edges. Second because it is very seldom that a single sweep identifies only one new persistent state which in turn means that the number of iterations performed is usually not correlated to the number of regress edges. Moreover, the upper bound we give here does not take into account caching effects that might further decrease the amount of disk accesses. This occurs when the destination state s of a forward edge is already present in T_{ins} when the edge is explored. Then the queue is unchanged.

4   Experimental Evaluation

We have implemented the external memory algorithm introduced in Sect. 3 in the ASAP verification platform [30] and experimented with models of the BEEM database [25]. We automatically derived a progress measure based on an off-line analysis of the full state spaces. Our progress measures project the state vector of the system to a subset of its components. This subset is selected in an heuristic way: each progress measure generated has a level ranging from 1 to 6 corresponding to a bound on the proportion of regress edges. At level 1 the progress measure is guaranteed to be monotonic and the proportion increases with the level to reach 20% at level 6.

We compared our external algorithm (denoted SL^{ext}) to the internal memory sweep-line algorithm of [23] (denoted SL) and to the external memory algorithms BFS^{ext} [10] and PART [3] combined with the dynamic partitioning strategy we introduced in previous work [15]. For each model, we first ran SL and SL^{ext}, and then BFS^{ext} and PART giving them the same memory amount that was used by SL^{ext}. The priority queue of SL^{ext} has been parametrised as follows: $\mu = 10$, $T = 20,000$, $B = 10,000$ and $K = 1,000$. We recall that the memory usage of the priority queue data structure is bounded by $T + K \cdot f$ where f is the maximal number of files simultaneously in use. We also experimented with different comparable (wrt. memory usage) parameter configurations but since this had few consequences we selected the configuration above.

The 43 instances we selected all have between 1,000,000 and 50,000,000 states and each instance has from 1 to 6 progress measures. This selection resulted in 125 pairs (model instance, progress measure) analysed. Out of these 125 pairs we only kept those for which SL^{ext} consumed significantly less memory than SL (selected to be 5 times less the consumption of SL) and leave out the other pairs. Keeping instances for which both algorithms consumed a comparable amount of memory would indeed not be relevant to study the performances of SL^{ext} and may moreover lead to a biased analysis. This second filtering resulted in 60 pairs of which we picked out a representative set of 16 instances to be presented in this section. These models are listed in Table 3 together with some experimental results obtained with algorithm SL^{ext}. Peak memory corresponds to the maximal number of states stored in internal memory during the search (regardless of their location). Revisit factor is the number of states visited by algorithm SL^{ext} relative to the number of states in the state space (i.e., column States). Columns Visited gives the number of edges visited by algorithm SL^{ext}. It may then be larger than the number of edges in the state space if the revisit factor is larger than 1. The last three columns give the distribution of these visited edges upon regress, forward and stationary edges.

Comparison of Memory Usage and Disk Access. Figure 4 compares SL^{ext} to SL with respect to peak memory usage and to PART with respect to state I/Os. We deliberately left out data of algorithm BFS^{ext} in Fig. 4 (and Fig. 5). As attested by Table 4, BFS^{ext} was not competitive on these models and including its results in the figures would have reduced their readability. We gave the data

Table 3. Statistics on selected models with experimental results of SL^{ext}

Model	States	Results of SL^{ext}					
		Peak memory	Revisit factor	Visited	Edges Reg.	Fwd.	Sta.
bakery.6	11,845,035	30,119	1.305	52,406,033	11.3 %	51.0%	37.6%
bopdp.7	15,236,725	32,244	2.566	100,779,572	1.0 %	37.6%	61.4%
brp.4	12,068,447	43,892	1.122	27,752,570	1.1 %	40.3%	58.6%
cambridge.6	3,354,295	39,392	12.360	106,771,249	3.5 %	39.8%	56.7%
elevator2.3	7,667,712	30,811	1.172	64,737,253	0.3 %	88.4%	11.2%
extinction.7	20,769,427	85,764	1.215	92,560,320	1.8 %	35.3%	62.9%
firewire_link.5	18,553,032	128,620	1.000	59,782,059	0.0 %	6.9%	93.1%
firewire_tree.5	3,807,023	22,837	1.000	18,226,963	0.2 %	80.8%	19.0%
iprotocol.6	41,387,484	89,480	1.724	239,771,446	3.8 %	22.8%	73.5%
leader_election.5	4,803,952	32,400	1.000	28,064,092	0.5 %	53.5%	46.0%
needham.4	6,525,019	30,420	1.000	22,203,081	0.0 %	30.5%	69.5%
peterson.4	1,119,560	38,338	5.286	19,974,479	1.8 %	46.7%	51.5%
pgm_protocol.10	29,679,589	25,142	1.324	81,985,078	2.5 %	55.7%	41.8%
plc.4	3,763,999	2,447	1.043	6,358,220	1.1 %	11.3%	87.5%
rether.6	5,919,694	31,599	1.496	11,902,295	5.5 %	47.4%	47.1%
synapse.7	10,198,141	203,448	1.333	24,201,729	11.2 %	66.9%	21.9%

observed with SL or PART a reference value of 1. For example, with instance firewire_tree.5, SL^{ext} used 5–6% of the internal memory used by SL and performed 10–12% of the state I/Os performed by PART.

The conclusions we can draw from Fig. 4 are rather positive as the general trend in that SL^{ext} consumes significantly less memory than SL while performing less disk accesses than PART. The comparison of SL and SL^{ext} confirm our initial intuition that SL is sometimes unable to significantly reduce the peak memory usage although the progress measure used efficiently divides the state space upon multiple progress layers. Out of the 16 instances we selected, our algorithm performed a comparable number of I/Os with respect to PART on 2 instances: elevator2.3 and synapse.7. The high proportion of forward edges (that increases disk accesses performed by SL^{ext}) combined with the special shape of their state space (wide and short) which makes them especially suited for PART can explain this difference. The figure indeed attests that the shape of the graph has an impact on the disk accesses performed by the two algorithms. The advantage of SL^{ext} over PART is more significant when the state space is long and narrow, e.g., for instances plc.4 or rether.6. If we only consider disk accesses, the performances of PART degrade for these models while SL^{ext} is insensitive to that parameter. For some models like cambrige.6 and (to a lesser extent) bopdp.7, Table 3 shows that, it is likely that the relatively high amount of state I/Os performed stems from the revisit factor of algorithm SL^{ext} (whereas PART does not revisit states).

Comparison of Execution Times. Figure 5 gives the execution times of algorithms SL, PART and SL^{ext} on the same instances. For each model we gave to the slowest algorithm a reference value of 1, and the execution times of the two other algorithms are expressed relatively to this one. We see a correlation between the disk accesses we previously observed and the execution times of SL^{ext} over PART. For most instances on which SL^{ext} performed significantly less disk accesses it outperformed PART. This is the case for instances brp.4, plc.4 or rether.6. Models firewire_link.5 and firewire_tree.5 go against this trend for reasons explained below. Nevertheless, the conclusions are somewhat disappointing in that the clear advantage of SL^{ext} over PART with respect to disk accesses is less significant when it comes to execution times even though we will see below that SL^{ext} is, on the average, faster than PART. One reason is that SL^{ext} visits more states that PART and the visit of a state implies some non-trivial operations like the computation of enabled events and the generation of successor states. We also profiled the code of some instances, and found out that comparing states according to their progress values — operations that are not performed by PART — contribute to degrade the relative performances of SL^{ext}. This operation is performed not only during state exploration but also during the merging of files operated for maintaining the priority queue. This explains the divergence between disk accesses and execution times for models firewire_link.5 and firewire_tree.5. On these two models, internal memory operations are the most time consuming operations and disk accesses play a lesser role.

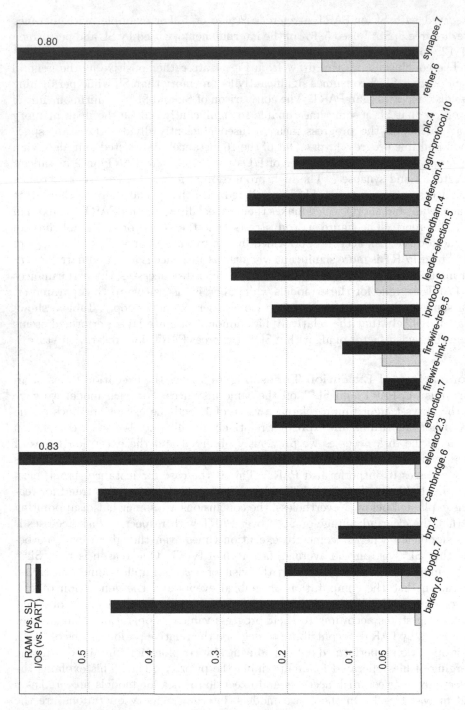

Fig. 4. Peak memory usage of SL^{ext} (this work) compared to SL [23] and state I/Os performed by SL^{ext} compared to PART [3] on the instances of Table 3

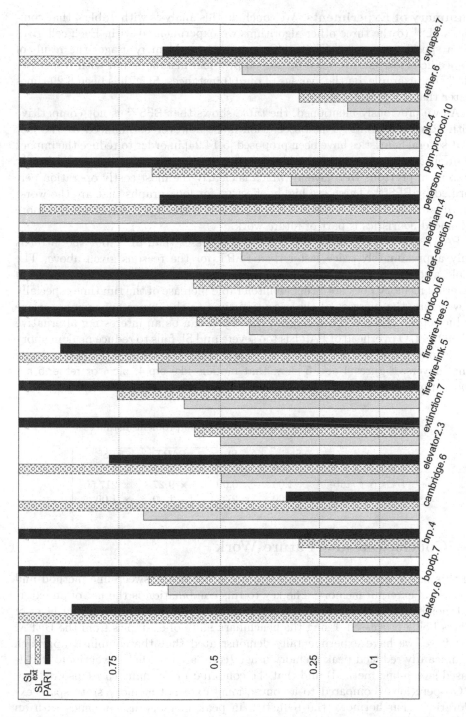

Fig. 5. Execution times of algorithms SL [23], SL^{ext} (this work) and PART [3] on the instances of Table 3

Summary of Experiments. We conclude this analysis with Table 4 that compares SL^{ext} to the three other algorithms we experimented with. Each cell gives for a specific parameter (Time, I/Os per state, or Memory usage) the result of a specific algorithm averaged on our 60 problem instances and with respect to SL^{ext}. For example, on the average of our 60 instances, SL^{ext} has been 8.29 times faster than BFS^{ext}.

As we previously mentioned, the table shows that BFS^{ext} is not competitive with other algorithms. This observation must however be nuanced by the fact that several heuristics have been proposed [5,14,24] in order to reduce the impact of duplicate detection (i.e., checking whether newly generated states are already present in previous BFS layers), which is clearly the most costly operation performed by BFS^{ext}. These are highly effective for long graphs that are the worst candidates for BFS^{ext}. A detailed comparison with BFS^{ext} based on the more advanced heuristics is part of future work.

PART generates significantly more disk accesses than SL^{ext} but the latter is only approximately twice faster than PART for the reasons given above. The table also shows that keeping the priority queue and the persistent states in external memory does not bring an intolerable increase of the run time especially if we relate the increase of the execution time to the important memory usage reduction we observe. This suggests that SL^{ext} can be an interesting alternative when the I/O overhead of PART is too severe and SL fails to reduce peak memory usage even if the progress measure efficiently splits the state space upon multiple small layers. Figures 4 and 5 show that models like brp.4, plc.4 or rether.6 are good application examples for our algorithm.

Table 4. Summary of performance on 60 problem instances

	SL^{ext}	SL	PART	BFS^{ext}
Time	× 1.00	× 0.40	× 1.88	× 8.29
I/Os per state	× 1.00	× 0.00	× 9.27	× 217.50
Memory usage	× 1.00	× 27.74	× 1.00	× 1.00

5   Conclusions and Future Work

In this paper we have explored the combination of the sweep-line method and the use of external memory. The key to this combination is the use of an external memory priority queue for storing states that are not in the current layer of states being processed. Using the benchmark suite of examples from the BEEM database, we have experimentally demonstrated that the combined approach significantly reduced peak memory usage (compared to the conventional RAM-based sweep-line method) and that the combination in many cases also reduces I/O operations (compared to a conventional external memory state space exploration). Furthermore, the reduction in peak memory usage comes with an acceptable run-time penalty caused by the external memory priority queue. A nice property of the combined approach is its compatibility with all existing sweep-line based algorithms as none of these rely on a particular implementation of the progress priority queue. In particular, it can therefore be used in the context of safety model checking [23]. We discuss below three areas of future work originating from the results presented in this paper.

LTL Model Checking. Checking LTL properties is, in an automata-based approach [29], reduced to a cycle detection problem and classical in-memory algorithms uses a depth-first search (DFS) for this purpose. Unfortunately DFS is not compatible with delayed duplicate detection in that the next state being processed is always the last generated. Hence, a variety of algorithms, that often come from the world of distributed memory model checking, have been designed for external-memory LTL model checking: [4,5,11,13]. The sweep-line LTL algorithm of [16] also follows the automata-theoretic approach. It searches for accepting cycles by using a variation of the MAP algorithm [8] that is compatible with our progress-first search order, and also combines well with any type of priority queue. A direct research perspective is thus to experimentally evaluate how well the sweep-line LTL algorithm of [16] equipped with an external memory priority queue competes with other external-memory algorithms for LTL model checking.

Quality of Progress Measures. With the use of an external memory priority queue our experiments demonstrate that we are able to unleash more of the potential of the sweep-line method and that reduction in peak memory usage can be significant. A follow-up research question is therefore whether the sweep-line method has more potential memory reduction that can be leveraged, i.e., how close are the provided/computed progress measures in terms of being optimal? For progress measures that are monotonic, the size of the largest strongly connected component is a lower bound on the reduction that can be obtained since all states belonging to a strongly connected component must have the same progress measure. For non-monotonic progress measures it is less obvious how to compute a good lower bound since the presence of regress edges must also be taken into account, and since optimality now needs to take into account both space (peak memory usage) and time (due to re-exploration caused by regress edges). Computing optimal progress measure hence remains an open and relevant aspect to explore as part of future work.

External-Memory Queues. In this paper we made the choice of external array-heaps [7] adapted from [2] to implement our algorithm. This was motivated by the simplicity of this data structure and its nearly optimal IO complexity. It is clearly of relevance to investigate the use of other forms of external priority queues. In that perspective, a first option is to combine our algorithm with the sequence heaps data structure [26] that according to [26] is a re-engineering of external array-heaps that is more efficient with respect to both I/Os and memory usage thanks to the explicit use of the different levels of memory. Second, external radix-heaps [7] seem to achieve better performance in practice than external array-heaps by relaxing the pre-requisites of the priority queue specification. Its design indeed makes the assumption that the priority queue is monotonic in the sense that the successive calls to *deleteMin* return a sorted sequence of items. Since a sweep explores states with increasing progress measures this assumption holds in our case and this structure thus seems to be an interesting alternative. Finally, we also observe that for preserving termination, it is only required that persistent states are identified during a sweep, put in a separate set, and ignored by the current sweep. The sweep-line can hence move backward and forward during a sweep. As long as regress edges are taken care of, the sweep-line will eventually converge and the sweep will terminate. This means that any form of queue can theoretically be used although a "strict" priority queue ensures that a sweep cannot revisit states (although states can then be visited multiple times during different sweeps). Starting from this observation, another research direction is to evaluate whether relaxing the priority queue requirements can further help reduce disk accesses. This can naturally come at the cost of state revisits meaning that a trade-off would have to be made.

References

1. Aggarwal, A., Vitter, J.S.: The Input/Output Complexity of Sorting and Related Problems. Commun. ACM 31(9), 1116–1127 (1988)
2. Ahuja, R.K., Mehlhorn, K., Orlin, J.B., Tarjan, R.E.: Faster Algorithms for the Shortest Path Problem. J. ACM 37(2), 213–223 (1990)
3. Bao, T., Jones, M.: Time-Efficient Model Checking with Magnetic Disk. In: Halbwachs, N., Zuck, L.D. (eds.) TACAS 2005. LNCS, vol. 3440, pp. 526–540. Springer, Heidelberg (2005)
4. Barnat, J., Brim, L., Šimeček, P.: I/O Efficient Accepting Cycle Detection. In: Damm, W., Hermanns, H. (eds.) CAV 2007. LNCS, vol. 4590, pp. 281–293. Springer, Heidelberg (2007)
5. Barnat, J., Brim, L., Šimeček, P., Weber, M.: Revisiting Resistance Speeds Up I/O-Efficient LTL Model Checking. In: Ramakrishnan, C.R., Rehof, J. (eds.) TACAS 2008. LNCS, vol. 4963, pp. 48–62. Springer, Heidelberg (2008)
6. Behrmann, G., Larsen, K.G., Pelánek, R.: To Store or Not to Store. In: Hunt Jr., W.A., Somenzi, F. (eds.) CAV 2003. LNCS, vol. 2725, pp. 433–445. Springer, Heidelberg (2003)
7. Brengel, K., Crauser, A., Ferragina, P., Meyer, U.: An Experimental Study of Priority Queues in External Memory. In: Vitter, J.S., Zaroliagis, C.D. (eds.) WAE 1999. LNCS, vol. 1668, pp. 346–360. Springer, Heidelberg (1999)
8. Brim, L., Černá, I., Moravec, P., Šimša, J.: Accepting Predecessors Are Better than Back Edges in Distributed LTL Model-Checking. In: Hu, A.J., Martin, A.K. (eds.) FMCAD 2004. LNCS, vol. 3312, pp. 352–366. Springer, Heidelberg (2004)
9. Christensen, S., Kristensen, L.M., Mailund, T.: A Sweep-Line Method for State Space Exploration. In: Margaria, T., Yi, W. (eds.) TACAS 2001. LNCS, vol. 2031, pp. 450–464. Springer, Heidelberg (2001)
10. Dill, D.L., Stern, U.: Using Magnetic Disk Instead of Main Memory in the Murφ Verifier. In: Vardi, M.Y. (ed.) CAV 1998. LNCS, vol. 1427, pp. 172–183. Springer, Heidelberg (1998)
11. Edelkamp, S., Jabbar, S.: Large-Scale Directed Model Checking LTL. In: Valmari, A. (ed.) SPIN 2006. LNCS, vol. 3925, pp. 1–18. Springer, Heidelberg (2006)
12. Edelkamp, S., Leue, S., Lluch-Lafuente, A.: Directed Explicit-state Model Checking in the Validation of Communication Protocols. STTT 5(2-3), 247–267 (2004)

13. Edelkamp, S., Sanders, P., Šimeček, P.: Semi-external LTL Model Checking. In: Gupta, A., Malik, S. (eds.) CAV 2008. LNCS, vol. 5123, pp. 530–542. Springer, Heidelberg (2008)
14. Evangelista, S.: Dynamic Delayed Duplicate Detection for External Memory Model Checking. In: Havelund, K., Majumdar, R. (eds.) SPIN 2008. LNCS, vol. 5156, pp. 77–94. Springer, Heidelberg (2008)
15. Evangelista, S., Kristensen, L.M.: Dynamic State Space Partitioning for External Memory State Space Exploration. Science of Computer Programming (in press, 2012)
16. Evangelista, S., Kristensen, L.M.: Hybrid On-the-Fly LTL Model Checking with the Sweep-Line Method. In: Haddad, S., Pomello, L. (eds.) PETRI NETS 2012. LNCS, vol. 7347, pp. 248–267. Springer, Heidelberg (2012)
17. Gallasch, G.E., Billington, J., Vanit-Anunchai, S., Kristensen, L.M.: Checking Safety Properties On-the-fly with the Sweep-Line Method. STTT 9(3-4), 371–392 (2007)
18. Gallasch, G.E., Han, B., Billington, J.: Sweep-Line Analysis of TCP Connection Management. In: Lau, K.-K., Banach, R. (eds.) ICFEM 2005. LNCS, vol. 3785, pp. 156–172. Springer, Heidelberg (2005)
19. Gallasch, G.E., Ouyang, C., Billington, J., Kristensen, L.M.: Experimenting with Progress Mappings for the Sweep-Line Analysis of the Internet Open Trading Protocol. In: CPN, pp. 19–38 (2004)
20. Godefroid, P., Holzmann, G.J., Pirottin, D.: State-Space Caching Revisited. In: Probst, D.K., von Bochmann, G. (eds.) CAV 1992. LNCS, vol. 663, pp. 178–191. Springer, Heidelberg (1993)
21. Gordon, S., Kristensen, L.M., Billington, J.: Verification of a Revised WAP Wireless Transaction Protocol. In: Esparza, J., Lakos, C.A. (eds.) ICATPN 2002. LNCS, vol. 2360, pp. 182–202. Springer, Heidelberg (2002)
22. Jabbar, S., Edelkamp, S.: Parallel External Directed Model Checking with Linear I/O. In: Emerson, E.A., Namjoshi, K.S. (eds.) VMCAI 2006. LNCS, vol. 3855, pp. 237–251. Springer, Heidelberg (2005)
23. Kristensen, L.M., Mailund, T.: A Generalised Sweep-Line Method for Safety Properties. In: Eriksson, L.-H., Lindsay, P.A. (eds.) FME 2002. LNCS, vol. 2391, pp. 549–567. Springer, Heidelberg (2002)
24. Lamborn, P., Hansen, E.A.: Layered Duplicate Detection in External-Memory Model Checking. In: Havelund, K., Majumdar, R. (eds.) SPIN 2008. LNCS, vol. 5156, pp. 160–175. Springer, Heidelberg (2008)
25. Pelánek, R.: BEEM: Benchmarks for Explicit Model Checkers. In: Bošnački, D., Edelkamp, S. (eds.) SPIN 2007. LNCS, vol. 4595, pp. 263–267. Springer, Heidelberg (2007), http://anna.fi.muni.cz/models/
26. Sanders, P.: Fast Priority Queues for Cached Memory. ACM Journal of Experimental Algorithmics 5, 312–327 (1999)
27. Schmidt, K.: LoLA A Low Level Analyser. In: Nielsen, M., Simpson, D. (eds.) ICATPN 2000. LNCS, vol. 1825, pp. 465–474. Springer, Heidelberg (2000)
28. Vanit-Anunchai, S., Billington, J., Gallasch, G.E.: Analysis of the Datagram Congestion Control Protocols Connection Management Procedures using the Sweep-line Method. STTT 10(1), 29–56 (2008)
29. Vardi, M.Y., Wolper, P.: An Automata-Theoretic Approach to Automatic Program Verification. In: LICS 1986, pp. 332–344 (1986)
30. Westergaard, M., Evangelista, S., Kristensen, L.M.: ASAP: An Extensible Platform for State Space Analysis. In: Franceschinis, G., Wolf, K. (eds.) PETRI NETS 2009. LNCS, vol. 5606, pp. 303–312. Springer, Heidelberg (2009)

A Compositional Minimization Approach for Large Asynchronous Design Verification

Hao Zheng[1], Emmanuel Rodriguez[1], Yingying Zhang[1], and Chris Myers[2]

[1] University of South Florida, Tampa FL 33620, USA
zheng@cse.usf.edu, erodrig9@gmail.com, yingyingz@mail.usf.edu
[2] University of Utah, SLC UT 84112, USA
myers@ece.utah.edu

Abstract. This paper presents a compositional minimization approach with efficient state space reductions for verifying non-trivial asynchronous designs. These reductions can result in a reduced model that contains the exact same set of observably equivalent behavior in the original model, therefore no false counter-examples result from the verification of the reduced model. This approach allows designs that cannot be handled monolithically or with partial-order reduction to be verified without difficulty. The experimental results show significant scale-up of the compositional minimization approach using these reductions on a number of large asynchronous designs.

Keywords: model checking, compositional verification, minimization, abstraction.

1 Introduction

Compositional verification is essential to address the state explosion problem in model checking large systems. The compositional methods can be roughly classified into *compositional reasoning* or *compositional minimization*. *Assume-guarantee* based compositional reasoning [2,8,13,14,18] does not construct the global state space. Instead, the verification of a system is broken into separate analyses for each module of the system. The result for the entire system is derived from the results of the verified individual modules. When verifying each module, assumptions about the environments with which the modules interact are needed for sound verification, and must be discharged later.

The success of compositional reasoning relies on the discovery of appropriate environment assumptions for every module. This is typically done by hand. If the modules have complex interactions with their environments, generating accurate environment assumptions can be challenging. Therefore, the requirement of manually finding assumptions has been a factor limiting the practical use of compositional reasoning. In recent years, various approaches to automated assumption generation for compositional reasoning have been proposed.

A. Donaldson and D. Parker (Eds.): SPIN 2012, LNCS 7385, pp. 62–79, 2012.
© Springer-Verlag Berlin Heidelberg 2012

In the *learning-based* approaches, assumptions represented by deterministic finite automata are generated with the L^* learning algorithm and analysis of local counter-examples [20,1,9,11,5]. The learned assumptions can result in orders of magnitude reduction in verification complexity. However, these approaches may generate assumptions with too many states and fail verification in some cases [20,1]. An automated interface refinement method is presented in [23] where the models of the system modules are refined, and the extra behavior is removed by extracting the interface interactions among these modules. Although the capability of these methods has been demonstrated by verifying large examples, it is difficult for them to handle inherently global properties such as deadlock freedom.

Compositional minimization [4,12,16], on the other hand, iteratively constructs the local model for each component in a system, minimizes it, and composes it with the minimized models of other components. Eventually, a reduced global model is formed for the entire system where verification is performed. To contain the size of the intermediate results, user-provided context constraints are required. The need for the user-provided context constraints may also be a problem because the user-provided constraints may be overly restrictive, thus resulting in real design errors escaping detection. Similar work is also described in [6,7].

The key to the success of compositional minimization is state space reduction. In the most existing work, reduction is conservative in that more behavior may be introduced, but no essential behavior may be removed during reduction. This is necessary since no real errors can be missed when verifying the reduced model. However, false errors may be introduced by reduction in the same time. When an error is found while verifying such a reduced model, it needs to be checked whether this error is real, typically done on the concrete model. This can be very time-consuming. If reduction is too conservative, the number of false errors may become too excessive, and checking these false errors can become the bottleneck.

In [22,27,28], methods are described for compositionally verifying asynchronous designs based on Petri-net reduction. These methods simplify Petri-net models of asynchronous designs either following the design partitions or directed by the properties to be verified, then verification is done on the reduced Petri-nets. However, these methods are limited to certain types of Petri-nets, and not easily extended to other formalisms.

This paper presents a number of state space reductions that can be used with compositional minimization. In this method, a design is modeled as a parallel composition of state graphs derived from the high-level descriptions of the components in a design. Before composing the component state graphs to form a global model for verification, these state graphs are reduced to lower the complexity. The reductions remove certain state transitions and states from a state graph in such a way that the observable behavior on the interface remains the same. At the end, a reduced state graph for the entire design, which is equivalent to the concrete model of the design in terms of observable behavior, is produced for verification. This method is sound and complete in that the reduced model is verified to be correct if and only if the concrete model is correct.

The reduction method presented in this paper is similar, in some degree, to the partial order reduction method[15] as both try to identify and remove certain transitions to eliminate equivalent paths. Partial order reduction determines the independent transitions such that the order of executing these transitions does not affect the verification results, and it removes all but one independent transition in each state during the state space traversal to avoid generating states and transitions that correspond to some equivalent paths. However, determining which transitions are independent requires the information of the global state space, which is not available during the state space traversal, therefore, the independent transitions are computed conservatively to ensure soundness of the verification results. This causes partial order reduction to be less effective or even useless in some situations. On the other hand, our method can effectively remove all transitions that correspond to equivalent paths in state space models because it considers the generated state space models where the necessary information is available for such reduction. Furthermore, our method can also remove states that do not affect the observable behavior after the equivalent paths are removed, while partial order reduction only tries to avoid generating the equivalent paths. Another difference is that partial order reduction is applied to the whole design, while the method in this paper builds a reduced global state space model compositionally.

This paper is organized as follows. Section 2 gives a brief overview of the modeling and verification of asynchronous designs. Section 3 presents the set of state space reductions for our compositional verification method. Section 3.1 describes a state space reduction approach that preserves the same observably equivalent behavior. Section 3.2 describes a set of techniques that remove redundant states and state transitions to augment the reduction presented in Section 3.1. Section 4 demonstrates our method on a number of non-trivial asynchronous design examples, and it analyzes the obtained results. The last section concludes the paper and points out some future work that can improve this method.

2   Preliminaries

2.1   State Graphs

This paper uses *state graphs* (SGs) to model asynchronous systems. The definition of state graphs is given as follows.

Definition 21 (State Graphs). *A state graph G is a tuple $(\mathcal{A}, S, R, init)$ where*

1. *$\mathcal{A}$ is a finite set of actions,*
2. *S is a finite non-empty set of states,*
3. *$R \subseteq S \times \mathcal{A} \times S$ is the set of state transitions,*
4. *$init \in S$ is the initial state.*

For an SG, $\mathcal{A} = \mathcal{A}^I \cup \mathcal{A}^O \cup \mathcal{A}^X$. $\mathcal{A}^I$ is the set of actions generated by an environment of a system such that the system can only observe and react. $\mathcal{A}^O$ is the set of actions generated by a system responding to its environment. $\mathcal{A}^X$ represents the internal behavior that is invisible at the interface, and it is usually denoted as ζ. In the above definition, S also includes a special state π which denotes the *failure state* of a SG, and it represents violations of some prescribed safety properties. The failure state π does not have any outgoing transitions. The set of actions enabled at a state $s \in S$ is denoted as $enb(s) = \{a \mid (s, a, s') \in R\}$. The set of state transitions leaving a state s, $\{(s, a, s') \in R\}$, is denoted by $out(s)$. In the remainder of this paper, $R(s, a, s')$ also denotes that $(s, a, s') \in R$.

A path ρ of G is a sequence of alternating states and actions of G, $\rho = (s_0, a_0, s_1, a_1, s_2, \cdots)$ such that $s_i \in S$, $a_i \in \mathcal{A}$, and $(s_i, a_i, s_{i+1}) \in R$ for all $i \geq 0$. A state $s_j \in S$ is *reachable from* a state $s_i \in S$ if there exists a path $\rho = (s_i, \cdots, s_j, \cdots)$ in G. A state s is reachable in G if s is reachable from the initial state $init$. The trace of path ρ, denoted by $\sigma(\rho)$, is the sequence of actions $(a_0, a_1, \cdots)$. Given a trace $\sigma(\rho)$ of a path $\rho = (s_0, a_0, \ldots, s_i, a_i, \ldots)$, its finite prefix, denoted by $\sigma(\rho, i)$, is $(a_0, \ldots, a_i)$. Two traces $\sigma = (a_0, a_1, \cdots)$ and $\sigma' = (a'_0, a'_1, \cdots)$ are *equivalent*, denoted by $\sigma = \sigma'$, iff $\forall_{i \geq 0} \, a_i = a'_i$. The set of all paths of G forms the language of G, denoted by $\mathcal{L}(G)$.

Given a trace $\sigma = (a_0, a_1, \ldots)$, its projection onto $\mathcal{A}' \subseteq \mathcal{A}$, denoted by $\sigma[\mathcal{A}']$, is obtained by removing from σ all the actions $a \notin \mathcal{A}'$ as shown below.

$$\sigma[\mathcal{A}'] = \begin{cases} a_0 \circ \sigma'[\mathcal{A}'] & \text{if } a_0 \in \mathcal{A}', \\ \sigma'[\mathcal{A}'] & \text{otherwise.} \end{cases}$$

where $\sigma' = (a_1, \ldots)$, and $\circ$ is the concatenation operator.
Given two paths, their equivalence is defined as follows.

Definition 22. *Let* $\rho = (s_0, a_0, s_1, a_1, \cdots)$ *and* $\rho' = (s'_0, a'_0, s'_1, a'_1, \cdots)$ *be two paths of* G. ρ *and* ρ' *are equivalent, denoted as* $\rho \sim \rho'$, *iff* $\sigma(\rho) = \sigma(\rho')$.

The SG of a system is obtained by composing the component SGs asynchronously. Asynchronous parallel composition is defined as follows. This definition is similar to that in [3] except that more rules are created for situations involving π. Given $G_1 = (\mathcal{A}_1, S_1, R_1, init_1)$ and $G_2 = (\mathcal{A}_2, S_2, R_2, init_2)$, the parallel composition of G_1 and G_2, $G_1 \| G_2 = (\mathcal{A}, S, R, init)$, is defined as follows.

1. $\mathcal{A} = \mathcal{A}_1 \cup \mathcal{A}_2$,
2. $S \subseteq S_1 \backslash \pi \times S_2 \backslash \pi \cup \{\pi\}$.
3. $R \subseteq S \times \mathcal{A} \times S$ such that all the following conditions hold:
   (a) For each $((s_1, s_2), a, (s'_1, s'_2)) \in R$,
      i. $a \in \mathcal{A}_1 - \mathcal{A}_2 \Rightarrow R_1(s_1, a, s'_1) \wedge s'_2 = s_2$,
      ii. $a \in \mathcal{A}_2 - \mathcal{A}_1 \Rightarrow R_2(s_2, a, s'_2) \wedge s'_1 = s_1$,
      iii. $a \in \mathcal{A}_1 \cap \mathcal{A}_2 \Rightarrow R_1(s_1, a, s'_1) \wedge R_2(s_2, a, s'_2)$,
   (b) For each $((s_1, s_2), a, \pi) \in R$,
      i. $a \in \mathcal{A}_1 - \mathcal{A}_2 \Rightarrow R_1(s_1, a, \pi)$,
      ii. $a \in \mathcal{A}_2 - \mathcal{A}_1 \Rightarrow R_2(s_2, a, \pi)$,

iii. $a \in \mathcal{A}_1 \cap \mathcal{A}_2 \Rightarrow ((R_1(s_1, a, \pi) \wedge a \in enb(s_2)) \vee ((R_2(s_2, a, \pi) \wedge a \in enb(s_1)),$

4. $init = (init_1, init_2).$

In the above definition, the composite state is the failure state if either component state is the failure state. When several components execute concurrently, they synchronize on the shared actions, and proceed independently on their invisible actions. If any individual SG makes a state transition to the failure state, there is a corresponding state transition to the failure state in the composite SG. In the actual implementation, when composing two SGs, a reachability analysis algorithm is performed from the initial composite state following the definition for transition relation R, and therefore, the resulting composite SG contains only the reachable states.

2.2   Correctness Definition

A path is referred to as a *failure* if it leads to the failure state π. The set of all failures in G is denoted as $\mathcal{F}(G)$ such that $\mathcal{F}(G) \subseteq \mathcal{L}(G)$ holds. A system is correct if $\mathcal{F}(G) = \emptyset$.

Given a failure $\rho' = (s_0', a_0, \cdots, s_i', a_i, \pi)$, the non-failure prefix of its trace is $\sigma(\rho', i)$. If another path ρ has the same non-failure prefix of ρ', ρ is also regarded as a failure. In such cases, path ρ is said to be *failure equivalent* to ρ'.

Definition 23. *Let* $\rho = (s_0, a_0, \ldots)$ *and* $\rho' = (s_0', a_0', \ldots)$ *be two paths. If* $\exists_{i>0} \; \sigma(\rho, i) = \sigma(\rho', i) \wedge s_{i+1}' = \pi$ *holds, then* ρ *is failure equivalent to* ρ', *denoted as* $\rho \sim_F \rho'$.

The definition of the abstraction relation between two SGs is given as follows.

Definition 24 (Abstraction). *Given SGs* G *and* G_1, G_1 *is an abstraction of* G, *denoted as* $G \preceq G_1$, *if and only if the following conditions hold:*

1. $\mathcal{A}^I = \mathcal{A}_1^I$ *and* $\mathcal{A}^O = \mathcal{A}_1^O$.
2. *For every path* $\rho \in \mathcal{L}(G)$, *there exists a path* $\rho_1 \in \mathcal{L}(G_1)$ *such that* $\rho[\mathcal{A}'] \sim \rho_1[\mathcal{A}']$ *or* $\rho[\mathcal{A}'] \sim_F \rho_1[\mathcal{A}']$ *where* $\mathcal{A}' = \mathcal{A}^I \cup \mathcal{A}^O$.

The abstraction relation defines that for any path in G, there exists a path in G_1 such that they are observably equivalent. For any failure in G, there exists an equivalent failure in G_1.

The equivalence relation between two SGs is more restricted than the abstraction relation.

Definition 25 (Equivalence). *Let* G *and* G_1 *be SGs.* G *is equivalent to* G_1, *denoted as* $G \equiv G_1$, *if and only if* $G \preceq G_1$ *and* $G_1 \preceq G$.

The equivalence relation defines that two SGs contain the same set of observably equivalent paths. Therefore, if $G \equiv G_1$, the following property holds.

$$\mathcal{F}(G) = \emptyset \quad \Leftrightarrow \quad \mathcal{F}(G_1) = \emptyset. \tag{1}$$

Intuitively, the above property states that the concrete model G is correct if G_1 is correct, and vice versa.

After a SG is generated, model checking can be applied for various properties to decide if they hold. In particular, our method checks the properties of safety and deadlock freedom of an asynchronous design. The correctness of a design is defined as the absence of failures caused by the violations of these properties. The failure state π in our method can be used to capture violations of various safety properties. A design is safe if π is unreachable. A design is said to deadlock if it cannot make progress in some state. It is defined as follows.

Definition 26 (Deadlock). *A SG is said to have a deadlock if* $\exists_{s \in S} enb(s) = \emptyset$.

A design is free of deadlock if no deadlock exists.

3   State Graph Reductions

In this method, it is assumed that a design consists of n components, the state graphs $G_i (1 \leq i \leq n)$ for these components are obtained using the method described in [25]. The state graph for the whole design is obtained by composing the two component SGs in parallel at a time for all components. However, directly composing G_i for verification defeats the purpose of compositional construction in that the interleaving of the invisible state transitions in G_i can explode quickly during the parallel composition. Therefore, this section presents a number of state space reductions to simplify the component SGs and the intermediate SGs generated during the composition process before they are composed to control the complexity. The reduced state graphs are observably equivalent to the original ones, which implies that any properties hold or fail in the reduced SGs if, and only if, they hold or fail in the original ones. These reductions remove the redundant paths from the original SG but do not introduce any extra paths that do not exist in the original SG. They play an important role in compositional minimization. The end of this section compares these reductions with another existing state space abstraction approach.

3.1   Observably Equivalent Reduction

Given a component, some of its outputs may become invisible to its neighbors when it is plugged into a larger system. In this case, the corresponding state transitions on these outputs in its SG can be converted to invisible transitions. The traditional abstraction techniques collapse the invisible state transitions into single states [6]. This may cause extra behaviors and thus may introduce false failures. This section provides a different reduction approach that compresses a sequence of invisible state transitions into a single visible state transition. This approach has certain desirable features over the previous approaches.

Let $(s_i, \zeta, s_{i+1}, \zeta, \cdots, s_{j-1}, \zeta, s_j, a_j, s_{j+1})$ be a subpath of a path in a SG G. After reduction, the whole subpath is replaced with state transition (s_i, a_j, s_{j+1}). This reduction is referred to as an *observably equivalent reduction*. This reduction is different from the previous approaches in the following ways.

1. Since the sequence of invisible state transitions on a path is replaced by a visible state transition, the number of reachable states of the reduced graph G may be reduced if some states have all their incoming state transitions on the invisible action. However, this may not always be the case, and the number of state transitions may be increased significantly.
2. This reduction shortens the existing paths, but no new paths are created. Therefore, no new failure traces are introduced.
3. Non-determinism may be introduced into the SG after reduction. Consider two subpaths $(s_i, \zeta, \cdots, s_{j-1}, \zeta, s_j, a_j, s_{j+1})$ and $(s_i, \zeta, \cdots, s_{k-1}, \zeta, s_k, a_j, s_{k+1})$. They are reduced to (s_i, a_j, s_{j+1}) and (s_i, a_j, s_{k+1}), respectively. This causes nondeterminism even though the original SG is deterministic. However, the nondeterministic transitions may be eliminated if s_{j+1} or s_{k+1} is redundant as described in the next section.

Let $\mathbf{reduce}(G)$ be a procedure for the observably equivalent reduction on a SG G as shown in Algorithm 1. The SG produced by $\mathbf{reduce}(G)$ in Algorithm 1 inherits every element of G except the updated R and S. The algorithm $\mathbf{reduce}(G)$ checks each invisible state transition (s_1, a_1, s_2) in G, and calls another function $\mathbf{oer}(G, s_1, s_2)$ if the start state s_1 of that invisible state transition has at least one incoming state transition that is visible. Function $\mathbf{oer}(G, s_1, s_2)$, as shown in Algorithm 2, searches forward bypassing each invisible state transition from s_2 in the depth-first manner until a visible transition or the failure state π is encountered. Then, new visible transitions are created to replace the sequences of invisible state transitions, and they are added into R. After all invisible transitions are handled, they are removed from G. Consequently, some other states and transitions may become unreachable, and they are also removed from G.

Algorithm 1. reduce (G)

---

1 **foreach** $(s_1, a_1, s_2) \in R$ **do**
2   **if** $a_1 = \zeta \land s_2 \neq \pi$ **then**
3   **if** $\exists_{(s,a,s_1) \in R}\ a \neq \zeta$ **then**
4              $\mathbf{oer}(G, s_1, s_2)$;
5 Remove all invisible state transitions from G;
6 Remove unreachable states and state transitions from G;

Fig. 1 shows an example how a SG in Fig. 1(a) is reduced by the observably equivalent reduction to become the one as shown in Fig. 1(b). In this example, suppose all invisible transitions are denoted by ζ. Then, for each visible transition in states s_{i+1}, s_{j+1}, and s_{k+1}, a new transition on the same action is created for states s_i, s_j, and s_k, respectively. Four new state transitions are added to preserve the same observable behavior. In this case, only three invisible transitions are removed. Therefore, without further reduction, the reduced SGs can actually be more complex with more transitions added. In the next section, redundancy

Algorithm 2. oer (G, s_1, s_2)

1 **foreach** $(s_2, a_2, s_2') \in R$ **do**
2   **if** $a_2 = \zeta \wedge s_2' \neq \pi$ **then**
3   oer(G, s_1, s_2');
4   **else**
5          $R = R \cup \{(s_1, a_2, s_2')\}$;
6   **return**;

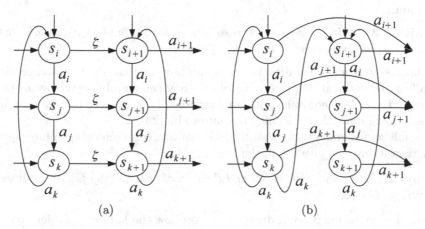

(a)   (b)

Fig. 1. (a) An example SG with invisible state transitions. (b) The SG from (a) after the observably equivalent reduction.

in the SGs is defined, and algorithms are described to identify and remove the redundancy to actually reduce the complexity of the SGs.

The following lemma asserts that reduce(G) is equivalent to G.

Lemma 1. *Given a SG G, $G \equiv$ reduce(G).*

Proof: The proof is based on how procedure reduce(G) works. It is straightforward to see that for every path ρ in G that does not include any invisible transitions, the same path also exists in reduce(G). For a path $\rho = (s_1, a_1, \ldots, s_i, \zeta, s_{i+1}, a_{i+1}, \ldots)$, there exists a path $\rho' = (s_1, a_1, \ldots, s_i, a_{i+1}, \ldots)$ in reduce(G), and $\rho \sim \rho'$ or $\rho \sim_F \rho'$.

Conversely, for every path $\rho' = (s_1, a_1, \ldots, s_i, a_{i+1}, \ldots)$ in reduce(G), either the same path exists in G, or it is reduced from a path $\rho = (s_1, a_1, \ldots, s_i, \zeta, s_{i+1}, a_{i+1}, \ldots)$ in G, and $\rho' \sim \rho$ or $\rho' \sim_F \rho$. This satisfies the conditions of the equivalence relation, therefore $G \equiv$ reduce(G). ∎

3.2   Redundancy Removal

From the example shown in the last section, it can be seen that the observably equivalent reduction can introduce nondeterminism. Nondeterminism exists if there are two state transitions (s, a, s_1) and (s, a, s_2) such that $s_1 \neq s_2$. This is a result from reduction while preserving observable equivalence. However, the introduced nondeterminism can potentially contain redundancy, and removing the redundancy can simplify the complexity of SGs.

If the failure state is involved in nondeterminism, redundant state transitions are identified based on the following understanding: if an action in a state may or may not cause a failure nondeterministically, it is always regarded as causing a failure. It is formalized as failure equivalent state transitions in the following definition.

Definition 31. *Given two state transitions (s, a_1, s_1) and (s, a_2, π) of a SG, (s, a_1, s_1) is failure equivalent to (s, a_2, π) if $a_1 = a_2$.*

The failure equivalent transitions are redundant in that their existence does not affect the verification results, therefore, they can simply be removed. After removing the failure equivalent state transitions, it is possible that some other states become unreachable leading to more reduction.

The following lemma states that the SG resulting from removing failure equivalent transitions is equivalent to the original SG.

Lemma 2. *Let G and G' be a SG and the one after removing failure equivalent transitions. $G \equiv G'$.*

Proof: The following proof is drawn based on how the failure equivalent reduction works. First, all paths in G also exist in G' except for paths $\rho = (s_1, a_1, \ldots, s_i, a_i, s_{i+1}, \ldots)$ in G such that there also exists a (s_i, a_i, π) in G. In other words, for every path $\rho = (s_1, a_1, \ldots, s_i, a_i, s_{i+1}, \ldots)$ in G, if (s_i, a_i, π) is also in G, there exists a path $\rho' = (s_1, a_1, \ldots, s_i, a_i, \pi)$, and we can see $\rho \sim_F \rho'$. This shows $G \preceq G'$.

Now, for every path ρ' in G', the path also exists in G if it does not end in the failure state. If ρ' ends in the failure state, the same path also exists in G. This shows that $G' \preceq G$. Therefore, $G \equiv G'$ holds.   ∎

Fig. 2 shows an example of failure equivalent transitions. Fig. 2(a) is an example SG. After observably equivalent reduction is applied, the reduced SG is shown in Fig. 2(b). In this reduced SG, transition (s_j, a_j, s_k) is failure equivalent to (s_j, a_j, π). After removing this failure equivalent transition, state s_k becomes unreachable, and it is also removed including all its outgoing transitions. The final reduced SG is shown in Fig. 2(c).

Next, a restricted case of redundancy is described. Let $incoming(s)$ be the set of state transitions (s', a, s) such that $R(s', a, s)$ holds.

Definition 32. *Let G be a SG, and $s, s_1,$ and s_2 be states of G. If the following conditions hold, then one of s_1 and s_2 is redundant.*

- *For every $(s, a, s_1) \in incoming(s_1)$, there exists a $(s, a, s_2) \in incoming(s_2)$.*
- *For every $(s, a, s_2) \in incoming(s_2)$, there exists a $(s, a, s_1) \in incoming(s_1)$.*

If such redundant states exist, one of them and its incoming and outgoing transitions can be removed as follows. Suppose s_1 is selected to remove.

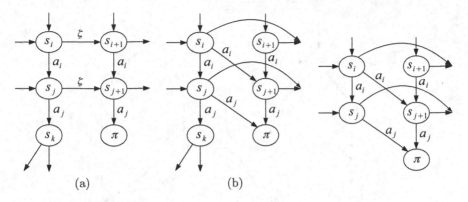

(a)   (b)

Fig. 2. (a) An example SG. (b) The SG from (a) after the observably equivalent reduction. (c) The SG from (b) after removing the failure equivalent transition (s_j, a_j, s_k) and the unreachable state.

- For each $(s_1, a_1, s_1') \in outgoing(s_1)$, add (s_2, a_1, s_1') into R.
- Remove all state transitions in $incoming(s_1)$ and $outgoing(s_1)$.
- Remove s_1.

Therefore, removing redundant states always results in a smaller number of states and state transitions. It is also obvious to see that $G \equiv G'$ where G' is the SG after redundant states are removed from G.

In the remaining part of this section, a more general definition of redundancy is given by checking all possible behaviors originating from two states. Basically, if all possible behaviors originating from these two states are equivalent, these two states are regarded as equivalent. Therefore, one of them is redundant, and can be removed. The state equivalence is formally defined as follows.

Definition 33. *Let s and s' be two states of a SG. s and s' are equivalent, denoted as $s \equiv s'$, if the following conditions hold.*

- *For each path $\rho = (s_0, a_0, s_1, a_1, \ldots,)$ such that $s_0 = s$, there exists another path $\rho' = (s_0', a_0, s_1', a_1, \ldots,)$ such that $s_0' = s'$, $\rho \sim \rho'$ or $\rho \sim_F \rho'$.*
- *For each path $\rho' = (s_0', a_0, s_1', a_1, \ldots,)$ such that $s_0' = s'$, there exists another path $\rho = (s_0, a_0, s_1, a_1, \ldots,)$ such that $s_0 = s$, $\rho \sim \rho'$ or $\rho \sim_F \rho'$.*

Fig. 3 shows two examples of SGs which contain equivalent states that possibly result from the reduction described in the previous section. In Fig.3(a), there are two loops. State s_i on one loop is equivalent to state s_i' on the other loop since the paths out of these states are equivalent. Similarly, the successor states of these two states are also equivalent. It can be shown that every state in one loop is equivalent to a corresponding state in the other loop. Fig. 3(b) shows a different case where equivalence exists. It can be shown that state s_0 is equivalent to s_k since each of these two states is the starting state of a path, and these two paths are equivalent.

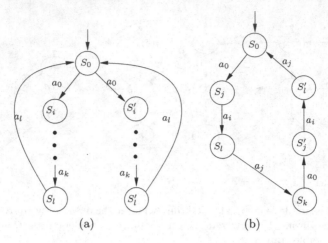

(a)   (b)

Fig. 3. Examples of equivalent states that can be resulted from reductions. States s_i and s_i' in (a) and s_0 and s_k in (b) are equivalent since the paths coming out of these states are equivalent.

The above observation directly leads to an algorithm to find equivalent states. To simplify the presentation, assume a SG with $\mathcal{A}^X = \emptyset$ after observably equivalent reduction is applied. The algorithm works as follows. Initially, the set Eq of all pairs of states is found such that for each $(s, s') \in Eq$, the following conditions hold.

- $\forall_{(s,a,s_1)\in outgoing(s)}\, \exists_{(s',a',s_1')\in outgoing(s')}\, a = a'$.
- $\forall_{(s',a',s_1')\in outgoing(s')}\, \exists_{(s,a,s_1)\in outgoing(s)}\, a = a'$.

Two states are obviously not equivalent if one has some enabled action that is not enabled in another state. This step excludes these obviously inequivalent states, and keeps the pairs that are potentially equivalent. Then, the algorithm iteratively removes from the set Eq any pairs (s, s'), until a fixpoint is reached, if one of the following conditions holds

$$\exists_{s_1\in succ(s)}\forall_{s_1'\in succ(s')}\, (s_1, s_1') \notin Eq \qquad (2)$$
$$\exists_{s_1'\in succ(s')}\forall_{s_1\in succ(s)}\, (s_1, s_1') \notin Eq \qquad (3)$$

where $succ(s)$ includes all states that are reachable in one transition from s. Finally, if Eq is not empty, then states in every pair $(s, s') \in Eq$ are equivalent. The correctness of the above algorithm is stated and proved in the following lemma.

Lemma 3. *For each pair* $(s, s') \in Eq$, $s \equiv s'$.

Proof: Suppose (s, s') is an arbitrary pair in Eq.

Let $\rho = (s_0, a_0, s_1, a_1, \ldots)$ be an arbitrary path such that $s_0 = s$. Since $(s, s') \in Eq$, there exists $(s', a_0, s_1') \in outgoing(s')$ corresponding to (s, a_0, s_1). Additionally, $(s_1, s_1') \in Eq$ because $(s, s') \in Eq$. Repeat the above argument

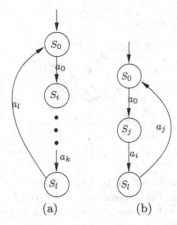

Fig. 4. SGs for the examples with redundant states in Fig. 3 after being reduced

for (s_1, s_1') and their successors recursively, we can construct another path $\rho' = (s', a_0, s_1', a_1, \ldots)$, and it is straightforward to see that for any path from s, there is another path ρ' such that $\rho \sim \rho'$.

Next, let $\rho' = (s_0', a_0, s_1', a_1, \ldots)$ be an arbitrary path such that $s_0' = s'$. By following the above steps similarly, we can conclude that for any path from s', there is another path ρ such that $\rho \sim \rho'$.

Therefore, for every pair $(s, s') \in Eq$, $s \equiv s'$ by Definition 33.   ∎

If $Eq(s, s')$ is not empty, for every pair (s, s') in the set, either s or s' and its outgoing transitions can be safely removed, and its incoming transitions are redirected to s' or s. In this case, the interface behavior of the transformed SG remains the same as that of the original one according to the definition of the state equivalence. The examples shown in Fig. 3 after being reduced are shown in Fig. 4.

3.3 Comparison between Reduction and Abstraction

Efficient and effective state space reductions are key to the success of compositional minimization. In [26], a different abstraction technique is presented. This section briefly compares it with the presented reductions in this paper.

The state-based abstraction in [26] removes every invisible state transition $(s_i, \zeta, s_j) \in R$ from an SG, and merges s_i and s_j to form a merged state s_{ij}. All state transitions entering s_i and s_j now enter s_{ij}, and all state transitions leaving s_i or s_j now leave s_{ij}. To preserve failure traces, if s_j is the failure state π, then the merged state s_{ij} is also the failure state. This abstraction can remove all invisible state transitions from an SG, which is illustrated in Fig. 5. It is efficient to simply remove one invisible transition at a time without checking any conditions as required in the paper. However, it may introduce a lot of extra behavior including failures. In Fig. 5(b), there is a path $\rho = (\ldots, a_k, s_{ij}, a_i, \ldots)$ that does not exist in the SG in Fig. 5(a). This extra path causes a false failure in the final reduced SG.

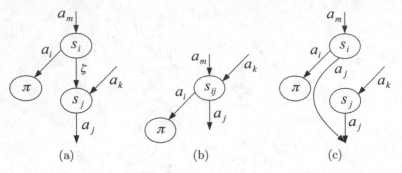

Fig. 5. Comparison of a traditional state space abstraction technique with the observably equivalent reduction. (a) An example SG. (b) The SG after the state space abstraction. (c) The SG after the observably equivalent reduction.

The observably equivalent reduction presented in this paper removes invisible state transitions while keeping the exact same set of observable paths in the original SG. Another example of this reduction is shown in Fig. 5(c). For an invisible state transition $(s_i, \zeta, s_j) \in R$, this reduction adds a new state transition (s_i, a_j, s_h) into R for every $(s_j, a_j, s_h) \in outgoing(s_j)$. Then, it removes (s_i, ζ, s_{i+1}). In Fig. 5(a), there exists a path $\rho = (\ldots, s_i, \zeta, s_j, a_j, s_h, \ldots)$, and in Fig. 5(c) there exists a path $\rho' = (\ldots, s_i, a_j, s_h, \ldots)$, and $\rho[\mathcal{A}'] \sim \rho'[\mathcal{A}']$ where $\mathcal{A}' = \mathcal{A}^I \cup \mathcal{A}^O$. For all other paths that do not involve (s_i, ζ, s_{i+1}), they are preserved after the reduction. This reduction does not introduce any extra paths that do not exist in the original. On the other hand, it may introduce a large number of redundant paths that may cause the reduced SG to be much larger than the original one. Fortunately, the redundancy removal techniques presented in this paper can help to remove a lot of these redundancy introduced by the observably equivalent reduction to significantly simplify the complexity of SGs.

4   Experimental Results

We have implemented a prototype of the automated compositional verification with the reductions described in this paper in a concurrent system verification tool *Platu*, an explicit state model checker. This model checker is programmed in Java, and can perform traditional depth-first search and compositional verification. Experiments have been performed on several non-trivial asynchronous circuit designs obtained from previously published papers. To verify a design using the compositional minimization method in this paper, all components in the design need to be converted to SGs first. The component SGs can be obtained using a compositional reachability analysis method as shown in [25]. Detailed description of this method is out of scope of this paper. In this paper, it is assumed that the component SGs are already obtained somehow.

The first three designs are a self-timed first-in-first-out (FIFO) design [17], a tree arbiter (ARB) of multiple cells [10], and a distributed mutual exclusion

Table 1. Comparison of the results from using the monolithic, partial-order reduction and the reduction methods. Time is in seconds, and memory is in MBs. $|S|$ is the numbers of states found. For the results under CompMin, $|S|$ is the number of states of the largest SG encountered during the whole course of compositional minimization.

Designs		Monolithic			SPIN			CompMin		
Name	$|V|$	Time	Mem	$|S|$	Time	Mem	$|S|$	Time	Mem	$|S|$
fig3a	6	0.044	2.7	20	0	2.195	20	0.037	3.14	10
arbN3	26	0.315	2.4	3756	0.015	2.781	3756	0.087	3.89	52
arbN5	44	8.105	61.538	227472	1.65	71.695	227472	0.18	4.3	52
arbN7	62	–	–	–	–	–	–	0.46	6.61	52
arbN9	80	–	–	–	–	–	–	0.89	7.43	52
arbN15	134	–	–	–	–	–	–	1.33	9.87	52
fifoN3	14	0.119	4.8	644	0	2.195	644	0.015	3.39	20
fifoN5	22	0.733	16.253	20276	0.08	6.593	20276	0.017	3.62	20
fifoN8	34	199.353	845	3572036	30.2	1087.211	3572036	0.11	4.03	20
fifoN10	42	–	–	–	–	–	–	0.08	4.38	20
fifoN20	82	–	–	–	–	–	–	0.11	4.7	20
fifoN50	202	–	–	–	–	–	–	0.35	6.14	20
fifoN100	402	–	–	–	–	–	–	0.76	7.67	20
fifoN200	802	–	–	–	–	–	–	1.56	11.1	20
fifoN300	1202	–	–	–	–	–	–	3.02	14.3	20
dmeN3	33	3.589	26.1	267, 999	0.265	19.706	117270	0.71	4.44	248
dmeN4	44	1235	1032	15.7M	15.5	553.421	4678742	0.8	5.74	248
dmeN5	55	–	–	–	–	–	–	2.23	10.19	248
dmeN8	88	–	–	–	–	–	–	3.57	16.4	447
dmeN9	99	–	–	–	–	–	–	5.86	20.9	900
dmeN10	110	–	–	–	–	–	–	58.9	46.6	3211
TU	48	–	–	–	4.37	144.984	786672	0.219	5.085	278
PC	50	–	–	–	–	–	–	0.842	7.567	864
MMU	55	–	–	–	–	–	–	0.688	10.143	2071

element (DME) consisting of a ring of DME cells [10]. Despite all these designs having regular structures to be scaled easily, the regularity is not exploited in our method, and all components are treated as black boxes. The fourth example is a tag unit circuit (TU) from Intel's RAPPID design [21]. This example is an unoptimized version of the actual circuit used in RAPPID with higher complexity, which is more interesting for experimenting with our methods. The fifth example is a pipeline controller (PC) for an asynchronous processor TITAC2 [24]. The last example is a circuit implementation of a memory management unit (MMU) from [19]. All examples are too large for traditional monolithic approaches to complete on a typical workstation.

In the experiments, DME, arbiter, and FIFO examples are partitioned according to their natural structures. In other words, each cell is a component. For the TU example, it is partitioned into three components, where the middle five blocks form a component, and gates on the sides of the component in the middle form the other two. The PC example is partitioned into five components, each of which contains ten gates. The MMU example is partitioned by following the structure provided in [19] such that each component defines an output that are used by other components.

All experiments are performed on a Linux workstation with an Intel dual-core CPU and 2 GB memory. The results are shown in Table 1. In Table 1, the first two columns show the design names and the number of variables used in the corresponding models. Since all examples are asynchronous circuits, the type of the variables used in the models is Boolean. Three different methods are used in the experiments for better comparison. The columns under Monolithic show the results from using the traditional DFS search method on the whole designs. The columns under SPIN show the results from using the SPIN model checker with the partial-order reduction turned on. The last three columns under CompMin show the results from using the compositional minimization method described in this paper. In these columns, Time is the total runtime, Mem is the total memory used, and $|S|$ shows the total number of states found. Specifically, the column $|S|$ under CompMin shows the total number of states in the largest SG found during the entire course of the compositional minimization process. The largest SGs are recorded because their sizes in general determine whether the whole process of compositional minimization can be finished or not, therefore, their sizes need to be carefully controlled. For examples which use too much memory, the corresponding entries are filled with $-$.

From Table 1, it can be seen that the traditional monolithic search method fails to finish quickly for most of the designs. This is understandable due to the state explosion problem. However, it is surprising to see that SPIN with partial-order reduction does not do any better. For all ARB and FIFO examples, SPIN cannot find any reduction, and the numbers of states found by SPIN are exactly the same as those found by the monolithic approaches for ARB and FIFO. For DME and TU, SPIN does slightly better in terms of reduction in of the number of states found. On the other hand, SPIN quickly blows up the 2 GB memory for most of the examples too. One possible explanation is that the partial-order reduction implemented in SPIN relies on the information about the independence among transitions, and this information is obtained by examining the structures of the Promela models. Since these examples are asynchronous circuit designs, the models for these examples are connections of descriptions of basic logic gates, and they may be difficult for SPIN to extract sufficient independence information for effective reduction.

On the other hand, the compositional minimization approach with all reductions described in this paper can finish all examples in the table quickly. For ARB and FIFO examples, the total runtime and memory usage grow polynomially in the number of components in the examples. For DME examples, the runtime and memory usage show a similar growth curve until the examples become too large. For dmeN10, there is a big jump on runtime and memory usage. This growth is due to an intermediate SG that contains too many state transitions after the equivalent reduction, and it takes a big part of total runtime to identify the equivalent states. The results for dmeN11 are not shown as the runtime for this example exceeds the 5 minute threshold. On the other hand, the memory usage still grows polynomially as the design size grows. For the three irregular designs, TU, PC and MMU, where SPIN also fails, they are finished with compositional minimization using very small amount of runtime and memory. For the PC example, a safety failure is found. The same safety failure is also found by the monolithic approach after about 30 minutes on a much more powerful machine.

From these results, one may conclude that compositional minimization works much better than partial-order reduction. This is true to some degree. For designs that do not contain any flaws, compositional minimization can prove the correctness very efficiently. On the other hand, for designs that contain one or more bugs, compositional minimization can also finish and return counter-examples quickly. However, as a lot of design details are removed during the minimization process, the returned counter-examples are very abstract, therefore not very useful for users to understand the causes of the bugs. In this case, concrete counter-examples corresponding to those returned by compositional minimization need to be generated. This can be done by the traditional search on the whole design guided by the returned counter-examples. Since these counter-examples are so abstract, the step of generating the concrete counter-examples may, in some cases, be as difficult as searching the state space of the whole design.

5 Conclusion

This paper presents a compositional minimization approach with a number of state graph reductions to lower the verification complexity while not introducing extra paths that might cause false failures nor reducing any essential behaviors. In other words, the reduction methods are sound and complete. Based on initial experimental results, these reductions work well on a number of asynchronous circuit examples. In the future, it is necessary to experiment on more diverse examples including communication protocols and multithreaded programs to fully demonstrate its potential. Additionally, it is necessary to develop efficient approaches that make abstract counter-examples in the reduced SG be concrete by recovering the reduced information for better debugging.

Acknowledgment. This material is based upon work supported by the National Science Foundation under Grant No. 0930510 and 0930225. Any opinions, findings, and conclusions or recommendations expressed in this material are those of the author(s) and do not necessarily reflect the views of the National Science Foundation.

References

1. Alur, R., Madhusudan, P., Nam, W.: Symbolic Compositional Verification by Learning Assumptions. In: Etessami, K., Rajamani, S.K. (eds.) CAV 2005. LNCS, vol. 3576, pp. 548–562. Springer, Heidelberg (2005)

2. Berezin, S., Campos, S., Clarke, E.M.: Compositional Reasoning in Model Checking. In: de Roever, W.-P., Langmaack, H., Pnueli, A. (eds.) COMPOS 1997. LNCS, vol. 1536, pp. 81–102. Springer, Heidelberg (1998)
3. Gheorghiu Bobaru, M., Păsăreanu, C.S., Giannakopoulou, D.: Automated Assume-Guarantee Reasoning by Abstraction Refinement. In: Gupta, A., Malik, S. (eds.) CAV 2008. LNCS, vol. 5123, pp. 135–148. Springer, Heidelberg (2008)
4. Bustan, D., Grumberg, O.: Modular minimization of deterministic finite-state machines. In: Proceedings the 6th International Workshop on Formal Methods for Industrial Critical Systems, FMICS 2001 (July 2001)
5. Chaki, S., Clarke, E., Sinha, N., Thati, P.: Automated Assume-Guarantee Reasoning for Simulation Conformance. In: Etessami, K., Rajamani, S.K. (eds.) CAV 2005. LNCS, vol. 3576, pp. 534–547. Springer, Heidelberg (2005)
6. Cheung, S., Kramer, J.: Context constraints for compositional reachability analysis. ACM Transations on Software Engineering and Methodology 5(4), 334–377 (1996)
7. Cheung, S., Kramer, J.: Checking safety properties using compositional reachability analysis. ACM Trans. Softw. Eng. Methodol. 8(1), 49–78 (1999)
8. Clarke, E., Long, D., McMillan, K.: Compositional model checking. In: Proceedings of the 4th Annual Symposium on Logic in Computer Science, pp. 353–362. IEEE Press, Piscataway (1989)
9. Cobleigh, J.M., Giannakopoulou, D., Păsăreanu, C.S.: Learning Assumptions for Compositional Verification. In: Garavel, H., Hatcliff, J. (eds.) TACAS 2003. LNCS, vol. 2619, pp. 331–346. Springer, Heidelberg (2003)
10. Dill, D.: Trace Theory for Automatic Hierarchical Verification of Speed Independent Circuits. PhD thesis, Carnegie Mellon University (1988)
11. Giannakopoulou, D., Păsareănu, C.S., Barringer, H.: Component verification with automatically generated assumptions. Automated Software Engineering, 297–320 (2005)
12. Graf, S., Steffen, B., Luttgen, G.: Compositional minimization of finite state systems using interface specifications. Formal Aspects of Computation 8(5), 607–616 (1996)
13. Grumberg, O., Long, D.: Model checking and modular verification. ACM Transactions on Programming Languages and Systems 16(3), 843–871 (1994)
14. Henzinger, T., Qadeer, S., Rajamani, S.: You Assume, we Guarantee: Methodology and Case Studies. In: Vardi, M.Y. (ed.) CAV 1998. LNCS, vol. 1427, pp. 440–451. Springer, Heidelberg (1998)
15. Holzmann, G.J., Peled, D.: An improvement in formal verification. In: Proceedings of the 7th IFIP WG6.1 International Conference on Formal Description Techniques VII, pp. 197–211. Chapman & Hall, Ltd., London (1995)
16. Krimm, J., Mounier, L.: Compositional State Space Generation from Lotos Programs. In: Brinksma, E. (ed.) TACAS 1997. LNCS, vol. 1217, pp. 239–258. Springer, Heidelberg (1997)
17. Martin, A.J.: Self-timed fifo: An exercise in compiling programs into vlsi circuits. Technical Report 1986.5211-tr-86, California Institute of Technology (1986)
18. Mcmillan, K.L.: A methodology for hardware verification using compositional model checking. Technical report, Cadence Berkeley Labs (1999)
19. Myers, C.J.: Computer-Aided Synthesis and Verification of Gate-Level Timed Circuits. PhD thesis, Stanford University (1995)
20. Nam, W., Alur, R.: Learning-Based Symbolic Assume-Guarantee Reasoning with Automatic Decomposition. In: Graf, S., Zhang, W. (eds.) ATVA 2006. LNCS, vol. 4218, pp. 170–185. Springer, Heidelberg (2006)

21. Stevens, K., Ginosar, R., Rotem, S.: Relative timing. In: Proc. International Symposium on Advanced Research in Asynchronous Circuits and Systems, pp. 208–218 (1999)
22. Thacker, R.A., Jones, K.R., Myers, C.J., Zheng, H.: Automatic abstraction for verification of cyber-physical systems. In: Proceedings of the 1st ACM/IEEE International Conference on Cyber-Physical Systems, ICCPS 2010, pp. 12–21 (2010)
23. Yao, H., Zheng, H.: Automated interface refinement for compositional verification. IEEE Transaction on Computer-Aided Design of Integrated Circuits and Systems 28(3), 433–446 (2009)
24. Yoneda, T., Yoshikawa, T.: Using partial orders for trace theoretic verification of asynchronous circuits. In: Proc. International Symposium on Advanced Research in Asynchronous Circuits and Systems. IEEE Computer Society Press (March 1996)
25. Zheng, H.: Compositional reachability analysis for efficient modular verification of asynchronous designs. IEEE Transactions on Computer-Aided Design of Integrated Circuits and Systems 29(3) (March 2010)
26. Zheng, H., Ahrens, J., Xia, T.: A compositional method with failure-preserving abstractions for asynchronous design verification. IEEE Transactions on Computer-Aided Design of Integrated Circuits and Systems 27 (2008)
27. Zheng, H., Mercer, E., Myers, C.: Modular verification of timed circuits using automatic abstraction. IEEE Transactions on Computer-Aided Design 22(9), 1138–1153 (2003)
28. Zheng, H., Myers, C., Walter, D., Little, S., Yoneda, T.: Verification of timed circuits with failure directed abstractions. IEEE Transactions on Computer-Aided Design 25(3), 403–412 (2006)

On Parallel Software Verification Using Boolean Equation Systems

Alexander Ditter[1], Milan Česka[2], and Gerald Lüttgen[1]

[1] University of Bamberg, 96045 Bamberg, Germany
{alexander.ditter,gerald.luettgen}@swt-bamberg.de
[2] Masaryk University, 602 00 Brno, Czech Republic
xceska@fi.muni.cz

Abstract. Multi- and many-core hardware platforms are today widely accessible and used to significantly accelerate many computationally demanding tasks. In this paper we describe a parallel approach to solve *Boolean Equation Systems* (BESs) in the context of *model checking*. We focus on the applicability of state-of-the-art, shared-memory parallel hardware – multi-core CPUs and many-core GPUs – to speed up the resolution procedure for BESs. In this setting, we experimentally show the scalability and competitiveness of our approach, compared to an optimized sequential implementation, based on a large benchmark suite containing models of software systems and protocols from industry and academia.

Keywords: formal verification, parallel model checking, boolean equation systems.

1 Introduction

In this paper we propose and evaluate a parallel approach to the resolution of *Boolean Equation Systems* (BESs) on parallel, shared memory systems, i.e., utilizing state-of-the-art multi-core and many-core processors – though not in a hybrid setting. Our goals are to (i) evaluate the scalability of our parallel approach with respect to an increasing number of parallel *processing units* (PUs), and (ii) prove its competitiveness in comparison with an optimized sequential algorithm, which we implemented as described in [1].

Motivation. Today, hardware manufacturers no longer increase clock rates but the number of available PUs of processors. Along with the evolving massively parallel, throughput oriented hardware architectures [13], this has led to an increasing interest in the parallelization of software. Indeed, this trend has already found its way into the field of software verification and model checking years ago [5,16,17] and must be considered further in order to push the limits of verification techniques further towards industrial strength, allowing one to deal with larger state spaces and providing rapid feedback to developers.

Modern processors can be divided into two main branches: (i) CPU-based multi-core processors with up to tens of cores and (ii) GPU-based many-core

A. Donaldson and D. Parker (Eds.): SPIN 2012, LNCS 7385, pp. 80–97, 2012.

processors with up to several hundreds of cores. The key differences are (i) the ability to efficiently deal with control flow at the expense of lower data through-put and, respectively, (ii) the ability to provide high data throughput rates at the expense of a lack of efficient, control-flow guided execution. We assume the trend to continue – see e.g., Intel's "Terra Scale Computing"[1] project – suggesting future hardware to consist of more, yet simpler PUs. With respect to parallel algorithms, current hardware development favors approaches that are geared towards the *single instruction multiple data* (SIMD) paradigm, since they can most easily take advantage of this type of parallel hardware. Therefore, it is inevitable to consider the applicability of massively parallel, SIMD-based (i.e., many-core) systems in our experiments.

Background. The standard model checking problem [9], $M \models \varphi$, can be encoded by a BES [23], where the solution of the BES is equivalent to the solution of the underlying model checking problem. The BES is obtained by the synchronous composition of a *Labeled Transition System* (LTS), corresponding to M, and a property φ (e.g., deadlock freedom) that is to be checked for this LTS. Consequently, the data dependencies within the resulting BES are closely related to the structure of the LTS from which it was generated. For our evaluation we rely on the well established VLTS benchmark,[2] which provides 40 LTSs – originating from academia and industry – that can be checked for deadlocks and livelocks, i.e., our resulting benchmark suite consists of a total of 80 BESs.

The average branching factor, i.e., the average number of outgoing edges per vertex, over all 40 LTSs in the benchmark is 5.73. With respect to parallelization, this number can be interpreted as an upper bound for the potential parallelism that is inherent to an LTS, as in our setting information needs to be propagated along edges. For workset based (i.e., bag of tasks) producer-consumer parallelizations [2] this means that (i) for each work item processed only few new work items are expected to be added to the workset, and (ii) synchronization is needed for concurrent operations on the dynamic data structure used to store the work items.

Due to this, our approach is not based on the producer-consumer paradigm that propagates only essential information, but on a more naive fixed point iteration. This promises a much higher potential for the utilization of parallel hardware as it does not require dynamic data structures. In our particular setting, data operations can even be implemented lock-free. Furthermore we do not have to populate a workset since we propagate all possible changes during a fixed point iteration, at the price of computational overhead, which is negligible considering the ever growing number of parallel PUs.

Cilk Plus and CUDA. Our approach is based on data-parallelization, which is commonly referred to as fine-grained parallelization (in contrast to task-parallelization, i.e., "coarse grained" parallelization). To efficiently parallelize this type of problem the choice of framework is very important, because it most

---

[1] http://techresearch.intel.com/ResearchAreaDetails.aspx?Id=27

[2] http://www.inrialpes.fr/vasy/cadp/resources/benchmark_bcg.html

significantly influences the overhead connected to context switches. In case of our multi-core parallelization the overhead of manual thread maintenance is not negligible since the amount of productive work per thread invocation is very limited. Therefore, the naive use of multi-threading environments, such as PThreads [26], is very likely to nullify the gain we expect from the parallelization itself. For this reason we chose Intel's Cilk Plus framework[3] which offers a work stealing based thread-pool and internally employs efficient scheduling and load balancing mechanisms. The scheduling of workers is not explicit and more lightweight than the manual management of threads.

For general purpose programming on GPUs, NVIDIA's *Compute Unified Device Architecture* (CUDA)[4] is the de facto standard framework for parallel computation. It provides an *Application Programming Interface* (API), allowing the utilization of NVIDIA's GPUs for massively parallel, throughput oriented applications beyond the scope of rendering graphics. Since the CUDA framework is tailored to applications with many data-parallel threads, light-weight computations per thread and frequent context switches [13], it is well suited for our application.

Contributions and Related Work. In the area of software model checking [9], the sizes of input problems become exceptionally large. For this reason, much research has been put into the development of techniques that can reduce the problem sizes by, e.g., applying abstractions, using efficient data structures such as Binary Decision Diagrams (BDDs) [8], or limiting the exploration of the problem domain to relevant parts only.

The approach advocated by us in this paper does not aim at reducing the problem size, but instead at exploiting modern parallel hardware for speeding-up the model checking of large problems. We parallelize a simple fixed point algorithm for BES solving on multi-core (CPU) and many-core (GPU) architectures. While our parallel approach is largely straightforward and its correctness is easy to understand, it gives rise to algorithms that – in the GPU case but not the CPU case – outperform an optimized sequential algorithm [1]. This standard algorithm for solving BESs is based on a workset data structure that propagates information during fixed point computation; however, in a parallel setting, synchronizations on this workset would lead to unacceptable overheads. In contrast, our approach does not require this workset; its higher computational costs are met by the higher number of PUs and their efficient utilization by us.

We extensively evaluate the performance of our workset-less multi-core and many-core algorithms when model checking deadlock and livelock properties on the large examples of the VLTS benchmark. More precisely, we used the tool "evaluator" distributed with the CADP toolset [24] to generate the BESs for our benchmark suite from the VLTS examples and the desired deadlock and liveness properties expressed as temporal logic formulae in the alternation-free μ-calculus [19]. For convenience, we restrict ourselves to the evaluation of the

---

[3] http://software.intel.com/en-us/articles/intel-cilk-plus/
[4] http://developer.download.nvidia.com/compute/cuda/4_0/toolkit/docs/
CUDA_C_Programming_Guide.pdf

solution step in the model checking process, since there exist several efficient and even parallel approaches for the construction of compact data representations in our setting [4,5,20], which can be used for preprocessing of input data.

Regarding closely related work, only two approaches on the parallel resolution of BESs are known to us. The first one [28] is based on a multi-core parallelization of the "Gaussian Elimination" as proposed in [23], which turns out not to be viable in practice due to its exponential space complexity. The second one [18] is tailored to distributed systems and aims at the resolution of extremely large BES instances. There exist further distributed implementations [7,14,16,22] but their general goal is, in contrast to our approach, to increase the total amount of memory in order to deal with larger problem instances, rather than to improve on their run-time performance, as network latency typically degrades the overall performance significantly.

The experimental evaluation of the parity-game based approach presented in [27], which performs a parallel resolution of μ-formulae on shared-memory multi-core systems, provides scalability results for up to eight workers. Yet, the range of examples is restricted to three *Sliding Window Protocol* (SWP) and two randomly generated instances, and their run-times are not related to existing sequential algorithms. In contrast, we present a parallel, shared-memory model checking approach that is based on a fixed point iteration used for the parallel resolution of BESs (cf. Sec. 3). Even though this approach is targeted at large BES instances, we are not only concerned about the capability to check large models, but also the improvement of run-time performance. The evaluation of our multi-core implementation confirms the scalability results presented in [27], extends them to a much larger set of different benchmark examples and, most importantly, puts them in relation to an optimized sequential BES solver (cf. Sec. 2). In addition, we show that our approach also scales on many-core architectures, boosting the run-time performance by one order of magnitude and outperforming the optimized sequential baseline significantly (cf. Sec. 4).

2 Fixed Points and Boolean Equation Systems

Fixed Points and the μ-Calculus. The μ-calculus [19] is a powerful formalism, e.g., subsuming the temporal logics LTL, CTL and CTL* [11], for expressing temporal properties. It features fixed point operators to express temporal properties such as liveness (i.e., something good will eventually happen) and safety (i.e., something bad will never happen). The following intuition describes the meaning of the least (μ) and greatest (ν) fixed point operators in the context of temporal-logic based model checking: μ is used to express liveness properties with the initial assumption that every state violates this property, and ν is used to express safety properties with the initial assumption that every state satisfies this property.

The syntax of the μ-calculus is defined by the following grammar:

$$\varphi ::= \top \mid \bot \mid x \mid \neg\varphi \mid \varphi \wedge \varphi \mid \varphi \vee \varphi \mid [a]\varphi \mid \langle a \rangle \varphi \mid \nu x.\varphi \mid \mu x.\varphi$$

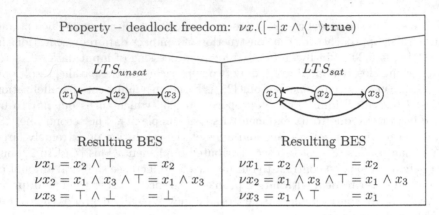

Fig. 1. Interpretation of μ-formula over LTSs

where Var is a set of propositional variables with $x \in Var$, and Act is a set of actions with $a \in Act$. In our setting, μ-formulae are used to express properties over LTSs as exemplary depicted in Fig. 1.

Boolean Equation Systems. BESs are sets of equations, resembling monotonic functions over the Boolean lattice $\{false < true\}$, of the form $\sigma x = \varphi$. Here, the *left hand side* (LHS) x is a Boolean variable from the set of propositional variables, $\sigma \in \{\mu, \nu\}$ is the least or the greatest fixed point operator, and the *right hand side* (RHS) is of the form $\varphi ::= \top|\bot|x|\varphi \wedge \varphi|\varphi \vee \varphi$.

In the context of model checking, BESs are the result of the interpretation of a μ-formula over an LTS. Since the formula has to be verified for every state of the LTS, the resulting BES is of size $|LTS| \times |\varphi|^k$, i.e., the size of the BES is proportional to the size of the LTS and exponential in the complexity of the μ-formula, where k is the alternation depth of ϕ which, roughly speaking, is the number of alternations of different fixed point operator types binding the same variables. Each fixed point operator of the formula is resembled by a so called *block* in the resulting BES, containing the set of equations associated with this operator. As is illustrated in Fig. 1, the resulting BESs for the deadlock freedom property with respect to the two displayed LTSs only contain one block, with three equations. This is because the corresponding formula only consists of one fixed point operator and each LTS comprises three states.

While equations may be reordered arbitrarily within a block, this is not the case for the ordering of blocks corresponding to alternating fixed point operators, as it may lead to the computation of a wrong fixed point. The order in which blocks have to be processed is defined by their nesting within the μ-formula. In this paper, we consider only alternation-free μ-formulae where the nesting of different fixed point operators binding the same variables is not allowed. Thus, dependencies between blocks form a tree [7] that can easily be constructed and yields the order (from leaves to root) in which the blocks have to be solved.

Optimized Sequential Resolution of BESs. To be able to conduct a fair evaluation of our parallel implementations for BES solving in terms of runtime competitiveness, we have implemented an optimized, sequential CPU-based algorithm in the style of the "chasing ones" as proposed in [1]. This approach is workset based and uses a queue to store work items, where a work item is equivalent to one equation of the BES. The computation in this algorithm starts at those equations where the LHS is directly assigned value *true* ($\top$) or *false* ($\bot$), and propagates this information to all equations relying on the value of these particular LHSs. For this purpose, equations must be enriched with information about such backward dependencies. As space and time complexity of this approach are linear in the size of the BES, it is well suited as a baseline for comparison with our parallel implementations.

3 Basic Fixed Point Algorithm and Parallelization

While a lot of effort has been put into the development and optimization of sequential model checking algorithms so as to fight computational complexity and state space explosion, our aim is to investigate whether a parallel approach can be more efficient and provide scalability not only on multi-core (CPU) architectures but also on many-core (GPU) architectures. For this purpose, we chose a fixed point iteration based algorithm, which we show to be well suited for such a parallelization. In this section we first present the algorithmic background of our approach, followed by the concepts of our parallel implementations.

Basic Fixed Point Algorithm. The listing of Algorithm 1 illustrates the fundamental idea of the fixed point computation that we employ for the resolution of BESs in our multi-core and many-core implementations.

Algorithm 1: FIXEDPOINT algorithm

Input : BES
Output: Solution of BES

1 Initialization of LHSs   `// true for` $\sigma = \nu$`; false for` $\sigma = \mu$
2 **foreach** *block B* **do**   `// block order matters`
3 | **do**
4 | | variablesChanged $\leftarrow$ `false`
5 | | **foreach** *equation* $E \in B$ **do**   `// equation order does not matter`
6 | | | LHS $\leftarrow$ EVALRHS(E)
7 | | | **if** LHSChanged **then**
8 | | | | variablesChanged $\leftarrow$ `true`
9 | **while** variablesChanged

This algorithm consists of two nested loops, the outer one over the BES-blocks (line 2) and the inner one over all equations within a block (line 5). The outer loop processes blocks in a sensible order, corresponding to the dependencies within the μ-formula (cf. Sec. 2). The inner loop computes the value of the LHS of an equation according to the evaluation of its respective RHS, where the RHS either consists of a terminal value (i.e., *true* or *false*) or LHS variables connected by Boolean operators. In the beginning, all LHSs are initialized depending on their associated fixed point operator σ, i.e., *false* in case $\sigma = \mu$ and *true* in case $\sigma = \nu$ (line 1). This *initial approximation* is derived from the Knaster-Tarski fixed point theorem [29], where $\mu f = \bigsqcup \{f^i(false) : i \in \mathbb{N}\}$ and $\nu f = \bigsqcap \{f^i(true) : i \in \mathbb{N}\}$. The termination of the fixed point computation is detected by a marker variable, indicating whether one or more LHSs have changed during an iteration (line 9).

The time complexity of Algorithm 1 is quadratic with respect to the size of the BES since, in the worst case, only one LHS is changed per iteration (one execution of the inner loop), whence the maximum number of iterations is equal to the total number of equations, where each iteration performs a linear amount of work.

Parallel Fixed Point Computation. The core idea for the parallelization of the basic fixed point algorithm is based on the parallel resolution of individual blocks by executing the inner loop of Algorithm 1 (line 5), computing the LHS value of an equation, in parallel. It is important to note that the order in which equations are evaluated does not matter within the loop, as our parallel frameworks are not aimed at the explicit scheduling of threads. Considering the fact that this operation needs to be executed for all equations during each iteration step, this approach exposes much potential for parallel computation, even within one iteration step, as we expect the number of equations to be very large, e.g., the largest LTS in the benchmark contains 33,949,609 states. The soundness of the approach is guaranteed by the fact that BESs resemble monotonic functions, i.e., even if the evaluation of a RHS depends on several other LHS variables – which in a parallel setting are potentially modified concurrently – the updated value of each LHS is available and thus can be propagated in the subsequent iteration. For complex μ-formulas the tree structure of BES-blocks can be exploited to increase the level of parallelization even further by processing all "leave blocks" in parallel.

Multi-core Data Structure. Data structures for multi-core systems have to follow two main objectives. On the one hand, they have to provide good data locality, i.e., data necessary for a computation should be closely grouped so that it can, ideally, be stored in the same cache line of a CPU. On the other hand, unrelated data should be separated in such a way that it does not interfere with each other in order to avoid harmful effects, such as cache thrashing, where independent data sets depend on and thus compete for the same cache lines. Due to these two factors and the structure of our input data (variable(s) $\in$ equation(s) $\in$ block(s) $\in$ BES) we have decided to use a nested data structure, where each aforementioned component is modeled by a structured type. In this layout, all data needed to evaluate one equation – the most frequent operation in our algorithm – is stored in a single structure resembling an equation, thus, accounting for good data locality. Clearly, this also provides good separation, and any further improvement would require machine dependent optimizations.

Multi-core Parallelization. For the parallelization of Algorithm 1 on CPUs we employ the Cilk Plus framework provided by the Intel C/C++ compiler.[5] We chose Cilk Plus because it is well suited for problems with fine-grained data-parallelism and irregular structure, as shown in [12], which also is the case in our setting. Cilk Plus maintains a pool of workers, each of which is mapped to a thread during execution, and supports work stealing, i.e., taking over work that was initially assigned to another worker. This is in contrast to having to create, manage and delete threads manually, inducing a much higher overhead.

The key idea of our multi-core implementation is the parallelization of the inner for-loop, iterating over the equations, by employing Cilk Plus' parallel version of a for-loop, *cilk_for*. The reasons why we do not require any locking and further modifications are (i) the monotonicity of the Boolean function, as mentioned before, and (ii) the fact that the variable *variablesChanged* indicating a change of LHSs is only reset outside the parallel loop (Algorithm 1, line 4) and set uniformly (only to *true*) inside the parallel loop (Algorithm 1, line 8), i.e., any worker that has observed a changing variable assigns this value and, thus, the value cannot become inconsistent.

Many-Core Data Structure. Data structures used for CUDA accelerated computation must be specially designed for this purpose. They must support independent thread-local data processing and, at the same time, they must also be compact enough to enable good data locality. This is to avoid high latency device-memory access and generally to reduce the usage of device-memory bandwidth that may otherwise become a performance bottleneck [21].

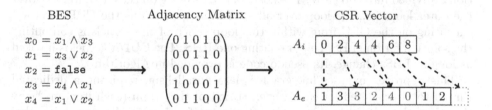

Fig. 2. Generation of adjacency list representation from BES

A BES may be interpreted as a directed graph where the LHSs are vertices and the dependencies on the RHSs are edges. Such a graph can be encoded as an adjacency matrix and stored using two vectors in *compressed sparse row* (CSR) format, as depicted in Fig. 2. Since this data structure has been demonstrated to be efficient for graph based algorithms in the context of CUDA accelerated

---

[5] http://software.intel.com/en-us/articles/intel-compilers/

computation [3,6,15] we employ it to store BESs. Each vertex stores the following information: a unique index, its value along with a flag indicating whether the Boolean value is already computed, and the *type* of Boolean operator (conjunction or disjunction).

In more detail, our representation uses two one-dimensional arrays A_i and A_e to encode the directed graph. For all vertices v_0 to v_n, the sum of outgoing edges is stored in A_i, such that the number of outgoing edges from a particular vertex v_j can be computed by $A_i[j + 1] - A_i[j]$. The idea of this encoding is that the value of an element $A_i[j]$ serves as an index to the second array A_e. The array A_e is a concatenation of ordered lists of target vertices of outgoing edges from individual graph vertices.

The sizes of the arrays A_i and A_e correspond to the sizes of the vertex set and the edge set of the graph, respectively. The array A_i does not only store the indices to the array A_e but also the aforementioned information (index, Boolean value, flag and type). Since the on-board memory of GPUs is very limited, we store this additional information in unused bits of A_i, thereby reducing the space requirement to 4 bytes per vertex.

Many-Core Parallelization. For our many-core parallelization we employ the CUDA framework, in which programs consist of two parts (i) *host code* that runs on the CPU and (ii) *device code* that runs on the GPU, the so called *kernels*. A kernel is executed concurrently in many independent data-parallel threads, where a group of threads, called a *warp*, executes on the same processor in a lock-step manner. When several warps are scheduled on a processor, memory latencies and pipeline stalls are hidden by switching to the execution of another warp. The CUDA framework is optimized for large numbers of simple parallel computations without explicit scheduling of threads.

For this reason the work-flow of our CUDA-accelerated fixed-point computation is divided into two parts. The host code, executing on the CPU, iterates over the outer loop, i.e., the loop over all BES-blocks, and calls the CUDA kernels executing on the GPU from within this loop. Each of the kernels is computing the solution for one LHS, i.e., evaluating one RHS. The CUDA kernel is invoked as long as LHSs change. Its pseudo code is provided in Algorithm 2.

This approach exposes fine-grained data-parallelism, requiring a dedicated thread to be executed for each vertex (LHS) of the graph (each item of Array A_i). Each thread first loads the data of a vertex from Array A_i (stored in global memory) into a local copy (line 1) and checks if the corresponding LHS has already been solved (line 2). Then, it processes all immediate successors (loop on line 6), representing the RHS of the corresponding equation. The algorithm employs a lazy evaluation of the equations. In case that a value within a RHS immediately determines the value of the LHS (i.e., the RHS is a purely disjunctive term where at least one variable is *true*, or a purely conjunctive term where at least one variable is *false*), the loop is broken (line 10). Finally, the Boolean value of the evaluation of the RHS (stored in *mySucc.value*) is compared to the Boolean value stored in the corresponding LHS (line 11). If the two values differ, the result of the evaluation is assigned to the respective LHS, written back to

---

Algorithm 2: FIXEDPOINT kernel – run in parallel for each LHS variable

---

Input : $g(lobal)A_e, g(lobal)A_i$, fixedPointFound

1   myVertex ← gA_i[tid]   // tid ∈ $[0, 1, ..., n]$ where n = sizeof(BES-block)
2   if myVertex.*solved* then
3 | return
4   first ← myVertex.*index*
5   last ← gA_i[tid + 1].*index*
6   foreach index ∈ first, . . . , last do
7 | targetVertex ← gA_e[index]
8 | mySucc ← gA_i[targetVertex]
9 | if mySucc.*value* ≠ myVertex.*type* then   // *type* ∨ ≡ 0 and *type* ∧ ≡ 1
10 | | break
11 if myVertex.*value* ≠ mySucc.*value* then
12 | myVertex.*solved* ← true
13 | myVertex.*value* ← mySucc.*value*
14 | gA_i[tid] ← myVertex
15 | fixedPointFound ← false

Array A_i (line 14), and the fixed point flag is set to *false* indicating that the fixed point is not yet reached.

Many-Core Optimizations. For the GPU-based implementation we have experimented with two optimizations.

The first one is the so called "intra-warp fixed point iteration." It is based on the observation that all threads within a warp have to load the required data from global memory into local copies. All operations are performed on the local copies, which are written back to global memory at the end of the execution of the warp. This means that updated LHSs do not become visible to other threads until the next iteration step and, thus, changes can only be propagated one step per iteration. The intra-warp fixed point iteration is intended to increase the number of propagations by performing multiple iterations on the equations bundled in a warp and thereby propagating changes of LHSs within this warp.

The second optimization is an extension to the intra-warp fixed point iteration. It utilizes the GPU's shared memory, which provides a fast local memory for single threads or warps, allowing the intermediate storage of data. We use this shared memory to optimize the execution of the kernel by copying the LHS variables contained in a RHS from global memory to shared memory. When the data of a LHS is required by the kernel, the copy in shared memory is utilized instead of the one in global memory. When the kernel returns, the copy is written back from shared to global memory. However, the indirection on line 8 potentially requires further LHSs; this data can either be read from global memory as before or also be copied to shared memory. This reduces access to global memory but requires additional load and store operations before and after each thread invocation.

4   Experimental Evaluation

In this section we experimentally evaluate the scalability of our parallel approach in its CPU and GPU variants and demonstrate the competitiveness of the GPU version when compared to the optimized sequential algorithm, using the VLTS benchmark suite.[6] We double-check the correctness of our implementations by observing that the results obtained from our sequential and parallel algorithms match those computed by CADP's sequential "bes_solve" tool [24].

To provide an outlook on the generality of our results, we also extend our evaluation using randomly generated BESs, thus analyzing the influence of the specific way in which BESs are derived from model checking problems. Furthermore, we evaluate the structure and density of the BESs generated from the benchmark suite. Besides the run-time based comparison we provide insights into the specifics of BESs in the context of model checking, i.e., we present heuristics for the order in which equations are to be solved, which may yield significant speed-ups for BES resolution in this context.

Benchmark Suite. Our experiments were conducted using the VLTS benchmark suite that was compiled within a joint project of CWI[7] and INRIA[8]. It consists of 40 examples from academia and industry, provided as LTSs with numbers of states ranging from 289 up to 33,949,609. The four largest examples of the benchmark were solved for the first time in 2005 [16].

Table 1. μ-Formulae of Properties

Property	μ-formula
Deadlock freedom	$\nu X.([-]X \wedge \langle - \rangle true)$
Livelock	$\mu X.(\langle - \rangle X \vee \nu Y.(\langle \tau \rangle Y))$

The backgrounds of the benchmark examples vary greatly; thus, different properties may be checked for individual examples. For our evaluation we use two representative properties, namely deadlock freedom and livelock, which can be checked for all examples of the benchmark suite (cf. Table 1 for their formalization). For these properties, results are also provided by the authors of the benchmark, thus allowing a direct verification of the correctness of the results obtained by our implementations.

The images of some exemplary BESs, as depicted in Fig. 3, show the significant variance in structure and density of the LTSs provided in the benchmark. The

---

[6] http://www.inrialpes.fr/vasy/cadp/resources/benchmark_bcg.html
[7] http://www.cwi.nl/
[8] http://vasy.inria.fr/

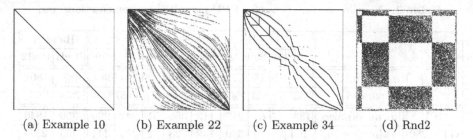

(a) Example 10   (b) Example 22   (c) Example 34   (d) Rnd2

Fig. 3. Visualization of benchmark examples as adjacency matrices

images are visualizations of the adjacency matrices of the respective BESs, with their origins, i.e., the LTSs' initial states, displayed on the top left.

In contrast to intuition, our experiments suggest that this information about structure and density does not usefully correlate with the scalability and/or run-time performance of our approach. This is the case for the following reasons: (i) the run-time generally depends on the question whether the property, for which the LTS is checked, is fulfilled or violated; (ii) our approach does not favor local propagation of changing variables, but globally propagates all possible changes during an iteration; (iii) our algorithms perform best in cases that expose large numbers of concurrent changes rather than sequential chains of changes, which in addition to a BES's structure depends on the initial distribution of terminal values. Unfortunately, none of these factors can be estimated sensibly nor be extracted from a BES in reasonable time, i.e., when compared to the time it takes to solve the BES.

Hardware. Our experiments were carried out on different hardware platforms for (i) the CPU and (ii) the GPU version of the implementation: (i) two interconnected Intel XEON E7-4830 processors @ 2,13 GHz, each with 8 physical cores and Hyper-Threading enabled (i.e., a total of 32 logical PUs) and 64 GB DDR3 RAM @ 1333 MHz, running Windows 7 64-bit, and (ii) one AMD Phenom II X4 940 processor @ 3,0 GHz, 8 GB DDR2 RAM @ 1066 MHz along with (a) one NVIDIA GeForce GTX 280 GPU with 1 GB of global memory, 16KB of shared memory per multiprocessor, providing 240 CUDA cores, and (b) one NVIDIA GeForce GTX 480 GPU with 1.5 GB of global memory, 48KB of shared memory per multiprocessor, providing 480 CUDA cores, running Debian 6.0 64-bit on kernel 2.6.39. Although the systems use different CPU types this fact does not affect our results since we did not evaluate a hybrid approach but only pure CPU and GPU versions of the respective algorithms.

Overview. Table 2 provides an overview of the run-times of the following algorithms: (i) the optimized sequential workset-based CPU implementation (the baseline for our comparison), (ii) the parallel Cilk Plus based CPU implementation, (iii) the unoptimized GPU implementation without any optimization, (iv) the GPU implementation with intra-warp iteration, and (v) the GPU implementation utilizing shared memory. In case of the GTX 280 GPU, we omitted the

Table 2. Overview of Run-Times for CPU and GPU Implementations [ms]

Algorithm		Benchmark Example									Random	
		10	21	22	31	32	33	34	35	39	Rnd1	Rnd2
CPU	(i) sequential	1	19	18	573	475	737	1	704	901	3891	7801
	(ii) parallel	2538	77	611	1564	1786	2764	279	4325	8170	7966	40576
GPU GTX 280	(iii) unoptimized	1336	17	68	217	113	359	51	242	290	350	1840
	(iv) intra-warp	104	22	69	320	149	528	52	404	344	493	2594
GPU GTX 480	(iii) unoptimized	703	6	33	75	46	105	6	98	125	178	992
	(iv) intra-warp	40	7	28	109	63	157	6	152	158	248	1391
	(v) shared mem	38	40	59	659	341	862	48	190	227	315	1800

results for (iv), the shared memory implementation, since this GPU does not provide a sufficient amount of shared memory for this optimization. Note that in the case of parallel CPU implementation we list the best runtimes available among the numbers of cores that have been utilized.

Because of layouting limitations, we restrict our selection of benchmark examples in Table 2 to those for which the run-time of the GPU implementation is sensibly measurable, i.e., larger than 5 [ms]; nonetheless we conducted our experiments for the entire benchmark suite. The numbering of the benchmark examples refers to their position in the table provided on the VLTS website,[9] which is sorted in ascending order relative to the number of states of the LTS; thus, Example 10 is *vasy_25_25*, Example 21 is *vasy_166_651*, Example 22 is *cwi_214_684*, Example 31 is *vasy_2581_11442*, Example 32 is *vasy_4220_13944*, Example 33 is *vasy_4338_15666*, Example 34 is *vasy_6020_19353*, Example 35 is *vasy_6120_11031* and Example 39 is *vasy_12323_27667*. In this naming scheme, the first number is the number of states divided by 1000, and the second number is the number of transitions divided by 1000.

Furthermore, all examples in Table 2 are checked for the deadlock freedom property since only eight of the 40 LTSs contain livelocks. Nonetheless, our general statements about scalability and competitiveness have been evaluated and are valid for the entire benchmark suite. To check whether the specific ways in which BESs were generated for and included in the VLTS benchmark have an influence on our performance results, we extend our evaluation to randomly generated BESs. We evaluate a total of five random examples with the number of states ranging from 1 to 10 million; Rnd1 and Rnd2 are two representatives illustrating our observations for this class of BESs.

We omit memory consumptions of our implementations in the table, since (i) our parallel versions operate on a static data structure that is linear in the size of the input BES (ranging from approximately 90 KB up to 4.5 GB) and (ii) it is not our aim to evaluate or optimize memory efficiency within the scope of this paper, especially since all benchmark examples easily fit our systems' memory.

---

[9] http://cadp.inria.fr/resources/benchmark_bcg.html#section-5

Multi-core Performance. The results in Table 2 clearly show that our multi-core implementation is outperformed significantly by the optimized sequential baseline. The reason for this is the low total number of parallel PUs (32 logical cores) and, thus, the computational overhead of the fixed point iteration is too large when compared to the amount of productive work and cannot be compensated by parallel processing power. This observation is supported by the two graphs in Fig. 4, which show the overall scalability of our CPU-based approach for an increasing number of parallel workers. This result is in accordance with [27] and extends their results to our much larger benchmark suite.

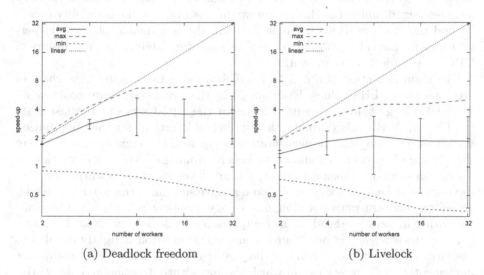

(a) Deadlock freedom   (b) Livelock

Fig. 4. Scalability of our multi-core implementation

The data for the two graphs in Fig. 4 is based on the median values of 10 runs for each of the 40 benchmark examples. It is evaluated separately for the two properties: deadlock freedom (Fig. 4(a)) and livelock (Fig. 4(b)). The average scalability (avg) is compiled from all 40 benchmark examples and is below linear for both properties. However the scalability is observable for up to eight workers, which corresponds to the number of physical cores of one CPU in our system. For the sake of completeness we also include the standard deviation for the average scalability, along with maximum (max) and minimum (min) scalability.

It is important that the shape of the two graphs, which suggests better scalability for LTSs that have been checked for the no deadlock property, is affected by the fact that there are 20 examples containing deadlocks, while only 8 examples contain livelocks. In the case of the trivial examples, i.e., those that do not contain deadlocks/livelocks, our algorithm needs to perform only one iteration, which has significant impact on scalability.

The super-linear speed-up in Fig. 4(a) can be explained by the parallel execution of workers. As the Cilk Plus framework may schedule the evaluation order of equations differently from the order in the BES, this may lead to a faster propagation of updated LHSs, requiring less iterations and thus result in the seemingly above linear boost in performance.

Many-Core Performance. The evaluation of our many-core implementation is aimed more at the competitiveness of our approach when compared to the optimized sequential baseline than at its scalability. Indeed, the scalability analysis is more difficult than for the multi-core implementation because we had to use different GPU devices that are not comparable with respect to some important specifications. Not only did the number of CUDA cores double from the GTX 280 to the GTX 480, but also the clock rate and the available amount of memory increased significantly. For this reason we did not evaluate the scalability aspect beyond the scope provided in Table 2, which shows a significant boost in performance for the GTX 480. Further evaluations of scalability, e.g., on clusters of GPUs, are subject to future work.

The main limitation of the GPU parallelization is the length of the chain of propagations of LHS values. Example 10 in the benchmark suite contains an artificially long chain of dependencies from the initial state to the last state (cf. Fig. 3(a)). For this example, the number of iterations for the unoptimized version of our many-core implementation is equal to the number of states , yet the example is a prime candidate to benefit from the intra-warp iteration as the changes can be propagated ideally within the equations of a warp. However, the remaining benchmark examples do not have such an extreme structure and, therefore, the intra-warp iteration, on average, does not provide any advantage but rather induces overhead as the comparison of run-times in Table 2 shows.

Since the efficiency of our shared memory optimization is tightly coupled to the intra-warp iteration, it can only improve the performance of the many-core implementation in those cases in which the intra-warp iteration actually works. Due to this reason, the results for this optimization in Table 2 are, not surprisingly, even worse than for the intra-warp iteration because the transfer times from and to shared memory degrade the run-time performance even further. Moreover, in order to use the shared memory, the required data (i.e., the part of a BES corresponding to a block) has to fit the limited size of the GPUs shared memory. The size of the data that has to be stored in the shared memory is given by the block size, the number of vertices in one block and the number of their successors. In case the average out-degree (i.e., the average number of RHS variables per equations) is high, we have to decrease the group size. This can lead to underutilization or low occupancy of the individual multiprocessors and, thus, significantly reduces the performance of our algorithm.

As documented in Table 2, our GPU implementation of BES resolution provides significant speed-ups for most cases of the benchmark examples and especially for the randomly generated BESs. Surprisingly, the GPU implementation with no optimizations yields the best results, since in most cases the structure of the inspected BESs does not allow one to benefit from our optimizations.

Ordering Heuristics. Table 3 provides a comprehensive overview of the total number of iterations for those examples of the benchmark, which have been

Table 3. Impact of Heuristics [Total Number of Iterations]

Heuristic	Benchmark Example																			
	4	5	7	10	15	16	18	19	21	22	25	27	30	31	32	33	35	37	38	39
Original	64	19	7	25219	19	33	23	18	33	208	24	7	56	32	23	34	33	20	29	29
Vectorized	64	19	7	25219	23	37	23	19	37	213	24	7	56	37	25	37	34	20	29	29
Reverse	2	4	3	2	7	8	8	5	8	8	10	2	3	7	4	6	4	5	5	5
Random	20	9	5	25219	10	12	6	11	11	63	7	3	6	8	5	8	16	10	9	9

checked for deadlocks and for which the initial approximation is not equal to the final solution, i.e., the total number of iterations is larger than one. Even though the available number of PUs increases with each hardware generation, it is still far from the point where a full iteration step can be computed fully in parallel. Thus, the processing order of equations within a block has a significant influence on the total number of iterations needed to compute the fixed point. Yet, our evaluation yields an interesting insight for an ideal "vectorized" parallelization, assuming that a fully parallel iteration step is possible; we model this by delaying the visibility of a changed LHSs until the next iteration step. Note that the lack of a suitable hardware architecture allowing such fully-parallel processing is the reason why we list the number of iterations instead of run-times in Table 3. Naturally the number of iterations is proportional to the run-times.

Our evaluation shows that this "Vectorized" approach does not increase the total number of iterations significantly, when compared to the "original" ordering, where equations are evaluated in their given order and changes of LHSs are directly visible in the following computations of the iteration (cf. Table 3). This result demonstrates that the penalty for a fully parallel computation is negligible regarding the total number of iterations needed to reach the fixed point.

As the application of advanced heuristics would require preprocessing of the data – causing a potentially high computational overhead – we restrict our evaluation to two simple cases that do not introduce any overhead. The first heuristics is called "Reverse" in Table 3 and takes the reverse order of equations within a BES-block, as proposed in [27]. It yields a significant improvement with respect to the total number of iteration needed to compute the fixed point (cf. Table 3). Yet, according to our observations, this heuristics only works for the examples generated from the benchmark's LTSs, but not for randomly generated BESs. This could be due to the way in which state spaces are enumerated in the CADP toolset, which in turn determines the order of equations in the VLTS examples.

The second heuristics, called "Random" in Table 3, is the randomized evaluation of equations within a BES-block. In our observations, this heuristics leads to a decrease in the number of iterations needed to solve a BESs when compared to the given ("Original") ordering. This result is of practical relevance as our parallel implementations rely on parallelizations in which the order of RHS evaluations is not under our control, but is determined by the runtime environment of CUDA and Cilk Plus. Thus, we expect an additional performance boost rather than a degradation, due to the parallelization frameworks.

5   Conclusions and Future Work

We implemented an approach to the parallel resolution of BESs on multi- and many-core systems, and evaluated them with respect to scalability and run-time performance in comparison to an optimized sequential algorithm. Our measurements confirm the scalability results of [27] for our multi-core implementation, yet this implementation's overall performance is not competitive when compared to our optimized sequential implementation. In contrast, the utilization of many-core hardware, not considered in [27], yields a significant speed-up and outperforms the optimized sequential implementation for most instances of the benchmark by almost one order of magnitude. Furthermore, the scalability of our many-core approach with respect to increasing numbers of PUs was demonstrated by us by (i) comparing the multi-core and many-core implementations and (ii) evaluating the many-core implementation for two GPU cards with 240 and 480 CUDA cores, respectively.

Future work will include further evaluation of the scalability results of the many-core implementation, e.g., by its distribution over a cluster of GPUs. Since BESs are not restricted to model checking, it is also promising to evaluate input BESs from other applications, such as data-flow analyzes in optimizing compilers [10]. Furthermore, the recently proposed many-core parallelization of graph algorithms [25] should be evaluated with respect to its suitability and potential impact on our work.

Acknowledgments. The second author has been partially supported by the Czech Grant Agency grants No. 102/09/H042 and GAP202/11/0312. We thank the anonymous reviewers for their valuable comments.

References

1. Andersen, H.R.: Model Checking and Boolean Graphs. Theoret. Comp. Sc. 126(1), 3–30 (1994)
2. Andrews, G.R.: Foundations of Multithreaded, Parallel, and Distributed Programming. Addison-Wesley (2000)
3. Barnat, J., Bauch, P., Brim, L., Češka, M.: Computing Strongly Connected Components in Parallel on CUDA. In: IPDPS, pp. 544–555. IEEE (2011)
4. Barnat, J., Bauch, P., Brim, L., Češka, M.: Designing Fast LTL Model Checking Algorithms for Many-Core GPUs. To app. in J. of Par. and Distrib. Comp. (2012)
5. Barnat, J., Brim, L., Ročkai, P.: Scalable Multi-core LTL Model-Checking. In: Bošnački, D., Edelkamp, S. (eds.) SPIN 2007. LNCS, vol. 4595, pp. 187–203. Springer, Heidelberg (2007)
6. Barnat, J., Brim, L., Češka, M., Lamr, T.: CUDA Accelerated LTL Model Checking. In: ICPADS, pp. 34–41. IEEE (2009)
7. Bollig, B., Leucker, M., Weber, M.: Local Parallel Model Checking for the Alternation-Free μ-Calculus. In: Bošnački, D., Leue, S. (eds.) SPIN 2002. LNCS, vol. 2318, pp. 128–147. Springer, Heidelberg (2002)
8. Bryant, R.E.: Symbolic Boolean Manipulation with Ordered Binary-Decision Diagrams. ACM Comput. Surv. 24(3), 293–318 (1992)

9. Clarke, E.M., Grumberg, O., Peled, D.A.: Model Checking. MIT Press (1999)
10. Gallardo, M.d.M., Joubert, C., Merino, P.: On-the-Fly Data Flow Analysis Based on Verification Technology. In: COCV. ENTCS, vol. 190, pp. 33–48 (2007)
11. Emerson, E.A.: Temporal and Modal Logic. In: van Leeuwen, J. (ed.) Handbook of Theoretical Computer Science, vol. B, ch. 16, pp. 995–1072. Elsevier (1990)
12. Ezekiel, J., Lüttgen, G., Siminiceanu, R.: To Parallelize or to Optimize? J. of Log. and Comput. 21, 85–120 (2011)
13. Garland, M., Kirk, D.B.: Understanding Throughput-Oriented Architectures. Commun. ACM 53, 58–66 (2010)
14. Grumberg, O., Heyman, T., Schuster, A.: Distributed Symbolic Model Checking for μ-Calculus. Form. Methods Syst. Des. 26, 197–219 (2005)
15. Harish, P., Narayanan, P.J.: Accelerating Large Graph Algorithms on the GPU Using CUDA. In: Aluru, S., Parashar, M., Badrinath, R., Prasanna, V.K. (eds.) HiPC 2007. LNCS, vol. 4873, pp. 197–208. Springer, Heidelberg (2007)
16. Holmén, F., Leucker, M., Lindström, M.: UppDMC: A Distributed Model Checker for Fragments of the mu-Calculus. In: PDMC. ENTCS, vol. 128, pp. 91–105. Elsevier (2005)
17. Holzmann, G.J., Bosnacki, D.: Multi-Core Model Checking with SPIN. In: IPDPS, pp. 1–8. IEEE (2007)
18. Joubert, C., Mateescu, R.: Distributed Local Resolution of Boolean Equation Systems. In: PDP, pp. 264–271. IEEE (2005)
19. Kozen, D.: Results on the Propositional mu-Calculus. Theoret. Comp. Sc. 27, 333–354 (1983)
20. Laarman, A., van de Pol, J., Weber, M.: Boosting Multi-Core Reachability Performance with Shared Hash Tables. In: FMCAD, pp. 247–255. IEEE (2010)
21. Lefohn, A., Kniss, J.M., Owens, J.D.: Implementing Efficient Parallel Data Structures on GPUs. In: GPU Gems 2, pp. 521–545. Addison-Wesley (2005)
22. Leucker, M., Somla, R., Weber, M.: Parallel Model Checking for LTL, CTL*, and L^2_μ. In: PDMC. ENTCS, vol. 89, pp. 4–16 (2003)
23. Mader, A.H.: Verification of Modal Properties Using Boolean Equation Systems. PhD thesis, Technische Universität München, Germany (1997)
24. Mateescu, R.: CAESAR_SOLVE: A Generic Library for On-the-Fly Resolution of Alternation-free Boolean Equation Systems. STTT 8(1), 37–56 (2006)
25. Merrill, D., Garland, M., Grimshaw, A.: Scalable GPU Graph Traversal. In: PPoPP, pp. 117–128. ACM (2012)
26. Nichols, B., Buttlar, D., Farrell, J.P.: PThreads Programming. O'Reilly (1996)
27. van de Pol, J., Weber, M.: A Multi-Core Solver for Parity Games. In: PDMC. ENTCS, vol. 220, pp. 19–34. Elsevier (2008)
28. Sailer, A.: Utilizing And-Inverter Graphs in the Gaussian Elimination for Boolean Equation Systems. Master's thesis, Hochschule Regensburg, Germany (2011)
29. Tarski, A.: A Lattice-Theoretical Fixpoint Theorem and its Applications. Pacific J. of Math. 5(2), 285–309 (1955)

Improving GPU Sparse Matrix-Vector Multiplication for Probabilistic Model Checking

Anton J. Wijs and Dragan Bošnački

Eindhoven University of Technology
P.O. Box 513, 5600 MB, Eindhoven, The Netherlands

Abstract. We present several methods to improve the run times of probabilistic model checking on general-purpose graphics processing units (GPUs). The methods enhance sparse matrix-vector multiplications, which are in the core of the probabilistic model checking algorithms. The improvement is based on the analysis of the transition matrix structures corresponding to state spaces of a selection of examples from the literature.

Our first method defines an enumeration of the matrix elements (states of the Markov chains), based on breadth-first search which can lead to a more regular representation of the matrices. We introduce two additional methods that adjust the execution paths and memory access patterns of the individual processors of the GPU. They exploit the specific features of the transition matrices arising from probabilistic/stochastic models as well as the logical and physical architectures of the device.

We implement the matrix reindexing and the efficient memory access methods in GPU-PRISM, an extension of the probabilistic model checker PRISM. The experiments with the prototype implementation show that each of the methods can bring a significant run time improvement - more than four times compared to the previous version of GPU-PRISM. Moreover, in some cases, the methods are orthogonal and can be used in combination to achieve even greater speed ups.

1 Introduction

Probabilistic model checking (e.g. [18,2,3]) was introduced for the analysis of systems that contain inherently probabilistic components. It has been applied to a broad spectrum of systems, ranging from communication protocols, like FireWire and Bluetooth, to various biological networks.

Unlike in standard model checking, in probabilistic model checking the correctness of the verified properties is quantified with some probabilities. Such properties are expressed in special logics which are extensions of traditional temporal logics. As a result, probabilistic model checking algorithms overlap with conventional ones in the sense that they require computing reachability of the underlying transition systems. Still, there are also important differences because numerical methods are used to compute the probabilities.

A. Donaldson and D. Parker (Eds.): SPIN 2012, LNCS 7385, pp. 98–116, 2012.

Modern General Purpose Graphics Processing Units (GPUs) are no longer dedicated only to graphics applications. Instead a GPU can be seen as a general purpose manycore processor. The idea to use GPUs for model checking in general, and for probabilistic model checking in particular, was put forth in [8,9]. The main goal was to speed up the numerical components of the algorithms. More precisely, it turned out that one can harness the massively parallel processing power of GPUs to accelerate linear algebraic operations, like sparse matrix vector multiplication (SpMV) and its derivatives, which are at the core of the algorithms. Significant speed ups, often of more than ten times in comparison to the sequential analogues, can easily be achieved.

In this paper, we describe three novel methods to improve SpMV and related algorithms. The methods exploit the specific structures of the matrices that arise in probabilistic model checking. The matrices contain transition probabilities for the underlying Markov chains, which are actually the state spaces of the probabilistic models. Therefore we first present an overview of the transition matrices/state spaces based on the examples that occur in the standard distribution of the probabilistic model checker PRISM [17].

The efficiency of the GPU computations crucially depends on the usage of the various types of memory that are on the device. The difference in speed between various memories can be up to 100 times. Therefore, we strive to achieve so called *coalesced* memory access, i.e. the active processors of the GPUs fetch data from addresses which are physically close to one another. It turns out that to obtain such efficient memory access patterns it is advantageous to have elements of the matrix grouped as close as possible to the main diagonal. To achieve this we develop a heuristic that assigns indices to the states of the Markov Chains based on breadth-first search.

We also present two new SpMV methods, each consisting of a new matrix storage format and accompanying SpMV algorithm. These are geared towards maximizing coalesced memory access, in particular for matrices stemming from probabilistic model checking problems.

In the first method, each thread processes one row of the matrix. The algorithm groups the threads in segments of rows that conform nicely with the logical and physical architecture of the GPU. The specially tailored storage format ensures efficient access to contiguous memory locations. The second method also groups the rows in segments, with the difference that each row is processed by two threads working in parallel. Again, its specific storage format ensures coalesced memory access of all threads accessing a row in the same segment.

We implemented the new methods in GPU-PRISM [10], an extension of the probabilistic model checker PRISM. Each of the efficient memory access methods can achieve runtime improvements with regard to the previous version of GPU-PRISM of at least factor 2, and improvements of factor 4.5 have been recorded too.

2 GPU Preliminaries

Harnessing the power of GPUs is facilitated by specific Application Programming Interfaces. In this paper, we assume a concrete NVIDIA GPU architecture and the Compute Unified Device Architecture (CUDA) interface [13]. Nevertheless, the algorithms that we present here can be straightforwardly extended to a more general context, i.e., for an architecture which provides massive hardware multithreading, supports the single instruction multiple thread (SIMT) model, and relies on coalesced access to the memory.

CUDA is an interface by NVIDIA which is used to program GPUs. CUDA programs are basically extended C programs. To this end CUDA features extensions like: special declarations to explicitly place variables in some of the memories (e.g., shared, global, local), predefined keywords (variables) containing the block and thread IDs, synchronization statements for cooperation between threads, run time API for memory management (allocation, deallocation), and statements to launch functions on GPU. In this section we give only a brief overview of CUDA. More details can be found in, for instance, [8].

CUDA Programming Model. A CUDA program consists of a *host* program which runs on the Central Processing Unit (CPU) and a CUDA *kernel.* The kernel, which describes the parallel part of the program, is executed many times in parallel by different threads on the GPU device, and is launched from the host program, which comprises the sequential part. Each GPU thread executes the same code. GPU threads are grouped in blocks. Each thread block is uniquely identified by its block ID and analogously each thread is uniquely identified by its thread ID within its block. The dimensions of the thread and the thread block are specified at the time of launching the kernel. The grid can be one- or two-dimensional and the blocks are at most three-dimensional.

CUDA Memory Model. Threads have access to different kinds of memory. Each thread has its own on-chip registers and off-chip local memory, which is quite slow. Threads within a block cooperate via shared memory which is on-chip and very fast. If multiple blocks are executed in parallel then the shared memory is equally split between them. All blocks have access to the device memory which is large (up to 6GB), but slow since, like the local memory, it is not cached. The host (CPU program) has read and write access to the global memory (Video RAM, or VRAM), but cannot access the other memories (registers, local, shared). Thus, the global memory is used for communication between the host and the kernel.

CUDA Execution Model. A GPU performs computations in SIMT (Single Instruction Multiple Threads) manner, which means that each thread is executed independently with its own instruction address and local state (registers and local memory). The threads of a block are executed in groups of 32 called *warps.* The threads in a warp execute instructions in a synchronous manner. These instructions can be different, but if they are all the same, the runtime is positively affected. Hence, our goal is to avoid execution divergence, i.e., to make the threads perform the same instructions as long as possible. Memory accesses of the threads in a single warp are also done simultaneously whenever possible, and if these accesses can be grouped together physically, i.e. if the accesses are coalesced, this greatly improves the runtime. For this reason, achieving as much coalesced memory access as possible in SpMV is the main objective throughout this paper. We developed algorithms where the memory accesses of threads in a warp can be grouped together.

3 Structures of Transition Probability Matrices and BFS Reindexing

To exploit the specifics of the transition matrices that arise in probabilistic model checking, we analyze some case studies from the literature. In particular, we consider the examples of probabilistic and stochastic models that are part of the standard distribution of PRISM. In the literature probabilistic and stochastic model checking often are used interchangeably. Usually a more clear distinction is made by relating the adjectives probabilistic and stochastic to the underlying model: discrete- (DTMC) and continuous-time Markov chain (CTMC), respectively. For the sake of simplicity in this paper our focus is on discrete-time Markov chains (DTMC), so we opted for consistently using the qualification "probabilistic". Nevertheless, the concepts and algorithms that we present here can be applied as well to continuous-time Markov chains. For the time being we do not consider models of the Markov decision processes type.

Since PRISM is probably the most widely applied probabilistic model checker, the examples that we consider give a fair representation of models that are used in applications. There are models from different areas, like probabilistic algorithms, queuing theory, chemistry, and biology.

Our first goal is to structurally examine the state spaces. Therefore, we make plots of the corresponding transition probability matrices. The existence of a probability greater than zero, i.e., a transition in the underlying Markov chain represented by the matrix element, is represented with a dot. The plots of the transition matrices are given on the left hand side of each pair of plots in Figures 2 and 3. Such plots can help identifying patterns in the elements which could be exploited in the algorithms.

In PRISM each state is given a number between 0 and $n - 1$, where n is the number of states in the underlying Markov chain. The plots on the left-hand side are based on the original indexing of the states as it is produced by (GPU-)PRISM. We explain below the plots on the right-hand side.

One can observe that there is often some regularity in the distribution of the non-zero elements. In most of the examples one can notice diagonal grouping of the elements. The diagonals are either parallel to the main matrix diagonal or they close some angle with it. The most notable in that regard are cluster, tandem, cell, and molecules, but also in the other examples (except herman) the diagonal structure is prevailing. The most remarkable of all is the matrix for herman which has some sort of "fractal" structure, reminiscent of the Sierpinski carpet or similar examples.[1]

3.1 Breadth-First Search Reindexing of the States

A diagonal grouping, similar to the one exhibited by the PRISM examples, has been exploited before in algorithms for SpMV to improve the runtimes [6,7,20]. This was based on the advantageous memory access pattern which arises from the distribution of the non-zero elements. Because of the diagonal structure, threads that belong to the same block access locations in the main memory which are close to each other. In the coalesced access the threads (preferably of the same block) access consecutive memory locations. This minimizes the number of accesses that are needed to provide data to all threads in the block. In the ideal case, all necessary data can be fetched simultaneously for all threads in the block.

For illustration, consider matrix M given in Fig. 1a in which the non-null and null elements are denoted with • and ○, respectively.

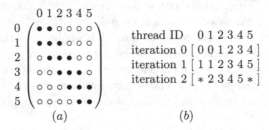

(a)   (b)

Fig. 1. (a) An example of a diagonally shaped matrix M. (b) A memory access pattern corresponding to the matrix.

We want to multiply M with a vector x. For simplicity, suppose that we use a kernel with a one dimensional grid. The grid consists of one block that contains six threads. Further, let each thread process one row in the multiplication algorithm by performing the inner product of the row with the vector. We assume that thread IDs range from 0 to 5 and that thread i processes row i, for $0 \leq i \leq 5$.

During the execution, we can observe the memory access pattern given in Fig. 1b. The top row of the pattern contains the thread IDs. The rest of the rows represent the access to the vector elements during the computation of the matrix vector product. Each of these rows corresponds to an iteration. In each row, the entry in a column corresponding to thread i contains the index of

---

[1] It would be worth investigating where this structure comes from and if there are also other examples of Markov chains, not necessarily in probabilistic model checking, that have this kind of a "fractal" structure. Considering that the fractals have been used for image compression, maybe one could develop an efficient compact representation of the transition matrices.

the element of vector x that is accessed in the iteration corresponding to the row. The special entry "*" denotes that the corresponding thread accesses no element during the iteration. In one iteration the thread k, corresponding to row k, computes the product of some non-zero element $M[k, l]$ of row k with element $x[l]$. For example, during iteration 0, both thread 0 and thread 1 access $x[0]$. For $2 \leq i \leq 5$, thread i uses $x[i-1]$. Element $x[5]$ is not used during iteration 0. The other rows of the pattern are interpreted in an analogous way. One can see that in most of the cases threads with consecutive ID numbers access consecutive

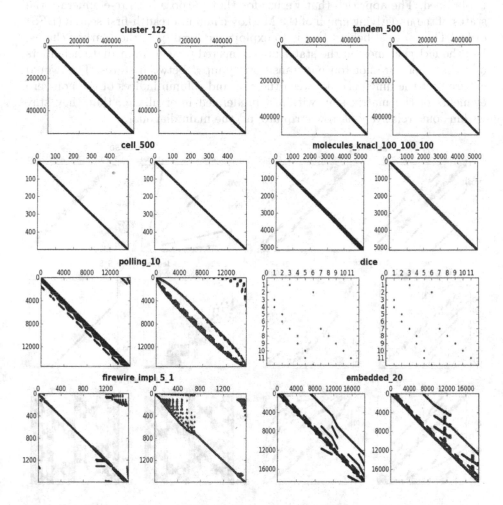

Fig. 2. Plots of transition matrices of models from the PRISM standard distribution. For each model two plots are given: the transition matrix produced by PRISM (left) and the transition matrix after the BFS reindexing (right). The numbers in the model names denote the values of the model parameters in the order they are asked by PRISM. The model names are (from left to right and top to bottom, respectively): `cluster`, `tandem`, `cell`, `molecules_knac`, `polling`, `dice`, `firewire_impl`, and `embedded`.

indices – and therefore consecutive memory locations – that correspond to the elements of vector x.

However, the access to the memory locations corresponding to the matrix elements is not contiguous. As we show in Section 4, contiguous access can be achieved to a significant extent by using an appropriate memory storage format for the matrix.

Considering the potential benefits of the diagonal structure, a natural idea is to try to permute the indices of the matrix such that a diagonal structure is obtained. The approach that we use for that purpose is to re-enumerate the states of the underlying graph of the Markov chain in breadth-first search (BFS) order. The rational behind this is to exploit the locality of the Markov chains, i.e., the fact that most of the states are connected to their immediate neighbors and that there are not too big transition "jumps" between states. This would ensure that the differences between the row and column indices of the non-zero elements of the matrix stay within a predefined interval, i.e., that they stay within some relatively narrow strip around the main diagonal.

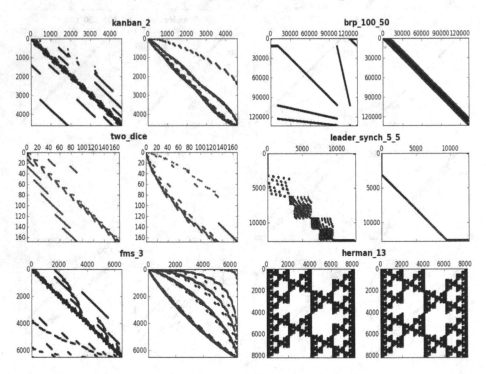

Fig. 3. (continued) Plots of transition matrices of models from the PRISM standard distribution. For each model two plots are given: the transition matrix produced by PRISM (left) and the transition matrix after the BFS reindexing (right). The numbers in the model names denote the values of the model parameters in the order they are asked by PRISM. The model names are (from left two right and top to bottom, respectively): kanban, brp, two_dice, leader_synch, fms, and herman.

The plots of the matrices after the BFS reindexing are given on the right-hand sides in Figs. 2 and 3. At least in two cases (brp and leader) the structure of the matrix has been "diagonalized", in the sense that different lines/diagonals are brought closer to each other. In the case of leader, the original "staircase" structure is transformed into a line parallel to the main diagonal. The matrices of kanban and two_dice have become more compact, in the sense that there are fewer "islands" in the state space. Such a grouping of the indices positively affects memory access in SpMV, similar to clustering around the main diagonal. Matrices such as cluster, tandem, cell, and polling, which already had a diagonal structure, maintained it. Finally, the "fractal" example, herman, stays the same under reindexing, as well as the small example dice.

4 Coalescing Matrix Data Access

As we saw in the previous section, by grouping the non-zero elements of the matrix in diagonal shapes, a contiguous access to the elements of the vector is made possible. However, to actually achieve this in practice, the matrix should be stored in a suitable way in the memory of the GPU. Once we have convenient storage formats, corresponding algorithms must be developed that can efficiently exploit these new data structures. In this section, we present two new storage methods and their accompanying algorithms.

4.1 Sparse Matrix Representation

The storage size of a matrix is $O(n^2)$, where n is the number of rows. Sparse matrices, however, can be significantly compressed. Matrix compression is a standard technique used for probabilistic model checking. For this, special matrix storage formats are used. In this section, we build on the so-called *modified sparse row/column format* (MSR) [16,5]. We illustrate this format with the example in Fig. 4.

The non-zero elements of the matrix are linearly stored in the array *non-zeros*. Elements belonging to the same row are stored in consecutive cells. The

$$
\begin{array}{c}
\;0\,1\,2\,3\,4\,5\,6 \\
\begin{array}{c}0\\1\\2\\3\\4\\5\\6\end{array}
\left(\begin{array}{ccccccc}
0 & a & b & 0 & 0 & 0 & 0 \\
0 & 0 & c & d & 0 & 0 & 0 \\
0 & 0 & 0 & 0 & e & 0 & 0 \\
f & 0 & 0 & g & 0 & 0 & 0 \\
0 & 0 & 0 & 0 & h & 0 & 0 \\
i & j & 0 & 0 & 0 & 0 & 0 \\
0 & 0 & k & 0 & 0 & 0 & 0
\end{array}\right)
\end{array}
$$

row-starts	0	2	4	5	7	8	10	11			
cols	1	2	2	3	4	0	3	4	0	1	2
non-zeros	a	b	c	d	e	f	g	h	i	j	k

Fig. 4. An example of the MSR storage format. The letters denote the non-zero elements of the matrix. On the right-hand side is the MSR representation of the matrix.

beginning of each row is given by the array *row-starts*. Array *cols* contains the column indices of the corresponding elements in *non-zeros*.

Algorithm 1 is the basic kernel of an SpMV algorithm that is executed by each of the threads. This kernel was developed based on the sequential implementation of PRISM (cf. [8,9]).

In this paper, we only present the kernels, i.e., the parts of the algorithms that are executed on the GPUs, since the host program, the CPU parts, are fairly standard. A generic host program can be found in its integral form in our previous papers on GPU model checking [8]. Such a host program can be used as is for all algorithms presented in this section.

Algorithm 1. Standard SpMV Kernel for MSR Matrices

Require: *row-starts, cols, non-zeros, n, x, x', BlockId, BlockSize, ThreadId*
1: $i := BlockId \cdot BlockSize + ThreadId$;
2: **if** $(i < n)$ **then**
3:   $d := 0$;
4:   $l := row\text{-}starts_i$;   // start of row
5:   $h := row\text{-}starts_{i+1}$;   // end of row
6:   **for** $(j = l; j < h; j++)$ **do**
7:     $d := d + non\text{-}zeros_j \cdot x_{cols_j}$;
8:   $x'_i := d$;

Algorithm 1 assumes the MSR memory storage format. Therefore, the input is an MSR representation (in three separate arrays) of a matrix, followed by the matrix size n, the vector x, as well as the GPU bookkeeping IDs, i.e. the ID of the current thread and the block to which the thread belongs, and the size of each block. Vector x', which is the output of the algorithm, is the result of the matrix-vector multiplication.

In line 1, the 'absolute' thread ID is computed since *ThreadId* is relative to the block. Variable i is used to determine the row that is processed by the thread. Line 2 is just a check whether this row number is within the matrix bounds. Variable d contains the temporary value of the inner product sum of the row i with vector x. In lines 4 and 5, we determine the start and the end, respectively, of the non-zero elements in *non-zeros* belonging to the designated row. The iteration in lines 6 and 7 computes the inner product which is stored in d and eventually assigned, in line 8, to the i-th element of the result x'.

A drawback of Algorithm 1 in combination with the MSR format is that, when the former is executed by the threads of a given block in parallel, the elements of array *non-zeros*, which are accessed by the threads, are not stored in consecutive memory locations. In the above example, assume a block size 4. Threads 0, 1, 2, and 3 of block 0, in their first iteration, need access to the elements of *non-zeros* which are the first elements of the corresponding rows. These are the elements a, c, e, and f, (at positions 0, 2, 4, and 5), respectively. As a result of such a non-contiguous access, several cycles might be needed to fetch all elements of *non-zeros.* In contrast, if the elements were in consecutive positions, i.e., if they could have been accessed in a coalesced way, just a single access cycle would have been sufficient.

Note that this problem occurs also with the diagonally shaped matrices discussed in the previous section. Although the elements of x, which are processed in the same iteration by the threads of the same block, can be accessed in a coalesced way, this is still not the case with the *non-zeros* elements, i.e., with the standard MSR format.

4.2   A Full-Warp SpMV Algorithm

To coalesce the memory accesses in SpMV, we focus on the fact that the GPU groups the launched threads into warps. If threads in the same warp can access the memory in a coalesced way, data fetching will be done for all those threads in a single cycle.

To achieve coalesced access of the elements in a matrix within a warp of threads, we reorder the MSR representation of the matrix such that the elements accessed in a warp are next to each other. First of all, to explicitly group the threads in warps, we introduce a new array named *seg-starts*, which partitions the matrix into segments, each containing as many consecutive rows as the warp size (apart from the last segment, possibly). Say the warp size is 4, then the example given earlier will now be rewritten as given below. The double vertical lines indicate the warp boundaries. Note that some "dummy" elements need to be added to keep the elements of the same row on equidistant intervals. However, as we will see later in the experiments, this increase of memory is usually of no significance, and it is amply compensated by improved runtimes.

seg-starts	0	8	14												
cols	1	2	4	0	2	3	-	3	4	0	2	-	1	-
non-zeros	a	c	e	f	b	d	0.0	g	h	i	k	0.0	j	0.0

To exploit the modified matrix storage format, we introduce Algorithm 2. The new algorithm is a modification of Algorithm 1 and features the same input and output, except for the fact that the matrix dimension n is replaced by two numbers n_s and n_{rem}. The former is the predefined number of segments, i.e. n divided by the number of threads in a warp, whereas n_{rem} is the number of rows in the last segment. The last segment does not necessarily have the same size as the other segments, depending on whether or not n is divisible by the warp size. If we assume for our running example matrix that we have just one block and a warp size 4, then this will result in $n_s = 2$ and $n_{rem} = 3$.

Like in Algorithm 1, we begin by computing the 'absolute' thread ID, which also determines the index of the processed row. Besides that, in line 2 the segment ID *segid* is computed. As mentioned above, for our running example we will have two segments. In line 3, *lane* is computed which is an index of the thread within the warp, or in our case, since the warp and segment size are the same, it is also an index within the segment. In line 4 the matrix dimension n is recovered from

---

Algorithm 2. SpMV Kernel for MSR Matrices reordered into warp segments

Require: $seg\text{-}starts$, $non\text{-}zeros$, n_s, n_{rem}, x, x', $BlockId$, $BlockSize$, $ThreadId$

1: $i := BlockId \cdot BlockSize + ThreadId$;
2: $segid := i/WarpSize$;   // segment index
3: $lane := ThreadId \ \& \ (WarpSize - 1)$;   // thread index in warp
4: $n = (n_s - 1) \cdot WarpSize + n_{rem}$;
5: **if** $(i < n)$ **then**
6: $\quad d := 0$;
7: $\quad$ **if** $segid < n_s - 1$ **then**   // determine segment size
8: $\quad\quad skip := WarpSize$;
9: $\quad$ **else**
10: $\quad\quad skip := n_{rem}$;
11: $\quad l := seg\text{-}starts_{segid}$;   // start of segment
12: $\quad h := seg\text{-}starts_{segid+1}$;   // end of segment
13: $\quad$ **for** $(j = l + lane; j < h; j = j + skip)$ **do**
14: $\quad\quad d := d + non\text{-}zeros_j \cdot x_{cols_j}$;
15: $\quad x'_i := d$;

---

the input values n_s and n_{rem}. The next difference compared to Algorithm 1 is in lines 7-10. This is because, unlike in the original MSR format, in the new format the $non\text{-}zeros$ elements, belonging to the same row (and therefore are accessed by the same thread), are not stored contiguously. Instead they are dispersed regularly in the $non\text{-}zeros$ array, i.e., separated by equal skip intervals. Note that in line 8 the skip for the last segment is set to n_{rem}, to take the possibly different size of the last segment into account. The start and end of the **for** loop are computed in lines 11 and 12, respectively, and they coincide with the start and end of the segment containing row i. The **for** loop in line 13 is started with offset $lane$ to take into account the relative position of the thread within the segment and the loop counter j is increased with step $skip$ to ensure that each thread i fetches the elements of row i.

One can see that for our running example with one block and two segments of size 4, threads 0, 1, 2, and 3 of the first segment will access in the first iteration through the **for** loop the first four elements of $non\text{-}zeros$, a, c, e, and f, respectively, i.e. the first elements of rows 0, 1, 2, and 3.

4.3   A Half-Warp SpMV Algorithm

The same coalescing approach can be used to obtain a matrix representation supporting multiple threads per row. If we set the segment size to half the warp size, assigning a warp of threads to each segment allows us to use two threads per row. This should be taken into account when rewriting the MSR representation of a matrix, in order to ensure that the elements of rows in a warp are grouped in pairs, as shown in the following example:

seg-starts	0	4	8	12	14									
cols	1	2	2	3	4	-	0	3	4	-	0	1	2	-
non-zeros	a	b	c	d	e	0.0	f	g	h	0.0	i	j	k	0.0

Algorithm 3. SpMV Kernel for MSR Matrices reordered into half warp segments

---

Require: *seg-starts, non-zeros, n_s, n_{rem}, x, x', BlockId, BlockSize, ThreadId*
1: __**shared**__ **volatile double** *shared*[*ThreadsPerBlock*/2];   // to store results
2: *i* := *BlockId · BlockSize + ThreadId*;
3: *segid* := *i/ WarpSize*;   // segment index
4: *lane* := *ThreadId* & (*WarpSize* − 1);   // thread index in warp
5: *row* := *i/2*   // row id
6: *n* = (n_s − 1) · (*WarpSize*/2) + n_{rem};
7: **if** (*row* < *n*) **then**
8:    *d* := 0;
9:    **if** *segid* < n_s − 1 **then**   // determine segment size
10:       *skip* := *WarpSize*;
11:    **else**
12:       *skip* := n_{rem} · 2;
13:    *l* := *seg-starts*$_{segid}$;   // start of segment
14:    *h* := *seg-starts*$_{segid+1}$;   // end of segment
15:    **for** (*j* = *l* + *lane*; *j* < *h*; *j* = *j* + *skip*) **do**
16:       *d* := *d* + *non-zeros*$_j$ · x_{cols_j};
17:    **if** *lane* % 2 **then**   // determine thread id in row
18:       *shared*[*ThreadId*/2] := *d*;
19:    **if** !(*lane* % 2) **then**   // accumulate results
20:       x'_{row} := *d* + *shared*[*ThreadId*/2];

Corresponding to the new storage format is the half-warp based Algorithm 3. This algorithm requires the same data as its full-warp counterpart, except that it is assumed that the matrix is stored in the "half-warp" storage format Algorithm 2. In line 1, array *shared*, which resides in the shared memory, is defined. Recall that the shared memory is accessible by all threads that belong to the same block and it is around two orders of magnitude faster than the main GPU memory in which both the matrix and the vector are stored. In this algorithm, the inner product of one row with the vector is done by two threads, so the final result should be the sum of the two partial sums produced by each of the thread. This requires communication between the threads assigned to the same row, and the *shared* array is used for this purpose.

The assignments in lines 2-4 are the same as in Algorithm 2, only this time, since two threads are processing one row, *i* does not correspond to the row index. We compute the latter in line 5, such that two threads are assigned to each row. The lines 6-16 are as in Algorithm 2, the only subtlety being that the segment size is halved, and the skip for the last segment is set to n_{rem} · 2. The main difference with Algorithm 2 is in lines 17-20. This piece of code actually checks if *lane*, the index of the thread within the segment, is even or odd. If the index is odd, then the end result (partial sum of the inner product) is saved in *shared* at the position corresponding to the row. Otherwise, the end result for the row is produced by adding the partial result from *shared* (of the other thread processing the same row) to the partial result obtained by this thread. There are no race conditions when accessing *shared*, since the threads in a warp execute their instructions in a synchronous manner, so the writing to *shared* is strictly done before the reading starts.

Again, one can see that the algorithm in combination with the matrix storage ensures coalesced accesses to the matrix elements of the threads within a segment.

5   Experimental Results

The BFS reindexing as well as the half and full-warp methods were implemented in GPU-PRISM 4.0 [10],[2] an extension of the model checker PRISM version 4.0. We conducted a number of experiments with our implementations on a 64-bit computer running Ubuntu 10.10 with CUDA version 4.1, both the Software Development Kit and the driver. It runs on an AMD Athlon(tm) 64 X2 Dual-Core Processor 3800+ running at 2 GHz with 4 GB RAM, and has an NVIDIA GPU GeForce GTX 480 with 1.5 GB global memory and 480 cores running at 1.4 GHz. As block size, we used 512 threads.

The data of the experiments were both represented in MSR format, and in the special *compact* MSR (CMSR) format [16], which was specifically designed to efficiently store matrices representing probabilistic models. These matrices tend to be not only sparse, but also contain a relatively small number of distinct values. This is exploited in CMSR by keeping these values in a separate array, and storing pointers to these values, instead of the values themselves, in the *non-zeros* array. In [16], it is remarked that besides memory benefits, CMSR also tends to speed up the computations, due to caching effects. Intuitively, in the GPU setting, the use of the CMSR format instead of the MSR format reduces the potential for coalesced memory access; the best one can do is reorder the pointers to the values, not the values themselves. Since CMSR is used by default in PRISM, and SpMV on a CPU with the CMSR format usually outperforms SpMV with MSR, it is crucial that we test the efficiency of the half- and full-warp methods with CMSR, as well.

All models that we used in our experiments were taken from the standard distribution of PRISM. Table 1 shows the common characteristics of the experiments. The first and the second column, respectively, contain the name and the instance (depending on the parameter values) of the model. The third column denotes the number of the property in the property file that comes with each model. The last two columns give the number of reachable states and the number of iterations required to solve the system of linear equations represented by the combination of the model and the property to check, using the Jacobi method.

---

[2] http://www.win.tue.nl/~awijs/software.html

Table 1. Information on the protocol properties

Model	Inst.	Prop.	n	Iterations
herman	15/5	3	32,768	245
cluster	320	1	3,704,340	5,107
cluster	464	1	7,776,660	23,932
tandem	1,023	1	2,096,128	16,326
tandem	2,047	1	8,386,560	24,141
kanban	5	1	2,546,432	663
fms	7	1	1,639,440	1,258
fms	8	1	4,459,455	1,438
polling	17	4	3,342,336	4,732
polling	18	4	7,077,888	4,880

Table 2 presents the results obtained when using standard GPU SpMV on both the original MSR matrices, as produced by PRISM, and the BFS-reindexed ones. As in the previous table, the first two columns give the name and instance of the model. The next column gives the consumed memory which is the same in both cases, since the data storage format is unchanged. Columns 4 and 5 contain the times with the PRISM and reindexed matrix, respectively. The last column gives the speed up factor which is obtained by dividing the original time with the time obtained with the reindexed matrix.

Table 2. Performance of standard SpMV on MSR and BFS-reindexed MSR data

Model	Inst.	mem.	orig. time	+BFS time	Factor
herman	15	165	15.50	12.46	1.24
cluster	320	305	45.45	44.79	1.01
cluster	464	642	440.16	443.06	0.99
tandem	1,023	139	39.56	43.91	0.90
tandem	2,047	559	228.18	255.57	0.89
kanban	5	347	14.78	15.34	0.96
fms	7	198	15.18	15.08	1.01
fms	8	560	52.14	50.28	1.04
polling	17	295	77.25	66.21	1.17
polling	18	646	184.12	160.77	1.15

In most of the cases there is some speed up which is probably due to the coalesced access to the vector elements. On the other hand, the best result is achieved for an instance of **herman**, which has the 'fractal' structure and it is invariant under the reindexing. This could be due to the fact that during the reindexing, the matrix and the correspondingly permuted vector are copied to a new data structure. Although the new structures are conceptually identical to the original MSR-based structures of PRISM, they might provide a faster memory access. Obviously, a more thorough analysis is needed to explain this

Table 3. Performance of SpMV(WL) and SpMV(HWL) on MSR data

Model	Inst.	Original matrix					BFS reindexed matrix				
		SpMV(WL)		SpMV(HWL)		Factor	SpMV(WL)		SpMV(HWL)		Factor
		mem.	time	mem.	time	(max.)	mem.	time	mem.	time	(max.)
herman	15	692	9.90	520	3.43	4.51	692	5.60	520	3.43	4.52
cluster	320	372	21.47	386	26.52	2.12	320	18.35	434	25.50	2.48
cluster	464	781	211.65	811	259.69	2.08	669	178.94	909	247.81	2.46
tandem	1,023	132	27.18	144	24.73	1.60	144	29.90	192	41.00	1.32
tandem	2,047	528	159.38	577	96.15	2.37	576	172.07	769	234.40	1.32
kanban	5	384	2.98	390	3.29	4.99	406	3.25	467	3.52	4.55
fms	7	248	3.88	242	4.30	3.91	261	3.93	261	4.30	3.86
fms	8	700	12.87	684	13.82	4.05	746	12.73	745	13.43	4.10
polling	17	329	20.43	329	23.31	3.78	496	25.86	505	30.42	2.99
polling	18	717	46.62	718	51.77	3.95	1,090	58.63	1,110	67.79	3.14

phenomenon. In general, although the results are not conclusive, it seems that the reindexing itself is able to produce some modest speed up.

Table 3 shows the results when applying the new algorithms using row segments to coalesce memory access. SpMV(WL) and SpMV(HWL) denote the algorithms with full- and half-warp segment size, respectively. For both algorithms, the memory use in megabytes, and run time in seconds are shown. The last column contains the maximal speed up factor with respect to the standard GPU-PRISM (without BFS reindexing), which can be found in Table 2.

For the original matrices, again the best speed up of 4.51 is obtained with **herman**, but this time this is paired with around the same factor of memory increase. The speed ups with the other models though are achieved with quite acceptable price in memory. It is important to note that the half-warp algorithm produces the best results only for the **herman** case; in all other cases the full-warp algorithm is the fastest. The **herman** matrices are relatively dense compared to the others, which supports the observation in related work, e.g. [6], that further parallelisation of individual row-vector multiplications, i.e. using multiple threads per row, often does not pay off for sparse matrices. In [6], this is related to assigning warps to rows, but here, even two threads per row does not outperform one thread per row, when typical sparse matrices of probabilistic models are used.

Table 3 also contains the results when using combinations of the new algorithms, i.e. first reindexing the matrix using BFS, and then partitioning the rows into segments. One can see that the results with **herman** are unaffected by the reindexing. This is in accord with our intuition since the transition matrix of this model is virtually invariant under the BFS reindexing. The results for **cluster** show that with the full-warp version of the algorithm, the BFS reindexing results in some gain in memory. Also the reindexing results in some additional speedup. For the other examples though, the reindexing causes deterioration of both the speed ups and the memory usage, suggesting that BFS reindexing is a technique which does not combine well with the improved SpMV methods.

Table 4. Performance of standard SpMV on CMSR and BFS-reindexed CMSR data

Model	Inst.	mem.	orig. time	+BFS time	Factor
herman	15	55	8.70	8.62	1.01
cluster	320	146	20.81	19.66	1.06
cluster	464	308	203.05	197.19	1.03
tandem	1,023	71	22.77	23.77	0.98
tandem	2,047	287	124.17	135.17	0.92
kanban	5	146	4.81	5.20	0.93
fms	7	86	5.75	5.76	1.00
fms	8	240	19.70	19.13	1.03
polling	17	189	35.65	41.44	0.86
polling	18	414	80.43	96.29	0.84

Table 5. Performance of SpMV(WL) and SpMV(HWL) on CMSR data

Model	Inst.	Original matrix					BFS reindexed matrix				
		SpMV(WL)		SpMV(HWL)		Factor	SpMV(WL)		SpMV(HWL)		Factor
		mem.	time	mem.	time	(max.)	mem.	time	mem.	time	(max.)
herman	15	231	5.48	173	3.56	2.44	692	5.60	520	3.43	2.54
cluster	320	159	17.05	164	24.57	1.22	142	15.09	152	23.93	1,38
cluster	464	335	175.40	346	255.72	1.16	298	162.17	319	253.89	1.25
tandem	1,023	64	23.77	68	39.34	0.96	68	25.22	68	39.85	0.90
tandem	2,047	256	139.42	273	230.46	0.89	272	146.78	273	231.25	0.85
kanban	5	152	2.18	154	2.84	2.21	159	2.37	161	3.05	2.03
fms	7	98	3.03	96	3.89	1.90	102	3.08	102	3.87	1.87
fms	8	276	9.92	271	12.64	1.99	291	9.69	291	12.06	2.03
polling	17	208	18.32	209	26.63	1.95	204	19.37	207	27.50	1.84
polling	18	455	37.89	456	58.48	2.12	447	42.89	453	58.16	1.88

Tables 4 and 5 show the results for the same model instances as Tables 2 and 3, but now using the CMSR data storage format. As expected, overall, the achieved speedups are not as high as when using MSR. BFS reindexing even shows a negative effect in combination with standard SpMV. It seems that the reindexing disturbs the optimization introduced by the CMSR storage format. Further research is required to determine the exact cause. The full-warp algorithm, however, still produces in most cases a speedup of two times. For the models cluster and tandem, it does not result in a speedup, which seems to be related to the fact that their matrices are perfect diagonals, and therefore probably already lead to relatively coalesced data access in SpMV. Finally, as when using MSR, the half-warp algorithm only outperforms the full-warp algorithm for the herman case.

6   Conclusions, Prospects and Related Work

We gave an overview and analysis of the state spaces that arise in probabilistic model checking, as represented by their corresponding transition probability matrices. Most of them show regular patterns and diagonally shaped matrices are prevailing. Based on this analysis, we suggested three methods for improving the run times of the model checking algorithms. All methods were implemented in GPU-PRISM, an extension of the probabilistic model checker PRISM.

Our first method performs a BFS-based reindexing of the states, which potentially leads to more compact representations of the matrices. The experiments with our implementation show that for some models the BFS reindexing can accelerate the model checking algorithms on GPUs.

Additionally, we proposed two methods that group the threads in segments. By choosing the segment size to coincide with a full or half-warp size, together with appropriate modifications of the data representation, one can achieve a coalesced access to the main GPU memory. The experiments showed that in some cases the model checking algorithms can be accelerated more than four times. Also combinations of the two coalescing methods with the BFS reindexing can produce some additional speed ups, but in most cases, the two techniques do not agree.

We intend to perform more experiments with different models from the PRISM set of examples as well as from other sources. It would also be worthwile to further investigate the state spaces structures. A special challenge in that direction could be the fractal-like structures which were observed in one of the examples. These can potentially be used to optimize the storage of the state spaces as well as the run times of the algorithms.

Related work. GPU model checking was a logical continuation of the concept of multi-core model checking [15]. Besides the above mentioned introductory papers on GPU (probabilistic) model checking [8,9,10], several algorithms for SpMV, which exist in the literature, were recently tested in the context of probabilistic model checking [12]. This work complements our previous work in [8,9] to a significant extent. The paper seems to confirm our hypothesis presented there that our algorithms for GPU probabilistic model checking from [8] are superior to the class of Krylov methods, representatives of which were tested in [12].

An overview of algorithms for SpMV can be found in [20]. Several methods for SpMV were discussed in [6,7]. Among them are methods for diagonally shaped sparse matrices, which could play an important rôle in probabilistic model checking. They consider algorithms which are analogous with our half-warp algorithm, in which several threads process one row. They conclude that this really gives results only if the matrices are dense. This is confirmed by our results with the half-warp algorithm. Often we do not get any improvement, even though a row is processed by only two threads. Compared to our work, they do not consider BFS reindexing, but the most important difference is that we group the rows in segments of one- and half-warp sizes, which is not the case in their work. Also our matrix and vector memory storage differs from the ones used by them.

In [19] the authors propose to speed up probabilistic model checking, by exploiting the structure of the underlying Markov chains, for sequential algorithms. It might be interesting to investigate a combination of the findings about the structure of the state spaces presented in this paper and theirs in the GPU context.

Previous algorithms for parallel probabilistic model checking were almost exclusively designed for distributed architectures, i.e., clusters [5,11]. They were focused on increasing the state spaces of the models instead of the run times and minimizing the communication overhead between the threads instead of the memory latency. In [1], a shared memory algorithm is introduced for CTMC construction, but the algorithms employed there are quite different from our approach.

There are other publications that deal with other kinds of model checking on GPUs that do not involve probabilities (e.g.,[4,14]). They use algorithms which are quite different from the ones presented in this paper, since they do not focus on parallelizing a numerical computation, but on parallelizing state space exploration.

References

1. Allmaier, S.C., Kowarschik, M., Horton, G.: State Space Construction and Steady-state Solution of GSPNs on a Shared-Memory Multiprocessor. In: Proc. 7th Intt. Workshop on Petri Nets and Performance Models, PNPM 1997, pp. 112–121. IEEE Comp. Soc. Press (1997)
2. Baier, C., Katoen, J.-P.: Principles of Model Checking, 950 p. MIT Press (2008)
3. Baier, C., Katoen, J.-P., Hermanns, H., Haverkort, B.: Model-Checking Algorithms for Contiuous-Time Markov Chains. IEEE Transactions on Software Engineering 29(6), 524–541 (2003)
4. Barnat, J., Brim, L., Ceska, M., Lamr, T.: CUDA Accelerated LTL Model Checking. In: IEEE 15th International Conference on Parallel and Distributed Systems, ICPADS 2009, pp. 34–41. IEEE (2009)
5. Bell, A., Haverkort, B.R.: Distribute Disk-based Algorithms for Model Checking Very Large Markov Chains. In: Formal Methods in System Design, vol. 29, pp. 177–196. Springer (2006)
6. Bell, N., Garland, M.: Efficient Sparse Matrix-Vector Multiplication on CUDA NVIDIA. Technical Report NVR-2008-004 (December 2008)
7. Bell, N., Garland, M.: Implementing sparse matrix-vector multiplication on throughput-oriented processors. In: Proceedings of the ACM/IEEE Conference on High Performance Computing, SC 2009. ACM (2009)
8. Bošnački, D., Edelkamp, S., Sulewski, D.: Efficient Probabilistic Model Checking on General Purpose Graphics Processors. In: Păsăreanu, C.S. (ed.) SPIN 2009. LNCS, vol. 5578, pp. 32–49. Springer, Heidelberg (2009)
9. Bošnački, D., Edelkamp, S., Sulewski, D., Wijs, A.J.: Parallel probabilistic model checking on general purpose graphics processors. STTT 13(1), 21–35 (2011)
10. Bošnački, D., Edelkamp, S., Sulewski, D., Wijs, A.J.: GPU-PRISM: An Extension of PRISM for General Purpose Graphics Processing Units (tool paper). In: Proc. Joint HiBi/PDMC Workshop, HiBi/PDMC 2010, pp. 17–19. IEEE Computer Society Press (2010)

11. Ciardo, G.: Distributed and Structured Analysis Approaches to Study Large and Complex Systems. European Educational Forum: School on Formal Methods and Performance Analysis, 344–374 (2000)
12. Cormie-Bowins, E.: A Comparison of Sequential and GPU Implementations of Iterative Methods to Compute Reachability Probabilities. In: Proc. of Workshop on GRAPH Inspection and Traversal Engineering, GRAPHITE 2012, Tallinn, Estonia, April 1 (to appear, 2012)
13. http://www.nvidia.com/object/cuda_home.html#
14. Edelkamp, S., Sulewski, D.: Model Checking via Delayed Duplicate Detection on the GPU, Technical Report 821, Universität Dortmund, Fachberich Informatik (2008) ISSN 0933-6192
15. Holzmann, G.J., Bošnački, D.: The Design of a multi-core extension of the Spin Model Checker. IEEE Trans. on Software Engineering 33(10), 659–674 (2007) (first presented at: Formal Methods in Computer Aided Design (FMCAD), San Jose, November 2006)
16. Kwiatkowska, M., Mehmood, R.: Out-of-Core Solution of Large Linear Systems of Equations Arising from Stochastic Modelling. In: Hermanns, H., Segala, R. (eds.) PROBMIV 2002, PAPM-PROBMIV 2002, and PAPM 2002. LNCS, vol. 2399, pp. 135–151. Springer, Heidelberg (2002)
17. Kwiatkowska, M., Norman, G., Parker, D.: PRISM: Probabilistic Symbolic Model Checker. In: Field, T., Harrison, P.G., Bradley, J., Harder, U. (eds.) TOOLS 2002. LNCS, vol. 2324, pp. 200–204. Springer, Heidelberg (2002)
18. Kwiatkowska, M., Norman, G., Parker, D.: Stochastic Model Checking. In: Bernardo, M., Hillston, J. (eds.) SFM 2007. LNCS, vol. 4486, pp. 220–270. Springer, Heidelberg (2007)
19. Kwiatkowska, M.Z., Parker, D., Qu, H.: Incremental Quantitative Verification for Markov Decision Processes. In: Proceedings of the IEEE/IFIP International Conference on Dependable Systems and Networks, pp. 359–370. IEEE (2011)
20. Vuduc, R.W.: Automatic Performance Tuning of Sparse Matrix Kernels. Ph.D. thesis, University of California, Berkeley (2003)

Gossiping Girls Are All Alike

Theo C. Ruys[1] and Pim Kars[2]

[1] RUwise, The Netherlands
theo.ruys@gmail.com
[2] Ordina, The Netherlands
pim.kars@ordina.nl

Abstract. This paper discusses several different ways to model the well-known *gossiping girls* problem in PROMELA. The highly symmetric nature of the problem is exploited using plain PROMELA, TOPSPIN (an extension to SPIN for symmetry reduction), and by connecting SPIN to *bliss* (a tool to compute canonical representations of graphs). The model checker SPIN is used to compare the consequences of the various modelling choices.

    This – tutorial style – paper is meant as a road map of the various ways of modelling symmetric systems that can be explored.

1   Introduction

In the early 1970s, the following puzzle (popularized by Paul Erdös) was circulated among mathematicians [12]:

> There are n girls, each of whom knows a unique piece of initial information. They communicate by telephone calls, and whenever two speak they share all the gossip that they know. The goal is to determine the minimum number of calls necessary for all of the girls to learn all of the initial information.

A number of researchers have independently proven that $2n-4$ calls are necessary and sufficient to achieve the goal. See [12] for an overview. A solution for $2n-4$ is straightforward. From [9]: "For $n \geq 4$, $2n-4$ conversations suffice. For four persons A, B, C and D, say, take conversations AB, and CD, followed by AC and BD. For every additional person P, schedule one conversation AP, before A, B, C and D interchange their knowledge, and another conversation AP afterwards."

Given the optimal $2n-4$ solution, it is clear that we are not really interested in using a model checker to compute this optimal solution. But given the highly symmetric nature of this problem, it is interesting to see whether the model checker SPIN can cope with this. And if not, what options do we have to improve SPIN's performance? We also want to explore different ways to model this problem. The first thing that comes to mind is to model each girl by a process and a telephone call by sending and receiving messages. But, as we will see, there are many ways to model the exchange of gossips between the girls.

Using the gossiping girls problem as a running example, we will show how a symmetric model can be analyzed with SPIN. Our goal is to inspire other

A. Donaldson and D. Parker (Eds.): SPIN 2012, LNCS 7385, pp. 117–136, 2012.
© Springer-Verlag Berlin Heidelberg 2012

verification engineers – when facing modelling challenges – to explore alternative modelling routes, especially in the case of a problem with apparent symmetries. The paper tries to retain the tutorial style of presentation of [18,20] to make the techniques easy to be adopted by intermediate to advanced SPIN users. The effectiveness of the techniques is illustrated by some experiments.

Related Work. In [22], Frits Vaandrager uses the gossiping girls problem to introduce the UPPAAL model checker. In [11], Joost-Pieter Katoen describes the gossiping girls problem as an example of gossiping networks. The paper itself focuses on the performance evaluation of such networks. Curiously, Katoen writes in a footnote: "The solution to instances of the gossiping girls example, e.g., can easily be computed using off-the-shelf model checkers in a few seconds." This might be true for small instances of the problem, i.e., $n \leq 6$, but does not scale up for slightly larger n, as we will see in this paper.

In [16], Arend Rensink reports on experiments with the GROOVE tool set on various highly symmetrical problems, including the gossiping girls problem. We will discuss GROOVE in more detail in Sec. 6, where we compare our results with GROOVE.

Two extensions to SPIN which exploit symmetry reductions for PROMELA models should be mentioned: SymmSPIN [1], a tool which lets the user specify symmetries through scalarsets and TopSPIN [2,28], a tool which can automatically detect symmetries in PROMELA models. In Sec. 4, we will use TopSPIN on a PROMELA model of the gossiping girls.

Overview. Sec. 2 presents two straightforward PROMELA specifications which model the problem. We also explain how to obtain the optimal solution to the problem with SPIN. In Sec. 3 we report on our most optimal model in *vanilla* PROMELA, i.e., without using external tools and/or embedded C code. Sec. 4 discusses a PROMELA model which we feed to TopSPIN. In Sec. 5 we use SPIN's embedded C extensions to connect our PROMELA model to *bliss*, a tool which computes canonical representations of graphs. Sec. 6 discusses the experiments that we performed with SPIN. Sec. 7 concludes the paper.

Source Code. This paper presents several PROMELA specifications which model the gossiping girls problem. All PROMELA models consider the problem for $n = 4$ girls. Of course, the models that we have used for our benchmark experiments have been parameterized in n, i.e., using the m4 macro processor [21]. All PROMELA models and the verification results as discussed in this paper are available from http://ruwise.nl/spin-2012/.

2   Initial Attempts

In this section we will discuss two straightforward approaches to model the gossiping girls problem in plain PROMELA. We will also explain how to find the minimal solution of the problem with SPIN.

```
byte knows[4] ;              /* bit vector of gossips    */
chan phone = [0] of { byte } ;   /* phone connections        */
byte calls ;                 /* number of telephone calls */

proctype Girl(byte x) {
  byte y;
  do
  :: atomic { phone ! x }
  :: d_step { phone ? y ->
       if
       :: knows[x] != knows[y] ->
              knows[x] = knows[x] | knows[y];
              knows[y] = knows[x];
              calls++;
       :: else
       fi;
       y=0;
     }
  od
}

init {
  atomic {
    knows[0]=1<<0; knows[1]=1<<1;
    knows[2]=1<<2; knows[3]=1<<3;
    run Girl(0); run Girl(1); run Girl(2); run Girl(3);
  }
}
```

Fig. 1. Promela model `girl-processes`

Girl Processes. Fig. 1 shows the PROMELA model `girl-processes`. The proctype `Girl` models the behavior of a single girl. The knowledge of a girl i is stored in the global bitvector `knows[i]`. If the j-th position (from the right) in `knows[i]` is set, it means that girl i knows the j-th gossip. Within `init`, the initial gossips are set using the bitshift-operator `<<`.

Each girl uses the channel `phone` to call one of the other girls. When two girls are connected, the mutual knowledge in `knows[x]` (the callee) and `knows[y]` (the caller) is exchanged and the total number of `calls` is updated; but only when new information has been exchanged. Exchanging the gossips themselves is easy: a simple bitwise-or (|) of the bitvectors suffices.

Due to the interleaving semantics of SPIN all possible sequences of calls between the `Girl` processes will be considered.

Single Process. A drawback of the `girl-processes` model is that, for each proctype instance, SPIN will allocate memory in the state vector. This is not really necessary as we are only interested in all possible configurations of the `knows` array.

In the model `single-process` as listed in Fig. 2 we resolve this drawback by exploiting SPIN's non-deterministic choice to generate all possible scenarios. There is only a single process `allgirls` which contains a do-loop. Each choice in the do-loop represents a call between two girls that do not yet share the same knowledge about the gossips. In this model the array of bitvectors is named `k`.

```
byte k[4];    /* bit vector of gossips      */
byte calls;   /* number of telephone calls */

active proctype allgirls() {
  k[0]=1<<0; k[1]=1<<1; k[2]=1<<2; k[3]=1<<3;
  do
  :: d_step { k[0] != k[1] -> k[0]=k[0] | k[1]; k[1]=k[0]; calls++; }
  :: d_step { k[0] != k[2] -> k[0]=k[0] | k[2]; k[2]=k[0]; calls++; }
  :: d_step { k[0] != k[3] -> k[0]=k[0] | k[3]; k[3]=k[0]; calls++; }
  :: d_step { k[1] != k[2] -> k[1]=k[1] | k[2]; k[2]=k[1]; calls++; }
  :: d_step { k[1] != k[3] -> k[1]=k[1] | k[3]; k[3]=k[1]; calls++; }
  :: d_step { k[2] != k[3] -> k[2]=k[2] | k[3]; k[3]=k[2]; calls++; }
  :: else -> break
  od;
}
```

Fig. 2. Promela model single-process

Another drawback of girl-processes is that we cannot easily express and exploit the fact that an exchange between girls i and j is not really different from an exchange between girls j and i. The single-process model easily allows to express this by always choosing girls i and j with $i < j$. This cuts away half of the outgoing transitions of a state, and consequently the number of states matched.

Finding the Optimal Solution. If we feed one of the PROMELA models to SPIN, a safety run will generate *all* possible states of the models. And due to SPIN's smart static analysis, the statement calls++; and the variable calls will even be removed from the model, as the variable calls is never used in the model.[1]

We can also use SPIN to find an optimal sequence of calls in the sense that the number of calls is minimal [20]. From Sec. 1 we know that for this optimal sequence the following holds: calls == 2*N-4. For the Promela models, we have defined a boolean expression ALLKNOW which is *true* when all girls know all gossips. For example, for the single-process model, this expression could be defined as follows (remember that $n = 4$, and 15 is decimal for 1111 binary):

```
#define ALLKNOW (k[0] == 15 && k[1] == 15 && k[2] == 15 && k[3] == 15)
```

The logical formula 'ALLKNOW $\Rightarrow$ calls >= 2*N-4' is invariant and holds for all states. To get an error trail to a state where calls == 2*N-4 *and* ALLKNOW both hold we could define the following PROMELA process:

```
#define P (ALLKNOW && calls == 2*N-4)
active proctype monitor() { atomic { P -> assert(!P)} }
```

The property P corresponds with the goal state. The process monitor is blocked on this condition P. At the moment P becomes *true*, the atomic sequence can

[1] One should not replace the statement calls++; by the semantically equivalent calls=calls+1; though. SPIN regards this latter statement as a usage of the variable calls and will thus retain the variable and statement in the system. With a blow-up of the number of states as a result.

be taken and the `assert` of the negation of P will trigger an error. If we had used `assert(!P)` instead of the `atomic` sequence, this would have doubled the number of states. See [19] for details.

The safety check using the proctype with the `assert` will *potentially* visit *all* states, as SPIN has to check the property for all states. We can do better though. Instead of a safety check, we can also use SPIN's liveness mode and check the following LTL property:

`(!ALLKNOW) U (calls > 2*N-4)`

The property corresponds with paths where condition `ALLKNOW` remains *false* until we reach a state where `calls > 2*N-4`. This property will be violated on paths where we reach a state where `ALLKNOW` is *true* and `calls > 2*N-4` is *false*, i.e., our goal state. The reason why this liveness property should be preferred over the safety check is the following: for each execution path for which the until-formula holds, SPIN will stop searching as soon as it hits a state for which `call > 2*N-4` holds.

Care should be taken when choosing the options for checking this liveness property: the until-operator in SPIN is the strong until-operator. This means that the property $p \cup q$ is violated on an infinite path where q never becomes *true*. In our `girl-processes` model there are infinite paths where the property `call > 2*N-4` never becomes *true*: paths containing 'calls' where no new information is being exchanged. For this reason, we should check the above LTL formula with 'acceptance cycle checking' disabled. Due to the monotonic nature of the variable `calls`, it is safe to do so: the state space has the shape of a tree, with self-loops for the calls that do not exchange information.

We could also have used the monotonic nature of `calls` in combination with SPIN's breadth-first-search (BFS) mode. In the presence of the process `monitor`, SPIN's BFS would then stop searching when the condition `ALLKNOW && calls == 2*N-4` is reached, without exploring any states where `calls > 2*N-4`. In practice, however, when searching for the optimal solution the BFS mode is typically slower than SPIN's default depth-first-search (DFS) exploration. The reason for this is that there are many 'symmetric' paths corresponding to an optimal solution; SPIN's DFS will hit one such solution much faster than SPIN's BFS can generate *all* states, for which `calls < 2*N-4` holds.

The techniques above use standard PROMELA and vanilla SPIN to find the optimal solution. Alternatively, one could use *directed model checking* techniques to find the optimal solution. A directed model checker use heuristic estimates and algorithms to direct the search into a specific error situation. In the realm of SPIN, HSF-SPIN [3] would have been a suitable candidate. We are, however, not really interested in getting the optimal solution as fast as possible; we are more interested in developing alternative, efficient PROMELA models for the problem at hand.

Preliminary Results. Table 1 shows the verification results of all PROMELA models of this paper and will be discussed in full in Sec. 6. For now, we are only interested in the first two columns of Table 1 which show the results of verifying

the girl-processes and single-process model. It is interesting to see that
the number of states grows very fast as the number of girls increase. SPIN still
manages to generate all states for $n \leq 6$. For greater n, the problem is infeasible
for SPIN (when limited to 2GB of memory). This is remarkable as the problem
at hand seems rather simple.

It should be clear that there is a lot of symmetry in these models. In fact,
if we have found a solution, any permutation on the set of girls gives rise to
new solution that is isomorphic to the original one. The tool to exploit this is
symmetry reduction, which we will further explore in Sec. 4. Before we do that,
we explore another line of reasoning to abstract from girl identity.

3   Channel of Knowledge

In the initial phase of our study, we constrained ourselves to 'pure' PROMELA
models and 'vanilla' SPIN. When experimenting with SPIN trying to solve the
problem more effectively, we noticed that there are many ways to incorporate
some notion of symmetry reduction into the model. In this section we discuss
our best approach – in vanilla PROMELA – so far. The central observation for
this model is that if girls i and j have the same knowledge,

- a conversation between girl i and girl j is not going to add anything
- a conversation between girl i and any girl k with different knowledge is the
  same as a conversation between girl j and girl k

So we might as well model equivalence classes of girls with the same knowledge. If we do so, we only have to record the number of girls in the equivalence
class. Denoting the size of an equivalence class with knowledge k by $size(k)$,
an exchange between girls with knowledge k_i and k_j then results in $size(k_i)$--,
$size(k_j)$-- and $size(k_i|k_j) = size(k_i|k_j)$+2. From an error trace with SPIN, we
can easily produce a trace of girls within each equivalence class.

Fig. 3 lists the PROMELA model chan-groups. Central to this solution
is the channel groups. The channel groups is a compressed representation
of the bitvector array knows of girl-processes: groups contains tuples
(*knowledge, size*). The *knowledge*-part is the bitvector representation of the gossips. The *size*-part specifies how many girls have this knowledge. For example,
the tuple (5,2) means that two girls have the knowledge 101. The channel
groups is used as a *sorted channel*. In this way we get a *canonical* representation of the knowledge information.

As with single-process, the do-loop is responsible for generating all possible
conversations between the girls. In the two select-statements[2], the variables i
and j are non-deterministically set to indices of elements within the groups
channel.

The subsequent invocations of the getgroup macro remove these tuples from
the channel and set the information of the tuples to (ki,si) and (kj,sj),

---

[2] The statement select is new in SPIN version 6. The statement select(i:
n..m); sets i non-deterministically to a value in the range n...m.

```
#include "chan-inlines.h"

chan groups = [4] of {short,byte};    /* fields: (knowledge, size)  */
byte maxgroup = 3;                     /* is equal to len(groups)-1  */
byte calls;                            /* number of calls            */

/* local, temporary variables of the process Girls: */
hidden byte i, j, ii, ki, kj, si, sj, kk, sk, kc, sc;

proctype Girls() {
  do
  :: if
     :: len(groups) == 1 -> break;
     :: else -> atomic {
          select(i: 0..maxgroup-1);
          select(j: i+1..maxgroup);
          getgroup(i,   ki, si);
          getgroup(j-1, kj, sj);

          kc = ki | kj;
          if
          :: kj == kc ->              /* only i has changed */
               remove(ki,si);
               groups !! kj,sj+1
          :: else ->                  /* i and j have changed */
               remove(ki,si);
               remove(kj,sj);
               if
               :: groups ?? [eval(kc),sc] -> /* existing group */
                    groups ?? eval(kc),sc;
                    groups !! kc,sc+2;
               :: else ->                    /* new group      */
                    groups !! kc,2;
                    maxgroup++
               fi
          fi;
          calls++;
          i=0; j=0; ii=0; ki=0; si=0; kj=0; sj=0;
          kk=0; sk=0; kc=0; sc=0;
        }
     fi
  od
}

init {
    groups !! 1<<0,1; groups !! 1<<1,1; groups !! 1<<2,1; groups !! 1<<3,1;
    run Girls();
}
```

Fig. 3. Promela model chan-groups

respectively. After exchanging the gossips, the most elaborate part of the process is storing the new knowledge back into groups. Note that due to fact that groups is sorted, kc will always be different from ki. When both the knowledge associated with i and j have changed, we use SPIN's *random receive* operator (??) to inspect whether there is already a tuple in groups which has the knowledge kc. If this is the case, two girls will be added to this tuple. Otherwise, a new tuple (kc,2) is added to groups.

```
inline getgroup(ix, kx, sx)
{
  ii=0;
  do
  :: ii < ix  -> groups ? kk, sk;
                 groups ! kk, sk;  /* put at the end */
                 ii++;
  :: ii == ix -> groups ? kx, sx;
                 do /* move remaining elements to end */
                 :: ii < len(groups) -> groups ? kk, sk;
                                        groups ! kk, sk;
                                        ii++
                 :: else -> break
                 od;
                 break;
  od;
  ii=0; kk=0; sk=0;
}

inline remove(kx, sx)
{
  if
  :: sx > 1  -> groups !! kx,sx-1
  :: else    -> maxgroup--
  fi
}
```

Fig. 4. Include file `chan-inlines.h`

Fig. 4 lists the definitions of the inline macros `getgroup` and `remove`. The macro `getgroup` is hairy as we need to get the i-th element out of the sorted FIFO-channel groups. The first $0 \ldots (\text{ix} - 1)$ elements of groups are copied to the end of groups using SPIN's regular send operation. Then, the ix-th element is stored into (`kx,sx`). Finally, the remaining elements are copied to the end of groups. In this way we keep the channel sorted without the need of an extra channel.[3] The macro `remove` removes one girl from the tuple (`kx,sx`). That is, if there are still remaining girls with knowledge kx, the tuple will be put back with sx-1. If sx==1, nothing will be put back into groups.

Semantically, the `hidden` variables i ... sc are local variables of the proctype `Girls`. They are only used within the `atomic` clause to compute the new groups. By defining these variables as `hidden` variables, they will not be stored in the state vector, and thus reducing each state by 12 bytes.

The model `chan-groups` is more effective than the previous attempts in the sense that it minimizes the outgoing transitions of states. Given two tuples (k_1, s_1) and (k_2, s_2) in groups, only a single conversation between a girl with knowledge k_1 and a girl with knowledge k_2 will be considered. Whereas in the corresponding state of the previous models, $s_1 \times s_2$ conversations would be considered.

Although this model outperforms the models of the previous section, it still does too much work. Even though we have abstracted from the identity of girls

---

[3] For our experiments we replaced the two calls to `getgroup` in `chan-groups` by a call to a more efficient (but even more verbose) macro `getgroups` which retrieves both tuples in a single walk over groups.

in the exchange part, we still are left with a symmetry in the identity of the gossips exchanged, which is encoded in the knowledge bitvectors. Although we tried hard, we did not succeed in exploiting this symmetry in a plain PROMELA model.

Finally, it should be noted that our approach bears similarities with the *counter abstraction* work of, e.g., [4,5,13,14]. In their approaches, however, the processes that are in the same location are being counted, whereas in our approach the variables that have the same values are being counted.

4   TopSPIN

In this section we will report on our ventures with TopSPIN to solve the gossiping girls problem. TopSPIN [2,28] is an automatic symmetry reduction tool for the SPIN model checker. TopSPIN is applied to a PROMELA model, and – provided that the model adheres to some restrictions – uses computational group theory to automatically determine a group of component symmetries associated with the specification. The tool automatically modifies the model checking algorithm employed by SPIN to exploit these symmetries during verification. We also considered the older symmSPIN package [1] but preferred TopSPIN because the tool is fully automatic and gives helpful explanations in cases when the tool cannot find symmetries in the model.

TopSPIN uses the GAP [24] computational algebra system to effectively detect state space symmetry from the associated PROMELA model. Furthermore, TopSPIN uses a prototype extension of the saucy program [26], which is used to compute symmetries of directed graphs. As mentioned, TopSPIN places some restrictions on the PROMELA model, including:

- All processes should be instantiated using run statements within init.
- The current version of TopSPIN does not support arrays of channels.
- TopSPIN is not yet compatible with the verification of liveness properties.
- For symmetry to be detected, it is important for proctypes to use their built-in _pid variable rather than a user-defined process identifier.
- TopSPIN does not support bitvectors in the sense that it recognizes a byte being used as an array from pid to bool.

Especially the last two restrictions forced us to rethink the representation of knowledge within our model. Fig. 5 lists the PROMELA model symm-girls. This model is a variation of the original girl-processes model. The behavior of each girl is represented by a Girl process. However, instead of using an arbitrary number to identify the girls, we now use the *process identifier (pid)* of a Girl process to identify the gossip that she originally knew.

Instead of using bitvectors to store the knowledge of the girls, we now encode the knowledge in sorted channels of *pid*'s. For each Girl with pid i, a channel ki is defined, which holds the pids of all gossips that this girl knows. When the processes are instantiated in the init process, the channel ki is passed to the Girl-process which will get pid i. This channel is stored in the Girl's know

```
chan phone = [0] of { chan };
chan k1    = [4] of { pid };    /* ki = knowledge of Girl with pid i    */
chan k2    = [4] of { pid };
chan k3    = [4] of { pid };
chan k4    = [4] of { pid };
chan tmp   = [4] of { pid };    /* temporary channel                    */
byte calls;                     /* number of telephone calls            */

proctype Girl(chan know) {
  pid  p;
  bool newinfo;
  chan friend = know;           /* outside of d_step, friend == know    */

  know ! _pid;
  do
  ::  atomic { phone ! know; }
  ::  d_step {
        phone ? friend;
        newinfo=false;
        do /* 1. move elements from friend to tmp */
        ::  empty(friend) -> break
        ::  nempty(friend) -> friend?p; tmp!p;
                              if
                              ::  know ?? [eval(p)] -> skip
                              ::  else -> newinfo=true
                              fi
        od;
        do /* 2. move elements from know to tmp */
        ::  empty(know)    -> break
        ::  nempty(know)   -> know?p;
                              if
                              ::  tmp ?? [eval(p)] -> skip
                              ::  else -> tmp!p; newinfo=true;
                              fi;
        od;
        do /* 3. move elements from tmp to friend and know */
        ::  empty(tmp)     -> break;
        ::  nempty(tmp)    -> tmp?p; friend!!p; know!!p
        od;
        if
        ::  newinfo -> calls++
        ::  else
        fi;
        p=0; friend=know; newinfo=false;
      }
  od
}

init { atomic { run Girl(k1); run Girl(k2); run Girl(k3); run Girl(k4); } }
```

Fig. 5. Promela model `symm-girls`

variable. Now, in combination with the symmetric version of the process Girl, TopSPIN will recognize that these channels can safely be permuted. As with the chan-groups model, we keep these channels sorted to obtain a canonical representation of the knowledge.

As before, the girls exchange information through the rendez-vous channel phone. The girls offer their own knowledge channel know on this channel phone. The *receiving* girl makes sure that knowledge is exchanged and that both her own knowledge channel (know) and the knowledge channel of the other girl (friend) get updated. Updating know and friend requires three steps. Firstly, all elements of friend are copied to the temporary channel tmp. Secondly, all elements of know which are not yet in tmp are copied to tmp. Now tmp contains the combined knowledge of the original friend and know channels. Thirdly, all elements of tmp are copied to friend and know using SPIN's sorted send operation. Note that we only update the variable calls if the conversation between the two girls revealed new information. At the end of the d_step we again reset all local variables.

The symmetric model for TopSPIN comes with a price, though. With respect to the information in the state vector, the symm-girls model is quite expensive, compared to the previous models. Instead of using an efficient array of bitvectors, $n+1$ channels of length of n are being used. Furthermore, exchanging information has become an expensive operation. Instead of using a single bitwise operator, a single conversation requires the copying of three of those channels.

As mentioned above, the current version of TopSPIN cannot yet deal with liveness properties. Therefore, for the verification runs to find the optimal solution to the problem, we had to resort to the slightly less effective assert statement.

5   Bliss

In this section we exploit SPIN's embedded C code extensions to encode the symmetries ourselves. This section assumes a working knowledge of SPIN's C code extensions, i.e., chapter of 17 of [6]. Basic knowledge of graph isomorphism theory is also assumed. The approach taken for this model is based on the abstraction techniques of [7].

The original PROMELA models of Sec. 2 use an array knows of bitvectors to store the knowledge within the system. This array knows is essentially the adjacency matrix of a graph representation of the knowledge: if a girl i knows the gossip of girl j, there is a directed edge from i to j. For this final PROMELA model, we exploit this graph representation. We will use the *bliss* tool to find the canonical representatives for these graphs.

bliss [10,23] is a tool for computing automorphism groups and canonical forms of graphs. It has both a command line user interface as well as C/C++ programming language APIs. Naturally, *bliss* does not use a polynomial-time algorithm for computing the authomorphism group of the graph (otherwise it would immediately imply a polynomial-time algorithm for the graph isomorphism problem). However, compared to other well-known tools for checking graph isomorphisms (e.g., nauty and saucy), *bliss* seems to perform quite well [10].

Two features of *bliss* which make the tool ideal for our purposes are the following: (i) *bliss* can work with directed graphs, and (ii) *bliss* can compute a canonical representation of the automorphism group of a graph. Given a graph G and its canonical representative graph $\rho(G)$ the following holds: for all graphs G' that are isomorphic with G, *bliss* will return the same representative graph, i.e., $\rho(G) = \rho(G')$.

Fig. 6 shows the PROMELA model bliss. The model is a variation of the single-process model: there is a single process allgirls, which enumerates

```
c_decl { \#include "bitmatrix.h" }
c_code {
  unsigned int automorph_partition[4];
  BitMatrix stack_adjmat;
  BitMatrix canonical_adjmat;
}
c_track "&automorph_partition"  "sizeof(unsigned_int)*4"   "StackOnly"
c_track "stack_adjmat.pbv"      "((4*4)/8+((4*4)%8>0))"    "StackOnly"
c_track "canonical_adjmat.pbv"  "((4*4)/8+((4*4)%8>0))"

#define SINGLE_CALL(x,y)                                        \
  c_expr { designated_partners(&stack_adjmat,                   \
                          automorph_partition, x, y) } ->       \
    calls++;                                                    \
    c_code {                                                    \
      merge_rows(&stack_adjmat, x, y);                          \
      comp_canonical(&stack_adjmat, &canonical_adjmat);         \
    };

byte calls=0;
active proctype allgirls() {
  c_code {
    init_bit_matrix(&stack_adjmat, 4);
    init_bit_matrix(&canonical_adjmat, 4);
  };

  do
  ::  c_code { comp_automorph_partition(&stack_adjmat,
                                    automorph_partition); };
      if
      ::  d_step { SINGLE_CALL(0,1) }
      ::  d_step { SINGLE_CALL(0,2) }
      ::  d_step { SINGLE_CALL(0,3) }
      ::  d_step { SINGLE_CALL(1,2) }
      ::  d_step { SINGLE_CALL(1,3) }
      ::  d_step { SINGLE_CALL(2,3) }
      ::  else -> break
      fi;
  od;
}
```

Fig. 6. Promela model bliss

all possible calls between the girls in a do-loop. We use an efficient bitmatrix to
store the knowledge of the girls. In fact, we use two bit matrices: stack_adjmat
and canonical_adjmat. The definition of the typedef BitMatrix can be found
in Fig. 7. The stack_adjmat is the adjacency matrix of the directed graph that
we work with in the body of the proctype allgirls. When a conversation
takes place between two girls, this adjacency matrix gets updated. However,
this adjacency matrix is never saved in the state space: it is only used in the
current state. Hence the decoration "StackOnly" next to the c_track declaration of stack_adjmat. Instead of stack_adjmat, we store the adjacency matrix
of its canonical graph: canonical_adjmat. Note that canonical_adjmat does
not have the "StackOnly" decoration within its declaration. In terms of [7],
canonical_adjmat is the *abstract* graph.

The BitMatrix library of Fig. 7 needs some more explanation. Essentially,
a BitMatrix is an efficient implementation of an array of bitvectors in C. The

```
typedef struct BitMatrix {
    char*   pbv;    /* pointer to bitvector */
    int     dim;    /* dimension of matrix */
} BitMatrix;

void init_bit_matrix(BitMatrix* g, int width);
void free_bit_matrix(BitMatrix* g);
void print_bit_matrix(BitMatrix* g);
int  all_bits_set(BitMatrix* g);
int  same_rows(BitMatrix* g, int v1, int v2);
void merge_rows(BitMatrix* g, int v1, int v2);

void comp_canonical(BitMatrix* src, BitMatrix* dst);
void comp_automorph_partition(BitMatrix* src,
                        unsigned int automorph_partition[]);
int  designated_partners(BitMatrix* src,
                        unsigned int automorph_partition[], int v1, int v2);
```

Fig. 7. Header file bitmatrix.h

first five functions of Fig. 7 are basic functions on a BitMatrix. The function same_rows checks whether the bitvector rows of v1 and v2 are the same; or in graph terms: whether the outgoing edges of v1 and v2 lead to the same nodes. The function merge_rows performs the familiar bitwise-or operator on the rows of v1 and v2. The last three functions of Fig. 7 implement the connection with *bliss*, and will be discussed in some more detail below.

Let us look at the macro SINGLE_CALL. The knowledge of the two girls x and y is merged using merge_rows. The function comp_canonical computes the canonical representation of stack_adjmat. First, in this function, the adjacency matrix of stack_adjmat is converted to *bliss*'s internal graph representation. Then, *bliss*'s function to compute the canonical representation of a graph is called. Finally, the internal graph representation is converted back to our BitMatrix representation.

An important part of SINGLE_CALL is the call to designated_partners. Converting the adjacency matrix to *bliss*' graph representation (and vice-versa), and especially the computation of the canonical representation of a graph are time-consuming procedures. To improve the running time of the verification with SPIN, it is important to eliminate, when possible, calls between girls that are guaranteed to lead to a canonical graph that has or will be covered by connecting two other girls. Given two potential partners x and y, the function designated_partners returns true, when:

- the knowledge of x and y is different
  (i.e., the rows of the bitvectors x and y differ), *and*
- if x and y belong to the *same* cell of the partition of the automorphism group, then x and y should both have the lowest indices of this cell, *or*
- if x and y belong to *different* cells of the partition of the automorphism group, they both should have the lowest indices within their respective cells.

A partition of a set V is a set of disjoint non-empty subsets of V whose union is V. The elements of a partition are called cells. Given a graph G, the automorphism group $Aut(G)$ of G can be represented by a partition $P(G)$ of the nodes V of G: the nodes in each cell of $P(G)$ can be *permuted*. For example, in the initial state of the model, when all girls only know their own gossip, the partition of the automorphism group consists of a single cell containing all nodes. It is enough to only consider a single conversation between two nodes of this cell. After the first transition, the partition consist of two cells: cell c_1 contains the two girls which just exchanged their gossips and cell c_2 contains the other girls. It is enough to only consider a conversation between two nodes of c_2 and a conversation between a node of c_1 and a node of c_2.

The partition is computed in comp_automorph_partition. Within this function, *bliss'* find_automorphisms function is called, which returns a set of generators for the automorphism group of the graph. Given this set of generators the cells can be computed. In Fig. 6 these cells are stored in the "StackOnly" array automorph_partition. If two nodes n_1 and n_2 belong to the same cell, automorph_partition[n_1] == automorph_partition[n_2].

Implementation. Although *bliss* has a well documented API, connecting the tool to SPIN took some considerable effort. Roughly 300 lines of C code were needed for this interface.

6   Experiments

This section discusses the experiments that we conducted with SPIN on the various PROMELA models. During our study, we carried out two types of experiments with SPIN: 'exhaustive' experiments where we used SPIN's standard *safety* mode to generate *all* reachable states for the given PROMELA model, and 'find the optimal sequence' experiments where we used SPIN's *liveness* mode to find a $2n-4$ solution to the gossiping girls problem.

We only report on the 'exhaustive' experiments. The 'find the optimal sequence' experiments show similar results though; except for the fact that in some cases SPIN could still find the optimal sequence where the corresponding 'exhaustive' experiment would run out of memory. These results, however, depend on SPIN's default DFS exploration order. Since version 5.1.x, SPIN supports several C compile time options (e.g., -DREVERSE, -DRANDOMIZE) which change the order of selecting outgoing transitions. Running the 'find the optimal sequence' experiments with any of these options will thus show different results. Therefore we decided that including the results of the second type of experiments was not very meaningful. Instead, we report on our experiments with the SWARM tool [8,27] to 'find the optimal sequence'.

Settings. All experiments were run on an Apple MacBook 2.66GHz Intel Core 2 Duo, with 8GB of RAM, running Mac OS X 10.6.8 (in single-user, console mode) and gcc 4.2.1. We used SPIN version 6.1.0 for all experiments, except for the TopSPIN experiments for which we used SPIN version 5.2.5. We used TopSPIN version 2.2.5, *bliss* version 0.50 and GROOVE version 4.4.5. For the TopSPIN

Table 1. Summary of exhaustive benchmark experiments

#girls		girl-processes	single-process	chan-groups	symm-girls SPIN	symm-girls TOPSPIN	bliss
$n = 4$	sv (bytes)	64	20	44	104	104	20
	states, stored	190	192	140	251	42	45
	states, matched	2,080	670	83	2,391	394	33
	time (sec)	0	0	0	0	0	0
	memory (MB)	131	131	131	131	131	131
$n = 5$	sv (bytes)	72	20	44	120	120	20
	states, stored	9,153	9,155	2,468	10,234	540	321
	states, matched	173,889	67,139	3,659	186,098	9,897	753
	time (sec)	0.08	0.01	0.01	0.36	0.06	0.03
	rate (s/sec)	114k	no data	no data	28k	9.0k	11k
	memory (MB)	131	131	131	132	131	131
$n = 6$	sv (bytes)	80	20	52	136	136	20
	states, stored	1,092,474	1,092,476	91,348	1,150,478	18,316	6,505
	states, matched	31,681,718	13,311,818	252,039	32,818,752	525,940	31,400
	time (sec)	13.4	3.0	0.8	70.5	4.8	1.2
	rate (s/sec)	81k	369k	114k	16k	3.8k	5.2k
	memory (MB)	197	172	137	272	133	131
$n = 7$	sv (bytes)	88	20	52	216	216	20
	states, stored	$> 28\,e6$	$> 37\,e6$	6,588,212	$> 13\,e6$	1,334,922	279,985
	states, matched	$> 11.4\,e8$	$> 6.6\,e8$	29,214,527	$> 5.3\,e8$	54,525,101	2,201,294
	time (sec)	541	195	96	1460	815	87
	rate (s/sec)	52k	191k	69k	9.0k	1.6k	3.2k
	memory (MB)	o.o.m.	o.o.m.	533	o.o.m.	325	142
$n = 8$	sv (bytes)			60		240	20
	states, stored			$> 27\,e6$		$> 11\,e6$	23,461,597
	states, matched			$> 17\,e7$		$> 62\,e7$	267,185,640
	time (sec)			595		14,300	11,100
	rate (s/sec)			47k		0.8k	2.1k
	memory (MB)			o.o.m.		o.o.m.	1026
exhaustive, solution found		$n \leq 7$	$n \leq 7$	$n \leq 7$	$n \leq 7$	$n \leq 7$	$n \leq 8$
swarm, solution found		$n \leq 8$	$n \leq 8$	$n \leq 10$	n.a.	$n \leq 6$	$n \leq 10$
modelling time		< 1 hour	< 1 hour	≈ 4 days	≈ 2 days		≈ 8 days

experiments we used TopSPIN's default *fast* symmetry reduction strategy (which is indeed fast, but does not yield canonical representations). For each verification run we reserved 2GB of memory. To compile SPIN's pan verifiers for safety runs we used the following options for gcc:[4]

```
gcc -O2 -o pan -DSAFETY -DNOCLAIM -DMEMLIM=2048 pan.c
```

Furthermore, for TopSPIN and *bliss*, we linked pan to the respective libraries, of course. We executed *all* pan verifiers using the following command-line:

```
./pan -m50000 -c1 -w24
```

Due to -w24, pan will always reserve 128MB of memory for the hash table.

---

[4] By default, SPIN's powerful and automatic partial-order-reduction (POR) optimization gets enabled. However, as there is no parellellism in the PROMELA models which POR can utilize, nothing is gained in terms of the number of states.

Effort. The last row of Table 1 shows an estimate of the modelling time for the various PROMELA models. Parameterizing the models in n (using the m4 macro processor) and setting up all experiments took us more than a week. Finally, *all* experiments can be executed in roughly 28 hours. All PROMELA models and verification results are available from http://ruwise.nl/spin-2012/.

Exhaustive experiments. Table 1 lists the results of letting SPIN compute *all* reachable states for the various models: we let SPIN perform safety verification runs where we only checked for invalid end-states. The columns correspond with the PROMELA models that have been discussed in this paper. The symm-girls model has been verified with both vanilla SPIN and with TopSPIN.

The rows 'time (sec)' list the *elapsed time* as reported by SPIN. The rows 'rate (s/sec)' list the number of states per second, again as reported by SPIN. When SPIN does not have enough memory to finish the verification, this is indicated with 'o.o.m.' (out-of-memory). We still report the output by SPIN though. For TopSPIN and *bliss* the 'rate (s/sec)' column needs clarification. Symmetry reduction involves computing a canonical representative for *every* state that is encountered. Every time TopSPIN or *bliss* processes a state, the tool is really processing a whole equivalence class of states.

From Table 1 we learn that our two initial PROMELA models are fast. Especially, the rate of the single-process model is high, compared to the rates of the other models. This is obvious as a transition in single-process only consists of a bitwise-or operation and two assignments. Moreover, the state vector of single-process consists of only 20 bytes.

Our best vanilla PROMELA model chan-groups behaves quite well. Compared to the two straightforward models, it succeeds in lowering the number of states without becoming too slow. It succeeds for $n = 7$.

Due to n processes and the $n + 1$ channels of length n, the state vector of the symm-girls model is large. We see that symm-girls exhibits poor results when veryfying the model with vanilla SPIN. Due to the expensive computation involving the knowledge channels, the rate is also quite low. On the other hand, in combination with TopSPIN, the symm-girls model fares quite well for $n \leq 6$. The rate is even lower, but this is no surprise due to the computation of canonical representatives. For $n \geq 7$ this computational overhead becomes significant.[5]

The 'winner' of our experiments is the bliss model. It is the only model which succeeds in generating all states for $n = 8$, albeit slowly. SPIN needs only slightly more than 1GB of memory to verify this model for $n = 8$. As with the TopSPIN model, we see that with increasing n, the verification rate for this model deteriorates. This is not surprising given all the operations that are executed within a single transition. Of these operations, with increasing n, the automorphism detection becomes the most dominant factor.

---

[5] We have discussed these verification results with Alastair Donaldson, the developer of TopSPIN. He suspects that the current version of TopSPIN does not handle *sorted send* channels in the most efficient way. A future version of TopSPIN should fix this.

Table 2. Summary of experiments with GROOVE

#girls	gossip-priorities				gossip-nested			
	states	trans.	time	memory	states	trans.	time	memory
$n = 4$	55	253	0.3s	6kB	13	66	0.2s	0.2MB
$n = 5$	382	1,852	1.1s	0.5MB	52	418	1.0s	0.3MB
$n = 6$	4,458	22,492	4.0s	1.5MB	361	4,749	3.2s	0.5MB
$n = 7$	80,459	409,372	44.7s	17.1MB	3,703	71,804	18.9s	2.6MB
$n = 8$	4,157,679	22,684,164	3099s	899MB	62,982	1,790,230	519s	54.9MB

Swarm. SWARM [8,27] is a tool, which – given a PROMELA model and some verification settings – generates a script that performs many small verification jobs with SPIN in parallel, that can increase the problem coverage for very large verification problems. SWARM's verification jobs use SPIN's bitstate hashing mode.

We have used SWARM on the PROMELA models to 'find the optimal sequence' using the LTL property as discussed in Sec. 2. For each PROMELA model (and for each $n \in \{4, \ldots, 10\}$) we first performed a test run with SPIN to get an estimate for the speed and the hash factor. These settings were then used to let SWARM run 60 minutes on each n-th version of the PROMELA models. We let SWARM terminate as soon as one of the parallel verifications would find an error trail (i.e., option -e). For $n \leq 6$ swarm would come up with an error trail within a few seconds. For $n \geq 7$ it took longer.

The one-but-last row of Table 1 summarizes our experiments with SWARM. For both chan-groups and bliss, SWARM succeeds in finding an optimal sequence for $n = 10$. Curiously, on symm-girls, the combination SWARM and TopSPIN only finds an error for $n \leq 6$. Perhaps the large state vector in combination with the slow speed are responsible for this. Obviously, if SWARM would have been given more time, it would probably have found more errors trails. This experiment just illustrates the power of SWARM in dealing with PROMELA models where exhaustive verification is not an option.

Groove. As mentioned in Sec. 1, the GROOVE tool set [15,25] has also been used for experiments with the gossiping girls problem [16]. GROOVE [25] is a project centered around the use of simple graphs for modelling several structures object-oriented systems, and graph transformations as a basis for model transformation and operational semantics. The GROOVE tool set includes an editor, a simulator, a generator for automatically exploring state spaces and a model checker.

One of the key features of the GROOVE tool set is its underlying, very efficient algorithm for isomorphy checking of graphs. With a symmetric model, such as the one for the gossiping girls, you get your symmetry reductions for free.

On the same machine that we ran our SPIN experiments, we have also ran the GROOVE generator to compute the state space. We allocated 2GB of memory for the JVM and used GROOVE's DFS mode. Table 2 shows the results of the GROOVE experiments. The results for *gossip-priorities* correspond with GROOVE models which use rule priorities [16], whereas the *gossip-nested* results correspond with improved GROOVE models which use a rule system with nested rules [17]. This rule system with nested rules has recently been added to GROOVE. We see that

GROOVE does not have any problems with $n = 7$ and clearly outperforms our PROMELA models for the exhaustive experiments.

7   Conclusions

We have explored several ways to model the gossiping girls problem along different points of view, trying to exploit the inherent symmetries of the problem. The main point of the paper is that alternative modelling routes with SPIN can lead to substantial better verification results.

We have seen that straightforward PROMELA models are easy to construct and show reasonable results, but are not very efficient in the terms of the number of states. However, we have also seen that even in vanilla PROMELA we can implement symmetry reductions to lower the number of states. Remember though that it took several modelling efforts to come up with the final chan-groups model that we discuss in this paper.

TOPSPIN is a fully automatic, user-friendly tool, but it requires some basic knowledge of group theory. And although TOPSPIN outperforms vanilla SPIN on the gossiping girls problem, for larger n one has to have patience. TOPSPIN requires a truly symmetric model. This might mean that you either have to rework your model or that you have to identify the symmetries yourself.

Although our PROMELA model which uses *bliss* shows the best results, it took quite some programming effort to get there. For the occassional symmetric model this route is therefore not recommended. However, whenever a very memory efficient model is required, this approach could be an option.

Due to its efficient algorithm for checking isomorphy, GROOVE performs best on the gossiping girls problem. The GROOVE tool set also includes CTL and LTL model checkers. So, if you have to verify a highly symmetric model – and you are not afraid to learn a new modelling formalism – GROOVE should be high on your list of potential candidates.

Finally, we witnessed the power of SWARM. The tool succeeds in finding the optimal sequence in PROMELA models where exhaustive verification surely would have failed. The results are not uniform for all PROMELA models though. More research with SWARM is needed.

We also intend to apply our modelling approach to other, larger symmetric problems to see in howfar our results can be generalised. Furthermore, we intend to extend our comparison with other model checkers.

Acknowledgements. We would like to thank Arend Rensink for providing us with the GROOVE models of the gossiping girls problem and with his assistance in running GROOVE. Gerard Holzmann is thanked for his help with SWARM. We would like to thank Joost-Pieter Katoen and especially Alastair F. Donaldson for their valuable comments and suggestions to improve the paper.

References

1. Bosnacki, D., Dams, D., Holenderski, L.: Symmetric SPIN. STTT 4(1), 92–106 (2002)
2. Donaldson, A.F., Miller, A.: A Computational Group Theoretic Symmetry Reduction Package for the SPIN Model Checker. In: Johnson, M., Vene, V. (eds.) AMAST 2006. LNCS, vol. 4019, pp. 374–380. Springer, Heidelberg (2006)
3. Edelkamp, S., Lluch Lafuente, A., Leue, S.: Directed Explicit Model Checking with HSF-SPIN. In: Dwyer, M.B. (ed.) SPIN 2001. LNCS, vol. 2057, pp. 57–79. Springer, Heidelberg (2001)
4. Emerson, E.A., Trefler, R.J.: From Asymmetry to Full Symmetry: New Techniques for Symmetry Reduction in Model Checking. In: Pierre, L., Kropf, T. (eds.) CHARME 1999. LNCS, vol. 1703, pp. 142–157. Springer, Heidelberg (1999)
5. Emerson, E.A., Wahl, T.: On Combining Symmetry Reduction and Symbolic Representation for Efficient Model Checking. In: Geist, D., Tronci, E. (eds.) CHARME 2003. LNCS, vol. 2860, pp. 216–230. Springer, Heidelberg (2003)
6. Holzman, G.J.: The SPIN Model Checker – Primer and Reference Manual. Addison-Wesley, Boston (2003)
7. Holzmann, G.J., Joshi, R.: Model-Driven Software Verification. In: Graf, S., Mounier, L. (eds.) SPIN 2004. LNCS, vol. 2989, pp. 76–91. Springer, Heidelberg (2004)
8. Holzmann, G.J., Joshi, R., Groce, A.: Tackling Large Verification Problems with the Swarm Tool. In: Havelund, K., Majumdar, R. (eds.) SPIN 2008. LNCS, vol. 5156, pp. 134–143. Springer, Heidelberg (2008)
9. Hurkens, C.: Spreading gossip efficiently. Nieuw Archief Voor Wiskunde 5/1(2), 208–210 (2000)
10. Junttila, T., Kaski, P.: Engineering an Efficient Canonical Labeling Tool for Large and Sparse Graphs. In: Applegate, D., Brodal, G.S., Panario, D., Sedgewick, R. (eds.) Proc. of ALENEX 2007, pp. 135–149. SIAM (2007)
11. Katoen, J.-P.: How to Model and Analyze Gossiping Protocols? ACM SIGMETRICS' Performance Evaluation Review 36(3), 3–6 (2008)
12. Liben-Nowell, D.: Gossip is Synteny: Incomplete Gossip and the Syntenic Distance between Genomes. Journal of Algorithms 43(2), 264–283 (2002)
13. Pnueli, A., Xu, J., Zuck, L.D.: Liveness with $(0, 1, \infty)$-Counter Abstraction. In: Brinksma, E., Larsen, K.G. (eds.) CAV 2002. LNCS, vol. 2404, pp. 107–122. Springer, Heidelberg (2002)
14. Pong, F., Dubois, M.: A New Approach for the Verification of Cache Coherence Protocols. IEEE Transactions on Parallel and Distributed Systems 6(8), 773–787 (1995)
15. Rensink, A.: The GROOVE Simulator: A Tool for State Space Generation. In: Pfaltz, J.L., Nagl, M., Böhlen, B. (eds.) AGTIVE 2003. LNCS, vol. 3062, pp. 479–485. Springer, Heidelberg (2004)
16. Rensink, A.: Isomorphism Checking in GROOVE. In: Zündorf, A., Varró, D. (eds.) Proc. of Graph-Based Tools, GraBaTs 2006, Natal, Brazil. Electronic Communications of the EASST, vol. 1 (2006)
17. Rensink, A., Kuperus, J.-H.: Repotting the Geraniums: On Nested Graph Transformation Rules. In: Boronat, A., Heckel, R. (eds.) Proc. of Graph Transformation and Visual Modeling Techniques, York, UK. Electronic Communications of the EASST, vol. 18 (March 2009)

18. Ruys, T.C.: Low-Fat Recipes for SPIN. In: Havelund, K., Penix, J., Visser, W. (eds.) SPIN 2000. LNCS, vol. 1885, pp. 287–321. Springer, Heidelberg (2000)
19. Ruys, T.C.: Towards Effective Model Checking. PhD thesis, University of Twente, Enschede, The Netherlands (March 2001)
20. Ruys, T.C.: Optimal Scheduling Using Branch and Bound with SPIN 4.0. In: Ball, T., Rajamani, S.K. (eds.) SPIN 2003. LNCS, vol. 2648, pp. 1–17. Springer, Heidelberg (2003)
21. Seindal, R.: GNU m4, version 1.4.16. Free Software Foundation, Inc., 1.4.16 edition (2011), http://www.gnu.org
22. Vaandrager, F.W.: A First Introduction to UPPAAL. In: Tretmans, G.J. (ed.) Quasimodo Handbook. Springer (to appear, 2012)
23. bliss – A Tool for Computing Automorphism Groups and Canonical Labelings of Graphs, http://www.tcs.hut.fi/Software/bliss/
24. GAP – system for computational discrete algebra, http://www.gap-system.org/
25. GROOVE – graphs for object-oriented verification, http://groove.cs.utwente.nl/
26. SAUCY2 – Fast Symmetry Discovery, http://vlsicad.eecs.umich.edu/BK/SAUCY/
27. SWARM - verification script generator for Spin, http://www.spinroot.com/swarm/
28. TOPSPIN, http://www.doc.ic.ac.uk/~afd/topspin/

Formal Verification of Hierarchically Distributed Agent Based Protection Scheme in Smart Grid

Shravan Garlapati and Sandeep K. Shukla

Virginia Polytechnic and State University, Blacksburg 24060, USA
{gshra09,shukla}@vt.edu

Abstract. In recent studies, hierarchically distributed non-intrusive agent aided transmission line distance relaying protection scheme has been proposed. This scheme is meant to provide the distance relays with situational awareness and improve their robustness against hidden failures. Distance relaying protection scheme is a part of safety critical cyber physical system (in particular, power system) and it operates with stringent timing requirements to remove the faulted line out of service. Before putting into practice, it is better to formally verify that the agent based relay supervisory scheme meets the specifications and its usage gives intended results and doesn't carry any negative side effects. Therefore, in this paper agent based relay supervision scheme is formally modelled, validated and its properties are verified using UPPAAL - a timed automata based formal verification tool.

1 Introduction

Power grid transmission lines are usually protected by distance relays which comprises of local primary relays (Zone 1), secondary relays (Zone 2) and remote back up relays (Zone 3) [1]. The main objective of the protection system is to isolate a fault as soon as possible to minimize the negative impact of the fault on the grid and also to minimize the amount of load shed because of the relay induced disconnection of lines. Remote back up relay is preferred to a local backup as a local backup shares the same electrical and communication infrastructure with primary relay; hence vulnerable to "Common Mode Failure" [2] [3]. Remote back up relay and primary relay are usually located in different substations and thus are less vulnerable to "Common Mode Failures". Compared with primary relays, remote backup relays operate with longer fault clearing times and also its operation to remove a fault may lead to larger area of load shedding. Therefore, transmission line distance relaying protection system is designed in such a way that the remote back up relay doesn't trip unless it is absolutely necessary i.e. when both zone 1 and zone 2 relays fail or their associated sensors or breakers simultaneously fail to clear the fault. After a thorough analysis of historical blackouts such as 1965 Great North-east blackout, 1977 New York blackout and the 1996 western blackout, North American Electric Reliability Council (NERC) concluded that a Zone 3 relay mis-operation is one of the major causes of cascading outages leading to blackout events [4].

A. Donaldson and D. Parker (Eds.): SPIN 2012, LNCS 7385, pp. 137–154, 2012.
© Springer-Verlag Berlin Heidelberg 2012

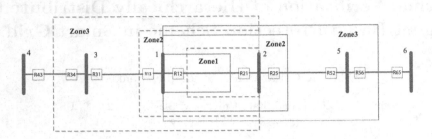

Fig. 1. Zones of Protection

Horowitz et. al. reanalyzed the distance relaying protection scheme and concluded that Zone 3 relay cannot be abandoned as its absence will put a power system at risk [2].

Zone 3 relays can incorrectly trip a line due to hidden failures [5][6]. A hidden failure is a defect (incorrect relay setting or software or hardware error) in a relay which may go unidentified for a long time and gets excited by another event leading to erroneous removal of circuit elements [7]. Because of hidden failures, Zone 3 relays may be extra sensitive to temporary line overloading due to transients, mistake it as a fault in a line and mis-trip even though it is not recognized as a faulty condition by Zone 1 or Zone 2 relay. At this instance, if power system is operating under stressed conditions, the hidden failure induced Zone 3 relay mis-trip may initiate other line trips leading to catastrophic failures like blackouts. One of the main objectives of the smart grid is that the power system will be enabled with communication and networking infrastructure to an unprecedented level, and wide area measurements and controls will provide the power system (transmission and distribution) with unprecedented robustness and prevent untoward incidents such as blackouts. In [8] an agent based relay supervision scheme is proposed to reduce the probability of hidden failure induced trips. Agents are hierarchically distinguished as master and slave agents. The real time communication between the master and slave agents aid Zone 3 relays to classify a fault as a true fault or a hidden failure induced fault and respectively to trip or not to trip.

In this paper we use UPPAAL [9] - a formal verification tool to formally verify and validate the agent based distance relaying protection scheme. Because of strict timing requirements (section 2) for the proper functioning of distance relays, time based formal models are needed, and UPPAAL allows us to model these in the form of timed automata, and allows model checking of timed properties on the models. To the best of our knowledge this is the first instance of applying formal verification to the protection scheme in a power system. Remainder of the paper is organized as follows. Section 2 explains distance relaying protection scheme. Summary of related research work is provided in section 3. Section 4 explains modelling of agent based distance relay protection scheme in UPPAAL. Section 5 discusses verification results and some observations are discussed in section 6. Section 7 concludes the paper.

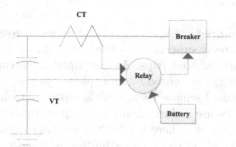

Fig. 2. Elements of a Protection System

2 Distance Relaying Protection Scheme

Distance relays operate based on the principle of impedance ratio, which is the ratio of the magnitude of voltage to that of the magnitude of current. The current and the voltage values measured respectively by current transformer (CT) and voltage transformer (VT) are communicated to the relay. With the current and voltage values as input, relay executes the relaying algorithm and concludes about the presence of a fault. If there is a fault then relay communicates with the breaker to trip the line out of service. If there is no fault, relay repeats the above procedure with the next set of current and voltage values. To account for the inaccuracies in sensing equipment (CT and VT), uncertainty in distance setting of relays and to make sure that there are no blind spots, multiple zones of protection (Zone 1, Zone 2) are employed for each transmission line. In the presence of a fault if the breaker associated with the Zone 1 or Zone 2 relay doesn't trip (due to a failure in CT, VT, relay or breaker), faulted line cannot be isolated from the system. Therefore a backup relay or Zone 3 relay is placed in the remote substation (bus). Thus there exists three different zones of protection i.e. Zone 1, Zone 2 and Zone 3 relays protecting a transmission line. It is already explained above that the remote back up relay is preferred to a local backup relay as the latter can be a victim of "common mode failure" along with the primary relay (Zone 1). Please refer to Fig 1 to see a pictorial representation of zones of protection. As shown in Fig 1 each transmission line is protected by relays at both ends. The internal circuitry of each of the rectangular boxes in Fig 1 is as shown in Fig 2. Dashed line shows protection in one direction of the transmission line and solid line in the other direction of the transmission line. In order to remove a faulted line out of service relays at both ends should trip. Zone 1 relay operates instantaneously i.e. within 2 cycles (32 ms). A coordination delay of 20 cycles (300 ms) is allowed before Zone 2 relay operates. Zone 3 relay or remote back up relay is allowed to operate with a coordination delay of 1 s(1000 ms). Coordination delays not only provide selectivity in isolating a faulted section but also ensure reliability of operation of the distance protection scheme [10]. Detailed explanation of zones of protection is out of the scope of this paper. Interested readers are referred to [1].

3   Previous Work

This section provides a brief summary of related previous research work. In [8] an agent based Zone 3 relay supervision scheme is proposed to reduce the probability of hidden failure induced trips. As explained in section 2, a fault in a single transmission line can be sensed by multiple relays under different zones of protection. In the proposed scheme each relay is associated with an agent(slave) which has the ability to sense and communicate fault status information to other agents. Fault status indicates if there is a fault in the transmission line protected by the relay or not. Based on the responsibilities assigned to them agents are hierarchically distinguished in a master/slave relationship. At any given instance the master agent has the complete information about the fault status sensed by all the relays (communicated by agents) protecting a transmission line. Whenever a relay senses a fault, its associated slave agent records it and queries the master agent to find out if the sensed fault is a true fault or a falsely perceived fault. Master agent compares the queried slave agent relay's fault status with the other slave agent relays protecting the same transmission line. In order to perform this comparison, master agent must know ahead of time which set of relays are protecting the transmission line. [11] provides an algorithm for the master agent to find out the set of relays protecting a transmission line. If majority of the other relays also sense fault, master agent classifies the fault as a true fault and acknowledges the queried slave agent relay to trip. On the other hand if majority of the other relays protecting the transmission line doesn't sense a fault, master agent categorizes the condition as non-faulty and sends a message to the Zone 3 slave agent relay not to trip. Thus, with the help of agent communication a relay can distinguish a true fault from a hidden failure induced fault. The entire process of sensors sensing the current and voltage values, relay algorithm execution to find the existence of fault, slave agent recording a fault and querying the master agent, master agent comparing fault statuses of different relays protecting a transmission line and acknowledging the queried slave agent relay has to be finished within the relay fault clearing time i.e. 1 s, 300 ms and 32 ms respectively for Zone 3, Zone 2 and Zone 1 relay. With the current state of the art in communication and networking technologies it may be difficult to meet the timing requirements of Zone 1 and Zone 2 relays but Zone 3 relay time constraint may be met. Hence we restrict our analysis to Zone 3 relay supervision i.e. only Zone 3 slave agent relay queries are answered by the master agent.

It is possible that a larger bus system is geographically wide spread around 100's to 1000's of miles. If a single master agent is employed to serve queries from all the Zone 3 slave agents in such a large power grid, the round trip communication delay over large distances can exceed the Zone 3 fault clearing time. This deceives the purpose of the agent based distance relaying protection scheme. To overcome this issue, in [12] a methodology is provided to divide a power system network into sub-networks with the objective of minimizing the number of master agents required to serve queries from all the Zone 3 slave agents such that the round trip communication timing requirements are met.

4 Modelling Behaviour

In UPPAAL the model of system's behaviour is expressed as the composition of the behaviour models of its individual components. The main components of the agent aided distance relaying protection scheme are sensors (CT and VT), Zone 1 relay, Zone 2 relay, Zone 3 relay, breakers, slave and master agents. There exist two different models for both the sensor and the breaker. The reason for this is as follows: Zone 3 relay operates when both Zone 1 and Zone 2 relay fail and/or their associated both breakers or sensors fail simultaneously. Practically it is possible that the Zone 3 relay and its sensor and breaker equipment can fail but we didn't consider this scenario in our model. The main reason being the probability of Zone 1, Zone 2 and Zone 3 relays failing simultaneously is very low. Moreover Zone 3 is the only backup available. If we consider the case where Zone 3 relay also fails along with Zone 1 and Zone 2 relay we cannot successfully verify the distance relaying scheme. Hence the case of either Zone 3 relay or its sensor or breaker failure is not considered. Therefore the Sensor 1 and the Breaker 1 models have *failed* state whereas the Sensor 2 and the Breaker 2 models do not have *failed* state. Sensor 1 and Breaker 1 model the behaviour of the sensor and the breaker associated with Zone 1 and Zone 2 relays. Whereas the behaviour of the sensor and the breaker of the Zone 3 relay are respectively presented in the Sensor 2 and the Breaker 2 automata.

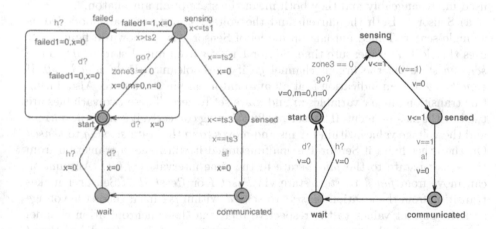

Fig. 3. Sensor1 automaton   **Fig. 4.** Sensor2 automaton

A reset transition moves an automaton from any state to the *start* state. The following two reset transitions are used by all the automatons described in this section. These two reset transitions are used multiple times to explain the behaviour of all the automata. Instead of rewriting these transitions many times they are just explained once here. At this point they may or may not be clearly understood but by the end of this section their relevance should become apparent.

1. *Reset I*: In our system model, when breakers at both ends of the line trip, a reset signal is sent via the broadcast channel d to all automatons to move to the *start* state. As shown in Fig 1 a transmission line is protected by Zone 1, Zone 2 and Zone 3 relays in both the directions. At least two relays i.e. one relay per direction have to trip in order to remove a faulted line out of service. In total there are at least six relays protecting a transmission line. Depending on which relay out of these six relays trip's last, any of the six breakers can send a reset signal via the urgent broadcast channel d to reset the whole system.

2. *Reset II*: If any of the Zone 3 relay senses no fault, then it moves from the location *calculate* to *nofault* transmitting a *nofault* signal via the broadcast channel *nf*. The remaining Zone 1, Zone 2 and Zone 3 relays receive the signal via the broadcast channel *nf* and move to *nofault* state. Zone 3 relay moves from *nofault* to *start* state by transmitting a reset signal on the broadcast channel h. All the automata move from their current location to *start* state after receiving a reset signal on the broadcast channel h.

In the following description of timed automata words "state" and "location" are used interchangeably and they both mean the state of an automaton.

a) Sensor 1: Both the current and the voltage transformer are modelled as a single sensor. Timed automaton model of Sensor 1 is as shown in figure 3. It uses the clock x to measure time. Sensor 1 moves from initial state *start* to the *sensing* state via the urgent channel *go* if the boolean variable *zone3==0*. If *zone3==0* it is an indication that all automatons are in start state. Also during this transition integer variables m and n are set to zero. These two variables are used by the master agent. If Sensor 1 is functioning correctly, it senses the current and the voltage values within *ts2* ms and moves from the state *sensing* to *sensed*. On the other hand if Sensor 1 is malfunctioned it will make a transition from the *sensing* state to the *failed* state in the time interval *(ts2,ts1)*. Automaton can move from *failed* to *start* state via *Reset I* or *Reset II*. If Sensor 1 makes transition from the location *sensing* to *sensed*, within *ts2* ms it sends the voltage and the current values to the respective relay via the synchronization channel a and moves to the committed location *communicated*. In networks of timed automata describing a system if any automaton is in a committed location next transition is from that location. Committed location is used in the execution of atomic sequence. From the committed location *communicated*, Sensor1 makes a transition to the *wait* state via the urgent channel *go*. Automaton can move from the *wait* to *start* state via *Reset I* or *Reset II*.

b) Sensor 2: The behaviour of the Sensor 2 is similar to that of the Sensor 1 except that the former doesn't have the *failed* state. Timed automaton of the Sensor 2 is as shown in figure 4.

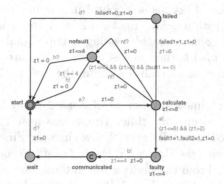

Fig. 5. Zone 1 Relay automaton

c) Zone 1 Relay: Timed automaton of Zone 1 Relay is as shown in figure 5. It uses the clock z to measure time. It receives the current and the voltage values from the Sensor 1 via the synchronization channel a and moves to the *calculate* state from the *start* state. Relay consumes $tz2$ to $tz3$ ms of processing time to find out if the transmission line protected by it is faulty or not. If there is a fault in the transmission line, Zone 1 relay moves from the state *calculate* to *faulty* within the time interval $(tz2,tz3)$. During this transition boolean variables *fault1, fault2* are set and a fault signal is sent to the slave agent associated with the relay via the communication channel e. It is aforementioned that in order to remove a faulted line out of service relays at both ends of the line have to sense and respective breakers have to trip. The Boolean variables *fault1* and *fault2* provide the fault status of the relays at both ends of the line. Initially both *fault1* and *fault2* are set to zero indicating a no fault condition. Whenever system (relay) senses a fault both *fault1* and *fault2* are set to one. The breaker trip at one end of the line resets *fault1* while the breaker trip at the other end of the line sets *fault2* to zero which removes the fault from the system.

On the flip side if there is no fault then relay makes a transition from the state *calculate* to *nofault* via *Reset II* if the Boolean variable *fault1* is not set. If *fault1* is already set, it is an indication that the system has already detected the fault via Zone 2 or Zone 3 relay and Zone 1 relay cannot move to *nofault* state. Zone 1, Zone 2 and Zone 3 relays all operate simultaneously until fault detection stage and detect the fault within the time interval $(tz2,tz3)$. The main difference in Zone 1, Zone 2 and Zone 3 relay models is the time instance at which they send tripping signal to their respective breakers. So, in the presence of a transmission line fault it is hard to predict which relay can first detect that fault and set the *fault1* variable. Thus it is necessary to check if *fault1* is set before moving from the state *calculate* to the state *nofault*. If Zone 1 Relay is malfunctioned, it does not respond in the time interval (tz2,tz3) and makes a transition to the *failed* state in time interval (tz3,tz1) and sets the Boolean variable *failed1* giving an indication that the relay has failed. Relay makes transition from the *failed* state to the *start* state when it receives a reset signal on the broadcast channel d via *Reset I*. During this transition it resets the Boolean variable *failed1*. A communication delay of tz4 ms is involved in sending a trip signal from a relay to the breaker. So, with a delay of tz4 ms Zone 1 Relay automaton moves from the state *faulty* to *communicated* sending a trip signal to its breaker via the synchronization channel *b*, then moves to the *wait* state via the urgent channel *go*. Automaton then makes a transition from the *wait* to the *start* state via *Reset I*.

d) Zone 2 Relay: Timed automaton of Zone 2 Relay is as shown in figure 6. It uses the clock z_2 to measure time. Transitions from the state *start* to *faulty* are similar to that of Zone 1 Relay with few changes. First, the Boolean variable *failed1* is replaced with the Boolean variable *failed2*. Second, the *faulty* state is a committed location. From the *faulty* state automaton makes a transition to the *wait1* state. If the breaker of Zone 1 Relay trips and resets the *fault1* variable, it is an indication that the system is fault free and Zone 2 relay moves to *start* state in time interval $[0, t2)$ ms by transmitting a signal via the urgent channel *zk* or by receiving a *Reset I*. If the breaker associated with Zone 1 relay doesn't trip within a communication delay of t_2 Zone 2 Relay moves to the *communicating* state from the *wait1* state to send a trip signal to its breaker. Zone 2 Relay automaton makes a transition from the *communicating* to the *communicated* state with a delay of tz4 ms. During this transition Zone 2 Relay sends a trip signal to its breaker via the synchronization channel *b*, and then moves to the *wait2* state via the urgent channel *go*. Automaton then makes a transition from *wait* to the *start* state via *Reset I*.

e) Zone 3 Relay: Timed automaton of Zone 3 Relay is as shown in figure 7. It uses the clock z_3 to measure time. Zone 3 relay automaton behaviour is almost similar to that of Zone 2 Relay, except that it doesn't have *failed* state. The other change is that the variable *t2* is replaced with the variable *t3*. When Zone 3 relay is in *wait1* state, within the coordination delay $[0, t3)$ if the breaker associated with either the Zone 1 or Zone 2 relay doesn't trip, Zone 3 relay moves to the *communicating* state and sends a signal to its breaker to trip the line out of service.

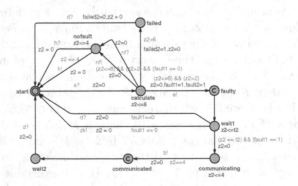

Fig. 6. Zone 2 Relay automaton

f) Breaker 1: Timed automaton of Breaker 1 is as shown in figure 8. Automaton uses the clock y to measure time. Breaker 1 is initially in the *start* location. Automaton receives a trip signal from its associated relay via the channel b and makes a transition from the location *start* to *received*. After receiving the trip signal from the relay, breaker and its associated electromechanical machinery trips a line out of service with a delay of tb1 ms. So, assuming that the breaker is functioning correctly automaton moves from the state *received* to the committed location *intermediate* in tb1 ms and resets the *fault1* variable, indicating that the line is tripped. If a transmission line is faulty then breakers at both ends of the line have to trip to remove the line out of service. So, to make a transition from the state *intermediate* to *tripped*, automaton performs a check to find out if the breaker on the other end of the line has tripped or not. If it is tripped *fault2* is reset otherwise *fault2* is set. Irrespective of whether *fault2* is set or reset automaton makes a transition from location *intermediate* to *tripped*. But if *fault2* is reset, automaton while making a move from the state *intermediate* to *tripped* transmits a faultfree signal via the channel c to the observer automata, giving an indication that the system is free of fault. When automaton is in *received* state, if the breaker doesn't respond for more than tb2 ms then it moves to *failed* state in time interval $[tb2, tb1)$. From the *failed* state breaker can make transition to the *start* state via *Reset I*. Transition from the location *tripped* to *start* occurs when both the Boolean variables *fault1* and *fault2* are reset. Also during this transition automaton sends a reset signal via *Reset I*.

g) Breaker 2: Timed automaton of Breaker 2 is approximately similar to that of Breaker 1 with the only change being Breaker 2 doesn't have a *failed* state. It is as shown in figure 9.

h) Observer automaton (OA): Observer automata captures the high level behaviour of the distance relaying protection scheme i.e. whether the system is *faultfree* or *faulty*. As shown in figure 10(a) observer automata has only 2 states i.e. *faultfree* and *faulty*. Automaton is initially in *faultfree* location. When Zone 1 or Zone 2 or Zone 3 Relay senses fault, they transmit fault signal n channel e. OA listen's it and moves to the *faulty* location. Transition from the state *faulty* to *faultfree* occurs when the automaton receives a reset signal via *Reset I*.

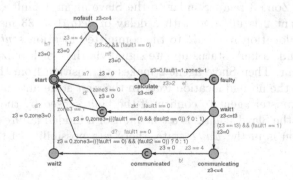

Fig. 7. Zone 3 Relay automaton

i) Helper automaton: As shown in figure 10(b) helper automaton has two transitions and one state. Whenever any automata has to make an urgent transition,
helper automata sends a signal via the urgent channel *go* and other automata
listens and makes a transition. Similarly Zone 2 and Zone 3 Relay make an urgent transition from the state *wait1* to the *start* state via the urgent channel
zk.

j) Slave agent: Similar to the sensor and the breaker models there exist two
different models for the slave agent. Slave agent 1 is used to model the behaviour
of the agent located at Zone 1 and Zone 2 relay. Timed automaton of the slave
agent 1 is as shown in figure 11(a). Slave agent 1 records the outcome of the relay
execution algorithm, records it and reports it to the master agent so that the latter's database is up to date. The current state of the art relays can communicate
at 30 times/s i.e. they can transmit new fault status every 33 ms. Therefore the
master agent receives a new fault status from a slave agent 1 every *delay*1 = 33
ms. In our model we declared a global variable *afault* for each slave agent and it
is updated with a delay of 33 ms. As slave agent's *afault* variable is declared as
global, master agent also has access to it. By declaring *afault* variable as global,
model is simplified as fault status value passing is avoided between the master
agent and the slave agent.

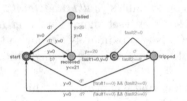

Fig. 8. Breaker1 automaton

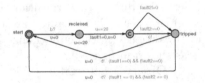

Fig. 9. Breaker2 automaton

Timed automaton of Slave agent 2 is as shown in figure 12. The behaviour of
the agent associated with Zone 3 relay is modelled by the Slave agent 2. Slave
agent 2 makes a transition from the state *start* to *received1* after receiving a fault
signal from the Zone 3 relay. Similar to the Slave agent 1 fault variable *afault*
of the Slave agent 2 is updated with a delay of *delay*1 = 33 ms. Automaton
moves from the location *received1* to the committed location *sent* with a delay
of 33 ms and sends a fault status update signal via the synchronization channel
f to master agent. Then Slave agent 2 makes a transition from the committed
location *sent* to the normal location *wait*. In the *wait* state automaton waits for
the reply from master agent to confirm if the fault sensed by the Zone 3 relay
associated with the Slave agent 2 is a true fault or a hidden failure induced fault.
When automaton is in the *wait1* state, there is a possibility of three different
transitions.

1. If either the Zone 1 or Zone 2 relay clears fault, Slave agent 2 makes a transition to the *start* state. When the master agent sends a signal to the Slave agent 2 via the synchronization channel *g* about whether the fault is a true fault or a hidden failure based fault, Slave agent 2 listens and moves from the location *wait* to the committed location *received 2*. Slave agent 2 then moves from the committed location *received2* to *start*. During the transition from the state *wait* to *received2* boolean variable *fault1* is updated by *function1()*. If the fault is a hidden failure induced fault, *function1()* resets *fault1* variable and if the fault is a true fault, *fault1* variable is set. It is aforementioned that a fault in a transmission line can be sensed by atleast six different relays. As each relay has a slave agent associated with it, atleast six slave agents report to the master agent about the fault status in a line. In *function1()* boolean variable *afault* of Slave agent 2 is compared with *afault* variables of five other slave agents. If at least half (3 out of 6) *afault* variables are set to 1, it is an indication that the transmission line is faulty and the boolean variable *fault1* is set to 1 and the breaker associated with the Zone 3 Relay can trip if both the Zone 1 and the Zone 2 relay breakers fail to trip. On the other hand if more than half (>3 out of 6) of the *afault* variables are set to zero, it is an indication that there is no fault in the line then the Boolean variable *fault1* is set to zero and it is not required for the Zone 3 relay's breaker to trip. If the sensor or the relay fails the respective slave agent's *afault* variable is not taken into consideration in the above decision making which is implemented by *function1()*.

2. If Slave agent 2 is waiting for an acknowledgement from the master agent, it is possible that a breaker associated with the Zone 1 or Zone 2 relay to trip. Therefore it is not required by the slave agent 2 to wait for the fault classification signal from master agent. In this case the transition from *wait* to *start* can occur in two different ways. If Zone 3 relay interprets that either the Zone 1 or Zone 2 relay has tripped and *fault1==0*, slave agent 2 receives a reset signal on the urgent broadcast channel *zk* and it moves from *wait* to *start* state. This is known as *Zone 3 Reset*. item The transition from *wait* to *start* state can occur via *Reset I*.

k) Master Agent: The behaviour of the master agent is modelled using two timed automatons. The master agent stores the requests in a queue as they are received and processes them based on the first in first out (FIFO) order. As

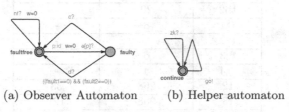

(a) Observer Automaton   (b) Helper automaton

Fig. 10. Different Automatons 1

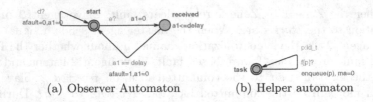

(a) Observer Automaton   (b) Helper automaton

Fig. 11. Different Automatons 2

shown in figure 11(b) the master agent receives requests from Slave agent 2 via the synchronization channel f and appends it to queue using the *enqueue()* function. The received request is processed by the master agent task execution timed automaton shown in figure 13. Whenever a request is received, length of the queue *len* is greater than zero and automaton moves from the initial location start to evaluate. There are three possible transitions from *evaluate* state:

1. While Slave agent 2 of Zone 3 relay is waiting to receive a trip/no trip signal from the master agent, breakers associated with either the Zone 1 relay or Zone 2 relay at both ends of the line may trip and reset *fault1* and *fault2* variables. In this case the master agent deletes from its queue the Zone 3 relay Slave agent 2 queries at both ends of the line and moves from the *send* to *start* state.
2. A slave agent is capable of transmitting new fault variable every 33 ms. Therefore a maximum delay of 33 ms is allowed for master agent to process a request. Also, a database query time of 100 ms is assumed in OPNET simulations [12]. A detailed justification is provided in [12] for the selection of database query and master agent service time. Hence the total master agent delay in processing a single query is 133 ms. Therefore the master agent automaton moves from *evaluate* to *send* state approximately in 133 ms.
3. The third possible transition is from *evaluate* to *start* state via the *Zone 3 Reset*.

Table 1. Timing values

Parameter	Before Scaling	After Scaling
ts1	2	-
ts2	1	-
tb1	21	-
tb2	20	-
tz1	8	-
tz2	2	-
tz3	6	-
tz4	4	-
t2	268	33
t3	968	121
delay	133	17
delay1	75	10

Automaton can move from the *send* state to *start* state via four different transitions.

1. Within *delay1* ms, master agent processes the next query in queue and sends a reset signal on the channel *g*.
2. The second possible transitions is via *Reset I*.
3. The other two possible transitions are due to *Zone 3 Reset*.

5 Verification

The description of the complete model can be downloaded from www.filebox.vt.edu /users/gshra09/agents.zip. This section explains the properties of the agent based Zone 3 relay supervision scheme that are verified. In UPPAAL Timed Computation Tree Logic (TCTL) is used to specify system properties. Sensor1t(2t,3t) and Breaker1t(2t,3t) are the sensor and the breaker associated with the Zone1t (Zone2t,Zone3t) relay protecting the line at one end whereas Sensor1f(2f,3f) and Breaker1f (2f,3f) are the sensor and the breaker associated with the Zone1f(Zone 2f,Zone3f) relay protecting the line at the other end. afault[0],afault[1],afault[2],afault[3],afault[4] and afault[5] are fault status recorded by slave agents of Zone1t, Zone1f, Zone2t, Zone2f, Zone3t and Zone3f respectively. The following properties are verified.

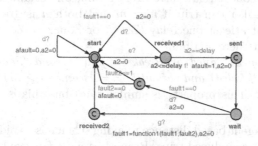

Fig. 12. Slave agent 2 automaton

Safety Property
a) *A [] no deadlock* i.e. system is deadlock free.
Bounded Liveness Property
b) *System.faulty* $\longrightarrow$ *((System.faultfree) and (System.w $\leq$ 153))* i.e. System is fault free within 153 ms. If there is a large range in timing, UPPAAL leads to state space explosion. Therefore timing values in slave agent to master agent communication, Zone 2 and Zone 3 waiting times are scaled by a factor of 8. Actually the system should be fault free within the Zone 3 fault clearing time of 1 s. A Zone 3 slave agent should receive a response from master agent within 968 ms, scaling this by 8 results in 121 ms. Remaining time of around 32 ms is

lost in communication delays between sensor and relay, relay and breaker. These values are not scaled as they are low. Not scaling these values doesn't have any effect on the scaled agent communication delays. Hence the total time available for the system to be fault free is $(121 + 32 = 153ms)$. The timing values before and after scaling are as shown in Table 1. '-' indicate that those values are not scaled.

Model Correctness Properties

c) $((Sensor1t.failed$ or $Z1t.failed$ or $Breaker1t.failed$ $)$ and $(Sensor2t.failed$ or $Z2t.failed$ or $Breaker2t.failed)$ and $(afault[4] == 1)$ and $(n < m)) \longrightarrow$ (not $(Breaker3f.tripped))$. Here 'n' is the number of slave agents with $afault = 1$ and 'm' is the number of slave agents with $afault = 0$. If Sensor1t or Zone1t relay or Breaker1t failed and Sensor2t or Zone2t or Breaker2t failed and Zone3t relay slave agent's Boolean variable $afault[4]$ is set to 1 then Zone 3 breaker cannot trip if $n < m$.

d) $((Sensor1f.failed$ or $Z1f.failed$ or $Breaker1f.failed$ $)$ and $(Sensor2f.failed$ or $Z2f.failed$ or $Breaker2t.failed)$ and $(n < m)$ and $(afault[5] == 1)) \longrightarrow$ (not $(Breaker3t.tripped))$.
This property is similar to property c) but this is verified at the other end of the line.

e) $((Sensor1t.failed$ or $Z1t.failed$ or $Breaker1t.failed$ $)$ and $(Sensor2t.failed$ or $Z2t.failed$ or $Breaker2t.failed)$ and $(afault[4] == 1)$ and $(n \geq m)) \longrightarrow$ $Breaker3t.tripped$.
If Sensor1t or Zone1t relay or Breaker t1 failed and Sensor2t or Zone2t or Breaker2t failed and Zone3t relay slave agent's Boolean variable afault[4] is set to 1 then Zone 3 breaker can trip if $n \geq m$ and both n is greater than one. $(n > 1)$ indicates that atleast one relay (Zone1 or Zone2 or Zone3) from both ends of line sense that there is a fault.

f) $((Sensor1f.failed$ or $Z1f.failed$ or $Breaker1f.failed$ $)$ and $(Sensor2f.failed$ or $Z2f.failed$ or $Breaker2f.failed)$ and $(afault[5] == 1)$ and $(n \geq m)$ and $(n > 1)$ $)$ $\longrightarrow$ $Breaker3f.tripped$. This property is similar to e) but this is verified at the other end of the line.

The main aim of the agent based distance relaying scheme is to aid Zone 3 relays to prevent hidden failure induced trips. Properties c,d,e,f prove that the model presented in this paper satisfies this criteria. Also the addition of agents should

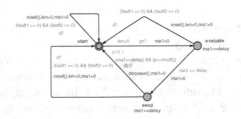

Fig. 13. Master agent task execute automaton

not disturb the actual operation of distance relaying scheme i.e. it should be deadlock free and be able to isolate faulted line within 1 s. Properties a,b verify that these two requirements are met. Therefore the above described six logical properties are sufficient to guarantee the correctness of our model.

6 Observations

In the above two sections agent based Zone 3 relay supervision scheme is formally modelled and verified for the simplest scenario of a single transmission line being protected by two Zone 3 relays. Depending on the power system network topology, it is possible that more than two Zone 3 relays may be protecting a transmission line. The following observations discusses how to handle this scenario.

1. Observation 1: The number 'N' of Zone 3 slave agent requests a master agent with an average service time of t_s can handle at any given time is upper bounded by $N \leq (1000 - t_r)/(t_s)$. Where t_r is the maximum round trip communication delay between any slave agent and master agent in the network. It is possible that a Zone 3 slave agent may not receive acknowledgement from the master agent with in its fault clearing time of 1 s. The two main reasons for this are network congestion and length of the queue at the master agent. In order to mitigate the network congestion problem, in OPNET simulations we designed the network with sufficient bandwidth [12]. Therefore the problem of network congestion can be neglected. As mentioned earlier, from OPNET simulations the average t_s is assumed to be 133 ms and t_r is 150 ms which results in $N \leq 6.4$.

It is well known that the transmission line fault occurrence is a rare event. Further the probability of a fault occurring simultaneously in more than one transmission line is very low. Therefore we restrict this analysis to a single transmission line fault. Also it is mentioned earlier that we restrict our analysis to Zone 3 relay supervision scheme. As discussed above, with $t_s = 133ms$ the maximum number of slave agent queries answered by a master agent in 1 s is 6. Table 2 shows the percentage of transmission lines in five different bus system networks protected by more than six Zone 3 relays. The percentage is around 18 for a 30 bus system and for remaining bus systems the percentage is less than 8. As the percentage of transmission lines with more than six Zone 3 relays is high, the master agent should be capable of handling more than 6 queries in a second. This can be achieved by doubling the query processing capacity of the server or arranging an extra server for query processing at the master agent. Either of these can result in the maximum number of slave agent queries answered by a master agent to be 12. It can be observed from Table 2 that the percentage of transmission lines in a given power system network protected by more than twelve Zone 3 relays is zero. Therefore for the power system networks shown in Table 2, a master agent capable of answering 12 queries per sec should be sufficient to meet the stringent timing requirements of Zone 3 relays. If the

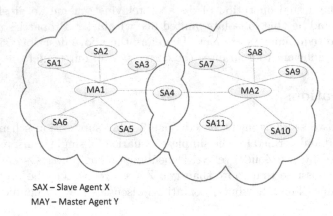

SAX – Slave Agent X
MAY – Master Agent Y

Fig. 14. Slave agent communication with multiple master agents

above discussed issues are taken into consideration, the formal models can be easily extended to a power system network of any size.

Table 2. Percentage of Zone 3 relays protecting a transmission line

Bus System	% of lines with $N > 6$	% of lines with $N > 12$
14	0	0
30	17.7	0
57	5.75	0
118	7	0.0025
127	3.25	0

2. Observation 2: It is aforementioned in section 3 that a larger bus system requires more than one master agent to answer queries from Zone 3 slave agents. Therefore a power system network is divided into sub-networks and a master agent is assigned to each sub-network to acknowledge queries from Zone 3 slave agents in that sub-network. It is possible that a network partitioned into sub-networks can be as shown in figure 14. If we can prove that both the sub-networks are disjoint, then the above described formal models and observation I can be applied to them to prove that both the sub-networks independently satisfy the properties verified in section 5. Therefore the entire power system network consisting of both these sub-networks can be assumed to satisfy the properties mentioned in section 5 . The only connection between the two sub-networks shown in figure 14 is that there exists some slave agent relays that are considered as a part of both these sub-networks. If these relays sense a fault, they can send queries to the master agents in both the sub-networks and fault classification depends upon the response from both the master agents. Thus, there exists some interconnection between both the sub-networks. The interconnection can be avoided by using

directional relays at the buses that are common to both the sub-networks. The directional relays can distinguish the fault i.e. in which sub-network the fault exists and based on that it can communicate with the corresponding master agent. Thus, the two sub-networks can be proved to be disjoint. If there are more than two sub-networks in a network, the same approach can be used to negotiate the interconnection between different sub-networks. As the sub-networks in a network are proved to be disjoint, each sub-network can satisfy the verification properties discussed in section 5 and observation I. Therefore the entire network can satisfy the properties discussed in section 5.

7   Conclusion

In this paper we used a formal verification tool called UPPAAL to formally verify and validate agent based back up relay supervision scheme for transmission line protection system. Time based abstract formal models that capture the behaviour of sensors, breakers, relays, master and slave agent are described. The informal requirements of the agent supervised transmission line protection system are formalized in 6 logical properties and are verified and validated successfully. To the best of our knowledge this is a first attempt to use formal verification in power system protection. One of the future plans include modelling the probabilistic behaviours of the relays and find the reliability with which the Zone 3 relay provides protection in the event of Zone 1 and Zone 2 failures. We plan to use PRISM model checker for this.

References

1. Phadke, A.G., Thorp, J.S.: Computer relaying for power systems, 2nd edn. Research Studies Press Ltd. and John Wiley & Sons (2009)
2. Horowitz, S.H., Phadke, A.G.: Third zone revisited. IEEE Transactions on Power Delivery 21(1), 23–29 (2006)
3. NERC. System Protection and Control Task Force. Report, Rationale for the Use of Local and Remote (Zone 3) Protective Relaying Backup Systems (February 2005), http://www.nerc.com/docs/pc/spctf/Zone3Final.pdf
4. Thorp, J.S., Phadke, A.G.: Protecting power systems in the post-restructuring era. IEEE Computer Applications in Power 12(1), 33–37 (1999)
5. Wang, H., Thorp, J.S.: Optimal locations for protection system enhancement: a simulation of cascading outages. IEEE Transactions on Power Delivery 16(4), 528–533 (2001)
6. Phadke, A.G.: Hidden failures in electric power systems. International Journal of Critical Infrastructures 1(1), 64–75 (2004)
7. Tamronglak, S.: Analysis of power system disturbances due to Relay Hidden Failures. PhD thesis, Virginia Tech, Dept of ECE, Blacksburg, VA, USA (1994)
8. Garlapati, S., Lin, H., Sambamoorthy, S., Shukla, S.K., Thorp, J.: Agent based supervision of zone 3 relays to prevent hidden failure based tripping. In: 2010 First IEEE International Conference on Smart Grid Communications, SmartGridComm, pp. 256–261 (October 2010)

9. Behrmann, G., David, R., Larsen, K.G.: A tutorial on uppaal, pp. 200–236. Springer (2004)
10. Horowitz, S.H., Phadke, A.G.: Power system relaying. Research Studies Press Ltd. (2004)
11. Garlapati, S., Shukla, S.K., Thorp, J.: An algorithm for inferring master agent rules in an agent based robust zone 3 relay architecture. In: North American Power Symposium, NAPS 2010, pp. 1–5 (September 2010)
12. Garlapati, S., Shukla, S.K.: Optimal location of master agents in an agent based zone 3 protection scheme designed for robustness against hidden failure induced trips. In: IEEE PES General Meeting (July 2012)

Parallelizing the Spin Model Checker

Gerard J. Holzmann

Laboratory for Reliable Software,
Jet Propulsion Laboratory, California Institute of Technology,
Pasadena, CA 91109, USA
gholzmann@acm.org

Abstract. We describe an extension of the Spin model checker that allows us to take advantage of the increasing number of cpu-cores available
on standard desktop systems. Our main target is to speed up the verification process for *safety* properties, the mode used most frequently, but
we also describe a small modification of the parallel search algorithm,
called the *piggyback* algorithm, that is remarkably effective in catching
violations for an interesting class of liveness properties at little cost.

Keywords: parallelism, concurrency, multi-core, model checking, Spin,
breadth-first search, safety, liveness, bounded search, software verification.

1 Introduction

We build on the infra-structure provided by the model checker Spin [5]. Although
the model checker targets the analysis of multi-threaded software applications,
until recently the tool itself performed its analyses single-threaded, using just a
single cpu. In 2005 a modification was introduced that allowed for the execution
of the depth-first search analysis on multiple cpu-cores [6]. This extension was
chosen because it can support both safety and liveness properties, yet for liveness properties the depth-first algorithm could only take advantage of parallel
execution on no more than two cpu-cores.

Parallelization of breadth-first search is often considered simpler, and could
lead to greater gains, so it is attractive to support also this option, even if it
means restricting it to the verification of safety properties alone. The parallel
version of the breadth-first search described in this paper requires virtually no
tuning or user adjustments and succeeds in providing an impressive performance
improvement in the model checking process. We also show that a simple extension of this algorithm suffices to support also the verification of an interesting
class of liveness properties without measurable overhead.

The remainder of this paper is organized as follows. In Section 2 we describe
the basic breadth-first search algorithm that is used in Spin. In Section 3 we
describe the parallelization of this algorithm, where we focus on the key issues
of load balancing, lock avoidance, and partial order reduction. In Section 4 we
discuss an extension that supports checks for liveness properties with a bounded
cycle search option.

A. Donaldson and D. Parker (Eds.): SPIN 2012, LNCS 7385, pp. 155–171, 2012.

Section 5 presents documents the performance of the new algorithm when applied to a range of verification problems. Section 6, concludes the paper and summarizes the key results.

2 Breadth-First Search

Figure 1 gives the basic sequential algorithm for performing a breadth-first in a reachability graph, as used in the Spin model checker. The algorithm uses three sets of states: S, Q[0], and Q[1]. Set S is the set of visited states, which is initially empty. Every new state that is encountered during the search is entered into this set, to avoid duplicate work when the state is revisited later. Set S is typically implemented as a hashtable.

```
1 global t = 0      // toggle bit 0..1
2 global S = {}     // statespace set
3 global Q[0] = {} // successor set
4 global Q[1] = {} // successor set
5 safety property f
6
7 add s0 to Q[0] and to S   // initial state
8
9 Search()
10   do {
11     for each s in Q[t]
12     { delete s from Q[t]
13       for each successor s' of s
14       { if s' not in S
15         { add s' to S
16           if s' violates f
17           { report safety violation
18           } else
19           { add s' to Q[1-t]
20     } } } }
21     t = 1 - t
22   } while (Q[t] is non-empty)
23 }
```

Fig. 1. Sequential breadth-first search

The breadth-first search proceeds by repeatedly generating the set of successor states (the 'next' generation) for a given set of states (the 'current' generation). These two sets are stored in successor sets Q[0] and Q[1]. As soon as all states in the 'current' generation of states have been processed, the roles of Q[0] and Q[1] switch, and what was the 'next' generation of states becomes the new 'current' generation, and the now empty former 'current' generation becomes the temporary holding place for the new 'next' generation of states. In Figure 1 this switch happens by toggling the value of t on line 21.

Every new state that is processed (i.e., each successor to one of the states from the 'current' generation of states) is first checked for its presence in S (line 14). If new, one or more safety properties can be checked for this state (line 16), and violations reported (line 17). In the absence of a violation, the state is added to the 'next' generation (line 19) for the future exploration of its successors.

The order in which the states from the current generation are processed (which is determined in Figure 1 by the selection on lines 11-12) is not important. This makes the parallelization of successor generation and processing simpler than it is in a depth-first search.

3   Parallel Breadth-First Search

One direct way to parallelize the search would be to keep the algorithm from Figure 1 as is, and to simply run it in parallel on all available cores. Clearly, access to the three shared sets S, Q[0], and Q[1], will then have to be protected with semaphores or locks, to avoid data corruption, but the main flow of the algorithm could remain unchanged. All cores then compete for states to process from the 'current' generation, and they coordinate their access to state S to lookup (line 13) and add states (line 14), and to include new states into the 'next' generation (line 18) when appropriate.

This strategy can be expected to achieve good load balancing, since all workers share a common work-queue, but it can also be expected to suffer from major delays in the wait for locks, which can significantly affect the overall performance of the algorithm, and can even make it run slower on multiple cores than it would run on a single core. The overhead of locking can be expected to get worse with every new core added to the system. This type of solution can therefore not be expected to scale.

3.1   Lock Avoidance

Our first goal is therefore to design the algorithm and its data structures in such a way that we can avoid the need for most locks, and achieve maximal decoupling between cpu cores.

To achieve lock avoidance we must be able to arrange that each core can retrieve states from a data structure that, at that point in the search, is not shared with any other core, and that it can deposit states for processing in the next round of the search into a data structure that, at that point in the search, is not shared with other cores. The key phrase here is "at that point in the search," and it can be achieved in a fairly simple manner.

The Q[0] and Q[1] data structures from Figure 1 are most naturally implemented as linked lists. Every element in the list holds the data associated with one unique state, plus a pointer to the next state in the list, or NULL if there is no next state. As noted, the ordering of states within the list is irrelevant to the correct functioning of the algorithm: there is no distinction or ordering implied between successor states that are part of the same generation of states (i.e., that are reachable in the same number of steps from the initial system state(s)).

This means that on an N-core system we can split each of the sets Q[0] and Q[1] into NxN subsets, with each subset reserved for the use of only one specific core to transmit states to one specific other core. When a successor state is generated we now have to choose which subset of the 'next' generation the new state is assigned to. Load balancing can be achieved here by simply randomly selecting this subset. Even though we must now support a quadratic number of sets (NxN on an N-core system), this does not impact the memory requirements in a significant way: the sets are merely linked lists, and we need only 2xNxN pointers instead of two. On a 32 core system this adds 2048 64-bit pointers, or 16 KB of memory: an insignificant amount compared to the Gigabytes of memory that are used to store the states of set S and the various subsets of Q for larger problem sizes. By sacrificing a relative small amount of memory we can reduce the runtime overhead with simple contention-free and lock-free data structures.

Figure 2 illustrates the main structure of the parallel version of the algorithm for N cores. The current and next generation of states are now stored in subsets of Q[0] and Q[1]. When the current generation is t, core w has uncompeted access to all subsets Q[t][w][1..N] from the current generation and subsets Q[1-t][1..N][w] from the next generation. As before, once all states have been processed, the current and next generations can be switched, but this time this switch has to be coordinated among all workers to make sure that the global breadth-first search discipline is maintained.

Note that while candidate states in subset Q[t][w][q] are being processed (lines 14-25) no further states can be added to this subset, and once the set is empty it will remain empty at least until all states in the current generation of successor states have been processed.

There are three places in the algorithm where coordination among the worker cores is required in the parallel version of the algorithm.

1. Access to the shared global state space S (lines 18 and 19) now has to be protected, to make sure that the entries cannot be corrupted by simultaneous access of different cores. To avoid a global lock, we can use a fine-grained strategy that avoids waits, using compare-and-swap instructions. We have adopted a lockless hashtable for this, as first described in [7], which has these properties.

2. The switch from one generation to the next (line 33) must be synchronized between the cores to make sure that a breadth-first search discipline is maintained and, importantly, also that exclusive access of each worker to its designated subsets of Q[0] and Q[1] is guaranteed. We explore this further in Section 3.2.

3. Finally, we need to be able to determine when all states have been explored and the cores can stop executing (line 30 and 39). This point too is explored further in Section 3.2.

```
1 global done = false
2 global t = 0
3 global S = {}                      // statespace set
4 global Q[0][1..N][1..N] = {} // successor set
5 global Q[1][1..N][1..N] = {} // successor set
6 global idle[1..N] = false      // all elements
7 safety property f
8
9 add s0 to Q[0][1][1] and to S // initial state
10
11 Search(w: 1..N)                     // N workers
12 { local ot = t
13   do {
14     for each q in 1..N
15     { for each s in Q[t][w][q]
16       { delete s from Q[t][w][q]
17         for each successor s' of s
18         { if s' not in S
19           { add s' to S
20             if s' violates f
21             { report error
22             } else
23             { w' = choose random 1..N
24               add s' to Q[1-t][w'][w]
25     } } } } }
26     idle[w] = true // one element
27     if (w == 1)
28     { wait until all idle[1..N] == true
29       { if (all Q[1-t][1..N][1..N] empty)
30         { done = true
31         } else
32         { idle[1..N] = false // all elements
33           t = 1 - t
34       } }
35     } else
36     { wait until t != ot or done
37       ot = t
38     }
39   } while !done
40 }
```

Fig. 2. Parallel breadth-first search for N cores

3.2 Synchronization and Termination

We designate one core to be the master of ceremony for each parallel verification run. It decides when all cores can advance from one generation of states to the next, and when the verification process can be terminated because all states have been processed. The core in charge is the same core that starts up all other worker processes (processes, not threads) at the start of the verification run.

The 'master' core (which is the core with (w==1)) checks if either type of synchronization is required when it has completed processing all states that were assigned to it in the last round, i.e., when it reaches line 26 in Figure 2.

The master core can reliably tell that all states from the current generation have been processed if all cores have set their idle flag to true (line 28).

When this condition is met, no further work can be performed by any of the corés and it is safe to switch the value of t (line 33) to make all states stored in the 'next' generation available as the new 'current' generation.

Before changing the value of the toggle variable t though, the master core checks if the search can be terminated. If the 'next' generation of states is empty at this point, then clearly there are no further states to be processed by any of the cores, and the search can be concluded. This termination check occurs on line 29.

All cores other than the master that conclude their processing of the current generation of states simply wait for either t to change or the global variable done to become *true* (line 36). Only the master core has write-access to global variables t and done, so race conditions on these variables cannot occur. Similarly, there can be no conflict on access to the global variable array idle, because simultaneous access by multiple cores is not possible.

3.3 Partial Order Reduction

Significant savings in the number of states that must be processed to perform an exhaustive search can be obtained with partial order reduction strategies. These methods were added to Spin in 1994 for the depth-first search [4], and later extended to cover also breadth-first search [3].

For the parallel version of the breadth-first search, the algorithm from [3] remains valid, the only difference being that states in the 'new' generation of states can now be found in multiple queues instead of a single one. A minor modification of the state storage method suffices: we only need to store one additional bit of information that indicates whether or not the state is currently *open* (i.e., is present in one of the 'next' queues) or *closed* (present only in hash-table S). The processing is minimal. Also here, we sacrifice a small amount of memory to store the additional information in return for potentially large savings in runtime.

4   An Extension for Liveness

Correctness properties are commonly divided into two broad categories: safety and liveness. As first shown in [1], properties of both categories can be combined to formulate virtually any type of correctness requirement.

In Manna and Pnueli's paper [9] it was argued that only three basic types of requirements could *"cover the majority of properties one would ever wish to verify."* In linear temporal logic, these three types of requirements from [9] correspond to the following types of formula:

1. []p (invariance),
2. [](p -> Xq) (response), and
3. [](p -> (q U r)) (precedence).

The first two properties can be classified as safety properties, and the last property as a liveness property.

Curiously, today we would normally formalize the response property differently from what was proposed in [9], namely as: [](p -> <> q). When formalized in this way, though, the response property becomes a liveness rather than a safety property. The difference is important because safety properties are simpler and less costly to verify than liveness properties. In Spin the difference can be quantified more precisely still: the verification of a liveness property with the nested depth-first search algorithm can increase the runtime by up to a factor of two [5].

No algorithm of comparable efficiency is known for the verification of liveness properties with a breadth-first search. Most attempts that have been explored to date carry a cost that can increase the cost up to quadratic (exploring up to N^2 reachable states instead of up to $2N$), which puts it beyond reach for larger problem sizes.

A linear time algorithm that can verify even a small sub-set of the liveness properties with a breadth-first search discipline can therefore be attractive. We will describe a small extension of the parallel breadth-first search algorithm that can do so. The subset that is covered is restricted, but the computational overhead required is so small that it can make a useful addition to a model checker's search capabilities.

In defining this method we take our clues from Manna and Pnueli's paper [9], where a small change of the formalization of the response property turns it from a liveness into a safety property. The resulting sub-class of liveness is known as *bounded liveness.*

We could modify the search to check for the satisfaction of a bounded liveness property with bound n, i.e., within n steps, but this also risks increasing the cost of verification by up to n. Instead we can also bound the search for ω-acceptance cycles to cycles of maximal length n. In this case we can make the extension without increasing the size of the search space significantly. Successor states of an ω-accepting state are tagged with the 'seed' (accepting) state and a counter that is initialized to n. With every new successor generation along this path the counter is decremented until either the seed state is revisited or the counter reaches zero, at which point the search stops. The counter itself is not stored in the state space, thus avoiding the n-fold increase. This choice comes down to a trade-off between precision and efficiency; we'll return to this shortly.

The extended algorithm, called the *piggyback* algorithm, is shown in Figure 3 as an extension of the sequential breadth-first search from Figure 1. The extension of the parallel version of the algorithm from Figure 2 is similar.

The lines with key changes from the algorithm shown in Figure 1 are marked with a asterix in the left margin.

Instead of storing single states in sets S, Q[0], and Q[1], we now store triples consisting of two states and a count (e.g., lines 20 and 32). The first element of each triple is the original successor state s' that was generated. The second element is a count, which measures the maximum length of the acceptance cycle that is checked to satisy a liveness property. The third element of the triple is the target accepting state that forms the 'seed' for the acceptance cycle search. The full value of this triple is stored in the queues Q[0] and Q[1] (line 32), so that it can propagate from one level in the search to the next (lines 12-13), but we abstract the value of the counter to one bit when the triple is stored in state space S, to indicate only if the counter is running or not running (line 20). Only this boolean result is now of relevance in the state matching (line 19).

The critical check is started at every accepting state that is reached (line 15) to see if that state can be revisited within BOUND steps (line 16). The counter, however, is only started if no cycle search is already in progress (line 21). We will return to the potential implications of this choice below.

Once the counter is set, it is decremented with each new generation of successor states generated (line 26). The counter is reset to zero when a match of the target accepting state is found (line 24), or it is left at zero when the count returns to its default value of zero.

It is not hard to see that the *piggyback* algorithm *can* indeed find violations of liveness properties, but it will also be clear that it will not be able to *guarantee* finding all such violations. In the version of the algorithm presented here, it could well be that a search for an accepting state that is not part of a cycle is in progress and prevents a new search for a different accepting state from starting (line 15), even if that second accepting state could turn out to be part of a cycle. We thus trade simplicity and low complexity for the potential of search incompleteness. The maximal increase in cost can be a factor of two, as in the nested-depth first search. Note that states could be visited up to twice if they are reachable within n steps both from an accepting state and from a non-accepting state.

Whether or not the *piggyback* algorithm succeeds can also subtly depend on the order in which states are explored, i.e., one cpu-core could generate intermediate states that are part of a cycle before the core exploring the cycle can reach those states and proceed towards the target seed state.

In all measurements we have done, the actual overhead of the algorithm tends to be near zero. We have also not yet encountered an example where a possible

```
 1 global t = 0       // toggle bit 0..1
 2 global S = {}      // statespace set
 3 global Q[0] = {} // successor set
 4 global Q[1] = {} // successor set
 5 safety property f
 6
 7 add (s₁,0,0) to Q[0] and to S // initial state
 8
 9 Search()
10 {
11   do {
12     for each (s,b,z) in Q[t]
13     { delete (s,b,z) from Q[t]
14       for each successor s' of s
15*      { if s' accepting ∧ b == 0
16*        { b = BOUND
17*          z = s'
18*        }
19          if (s',(b>0),0) not in S
20          { add (s',(b>0),z) to S
21*            if b > 0
22*            { if s' == z ∧ b < BOUND
23*              { report liveness violation
24*                b = 0
25*              } else
26*              { b = b-1
27*                if b == 0 { z = 0 }
28*              } }
29            if s' violates f
30            { report safety violation
31            } else
32            { add (s',b,z) to Q[1-t]
33     } } }
34   }
35   t = 1 - t
36 } while (Q[t] is non-empty)
37 }
```

Fig. 3. *Piggyback* Algorithm for Limited Liveness Detection

liveness violation was not reported by the *piggyback* algorithm, although knowing the specifics of the algorithm it would not be too difficult to construct such a case.

As noted, the choice made here is between a complete solution with an unacceptably high overhead (e.g., the potential for a quadratic increase in the size of the statespace), which is of very limited practical value, and a bolder algorithm that is well-behaved for all problem sizes, but that cannot guarantee success in all cases. The *piggyback* algorithm is in this sense comparable in its tradeoff to the bitstate hashing algorithm, introduced in 1987 (cf. [5]), which has proven to be of significant value in large model-checking applications despite its potential incompleteness.

We provide performance data for the *piggyback* algorithm in Section 5.4.

5   Measurements

5.1   Beem Models

We first perform a comparison with the performance of the two leading competing tools in distributed model checking: the Divine model checker [2] and the Ltsmin tool [7],[8]. We have used the latest available version of each tool: Divine version 2.5.2 and Ltsmin version 1.7.1, in our comparison with Spin version 6.2.0. Each tool was compiled and installed on the same Ubuntu 11.10 system, with 32-cores (using two AMD 16-core chips) and 64 GBytes of main memory, to make sure that the performance results are directly comparable. Generally in our tests we avoid using all available cores for a verification run, to avoid boundary effects that may be introduced by the operating system performing unrelated tasks on the system. We leave at least one cpu-core free for such tasks, reducing the maximum number of cores used in these tests to 31.

Naturally, there are many differences between the three tools, with each supporting a different specification language. Spin's specification language is the most general, which requires implementation choices that can affect overall performance. We measure the basic performance of each tool on models that lie within the intersection of the input languages of the three tools, and that have closely comparable complexity (measured as the number of reachable states that must be searched to complete a exhaustive verification).

We focus here on three models taken from the BEEM database [10], that were selected in [7] (Fig. 2), to compare the performance of Divine, Ltsmin, and the earlier multi-core version of Spin version 5.2.4 using parallel depth-first search [6]. The measurements from [7] showed a decisive advantage for Ltsmin.

The three models that were selected for comparison in [7] were

1. anderson.6: a queue lock mutual exclusion algorithm with 6 processes,
2. at.5: a timing-based mutual exclusion algorithm with 5 processes, and
3. bakery.7: a model for Lamport's bakery algorithm with 7 processes.

Table 1. Anderson.6 – RunTimes in seconds

#Cores	1	2	4	8	16	31
Divine	88.10	56.88	38.49	23.31	14.01	20.14
LTSmin Unix time	51.82	33.06	21.24	14.73	12.80	11.88
LTSmin self-reported	44.23	25.14	13.21	6.74	4.72	3.95
Spin Unix time	42.55	27.74	16.01	10.61	7.31	6.69
Spin self-reported	42.20	27.30	15.70	10.20	6.06	4.63
Linear	42.20	21.10	10.55	5.28	2.64	1.36

Table 2. At.5 – RunTimes in seconds

#Cores	1	2	4	8	16	31
Divine	146.20	91.83	57.79	33.47	21.12	19.38
LTSmin Unix time	58.09	35.34	21.00	14.72	11.81	10.28
LTSmin self-reported	52.02	28.77	14.57	8.29	5.16	3.76
Spin Unix time	74.55	50.97	28.29	18.81	13.38	11.38
Spin self-reported	74.10	50.40	27.90	18.10	11.80	8.42
Linear	74.10	37.05	18.53	9.26	4.63	2.39

Table 1 reports the time taken by Divine, Ltsmin, and Spin to complete the safety verification of the anderson.6 protocol as measured by the standard Unix 'time' tool.

Both Ltsmin and Spin (but not Divine) also report the time taken by each tool for the search itself, leaving out unrelated tasks, e.g., to clean up and release shared memory. If we use these self-reported times, the results look slightly different, as also shown in Table 1. Curiously, for Unix wall-clock times Spin can be seen to perform the best, but for the self-reported times Ltsmin comes out first.

Table 2 shows the results for the at.5 protocol, and Table 3 similarly for the bakery.7 model. The results for the bakery.7 protocol are similar to those for the anderson.6 model, with the best performance differing for wall-clock and self-reported runtimes. For the at.5 protocol Ltsmin has an edge for the Unix wall-clock times, and a larger advantage for the self-reported times.

Both the Ltsmin and the Spin tool scale reasonably well with increasing numbers of cores, though not perfectly. The Divine tool shows good scaling behavior as well, though the runtimes are longer, with a single anomaly for the anderson.6 protocol on 31 cpu cores.

5.2   Additional Spin Models

We measured the performance of the parallel breadth-first search algorithm on five additional verification models from the standard Spin distribution, and on four larger verification models that were also used in previous studies. The models from the Spin distribution are:

Table 3. Bakery.7 – RunTimes in seconds

#Cores	1	2	4	8	16	31
Divine	42.59	34.48	31.84	25.97	31.59	24.84
LTSmin Unix time	56.64	33.77	22.48	15.82	13.60	12.46
LTSmin self-reported	48.60	26.09	14.06	7.51	5.13	4.20
Spin Unix time	43.73	31.71	19.20	11.89	8.94	9.28
Spin self-reported	43.20	30.90	18.70	11.10	7.12	5.94
Linear	43.20	21.60	10.80	5.40	2.70	1.39

1. a leader election protocol with 8 processes,
2. Peterson's algorithm with with 4 processes,
3. a sliding window protocol with window size 5,
4. a dining philosophers model with 9 processes,
5. a model of a telephone switch (tpc).

Each of these models were also used for measurements reported in our earlier work, e.g., [6].

In each data set recorded, we compare the performance with the one that would be achieved with the theoretically optimum scaling performance: linear scaling, indicated by a dashed curve. The results are summarized in Figure 4 by showing the relative speedup-ratios that are achieved in each of these tests.

The measurements for these applications are fairly consistent. They show good, though not perfect, scaling behavior.

All applications show a drop in performance near the maximum number of cpu cores. Earlier (cf. [6]) we noticed the same phenomenon on a smaller system with just 8 cores, and a similar effect can be seen when measurements are performed on a 12 core system. We observed the same general effect for the examples we verified with the Ltsmin and Divine tools so we suspect a more general trend that is independent of the specific verification method used. In all cases though, the best performance, i.e., the shortest overall runtime, is realized when the largest number of cores is used.

Background Load. To study the tapering off of performance near the maximum number of cores in more detail we performed some additional tests. For this test we used the at.5 model also used in the measurements from Section 5.1. We earlier measured the reduction in runtimes when between 1 and 31 cores are used to perform the parallel breadth-first search. In the new experiment we again run between 1 and 31 cores, but we arrange it such that only *one* of the cores will perform *all* state explorations, by assigning all successor states in each successive generation of states back to itself.

We should expect to see a flat performance curve, since the same work is done by the same cpu-core in each run, with all other cpu-cores (from 1 to 30) merely waiting for states to process that never arrive. We see a different effect of this

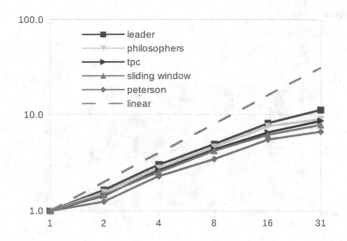

Fig. 4. Speedup ratios for the five additional Spin models

background load though, that may be caused by interference on shared memory usage e.g., for polling the shared queues for states.

The experiment shows a notable increase in the time to process states from 71.9 seconds with one process running to 101 seconds with 31 processes running. Most of the increase occurs when more than 8 cpu-cores are used, as shown in Figure 5. This background effect influences how well our search method can scale under ideal conditions, and it could mean that the speedup ratios shown in Figure 4 are near the maximum that can be obtained on the hardware used.

5.3   Larger Models

The four large verification models represent additional applications where a parallel search technique can prove most valuable in practice. They are:

1. a verification model of the DEOS operating system developed at Honeywell Laboratories,
2. a large call processing application (CP),
3. a model of and ad hoc network structure developed by a Spin user (Gurdag),
4. a model of an autonomous planning subsystem that was used on NASA's EO1 spacecraft.

Each of these larger models was also used in the measurements in [6].

The results for the larger models is summarized in Figure 6. To make it easier to interpret the scaling behavior for these models with very different runtime requirements, we captured the number of reachable states that is processed per second, normalized to the same base for all models, as was also done in [6], to obtain the speedup ratios.

Also here we see performance drop as we near the system capacity of 32 cores, and very good scaling up to eight cores (cf. Figure 4 and Figure 5). In the two

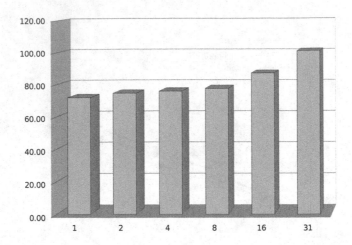

Fig. 5. Runtime Decay when other processes are present and idling

best cases (for the DEOS and CP verification model) the improvement measured was a speedup of 9-fold on 31 cores. In the worst case (for the EO1 model) only a 6-fold speedup was measured.

For comparison, in our earlier work on the parallelization of the *depth-first* search algorithm of safety properties, we measured a speedup of 7.8x for the EO1 model on an 8-core system [6], outperforming the parallel breadth-first search from this paper.

For the DEOS model though, the parallel *depth-first* search achieved a speedup of no more than 1.6-fold on 8 cores, where the parallel breadth-first method from this paper achieves a 6-fold speedup on 8 cores.

5.4   Liveness

To study the capabilities of the piggyback liveness detection algorithm we consider two examples from the BEEM database of models that were also studied in [2] (Table 1). The only model studied in [2] that contains an acceptance cycle is the anderson.6 model. We earlier reported measurements for this model in Table 1.

The LTL property for this model, in Spin syntax, is `[] (<>(P[2]@CS))`, which states that process P[2] (arbitrarily chosen) can always eventually enter its critical section.

An exhaustive exploration of this model visits about 49 Million reachable system states (which is about three times the number of states reached without applying the LTL property), and takes 151 seconds of cpu-time. An exhaustive run of the nested-depth first search algorithm (executed on one single cpu, and without stopping at the first cycle detected) explores the same state space, but each state can now be visited up to twice, which increases the runtime to 222 seconds. An acceptance cycle can of course be detected early or late in the search.

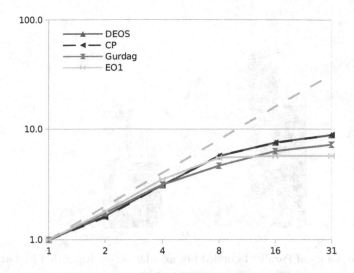

Fig. 6. Measured speedup ratios for four large verification models – using normalized performance captured as the total number of reachable states processed per second

In this case, the nested depth-first search algorithm detects a first accept-cycle after having explored just 142,027 states in 0.31 seconds.

The parallel breadth-first search algorithm, when applied to the same model and LTL property also explores about 49 Million states. On 31 cpu-cores it takes 44.5 seconds to do so, with the scaling behavior on fewer cores again matching that for pure safety properties, cf. Table 1.

If we add the piggyback liveness detection method, the number of reachable states that is explored in the parallel search does not change, and neither does the runtime. For an exhaustive run that is not stopped at the first counter-example the time measured 43.8 seconds, which is close to the earlier measurement without liveness detection enabled.

The *piggyback* algorithm discovers a first acceptance cycle relatively late in the search in this case, after having explored nearly all 49 Million states. But as can be expected, the cycle that is uncovered in the parallel search is shorter than the one found in the depth-first search: 28 steps instead of 58 steps in this case, and therefore potentially of greater interest. The most interesting aspect of this search is that it does not measurably increase the runtime. We see this effect repeated also in cases where there is no acceptance cycle to be found: the case where the nested depth-first search algorithm can incur up to a doubling of its runtime.

The second example model from [2], with no acceptance cycles, is the elevator2.3 model. The LTL property given in the BEEM database states that after the elevator has been called at level 0, the elevator passes that level at most once without serving it. The property is satisfied for the model provided, so no counter-example acceptance cycles exist.

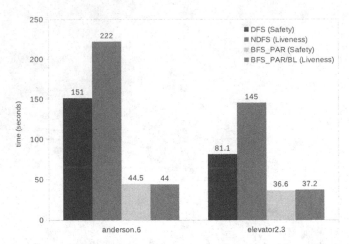

Fig. 7. Performance of Parallel Bounded Liveness Detection Algorithm for larger models with (left) and without (right) acceptance cycles

An exhaustive exploration of the model with a standard depth-first search visits a total of approximately 27 Million states in 81.1 seconds, on a single cpu. If instead we use the nested depth-first search algorithm, the same number of states is explored, but some are visited twice. As a result, the runtime for the depth-first search increases to 145 seconds.

With the parallel breadth-first search algorithm the number of states explored in an exhaustive search remains approximately 27 Million states. On 31 cpu-cores the runtime required to complete this search is 36.6 seconds, and again the scaling behavior on fewer cores is similar to that reported before. With the *piggyback* algorithm added, the number of explored states and the runtime remain unchanged. We measured 37.2 seconds for this search. The results are illustrated in Figure 7.

6   Conclusion

We have described the design and implementation of a new parallel breadth-first search option for the Spin model checker. The original motivation for this algorithm was that most properties of interest that model checkers are used for are safety properties. These types of properties, including those specified in linear temporal logic, can readily be verified with a breadth-first search algorithm. The breadth-first search option has the additional advantage of locating the shortest possible counter-examples.

We also described a relatively simple extension of the breadth-first search that can allow us to intercept not only safety properties but also an interesting class of liveness properties, Fig. 3. The algorithm, which is based on a bounded *search* for cycles, can catch any liveness violation (not just violations of bounded liveness properties), provided that there exists a cycle shorter than the bound given. The extension carries no significant computational overhead, but cannot guarantee completeness. In the tests we performed the algorithm succeeded in locating non-trivial counter-examples in a broad range of applications, which can make it of some practical interest.

We have shown that the performance of the new parallel breadth-first search algorithm scales reasonably well with increasing numbers of cpu-cores, cf. Figs. 4 and 6, and is comparable to, and in some cases better than, that of other leading tools, e.g. [2] and [7].

We have also identified a factor that limits the benefit that can be obtained from multi-core algorithms, cf. Figure 5. The effect is especially pronounced for larger numbers of cpu-cores.

Acknowledgements. The research described in this paper was carried out at the Jet Propulsion Laboratory, California Institute of Technology, under a contract with the National Aeronautics and Space Administration. The work was supported in part by the NSF Expeditions Project on Computational Modeling and Analysis of Complex Systems (CMACS).

References

1. Alpern, B., Schneider, F.B.: Defining Liveness. Information Processing Letters 21, 181–185 (1985)
2. Barnat, J., Brim, L., Rockai, P.: Scalable shared memory LTL model checking. Int. Journal on Software Tools for Technology Transfer (STTT); special section with papers from the Spin 2007 Workshop 12(2), 139–153 (2010)
3. Bošnački, D., Holzmann, G.J.: Improving Spin's Partial-Order Reduction for Breadth-First Search. In: Godefroid, P. (ed.) SPIN 2005. LNCS, vol. 3639, pp. 91–105. Springer, Heidelberg (2005)
4. Holzmann, G.J., Peled, D.: An Improvement in Formal Verification. In: Proc. Formal Description Techniques, FORTE 1994, pp. 197–211. Chapman Hall, Berne (1994)
5. Holzmann, G.J.: The Spin Model Checker: primer and reference manual. Addison-Wesley (2004)
6. Holzmann, G.J., Bosnacki, D.: The design of a multi-core extension to the Spin model checker. IEEE Trans. on Softw. Eng. 33(10), 659–674 (2007)
7. Laarman, A.W., van de Pol, J.C., Weber, M.: Boosting multi-core reachability performance with shared hash-tables. In: Proc. 10th Int. Conf. on Formal Methods in Computer Aided Design, Publ. IEEE Computer Society, Lugano (2010)
8. Laarman, A., van de Pol, J., Weber, M.: Parallel Recursive State Compression for Free. In: Groce, A., Musuvathi, M. (eds.) SPIN Workshops 2011. LNCS, vol. 6823, pp. 38–56. Springer, Heidelberg (2011)
9. Manna, Z., Pnueli, A.: Tools and rules for the practicing verifier, Stanford University. Technical Report STAN-CS-90-1321, 35 pgs (July 1990)
10. Pelánek, R.: BEEM: Benchmarks for Explicit Model Checkers. In: Bošnački, D., Edelkamp, S. (eds.) SPIN 2007. LNCS, vol. 4595, pp. 263–267. Springer, Heidelberg (2007)

Parallel Model Checking Using Abstraction

Ethan Burns[1] and Rong Zhou[2]

[1] Department of Computer Science
University of New Hampshire, Durham, NH 03820 USA
eaburns@cs.unh.edu
[2] High Performance Analytics Area
Palo Alto Research Center, Palo Alto, CA 94304 USA
rzhou@parc.com

Abstract. Many model checking techniques are based on enumerative graph search, a procedure that is known to be prohibitively time and memory consuming. Modern multi-core processors rely on parallelism instead of raw clock speed to provide increased performance, so it is necessary to leverage this parallelism to achieve better performance in model checking. In this work, we compare hash-distributed search, a well-known parallel search technique for model checking, with an algorithm from the automated planning and heuristic search community called Parallel Structured Duplicate Detection (PSDD). We show that PSDD has two major advantages over hash-distributed search for multi-core model checking. First, PSDD is able to perform full partial-order reduction where hash-distributed search must be conservative and subsequently miss reduction opportunities in many cases, causing it to search a much larger space. Second, PSDD performs duplicate detection on states immediately, avoiding the need to store duplicate states for inter-thread communication. We have implemented and compared both techniques in the Spin model checker; our results show that PSDD uses significantly less memory than hash-distributed search, can be faster and give better parallel speedup than both hash-distributed search and Spin's built-in parallel depth-first search. Finally, we show how PSDD can use external memory, such as disk storage, to greatly reduce its internal memory requirements.

Introduction

Model checking is a fundamental tool used in the creation and verification of asynchronous and distributed systems. Since the actions performed by each component of such a system may be interleaved in many ways, there can be a large number of configurations of the system as a whole. Given an abstract model of a system, a model checker can enumerate all reachable configurations of the model in order to aid in verification of its correctness. During enumeration, the model checker can ensure that the model does not exhibit any invalid behaviors or reach any invalid states. If such an error is found then a trace of the actions leading to it can be reported back to the user. This trace information is invaluable when creating and debugging a new system. Additionally, if the model checker is unable to find any invalid behaviors then it is evidence that the system is in fact correct.

A. Donaldson and D. Parker (Eds.): SPIN 2012, LNCS 7385, pp. 172–190, 2012.

To enumerate all possible states of an asynchronous system, many popular model checkers treat the configuration space as an implicitly defined graph where nodes correspond to system states and edges are the possible transitions of each component. A path through this graph gives one possible interleaving of the actions that the system may perform. Once the graph is defined, an exhaustive search algorithm can then explore all reachable states of the system looking for ones that violate certain properties. As is typical with implicit graphs, however, there can be a very large number of nodes causing the search to take a prohibitive amount of time or memory.

The model checking community, the heuristic search and automated planning communities have all been quite successful in developing new search frameworks that take advantage of modern multi-core processors. These frameworks have enabled them to improve the performance of their algorithms and have also been shown to be successful at offloading a significant portion of the memory requirement of a large graph search to external storage devices such as hard disks. However, some of the most successful techniques used by the heuristic search and planning communities have yet to be tested for model checking. Because of their success on other types of search problems, we would like to compare these approaches to those commonly used to parallelize search in model checking.

We have implemented two techniques for parallelizing breadth-first search in the Spin model checker [7]. The first technique is based on a common approach for parallel model checking that distributes states among different searching threads by using a hash function [18,12]. We call our implementation of this algorithm hash-distributed breadth-first search (HD-BFS). The second method comes from the heuristic search and planning communities called parallel structured duplicate detection (PSDD) [20]. We show that PSDD has some major advantages over hash-distributed search for model checking. First, HD-BFS uses delayed duplicate detection [16,13] and must store duplicate search nodes temporarily while they are being communicated between threads. PSDD is able to detect duplicate states immediately after they are generated thus abolishing the need to use extra memory in order to store them. Second, PSDD is able to preserve Spin's ability to perform partial-order reduction – a technique used by model checkers to decrease the size of the search space. This means that, when using multiple threads, PSDD is often able to search a significantly smaller space than both HD-BFS and Spin's built-in multi-core depth-first search, both of which must be more conservative when performing partial-order reduction. Overall, the results of our experiments demonstrate that PSDD is faster and able to achieve greater parallel speedup than both HD-BFS and Spin's state-of-the-art multi-core depth-first search.

In addition to improving the performance of breadth-first search, we show some preliminary results demonstrating that PSDD can also successfully reduce the memory requirements of model checking by making use of external storage devices. In one experiment PSDD is able to reduce the memory requirement of the search by over 500% when using a hard disk to supplement internal memory.

Depth-First versus Breadth-First Search

Two of the most well-known graph search algorithms are depth-first search and breadth-first search. Depth-first search generates the successors of nodes in the graph (we call the generation of successors of a node 'expanding the node') in deepest-first order. This means that one of the most recently generated nodes will be the next node that is expanded. Breadth-first search, on the other hand, expands nodes in shallowest-first order. Spin uses depth-first search by default as it is able to check both safety properties (typically used to verify that something undesirable will not happen) and liveness properties (typically used to verify that something desirable will eventually happen) whereas Spin's breadth-first search algorithm is only able to verify safety properties.

Breadth-first search for model checking is guaranteed to find shortest counterexamples if the model violates a safety property. This is significant because, many important properties of an asynchronous system are safety properties and when debugging a system one must understand the counterexample provided by the model checker in order to determine why the system is not behaving as desired. Depth-first search pays no heed to the number of steps used to reach a node in the state space and therefore may produce a counterexample that is many steps longer than necessary. These long traces can be extremely hard to interpret as they may contain a lot of transitions that are not necessary to produce the faulty behavior. To put this in perspective, on one model we have observed that depth-first search finds a deadlock and provides a trace consisting of 9,992 steps where breadth-first search finds a trace for the deadlock with the smallest number of possible steps: 42.

While breadth-first search cannot be used directly to verify liveness properties, there has been work on efficient translations of liveness checking problems into safety checking problems, which can subsequently be verified by breadth-first reachability analysis [1,17]. Given depth-first search's inherently sequential nature [15], checking liveness property using a breadth-first, instead of depth-first, strategy can better leverage the latest multi-core processors for greater parallel speedups.

Hash-Distributed Breadth-First Search

Burns et al. [3] discuss the difficulties in parallelizing best-first search algorithms such as breadth-first search[1] and they show that many naïve implementations of parallel search actually perform worse than their serial counterparts.

In order to successfully search a graph in parallel the graph should be divided in a way that each thread performing the search can operate on an independent portion of the graph. A simple way to achieve this is to divide the nodes of the graph statically using a hash function; as each new node is generated, its hash value is computed and it is distributed to the thread with the thread ID equal to the hash value modulo the number of threads. If a node is generated multiple times, each duplicate will be assigned to the same thread so duplicate detection can be performed locally within each thread. This framework is called hash-distributed search and was originally proposed as a method for parallelizing the A* algorithm [6] and was later discovered by Stern and Dill [18] in the context of model checking and then by Kishimoto et al. [12] who called the algorithm hash-distributed A* (HDA*) and applied it to automated planning problems.

We have implemented a hash-distributed breadth-first algorithm, based on HDA*. We call this algorithm hash-distributed breadth-first search (HD-BFS). HD-BFS works

---

[1] Breadth-first search can be viewed as a special best-first search where all edges have unit cost.

in layers by expanding the nodes at a given depth from the root in parallel until all nodes at the current depth have been expanded. When a depth layer has been completely expanded, all threads proceed synchronously to the next depth and begin searching there.

Each HD-BFS thread uses a pair of queues to represent the search frontier. One queue, called the *current queue*, contains all nodes assigned to the thread that are at the current search depth. The second queue, called the *next queue*, contains all nodes assigned to the current thread that are at the next search depth. Each thread also has a hash table containing all nodes that it has previously expanded. This table is used to prevent the search from expanding the same nodes multiple times. Note that, because all duplicates of a search node will be assigned to the same thread by the hash function, no node resides in more than a single hash table.

When searching, each thread expands the nodes from its current queue one-at-a-time. When a successor node is assigned by the hash function to a different thread than the one that generated it, it must be sent there using inter-thread communication. Otherwise, when a successor node is assigned back to the same thread that generated it, it is immediately checked for membership in the local hash table to determine if it is a duplicate and if it is not a duplicate then it is added to the next queue for the local thread; no communication is required. Our implementation of HD-BFS uses the communication scheme from Burns *et al.* [3] to send nodes between threads asynchronously using shared-memory queues.

After receiving a new node sent from a different thread, the receiving thread checks to see if the node is a duplicate by testing it for membership in its local hash table. If the node is not a duplicate then it is placed on the thread's next queue. This is the appropriate queue because all threads are expanding nodes at the same depth from the root and therefore any generated node resides at the next depth regardless of which thread generated it.

If all threads have empty current queues and no nodes are in transit between threads, then the current depth layer has been completely expanded. When this happens, all threads synchronously swap their next queue with their current queue and begin searching nodes at the next depth. If all current queues are still empty after swapping to the next depth then the search space has been exhausted and the algorithm terminates.

Disadvantages

We have found that there are two major disadvantages to hash-distributed search when applied to model checking. The first is that hash-distributed search delays the detection of duplicate nodes when they are communicated between threads. When nodes are sent to another thread they are placed on the receiving queue for that thread and sit there until they are eventually received and checked against the receiving thread's hash table. This delayed detection of duplicate nodes can cause the search to require more memory as the duplicates reside in the receiving queue instead of immediately having their memory freed for reuse. As we will see, the extra memory overhead created by delaying duplicate detection can be quite substantial.

The second disadvantage of hash-distributed search is that it must be conservative when applying partial-order reduction [9], a technique used in model checking to reduce the size of the search graph. When expanding a node while using partial-order reduction, only a subset of the successors are considered and the rest are discarded. While performing breadth-first search with partial-order reduction, Spin uses a test called the Q *proviso* [2] to prevent reduction in cases where completeness cannot be ensured.

The Q proviso tests if a newly generated node is placed on the breadth-first search queue or if it was already on the queue from a previous generation. If the Q proviso is satisfied then the reduction can take place, otherwise the full expansion must happen. Bošnački *et al.* [2] proved that this simple test allows breadth-first search to remain complete under partial-order reduction when searching for safety property violations and deadlocks.

With hash-distributed search, the successors of a node may not be assigned to the expanding thread. When this happens, the expanding thread does not have the ability to test if the successors are on or end up on the queue because this queue is owned by a different thread. To preserve completeness, HD-BFS must be conservative and assume that all nodes that are sent to different threads do *not* pass the Q proviso. This reduces the chances of successfully performing partial-order reduction because, in order to reduce, a thread must generate a successor that is assigned to itself and also passes the Q proviso. As we will show in our experimental results, with a greater number of threads the chance that successors will not be assigned to the expanding thread increases, so as the number of threads increases the size of the search space will increase too. Because of this, HD-BFS using multiple threads can actually perform worse than a serial breadth-first search because the former must search a significantly larger space to guarantee completeness.

Abstraction-Based Hashing

Both of the previous issues with hash-distributed search stem from the fact that the hash function used to assign nodes to threads is designed to uniformly distribute the nodes. This is beneficial from a load balancing perspective, however, it means that it is uncommon for the successors of a node to be assigned to the thread that generated them. Burns *et al.* [3] present a novel modification to hash-distributed search that can be used to help alleviate this issue at the cost of possibly decreasing load balancing. Instead of using a hash function that distributes the nodes uniformly, a homomorphic abstraction function can be used to distribute the nodes in a more structured fashion. Each thread is responsible for a set of nodes in an abstract representation of the search graph. When a node is generated, its abstract representation is computed and it is assigned to the thread responsible for this abstract node.

The advantage of this approach, when using a carefully created abstraction, is that the successors of a search node will tend to be assigned back to the same thread that generated them. This means that the need for communication is reduced as newly generated nodes can often be handled locally. The disadvantage is that the search load may not be evenly balanced among the threads. Burns *et al.* show that, in practice, using an abstraction instead of a uniformly distributed hash function can greatly increase the performance of HDA* on puzzle solving and planning problems.

For model checking, fewer communications mean fewer duplicate nodes that reside in memory. It also means that there are more chances to perform partial-order reduction. As we will see, this approach can greatly reduce the memory requirements and the size of the search space explored by hash-distributed search. Unfortunately, because the nodes are no longer distributed uniformly among the threads, this abstraction-based implementation of HD-BFS (which we call AHD-BFS) gives very brittle performance for different numbers of threads. We suspect that the nodes tend to be distributed unevenly causing some threads to be very busy and some threads to starve for work. This behavior hinders the ability of the search to fully exploit the available parallelism.

Parallel Structured Duplicate Detection

Instead of assigning nodes to threads *a priori* by using a hash function, Zhou *et al.* [20] developed a framework called *Parallel Structured Duplicate Detection* (PSDD) that allows threads to dynamically divide the search effort. PSDD uses a homomorphic abstraction to map nodes in the search graph to nodes in an abstract representation of the search graph. The abstraction is a many-to-one mapping that is typically created by projecting away some of the state information of each search node. The abstract node to which a search node maps is called the *image* of the search node under the abstraction.

Given a search graph and a homomorphic abstraction function, an *abstract graph* is constructed as follows.

1. The set of nodes, called *abstract nodes*, in the abstract graph corresponds to the set of abstract states.
2. An abstract node y' is a successor of an abstract node y if and only if there exist two states x' and x, such that
   a. x' is a successor of x, and
   b. y' and y are images of x' and x, respectively.

The abstract graph is used during search to locate portions of the search space that are disjoint. More formally, let abstract node $y = \phi(x)$ be the image of state x under a homomorphic abstraction function $\phi(\cdot)$ and let $succ(y)$ be the set of abstract successor nodes of y in the abstract graph.

Definition 1. *The* duplicate-detection scope *of a state x under a homomorphic abstraction function $\phi(\cdot)$ corresponds to the union of sets of stored nodes that map to an abstract node y' such that $y' \in succ(\phi(x))$, that is,*

$$\bigcup_{y' \in succ(\phi(x))} \phi^{-1}(y')$$

where $\phi^{-1}(y')$ is the set of stored nodes that are pre-images of y'.

Proposition 1. *The duplicate-detection scope of a node contains all stored duplicates of the successors of the node.*

Definition 2. *The duplicate-detection scopes of states x_1 and x_2 are disjoint under a homomorphic abstraction function $\phi(\cdot)$, if and only if the set of abstract successors of x_1's image is disjoint from the set of abstract successors of x_2's image in the abstract graph, that is, $succ(\phi(x_1)) \cap succ(\phi(x_2)) = \emptyset$.*

Proposition 2. *Two states cannot share a common successor if their duplicate-detection scopes are disjoint.*

Proposition 2 provides an important guarantee that a parallel model checker can leverage to reduce the amount of synchronization needed in parallel graph search. In particular, multiple threads can search disjoint portions of the graph, which correspond to disjoint duplicate-detection scopes, without the need for communication. Unlike HD-BFS, duplicate states are detected in PSDD as soon as they are generated.

As with HD-BFS, the search proceeds in layers. Each node in the abstract graph has two queues, one for the current depth-layer and one for the next. These queues contain the frontier nodes of the search graph that map to the given abstract node. Each abstract node also has a hash table containing all of the previously expanded search nodes that map to it.

Threads acquire access to expand all of the search nodes at the current depth for a single abstract node at a time. Because the abstraction is homomorphic, the successors of a search node will either map to the same abstract node or to one of the successors in the abstract graph. By claiming exclusive access to an abstract node and its successors, a thread can expand from the abstract node and perform immediate duplicate detection on the generated successors using only the data structures to which it has exclusive access. We call the set of nodes corresponding to an abstract node and its successors a *duplicate detection scope* (see Def. 1) or just a *scope* for short.

The left image in Fig. 1 shows an example graph in light gray with a possible abstraction of the graph drawn in dark black on top of it. This abstraction groups together sets of four nodes. There is an edge in the abstract graph between each pair of abstract nodes for which there exists a pair of nodes in the underlying graph that are connected by an edge and whose images correspond to each respective abstract state. The right image in Fig. 1 shows two duplicate detection scopes in this graph, each defined by the gray nodes and surrounded by a dashed line. Both duplicate detection scopes consist of the gray nodes and all nodes that map to the successors of their image in the abstract graph. When expanding any of the gray nodes, all successors will correspond to a node that resides in the same duplicate detection scope.

To perform parallel search, each thread will use the abstract graph to locate a duplicate detection scope that does not overlap the scopes being used by other threads. Given Proposition 2, these *disjoint duplicate detection scopes* may be searched in parallel without requiring communication. With this scheme, the only time that threads must synchronize is when multiple threads require access to the abstract graph at the same time. Only a single mutex is required to serialize access to the abstract graph and operations on the abstract graph tend to be quick.

The two duplicate detection scopes shown on the right half of Fig. 1 are disjoint as they do not share any nodes.

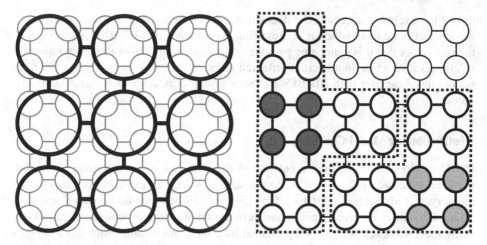

Fig. 1. A graph along with one of its possible abstractions (left) and two disjoint duplicate detection scopes of this graph (right)

When a thread completes the expansion of all open search nodes mapping to its current abstract node, it can release its duplicate detection scope, marking all abstract nodes in the scope as free to be re-acquired. Then the thread can try to acquire a new scope to search. If there are no free scopes with open search nodes at the current depth then the thread attempting to acquire a new scope must wait until another thread finishes expanding and releases its abstract nodes. This wait time can be reduced by using a finer-grained abstraction with sufficiently many disjoint duplicate detection scopes. In practice, we find that abstractions can typically be made large enough that wait times are insignificant.

Eventually, as open search nodes become exhausted in the current depth-layer, there will be only a single thread actively searching as the other threads wait for abstract nodes to become free. When the final non-waiting thread releases its duplicate detection scope and finds that there are no free scopes with open nodes it will progress the search to the next depth layer. To do this, the current and next queues for each abstract node are swapped, all abstract nodes with open nodes in their new current layer are marked as free, waiting threads are woken up and the search resumes. If the new depth-layer contains no open search nodes then the search space has been exhausted and the threads can terminate.

PSDD provides at least two advantages over hash-distributed search: 1) there may be less synchronization between threads in PSDD because threads only need to synchronize access to the abstract graph when releasing and acquiring a new duplicate detection scope and 2) duplicates can be checked immediately instead of using extra memory to store duplicate nodes before they can be checked against the hash table.

PSDD provides an additional benefit when applied to model checking: it does not need to be conservative when performing partial-order reduction. Recall that HD-BFS did not have access to test if successor nodes reside on the breadth-first queue when the successors were not assigned to the expanding thread. In PSDD, however, the expanding

thread has exclusive access to the data structures for the duplicate detection scope of
the abstract node from which it is expanding. This means that PSDD is able to test if
the successors that it is generating pass the *Q proviso* and therefore it does not need to
be conservative when doing partial-order reduction. As we will see, this gives PSDD a
major advantage over both HD-BFS and Spin's multi-core depth-first search on many
models.

Abstraction for Model Checking

PSDD requires an abstract representation of the state-space graph in order to exploit
the local structure of the space. Since the state space is not explicitly represented in
memory, this abstraction must be a function that can be computed on each node. In
Spin, each state in the search space consists of the set of processes whose executions are
being modeled. Each process is represented by a finite automaton which has a current
state and a set of transitions. The abstraction that we used in our implementation of
PSDD is: given any state, consider only the process type and the automaton state of
a fixed subset of the process IDs. For example, consider a state with seven processes
numbered 0–6. One possible abstraction is to consider only the automaton states of the
first two process IDs. This effectively 'projects away' process IDs 2–6, leading to a
much smaller set of abstract nodes.

We use the transitions of the finite automaton to determine the predecessor and successor relations in the abstract graph. Because only the state of a single component
automaton will transition between a node and its successors[2], the successors in the abstract graph are all of the possible single transitions of the process IDs that have not
been removed in the abstraction. For efficiency, we generate the abstract graph lazily
as needed during the search. This provides the benefit of only instantiating the portions
of the graph that are actually used and it also constructs the graph in parallel with the
execution of the search instead of doing it serially as a pre-processing step.

Experimental Results

In this section we present the results of a set of experiments that we performed to evaluate the two methods of parallelizing breadth-first search. In addition, we compare to
Spin's built-in multi-core depth-first search where applicable. The machine used in our
experiments has two 3.33GHz Xeon 5680 processors, each having six cores, and 96GB
of RAM.

Multi-core Depth-First Search

Spin comes, by default, with a state-of-the-art multi-core depth-first search algorithm
[8]. The algorithm connects each of the threads performing the search in a ring. Nodes

---

[2] For Spin, this is not strictly true when using 'never claims.' Our implementation requires that
never claims are not considered by the abstraction, thus ensuring that only a single component
automaton will change across a transition.

may be passed from one thread to another around the ring in a single direction. Each thread is then responsible for expanding all of the nodes that fall within a particular depth-interval. When the successors of a node fall outside of an interval assigned to the current thread, the newly generated successors must be passed to the neighboring thread along the ring using a shared memory queue. This neighboring thread may then receive the nodes from the queue and begin expanding them.

Using this technique, Holzmann et al. [8] were able to achieve speedups of just over 1.6x at two threads on a set of benchmark models and almost perfect linear speedup for two threads on a reference model that provided a set of tunable parameters. In their results, however, they show that this technique must be conservative when doing partial-order reduction. So, as with HD-BFS, the performance of multi-core depth-first search can actually be worse than serial search when partial-order reduction is used.

In the following experiments, we compare to Spin's multi-core depth-first search on models that do not contain safety property violations. The reason is that, on models with safety violations, depth-first search may find these violations via suboptimal paths, whereas breadth-first search must return optimal-length traces and thus may be forced to perform significantly more work. This renders the comparison unfair. On models without safety property violations, however, all algorithms must exhaust the search space and therefore will do a comparable amount of search.

Spin provides many parameters that may be tweaked to tune the search performance for different models. We compiled the multi-core depth-first with the

```
-DFULL_TRAIL -DSAFETY -DMEMLIM=64000
```

options on all models. For each individual model we also used any additional parameter settings that were recommended by Spin after running with the default parameter set.

Effect of Delaying Duplicate Detection

To compare the effects of the immediate duplicate detection of PSDD with the delayed duplicate detection of HD-BFS we looked at the memory usage of the two algorithms. Our hypothesis was that HD-BFS would require more memory in order to store duplicate search nodes during communication before they can be checked against the hash table by the receiving thread. The model that we choose for this experiment is a model of the dining philosophers problem with 10 philosophers. The model is constructed to avoid the classic deadlock situation and therefore the entire search space will be exhausted by the search algorithms. This removes the effects of tie-breaking that may be encountered when searching a model that contains an error. Also, with this model, the same number of states are expanded by all algorithms regardless of whether or not partial-order reduction is used and therefore we can conclude that any difference in memory usage must be attributed to immediate detection of duplicate nodes or lack thereof.

Figure 2 shows the memory usage reported by Spin for the 10 philosophers problem. The x axis gives the number of threads from 1–12 and the y axis shows the number of Gigabytes used to complete the search. Each line gives the mean of five runs at each thread count and the error bars (which are so tight that they are hardly even visible in this plot) show 95% confidence intervals on the mean. Breadth-first search only uses a

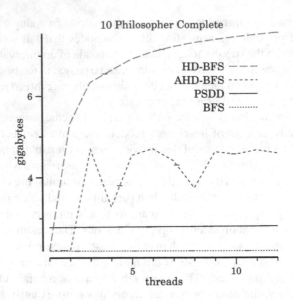

Fig. 2. Memory usage of PSDD, HD-BFS, AHD-BFS and BFS

single thread but we have extended the line for its single threaded performance across the x axis to ease comparison.

From this figure, we can see that breadth-first search and PSDD both used less than 3 Gigabytes of memory. The memory usage for PSDD remained nearly constant in the number of threads that performed the search. HD-BFS, however, required significantly more memory on this model when run with more than a single thread. The amount of memory required by HD-BFS increased sharply for up to six threads where it begun to even out. As mentioned above, this can be attributed to the fact that HD-BFS was required to store duplicate nodes in memory during communication instead of detecting them immediately. Due to the reduction in inter-thread communication, AHD-BFS used less memory than HD-BFS, however it still required more memory than breadth-first search and PSDD for more than two threads.

In addition to the results shown here, we have observed that HD-BFS required a lot more memory on all of the models that we have used in our experiments. Presumably, this is because of duplicate nodes, however, for other models the conservative partial-order reduction may also be a factor as we will see next.

Effect of Conservative Partial-Order Reduction

To evaluate the performance degradation that hash-distributed search and Spin's multi-core depth-first search suffer from due to conservative partial-order reduction we performed an experiment using a model of the semaphore implementation from the "Plan 9 from Bell Labs" operating system (Plan 9) [14][3]. The model is of particular interest

---

[3] The model was available from http://swtch.com/spin/

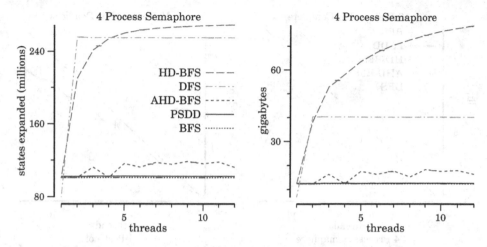

Fig. 3. States expanded and memory used by PSDD, HD-BFS and BFS

because, unlike the philosopher model used in the previous experiments, the semaphore model was taken from a real-world model checking problem. Partial-order reduction is able to reduce the size of the state space of this model by approximately a factor of three, so failure to perform the full reduction has a significant impact on performance.

Figure 3 shows the number of states expanded (left) and the amount of memory used (right) by PSDD, HD-BFS, breadth-first search and Spin's multi-core depth-first search on the semaphore model with four separate processes contending for the semaphore. The format of the plot is the same as that of Fig. 2. We can see that breadth-first search expanded the fewest nodes and used the least amount of memory in order to exhaust the configuration space of this model. PSDD expanded only slightly more nodes than breadth-first search and used approximately the same amount of memory. The reason that PSDD and breadth-first search expanded slightly different numbers of nodes is that they may expand nodes within the same depth layer in a different order. This differ-ence in tie-breaking can have a small effect on the partial-order reduction by slightly increasing or decreasing the number of nodes that must be expanded.

With a single thread, HD-BFS expanded about the same number of nodes and used about the same amount of memory as breadth-first. As the number of threads was increased, however, the number of expansions and memory requirement of HD-BFS rapidly increased. HD-BFS required almost 80GB of memory when run with 12 threads. The reason for the steep increase is that HD-BFS required more communications as the nodes were divided up between more threads. Each time a node is communicated the search conservatively assumed that it could not perform partial-order reduction and therefore many redundant paths were explored that were not pursued by the other two algorithms. The plot also shows this same effect happens with Spin's multi-core depth-first search. The depth-first search suffers from the same conservative partial-order re-duction as HD-BFS and for more than a single thread it expanded many more states than PSDD and breadth-first search.

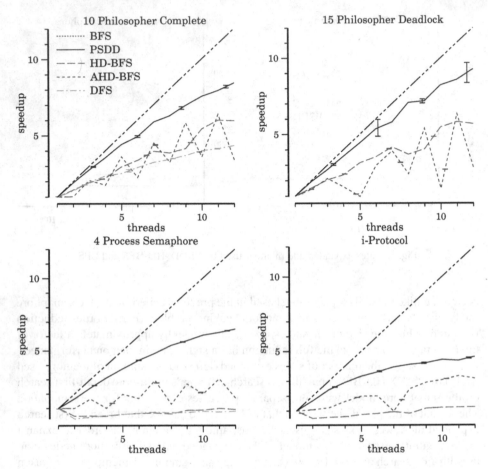

Fig. 4. Parallel speedup for PSDD, HD-BFS, AHD-BFS, and parallel depth-first search

Overall Performance

Next we show the overall performance in terms of parallel speedup and wall-clock time for the different algorithms on four models. For PSDD and AHD-BFS, which both require an abstraction, we choose the fixed subset of processor IDs used in the projection experimentally. For each model we ran the algorithms using a small set of hand-chosen process ID sequences from 0–n and 1–n for small values of n (up to 7). The sequence that gave the best performance for each model was used in the following comparisons. We believe that the good performance exhibited by PSDD in the following results when using such a simple abstraction is strong evidence that finding a good abstraction for PSDD is not a difficult task.

Figure 4 shows the parallel speedup and Figure 5 shows the total wall-clock time that the algorithms required to search four different models using 1–12 threads. As in the previous plots, each line shows the mean performance across five runs with error bars giving the 95% confidence intervals. The x axis show the number of threads used

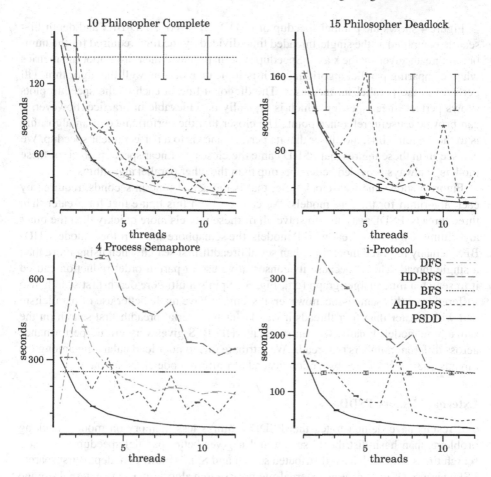

Fig. 5. Wall-clock seconds for PSDD, HD-BFS, AHD-BFS, parallel depth-first search, and serial breadth-first search

from 1–12 and in Fig. 5 the performance of breadth-first search is drawn across the x axis of each plot even though it was only run serially. The models used were the dining philosopher problem with 10 philosophers and no deadlock, the dining philosophers problem with 15 philosophers and a deadlock which is reachable in 42 steps, the Plan 9 semaphore with 4 contending processes, and the 0-level abstraction of the GNU i-Protocol model from Dong et al. [4][4] which contains a live-lock that is reachable in 72 steps, modified to avoid rendezvous as Spin complains that these do not maintain completeness with breadth-first search. Spin's multi-core depth-first search algorithm is not shown on the 15 philosopher model or the i-Protocol model because they both exhibit errors for which depth-first search does not find shortest counterexamples and therefore does not perform a comparable amount of search.

---

[4] Available from http://www.cs.sunysb.edu/~lmc/iproto/

Figure 4 shows the parallel speedup of PSDD, HD-BFS, AHD-BFS and depth-first search, computed as the single-threaded time divided by the time required for the number of threads given on the x axis. Speedup is perhaps one of the most important metrics when comparing parallel algorithms as it is indicative of how well the algorithm will perform as the parallelism increases. The diagonal line in each of the speedup plots shows perfect linear speedup which is typically unachievable in practice, however, it can provide a useful reference point. The closer that the performance of an algorithm is to the diagonal line, the closer that its performance is to a perfect linear speedup. We can see from these figures that PSDD came the closest to linear speedup on all of these models; it always provided better speedup than the other parallel algorithms.

Figure 5 shows the wall-clock time, that is the actual time in seconds, required by each algorithm for the four models. We can see from this figure that for greater than three threads, PSDD was able to solve all of these models more quickly than the other algorithms. On the two 'real-world' models, the semaphore and i-Protocol models, HD-BFS actually required more time than serial breadth-first search when using more than a single thread. This is because its conservative use of partial-order reduction caused it to search a much larger graph (c.f., Fig. 3). Spin's multi-core depth-first search also suffered from this same issue, however, it seems to have made better use of parallelism and with greater than four threads it was faster than serial breadth-first search on the semaphore model. Finally, we can see that AHD-BFS gives very erratic performance across different numbers of threads. We attribute this to poor load balancing among the threads due to use of the abstraction instead of uniform node distribution.

External-Memory PSDD

Our results have demonstrated that PSDD requires less memory on model checking problems than hash-distributed search and it gives better parallel speedup and faster search times than both hash-distributed search and Spin's multi-core depth-first search. PSDD is also able to act as an external-memory search algorithm where external storage such as a hard disk is used to supplement core memory. In fact, the PSDD framework was originally developed by Zhou *et al.* for external-memory search [19]. External-memory PSDD [20] (external PSDD for short) works just like PSDD, however, when an abstract node is not in use by one of the threads, it can be pushed off to external storage. This reduces the memory usage of the search algorithm from that of the entire search graph to just the size of the duplicate detection scopes acquired by each thread.

As a preliminary experiment, we implemented external PSDD in Spin and used it to solve the deadlock-free 10 philosophers model. We ran on a machine with eight cores and four disks configured in a RAID 0 array. A limitation of our setup was that I/O operations were serialized via a single disk controller, therefore when using all eight cores external PSDD did not benefit from parallelism. When using a single thread, standard PSDD used an average of 233 seconds to complete its search and external PSDD required 1,764 seconds on average (both times had very little variance). With a more sophisticated machine, external PSDD will show improved performance when using parallelism, for example, Zhou and Hansen [20] show performance improvements for up to four threads with external PSDD for automated planning. Even given this limitation with our experimental setup, the real benefit of external PSDD is still realized:

external PSDD was able to reduce the memory usage of search from 2.5 Gigabytes with standard PSDD down to around half of a Gigabyte when using a single thread. This is a 500% reduction in the memory requirement of the search. In many cases this reduction in the memory requirement is much more important than reducing the search time because it is easier to wait longer for the search to complete, however, it may not be possible to add more memory. Because of this, the memory requirement is often the limiting factor determining whether or not a model can be validated with a model checker.

Discussion and Related Work

In a preliminary experiment we have seen that external-memory PSDD is able to reduce the memory requirement of search by a substantial amount. The penalty for external-memory PSDD, however, is that it can take a lot longer than serial search as it has to access hard disk storage. We suspect that the performance of external PSDD can be increased substantially by using multiple RAID arrays in order to exploit parallelism.

In our current implementation, external PSDD uses more memory when run with more than a single thread as each thread must have its own duplicate detection scope in RAM. With eight cores, external PSDD used around the same amount of memory as standard PSDD which does not use hard disk storage at all. A new technique called edge partitioning [22] may be able to fix this problem. Edge partitioning reduces the size of a duplicate detection scope to be only those search nodes that map to a single abstract node. This can be a very significant reduction that will enable external PSDD to use multiple threads while still having a very small memory footprint.

Until now, we have not discussed, in detail, how the chosen abstraction effects the performance of PSDD. For our experiments, the abstraction was selected by evaluating a small set of different abstractions on each model and choosing the one that gave the best performance. If the abstract graph is too small or is too strongly connected then PSDD can suffer as it will be unable to find a sufficient number of disjoint scopes to search in parallel. We have found that the simple abstractions used in our experiments have provided a sufficient amount of parallelism. Recent work, however, has shown that PSDD can greatly benefit from a dynamic search space partitioning that changes the abstraction during search [21]. By using dynamic partitioning, the algorithm would be able to select an abstraction that is more balanced, reducing the peak memory requirement of external search, and less connected, increasing its ability to exploit parallelism.

Given its rising importance, search parallelization has been the subject of focus for a number of related work done in the field of model checking. In [11], Jabbar and Edelkamp describe a parallel extension of External A*, which is a disk-based heuristic search algorithm. Like HD-BFS, Parallel External A* also uses delayed duplicate detection, which can be less efficient than structured duplicate detection for reasons discussed in this paper. Unlike both HD-BFS and PSDD, Parallel External A* is designed only for directed model checking, since it relies on both the g-value (the distance from the start state) and the h-value (an estimate on the distance to go) of a state to partition the search space. Thus, depending on whether an informative heuristic function is available, Parallel External A* can sometimes be less efficient. On the other hand, since

PSDD makes no assumption about the availability of a heuristic function, it is applicable to both directed and undirected model checking. Furthermore, Parallel External A* seems inherently disk-based, since "all communication between different processes [of Parallel External A*] is done through shared files" (page 7 of [11]). Thus, whether there exists an efficient implementation of Parallel External A* that only uses RAM remains to be seen. As for PSDD, since it does not rely on any file system for inter-process communication, both internal and external-memory versions of PSDD have been successfully applied to STRIPS planning, as shown in [20]. Fortunately, the same is true for model checking, as we show in this paper.

Besides systematic approaches, non-systematic parallel search techniques such as [5,10] have also been proposed and successfully applied to model checking large verification problems. In [5], the Parallel Randomized State-space Search (PRSS) technique was shown to reduce the cost of finding an error in Java code by factors ranging from 2 to well over 1,000. In [10], experiments show the Swarm Tool can dramatically reduce runtime and increase coverage over the standard method of a single depth or breadth first search. Both PRSS and Swarm parallelize search by isolating the threads, allowing them to search independently without any communication. It is this isolation, however, that makes it difficult for either technique to prove the correctness of a model. In the absence of communication, the only time either algorithm will converge (i.e., declare the model is bug-free) is if a single thread exhausts the entire search space – a rarity for large verification problems. On the other hand, a systematic search technique such as PSDD can detect global convergence and terminate both in the presence of bugs or in their absence.

Conclusion and Future Work

We have compared two techniques for parallelizing the breadth-first search algorithm used to find deadlocks and safety property violations in model checking. Our results showed that Parallel Structured Duplicate Detection provides benefits over both hash-distributed search and Spin's multi-core depth-first search because it gives better parallel speedup and it requires significantly less memory. We have also demonstrated that external PSDD can reduce the memory requirements of model checking even further by taking advantage of cheap secondary storage such as hard disks. As CPU performance relies more on parallelism than raw clock speed, the techniques presented in this paper enable model checking to better exploit the full capabilities of modern hardware.

Partial-order reduction is a widely used technique for tackling the state-space explosion problem found in model checking. However, combining it with parallelization techniques has been a challenge in the past. In this paper, we show that not only PSDD is effective for parallel reachability analysis, but it also preserves the full power of Spin's partial-order reduction algorithm. As for future work, we will apply PSDD to other model checkers to show its generality and effectiveness in speeding up search with full partial-order reduction.

References

1. Biere, A., Artho, C., Schuppan, V.: Liveness checking as safety checking. In: FMICS 2002: Formal Methods for Industrial Critical Systems. ENTCS, vol. 66(2) (2002)
2. Bošnački, D., Holzmann, G.J.: Improving Spin's Partial-Order Reduction for Breadth-First Search. In: Godefroid, P. (ed.) SPIN 2005. LNCS, vol. 3639, pp. 91–105. Springer, Heidelberg (2005)
3. Burns, E., Lemons, S., Ruml, W., Zhou, R.: Best-first heuristic search for multicore machines. Journal of Artificial Intelligence Research 39, 689–743 (2010)
4. Dong, Y., Du, X., Holzmann, G.J., Smolka, S.A.: Fighting livelock in the GNU i-Protocol: A case study in explicit-state model checking. International Journal on Software Tools for Technology Transfer (STTT) 4(4), 505–528 (2003)
5. Dwyer, M.B., Elbaum, S., Person, S., Purandare, R.: Parallel randomized state-space search. In: Proceedings of the 29th International Conference on Software Engineering, ICSE 2007, pp. 3–12 (2007)
6. Evett, M., Hendler, J., Mahanti, A., Nau, D.: PRA* - massively-parallel heuristic-search. Journal of Parallel and Distributed Computing 25(2), 133–143 (1995)
7. Holzmann, G.J.: The Spin Model Checker: Primer and Reference Manual. Addison-Wesley (2004)
8. Holzmann, G.J., Bošnački, D.: The design of a multicore extension of the spin model checker. IEEE Transactions on Software Engineering 33(10), 659–674 (2007)
9. Holzmann, G.J., Peled, D.: An improvement in formal verification. In: Proceedings of the 7th IFIP WG6.1 International Conference on Formal Description Techniques, FORTE 1994 (1994)
10. Holzmann, G.J., Joshi, R., Groce, A.: Tackling Large Verification Problems with the Swarm Tool. In: Havelund, K., Majumdar, R. (eds.) SPIN 2008. LNCS, vol. 5156, pp. 134–143. Springer, Heidelberg (2008)
11. Jabbar, S., Edelkamp, S.: Parallel External Directed Model Checking with Linear I/O. In: Emerson, E.A., Namjoshi, K.S. (eds.) VMCAI 2006. LNCS, vol. 3855, pp. 237–251. Springer, Heidelberg (2005)
12. Kishimoto, A., Fukunaga, A., Botea, A.: Scalable, parallel best-first search for optimal sequential planning. In: Proceedings of the Nineteenth International Conference on Automated Planning and Scheduling, ICAPS 2009 (2009)
13. Korf, R.: Linear-time disk-based implicit graph search. Journal of the ACM 35(6) (2008)
14. Pike, R., Presotto, D., Dorward, S., Flandrena, B., Thompson, K., Trickey, H., Winterbottom, P.: Plan 9 from Bell Labs. Computing Systems 8(3), 221–254 (1995)
15. Reif, J.H.: Depth-first search is inherently sequential. Information Processing Letters 20(5), 229–234 (1985)
16. Roscoe, A.W.: Model-checking csp. In: A Classical Mind, Essays in Honour of CAR Hoare, pp. 353–378. Prentice-Hall (1994)
17. Schuppan, V., Biere, A.: Efficient reduction of finite state model checking to reachability analysis. International Journal on Software Tools for Technology Transfer (STTT) 5(2-3), 185–204 (2004)
18. Stern, U., Dill, D.: Parallelizing the Murϕ Verifier. In: Grumberg, O. (ed.) CAV 1997. LNCS, vol. 1254, pp. 256–267. Springer, Heidelberg (1997)
19. Zhou, R., Hansen, E.A.: Structured duplicate detection in external-memory graph search. In: Proceedings of the Nineteenth National Conference on Artificial Intelligence, AAAI 2004, pp. 683–688 (July 2004)

20. Zhou, R., Hansen, E.A.: Parallel structured duplicate detection. In: Proceedings of the Twenty-Second Conference on Artificial Intelligence, AAAI 2007, pp. 1217–1223 (2007)
21. Zhou, R., Hansen, E.A.: Dynamic state-space partitioning in external-memory graph search. In: Proceedings of the Twenty-First International Conference on Automated Planning and Scheduling, ICAPS 2011, pp. 290–297 (2011)
22. Zhou, R., Schmidt, T., Hansen, E.A., Do, M.B., Uckun, S.: Edge partitioning in parallel structured duplicate detection. In: The 2010 International Symposium on Combinatorial Search, SOCS 2010, pp. 137–138 (2010)

McPatom: A Predictive Analysis Tool for Atomicity Violation Using Model Checking

Reng Zeng, Zhuo Sun, Su Liu, and Xudong He

School of Computing and Information Sciences
Florida International University Miami, Florida 33199, USA
{rzeng001,zsun003,sliu002,hex}@cis.fiu.edu

Abstract. Multi-thread programs are prone to bugs due to concurrency. Concurrency bugs are hard to find and reproduce because of the large number of interleavings. Most non-deadlock concurrency bugs are atomicity violation bugs due to unprotected accesses of shared variables by multiple threads. This paper presents a dynamic prediction tool named McPatom for predicting atomicity violation bugs involving a pair of threads accessing a shared variable using model checking. McPatom uses model checking to ensure the completeness in predicting any possible atomicity violation captured in the abstract thread model extracted from an interleaved execution. McPatom can predict atomicity violations involving more than three accesses and multiple subroutines, and supports all synchronization primitives. We have applied McPatom in predicting several known bugs in real world systems including one that evades several other existing tools. We provide evaluations of McPatom in terms of atomicity violation predictability and performance with additional improvement strategies.

1 Introduction

Multi-core hardware is a growing industry trend, for both high performance servers and low power mobile devices. Multi-thread programs can exploit multi-core processors at their full potential. In the real world, most servers and high-end critical software are multi-thread. Unfortunately, multi-thread programs are prone to bugs due to the inherent complexity caused by concurrency. It is difficult to detect concurrency bugs due to the huge number of possible interleavings. Many concurrency bugs escape from testing into software releases and cause some of the most serious computer-related accidents in history, including a blackout leaving tens of millions of people without electricity [1].

Among different types of concurrency bugs, atomicity violation bugs are the most common one. Atomicity violation bugs are caused by violations to the atomicity of certain code regions without proper synchronization. They widely exist in the real world systems and contributed to about 70% of the examined non-deadlock concurrency bugs [2]. Therefore, techniques for detecting atomicity violation bugs are extremely important.

A. Donaldson and D. Parker (Eds.): SPIN 2012, LNCS 7385, pp. 191–207, 2012.

This paper presents a dynamic prediction tool McPatom to predict atomicity violation bugs involving a pair of threads accessing a shared variable using model checking, based on binary executables that use POSIX thread library. McPatom uses memory access patterns instead of subroutine atomicity. The only input needed by McPatom is a binary executable, while source code is optional for locating bugs.

The McPatom framework contains the following major steps: (1) using Pin [3] to instrument an interleaved execution of a multi-thread program and to record an interleaved trace containing only atomicity violation impacting events including all shared variable accesses and all synchronization routines (locks, condition variables, barriers and thread management events); (2) projecting the single interleaved trace into a partial order thread model of abstract threads, which maintains the causal relation within actual threads imposed by the synchronization routines; (3) automatically translating the partial order thread model into a Promela program for model checking in Spin [4]; (4) defining a complete set of atomicity violation patterns involving a pair of threads accessing every single shared variable and automatically translating them into temporal logic formulas; (5) using Spin to model check the atomicity violation patterns; and (6) mapping the violation reported in Spin to the execution trace in the original multi-thread program. Figure 1 gives an overview of McPatom framework.

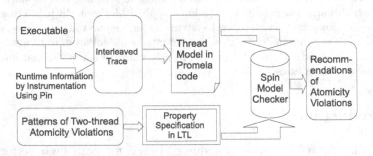

Fig. 1. Overview of McPatom Framework to predict atomicity violation bugs using model checking

Our work makes the following contributions:

1. A method to extract a thread model from an instrumented interleaved trace that only records events related to atomicity violations. Such an interleaved trace is much smaller than the program behavior in a complete execution. Furthermore the extracted thread model enables the checking of all alternative traces with the same causal relationships as the interleaved trace. The completeness of instrumented interleaved traces and the extracted thread models is proved.

2. A complete set of the patterns of unserializable interleavings involving two threads (most concurrency bugs involve only two threads [5]) containing any number of accesses to a shared variable (either user defined or every word sized dynamically allocated memory accessed by multiple threads). These patterns generalize and cover the three accesses proposed in [2][6]. These atomicity violation patterns become property specifications to be checked.

3. A unique prediction tool - McPatom, for detecting atomicity violation bugs through model checking. McPatom instruments interleaved executions, extracts thread models from interleaved traces, automatically converts (1) thread models into Promela programs and (2) atomicity violation patterns into property specifications. By constraining the checking within a pair of threads involving one shared variable at a time, the interleaving space to be checked is vastly reduced. As a result, McPatom is applicable to large software systems. McPatom can predict atomicity violations that do not manifest during testing or runtime.

We applied McPatom to predict several known atomicity violations in real world systems as well as an atomicity violation that cannot be detected by several existing tools. We obtained favorable experimental results with regard to atomicity violation predictability, accuracy and performance of using McPatom. McPatom ignores data-flow in the thread model, thus may report false positives.

2 Extracting Partial Order Thread Models from Multi-thread Program Executions

2.1 Description of the Partial Order Thread Model

A multi-thread program has a set of threads and a set of shared variables. Shared variables are addresses of global variables and every word sized dynamically allocated memory accessed by multiple threads. The same memory address is considered as another shared variable if it is released and reallocated through the invocations of memory functions. An execution $\sigma = s_1, ..., s_n$ of a multi-thread program P is a sequence of executed statements. A trace is the projection of an execution to a sequence of annotated shared variable accesses and synchronization events. Formally, a trace, $\tau = e_1, ..., e_m$ is a sequence of events where each event $e_i (1 \leq i \leq m)$ is a tuple $\langle tid_i, timestamp_i, action_i \rangle$ in which tid_i is a thread handle, $timestamp_i$ is a time stamp based on real time and $action_i$ is one of the following: (read/write, a shared variable), (a synchronization routine, a synchronization variable) or (a thread management operation, a thread handle). McPatom uses POSIX Threads in which a synchronization routine is a routine related to semaphores, mutex locks, condition variables and barriers, does not handle user-defined synchronization primitives. McPatom also assumes a shared variable as a synchronization variable if it is accessed by synchronization routines, thus does not treat its accesses as shared variable accesses.

Lemma 1. *A trace* $\tau = e_1, ..., e_m$ *extracted from an execution sequence* $\sigma = s_1, ..., s_n$ *is sound and complete with respect to* σ *in terms of atomicity violation predictability.*

Proof sketch. (1) Soundness: An atomicity violation revealed in τ must exist in σ. This is obvious since τ is a projection of σ. An atomicity violation pattern appearing in τ exists in σ.

(2) Completeness: Any existing atomicity violation in σ remains in τ. Since atomicity violations do not depend on general program states, and only depend on the execution orders of shared variable accesses and synchronization events, that are completely captured in τ.

Definition 1. *Given a trace* $\tau = e_1, ..., e_m$ *containing shared variable accesses and synchronization events, a partial order thread model* $(E_\tau, \prec)$ *is defined as follows:*

1. $E_\tau = \{e_i \mid e_i \ in \ \tau\}$
2. $\prec$ *is a partial order relation such that, for any* $e_i, e_j \in E$ $(i \neq j)$, $e_i \prec e_j$ *iff*
    (a) $tid_i = tid_j$ *and* $i < j$, *or*
    (b) $tid_i \neq tid_j$, $action_i = (Signal, cvar)$, $action_j = (Wait, cvar)$ *and* $\forall k$. $((j < k < i) \wedge (action_k \neq (Signal, cvar)))$ *in which cvar is a condition variable, or*
    (c) $tid_i \neq tid_j$, $action_i = (Wait, bvar)$ *and* $(i < j) \wedge \exists k . ((tid_k = tid_j) \wedge (k < j) \wedge action_k = (Wait, bvar) \wedge \forall h . ((tid_h = tid_k) \Rightarrow \neg(k < h < j)))$ *in which bvar is a barrier variable, or*
    (d) $tid_i \neq tid_j$, $action_i = (Create, tid_j)$, *or*
    (e) $tid_i \neq tid_j$, $action_j = (Join, tid_i)$.
3. *Mutual exclusion: for any* $e_i, e_j, e_m, e_n \in E$ $(i \neq j \neq m \neq n)$, $e_j \prec e_m$ *or* $e_n \prec e_i$ *iff*
    (a) $tid_i = tid_j$, $action_i = (Lock, lvar)$, $action_j = (Unlock, lvar)$, *and*
    (b) $tid_m = tid_n$, $action_m = (Lock, lvar)$, $action_n = (Unlock, lvar)$.

The above partial order relation (or simply causal relation) is similar to the happened-before relation given in [7]. From the above definition, we have (1) shared variable accesses within the same thread are ordered, and (2) a pair of shared variable accesses from two different threads are only ordered if and only if they are constrained by some intermediate synchronization events such as one thread creating the other.

While the partial order thread model $(E_\tau, \prec)$ respects the causal relation in trace τ, it captures an equivalent class of alternative traces that obey the same causal relation as τ, in which each alternative trace τ' is a result of rearranging some shared variable accesses not constrained by $\prec$. The partial order thread model allows us to explore all possible alternative traces that correspond to a set of feasible interleavings in a multi-thread program, however, the model provides an over-approximation without considering data-flow, thus cannot guarantee each permissible trace in the model is covered by some feasible interleaved execution in the multi-thread program P.

2.2 Implementation of the Partial Order Thread Model

Capturing Runtime Traces and Related Source Code. McPatom uses Pin binary instrumentation framework [3] to collect runtime trace information, specifically including, every access to every shared variable and every synchronization event using POSIX Thread (locks, condition variables, barriers, thread joining and etc.). For each collected event, McPatom also finds the corresponding source code information including file name and line number. The source code information can be used to help locating the predicted bugs. A sample of a partial trace is shown in Fig. 2.

```
3047143104,  1,  thread.c-624,  Read,   threads
3047143104,  1,  thread.c-172,  Create,  3020999536
3020999536,  1,  thread.c-240,  Lock,   init_lock
3020999536,  1,  thread.c-241,  Read,   init_count
3020999536,  1,  thread.c-241,  Write,  init_count
3020999536,  1,  thread.c-242,  Signal,  init_cond
3020999536,  1,  thread.c-243,  Unlock,  init_lock
```

Fig. 2. A Sample of a Partial Trace (The format of each line: thread handle, timestamp, file name - line number, action)

Automatically Encoding Traces to Promela Code. McPatom uses Spin model checker to detect atomicity violations in a partial order thread model. This section shows how we realize a partial order thread model from a recorded trace in Spin's underlying language Promela.

Defining Shared Variable Accesses. McPatom defines every shared variable v as a *short* in Promela, automatically assigns a unique value for all reading accesses and a unique value for all writing accesses in each thread. Formally, let $rw \in \{r, w\}$ and *tid* be thread ID, each access of v is defined as $v=rw+tid$. Since the maximum number of threads per process is limited to 64 in POSIX threads, McPatom sets r to 0, and w to 64. For example, given two threads: $t1(tid=1)$ and $t2(tid=2)$, and a shared variable v, McPatom makes the following assignments :

1. $v = 64+1$ for each writing access of v in thread $t1$,
2. $v = 1$ for each reading access of v in thread $t1$,
3. $v = 64+2$ for each writing access of v in thread $t2$,
4. $v = 2$ for each reading access of v in thread $t2$.

Defining Synchronization Primitives. McPatom automatically generates Promela code for all synchronization primitives. Due to space limit, we only present Promela code for mutex locks. McPatom models synchronization events to capture the causal relationships between threads, to prune infeasible interleavings. The Promela code shown in Fig. 3 models the POSIX Thread routines *pthread_mutex_lock* and *pthread_mutex_unlock*. The atomic construct groups indivisible statements together to ensure no interleaving within an atomic sequence. *Lock* inline function accepts a lock l as its argument. If lock l is not locked, *Lock* function locks it and sets the owner to the thread that is the predefined variable *_pid* for the executing process in Promela. If lock l is in locked status, no guards are executable so that the thread is blocked until lock l is available according to Promela semantics. *Unlock* inline function simply sets lock l to unlocked status. It is exactly what is required to model locking and unlocking of a mutex lock.

```
#define NUM_LOCKS 100
short locked[NUM_LOCKS] = -1;
inline Lock(l) {
 if
 ::atomic{(locked[l] == -1) -> locked[l] = _pid}
 fi;
}
inline Unlock(l) {
 assert(locked[l] == _pid);
 locked[l] = -1;
}
```

Fig. 3. Promela Code Modeling Mutex Locks

Defining Threads. All events with regard to a particular thread from the recorded trace are grouped into a Promela process in which each event is represented by its corresponding Promela code defined in previous steps as shown in Fig. 4. Since the maximum number of threads per process in POSIX threads is 64, which is well below the maximum number (256) of processes allowed in Promela, we do not have problem to encode all possible threads occurring in a recorded trace. The interleaved execution of processes in the Promela program generates all alternative permissible traces in the partial order thread model.

3   Defining and Encoding Unserializable Interleaving Patterns between Two Threads

Atomicity is a semantic correctness property for concurrent programs. A thread interleaving is serializable if and only if it is equivalent to a serial execution, which executes a code region without other threads interleaved in between. The code region is typically enforced as atomic explicitly in the code. When proper synchronization is missing to enforce atomicity, atomicity violation bugs may occur. [8] proved that a thread interleaving is serializable if and only if its conflict graph is acyclic.

```
proctype t1() { ... }
proctype t2()
{
  Lock(init_lock);       /* thread.c - 240 */
  init_count = 0 + 2;    /* thread.c - 241 */
  init_count = 64 + 2;   /* thread.c - 241 */
  Signal(init_cond);     /* thread.c - 242 */
  Unlock(init_lock);     /* thread.c - 243 */
  ...
}
init
{
  run t2();     /* thread.c - 172 */
  ...
}
```

Fig. 4. A Sample of Partial Promela Code

Most concurrency bugs involve two threads, instead of a large number of threads, based on the study in [5], in which 101 out of 105 bugs involved only two threads. Thus atomicity violation bugs in a multi-thread program can be explored through every pair of threads. Our work is inspired by the works in [2][6], which addressed a special case of unserializable interleavings with three accesses of the same shared variable. However, as Fig. 5 shows, there are real world bugs involving four accesses of the same shared variable. Furthermore, there can be more accesses involved, such as reading accesses of a shared variable for logging purpose. The patterns given in this paper cover atomicity violation bugs involving any number of accesses of a shared variable between a pair of threads.

3.1 Three-Access and Four-Access Atomicity Violation

Many recent works focused on three-access atomicity violations [2][6][5], which involve one shared variable, two threads and three accesses to the variable. For simplicity, two threads are referred as a local thread (Thread 1) and a remote thread (Thread 2), the opposite view is also explored during the detection process. If two consecutive accesses of a shared variable in a local thread are interleaved with an access to the variable from a remote thread, the interleaving is a potential unserializable one. In practice, unserializable interleavings indicate the presence of atomicity violation bugs. The explanation of unserializable interleavings of three accesses and many real world atomicity violation bugs can be found in [2].

Three-access atomicity violations are chosen by tools above because (1) there are many real world atomicity violation bugs involving only three accesses, and (2) checking only two accesses (current access and previous access) in a thread can reduce the complexity of algorithms. However, some atomicity violation bugs involve more than three accesses. A real world example [9] is shown in Fig. 5. The shared variable accesses in Thread 1 must be in an atomic region; otherwise, a possible interleaving may result in HandleEvent function of Thread 2 returning with a missing event. PSet [9] detected this bug (incorrect interleaving 1) since PSet keeps track of either the last writer or the set of last readers for every memory location. However PSet cannot detect the mutant of the bug (incorrect interleaving 2) because in PSet's view the mutant only involves a set of last readers and the current reading access. AVIO [2] cannot detect this bug because it involves more than three accesses.

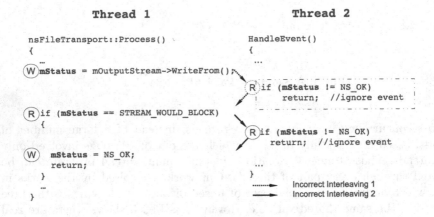

Fig. 5. A four-access atomicity violation bug [9] in Mozilla (Incorrect interleaving 1 was detected by PSet [9] and missed by AVIO [2], while incorrect interleaving 2 cannot be detected by either PSet or AVIO)

3.2 Patterns of Two-Thread Atomicity Violations involving any Number of Accesses

In the sequel, a two-thread atomicity violation refers to a two-thread atomicity violation involving any number of accesses of a shared variable, and $A \in \{Read, Write\}$, $R = Read$, $W = Write$, A^* denotes zero or more A, A^+ denotes one or more A, R^* denotes zero or more R and R^+ denotes one or more R. This section gives a set of patterns covering all possible two-thread atomicity violations.

Figure 6 shows all possible scenarios of unserializable interleavings with only one access from Thread 2. If any of the unserializable interleaving patterns is matched, it indicates a potential atomicity violation.

Theorem 1. *The set of patterns in Fig. 6 is complete, i.e. they cover all possible unserializable interleavings between two threads.*

Proof. Let $A_1^{t_1}, A_2^{t_2}, ..., A_n^{t_n}$ be a sequence of atomic accesses in an interleaved execution of two threads, in which $A_i^{t_i}$ ($t_i \in \{1,2\}$, $A_i^{t_i} \in \{Read, Write\}$, $1 \le$

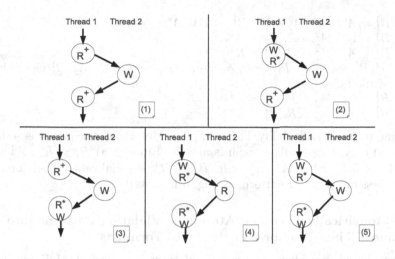

Fig. 6. Unserializable Interleavings with two threads. In (1)(2)(3)(5), W in Thread 2 unexpectedly changes the value; In (4), An intermediate value in Thread 1 is read by Thread 2.

$i \leq n$) denotes an atomic access from thread t_i to the same shared variable. Let every subsequence of $A_1^{t_1}, A_2^{t_2}, ..., A_n^{t_n}$ be of the form B_1^1, B_2^2, B_3^1 where B_1^1 and B_3^1 of Thread 1 are sequences of $A_i^{t_i}(t_i = 1)$, B_2^2 of Thread 2 is a sequence of $A_i^{t_i}(t_i = 2)$. Let P_i be pattern i. B_2^2 is assumed to be or can be reduced to a single access A_2^2. If B_1^1, A_2^2, B_3^1 does not match with any of the patterns in Fig. 6, B_1^1, A_2^2, B_3^1 satisfies $\neg P_1 \wedge \neg P_2 \wedge \neg P_3 \wedge \neg P_4 \wedge \neg P_5$. Since operator $\wedge$ is commutative, we can select a specific order and carry out an incremental analysis of possible B_1^1, A_2^2, B_3^1 based on each of $P_i (1 \leq i \leq 5)$.

1. B_1^1, A_2^2, B_3^1 satisfies $\neg P_1$. B_1^1, A_2^2, B_3^1 can only be one of the following:
   (a) $B_1^1 = A^*WA^*$, $A_2^2 = W$, $B_3^1 = A^+$
   (b) $B_1^1 = A^+$, $A_2^2 = W$, $B_3^1 = A^*WA^*$
   (c) $B_1^1 = A^+$, $A_2^2 = R$, $B_3^1 = A^+$
2. B_1^1, A_2^2, B_3^1 satisfies $\neg P_1 \wedge \neg P_2$. B_1^1, A_2^2, B_3^1 can only be one of the following:
   (a) $B_1^1 = A^*WA^*$, $A_2^2 = W$, $B_3^1 = A^*WA^*$
   (b) $B_1^1 = A^+$, $A_2^2 = W$, $B_3^1 = A^*WA^*$
   (c) $B_1^1 = A^+$, $A_2^2 = R$, $B_3^1 = A^+$
3. B_1^1, A_2^2, B_3^1 satisfies $\neg P_1 \wedge \neg P_2 \wedge \neg P_3$. B_1^1, A_2^2, B_3^1 can only be one of the following:
   (a) $B_1^1 = A^*WA^*$, $A_2^2 = W$, $B_3^1 = A^*WA^*$
   (b) $B_1^1 = A^*WA^*$, $A_2^2 = W$, $B3 = A^*WA^*$ which is equivalent to above one.
   (c) $B_1^1 = A^+$, $A_2^2 = R$, $B_3^1 = A^+$
4. B_1^1, A_2^2, B_3^1 satisfies $\neg P_1 \wedge \neg P_2 \wedge \neg P_3 \wedge \neg P_4$. B_1^1, A_2^2, B_3^1 can only be one of the following:

(a) $B_1^1 = A^*WA^*$, $A_2^2 = W$, $B_3^1 = A^*WA^*$
(b) $B_1^1 = R^+$, $A_2^2 = R$, $B_3^1 = A^+$
(c) $B_1^1 = A^+$, $A_2^2 = R$, $B_3^1 = R^+$

5. B_1^1, A_2^2, B_3^1 satisfies $\neg P_1 \wedge \neg P_2 \wedge \neg P_3 \wedge \neg P_4 \wedge \neg P_5$. B_1^1, A_2^2, B_3^1 can only be one of the following:
   (a) $B_1^1 = R^+$, $A_2^2 = R$, $B_3^1 = A^+$
   (b) $B_1^1 = A^+$, $A_2^2 = R$, $B_3^1 = R^+$

According to the Serializability Theorem [8], an interleaved sequence is serializable if and only if its conflict graph is acyclic. Either 5(a) $B_1^1 = R^+$, $A_2^2 = R$, $B_3^1 = A^+$ or 5(b) $B_1^1 = A^+$, $A_2^2 = R$, $B_3^1 = R^+$ is serializable. Therefore, the completeness of the set of patterns in Fig. 6 is proved.

3.3 Automatically Encoding Atomicity Violation Patterns into Linear Time Temporal Logic (LTL) Formulas

For every shared variable and every pair of threads $t1$ and $t2$, McPatom automatically defines a LTL formula (3.1) for each pattern in Fig. 6 and another LTL formula (3.2) reversing the view of t_1 and t_2. Let v be a shared variable, $r = 0$ and $w = 64$ as defined in section 2.2, $A_i \in \{r, w\}$, and tid_i, $\overline{tid_i} \in \{1, 2\}$.

$$\begin{aligned}
[]! <> ((v == A_1 + tid_1)\&\& \\
X((v == A_2 + tid_2)U((v == A_3 + tid_3)\&\& \\
X((v == A_4 + tid_4)U(v == A_5 + tid_5)))))
\end{aligned} \tag{3.1}$$

$$\begin{aligned}
[]! <> ((v == A_1 + \overline{tid_1})\&\& \\
X((v == A_2 + \overline{tid_2})U((v == A_3 + \overline{tid_3})\&\& \\
X((v == A_4 + \overline{tid_4})U(v == A_5 + \overline{tid_5})))))
\end{aligned} \tag{3.2}$$

where "[]" denotes *Always*, "!" denotes *Logical Negation*, "<>" denotes *Eventually*, "X" denotes *Next* and "U" denotes *Until*. These formulas specify that the atomicity violation patterns do not occur.

Using Fig. 6 (2) as a concrete example, one formula in LTL is shown below:

$$\begin{aligned}
[]! <> ((v == w + 1)\&\& \\
X((v == r + 1)U((v == w + 2)\&\& \\
X((v == w + 2)U(v == r + 1)))))
\end{aligned} \tag{3.3}$$

$(v == w+2)U(v == r+1)$ is true if and only if $v == w+2$ holds until $v == r+1$ is true or simply $v == r + 1$ holds without $v == w + 2$ holds. This subformula captures $W_2^*R_1^+$ in which W_2^* means zero or more writing accesses from Thread 2, R_1^+ means one or more reading accesses from Thread 1. Furthermore, $(v == w + 2)\&\&X((v == w+2)U(v == r+1))$ captures $W_2^+R_1^+$ and $(v == r+1)U((v == w + 2)\&\&X((v == w + 2)U(v == r + 1)))$ reflects $R_1^*W_2^+R_1^+$. Therefore, (3.3) captures $[]! <> W_1R_1^*W_2^+R_1^+$ and ensures that pattern $W_1R_1^*W_2R_1^+$ in Fig. 6 (2) does not occur in the partial order thread model. The reason that the LTL formula contains W_2^+ instead of W_2 is that there can be synchronization events between W_2 and R_1^+, for each of those events, W_2 needs to hold.

4 Predictive Analysis of Atomicity Violation Using Model Checking

In this section, we discuss McPatom framework's general merits in terms of its soundness and completeness as well as specific ways in using Spin model checker [4] to show its applicability.

4.1 Soundness and Completeness of McPatom

An important feature of a prediction method is its capability to predict as many violations as possible. Since the majority of existing prediction methods uses an abstract model extracted from one interleaved execution at a time from a multi-thread program, a prediction method's capability rests on the quality of the abstract model built and its thoroughness in exploring the permissible traces in the abstract model. McPatom extracts the least constrained partial order thread model respecting the causal relation from the observed interleaved execution and uses model checking to explore all permissible traces in the partial order thread model.

Theorem 2. *McPatom ensures the completeness of its prediction - any possible atomicity violation involving a pair of threads accessing one shared variable in the partial order thread model can be detected.*

Proof sketch. McPatom encodes all possible atomicity violation patterns involving a pair of threads accessing one shared variable (Theorem 1) into linear time temporal logic formulas. McPatom uses model checking to exhaustively check whether any temporal logic formula fails in the partial order thread model. Thus none of possible atomicity violation will be undetected.

In general, McPatom cannot guarantee the soundness of its prediction, i.e., each predicted atomicity violation is covered by a feasible execution, since data-flow is ignored in the partial order thread model.

One major potential problem using model checking is the state explosion problem. Fortunately, the state explosion problem will not occur in atomicity violation prediction due to the following reasons (1) the partial order thread model (capturing only shared variable accesses and synchronization events) used for model checking is drastically smaller compared to the original multi-thread program, (2) each atomicity violation pattern to be checked involves only one shared variable, and (3) checking each atomicity violation pattern does not depend on the value of the shared variable. Another possible problem with model checking is the potential exponential number of possible interleavings due to the number of threads involved and the number of shared variable accesses. This problem is partially resolved (1) due to our focus on checking atomicity violations involving only two threads, (2) due to the constraints imposed by causal relations that drastically reduce the number of potential interleavings generated by the number of shared variable accesses, and (3) due to our implementation strategies of grouping all reading event sequences in each thread into atomic blocks in Spin to achieve partial order reductions and enforcing the wait/signal order of condition variables in the observed execution while exploring alternative interleavings. Our experiment results show very good performance using model checking.

4.2   Using Spin Model Checker to Find Atomicity Violation Traces

McPatom selects Spin model checker [4] based on its maturity, popularity, and capability. Spin is used to check every atomicity violation freedom property involving every pair of threads accessing every single shared variable one at a time in the partial order thread model extracted from a single interleaved trace recorded through instrumentation using Pin. Based on the partial order thread model encoded in Promela in section 2.2, and the atomicity violation freedom property encoded in LTL formulas in section 3.3, McPatom uses Spin to find atomicity violation traces or report no atomicity violations. Figure 7 gives an example of atomicity violation reported by Spin, which is mapped to real code in the original program.

```
70: proc  2 (t13) spin_av.pml:551 (state 28) [sharedvariable
    = (0+13)]
72: proc  3 (t48) spin_av.pml:591 (state 31) [sharedvariable
    = (64+48)]
76: proc  2 (t13) spin_av.pml:552 (state 29) [sharedvariable
    = (0+13)]
```

Fig. 7. A Sample of Atomicity Violation Trace Reported by Spin

Spin can be configured to search all errors or stop at the first error. McPatom chooses to stop at the first error, thus McPatom reports no atomicity violation if there exists no atomicity violation; when McPatom reports some atomicity violation traces, there may be additional atomicity violations not yet reported, which can be detected by re-running McPatom after grouping the previously reported violation related accesses into an atomic region so that it will not cause a new violation in the next run. For each shared variable and each pair of threads, an atomicity violation is recorded in a Spin trail file for each pattern if it exists. The Spin trail file can be simulated by Spin to give a clear view of those accesses involved in the atomicity violation, as shown in Fig. 7.

4.3   Mapping the Violations Reported in Spin to the Original Program

Atomicity violations reported in Spin, as shown in Fig. 7 as an example, are mapped to real code in original program. McPatom automatically identifies the related lines in Promela files, in which the comments of each line in Promela are

file names and line numbers of the corresponding source code. Figure 8 shows
the Promela code at the left and the corresponding real code at the right, for
the atomicity violation in Fig. 7.

```
sharedvar=0+13;  /*mod_log_config.c-1353*/  |if (len+buf->outcnt>LOG_BUFSIZE)
 sharedvar=64+48; /*mod_log_config.c-1373*/|    buf->outcnt += len;
sharedvar=0+13;  /*mod_log_config.c-1369*/  |s = &buf->outbuf[buf->outcnt]
```

Fig. 8. Promela code and the corresponding real code in the original program

5 Evaluation

We have used several real-world systems with known bugs listed in Table 1
(the issue numbers are the IDs in corresponding Bugzilla Databases) ([2],[9])
to examine our tool's bug prediction capability, as well as four programs [2]
without atomicity violations in SPLASH-2 parallel benchmark suite [10] to test
the accuracy of our tool (no false positives are reported).

Table 1. Bug List

Bug #	Program	Issue Number
1	Apache	25520
2	Apache	21287
3	Apache	21285
4	MySQL	644
5	MySQL	791
6	Mozilla-extract	Fig. 5

Table 2. Performance

	Program	Program Input	Trace Size (MB)	Time to Check (mins)	Number of Shared Variables	Number of Properties	Average Time per Property (secs)
1	fft	-p2 -m1024	4.3	304	3656	36560	0.499
2	fmm	Particles : 64 Processors : 2	10.8	183	1248	12480	0.88
3	lu	-p2 -n16	0.3	0.44	5	50	0.53
4	radix	-p2 -n10	3.7	328	3094	30940	0.636
5	Apache	2 concurrent httperf	9.4	15.68	151	3360	0.005

Table 3. Performance (Continue)

	Program	The Shared Variable with Maximum Number of Accesses		
		Number of Accesses	Maximum Number of States	Time to Check (secs)
1	fft	1041	3294	0.04
2	fmm	20064	9996	0.08
3	lu	282	941	0.02
4	radix	81	433	0.01
5	Apache	1415	16	less than 0.01

Bug Prediction Capability. McPatom has successfully predicted all the known bugs listed in Table 1, especially bug number 6 - an extraction of a real world atomicity violation bug reported in [9], which evades PSet [9] because this bug involves a set of last readers and the current reading access, and AVIO [2] because this bug involves more than three accesses.

Accuracy. We have chosen four programs (also used in [2]) without atomicity violations in SPLASH-2 parallel benchmark suite [10] to test whether McPatom produces violation predictions, which would certainly be false positives. Mc-Patom passed this test without reporting any violations.

Performance. Since McPatom framework uses model checking as the underlying atomicity violation prediction method and relies on a third party tool, Spin, to perform the model checking, it is extremely important to demonstrate the applicability of McPatom. We conducted the experiments[1] on a PC with dual core 2.33GHz CPU and 2GB memory. Performance data are given in Table 2 and Table 3, where time to check included automatically running Spin, compiling generated pan.c and model checking properties for all shared variables. There are ten properties to check for each pair of threads accessing a shared variable based on five violation patterns and their mutants. Apache program contains more than two threads and results in more properties to be checked. Instrumentation overhead was similar to that given in [2]. Table 3 shows the shared variable with maximum number of accesses in each program. From Table 2 and Table 3, it shows that the number of states does not explode when the number of accesses increases since checking the shared variable with maximum number of accesses took less than 0.01 seconds (not including the time to run Spin and compile generated pan.c) while checking any shared variable on average took 0.005 seconds. These preliminary experimental results are very encouraging and demonstrate the scalability of McPatom. These results also confirm our belief that although the total number of possible interleavings to check can explode quickly as the number of accesses increase; however, the number of actual interleavings are drastically smaller due to the constraints imposed by causal

---

[1] Data available at
http://users.cs.fiu.edu/~rzeng001/spin12/

relationships between threads. Other major reasons, which also vastly reduce the possible interleavings, are that McPatom takes advantage of the nature of atomicity violations and considers only a pair of threads and accesses to a single shared variable at one time, groups all reading event sequences in each thread into atomic blocks in Spin to achieve partial order reductions , and enforces the wait/signal order of condition variables in the observed execution while exploring alternative interleavings. Table 2 and Table 3 show that the experiment with Apache has even better performance than others, due to Apache's heavy use of condition variables. Since atomicity violations involving a single shared variable can be checked independently from violations involving other shared variables, we can significantly reduce the duration (not the cumulative time) of model checking by using multiple machines.

6 Related Works

There are many recent works on tackling atomicity violations. Some works proposed techniques to detect atomicity violations on actual program executions through testing [11] or runtime monitoring ([2], [12], and [13]). Other works developed methods to predict atomicity violations that may evade testing and runtime monitoring. In this section, we mention some recent works most relevant to ours on dynamically predicting atomicity violations. Most of these works share the following fundamental process: (1) instruments a multi-thread program P to record atomicity relevant events, (2) extracts a trace τ of atomicity relevant events from an interleaved execution σ of P, (3) projects trace τ into a partial order model M based on a causal relation defined on P, (4) explores various alternative trace τ' in M to predict potential atomicity violations in a possible corresponding interleaved execution σ' in P. Various methods and their supporting tools differ with regard to the strategies used in the above process.

How to abstract a partial order model M from a trace τ is critical. If the model is too restrictive, many feasible atomicity violations cannot be explored. If the model is too permissible, the prediction may not be sound, i.e. a predicted atomicity violation may not be a feasible interleaved execution of P. Penelope [14] ignores some causal relationships in building a partial order model and thus requires additional feasibility checking of a predicted atomicity violation. Fusion [6] abstracts a partial order model called concurrent trace program (CTP) that ignores the causal relation between different threads. Linearized atomicity violation traces in CTP are symbolically checked with additional order information from source codes to ensure their feasibility. In [15], a theoretical study was conducted to analyze the complexity of predicting atomicity violations, in which two simplified partial order models are considered. The first one ignores all synchronization and the second one only considers lock-based synchronization. It shows the tradeoffs between efficiency and accuracy. jPredictor [16] defines a partial order model based on a concept of sliced causality and lock-atomicity, which may predict some infeasible violations. Our work abstracts a partial order model respecting the causal relationships imposed by all synchronization constructs, but without considering data-flow, our work also may produce some infeasible violations.

A variety of techniques have been proposed to explore atomicity violation traces from an abstract partial order model. CTrigger [5] and Penelope [14] developed different algorithms to generate potential violation schedules and to prune away many infeasible ones. However these algorithms may report infeasible atomicity violation traces as well as miss feasible ones. jPredictor [16] uses model checking to exhaustively check a property in the partial order model and is capable to predict other concurrency bugs in addition to atomicity violations. Fusion [6] encodes the partial order model, the source program, and three access atomicity violation patterns into a logic formula; and uses a satisfiability modulo theory solver to check the feasible interleavings for atomicity violations. Our work converts the partial order model into a Promela program, defines a complete set of atomicity violation patterns as temporal logic formulas, and then uses Spin model checker to produce atomicity violation traces.

7   Conclusion

Concurrency bugs are extremely hard to detect using testing techniques due to huge interleaving space. This paper presents a tool McPatom using model checking to predict atomicity violation concurrency bugs. McPatom is powerful and can explore a vast interleaving space of a multi-thread program based on a small set of instrumented test runs. McPatom is applicable to large real-world systems.

McPatom focuses on atomicity violations involving each single shared variable, and thus cannot find atomicity violations involving multiple variables. Another limitation is that redundant model checking may be performed if two recorded interleaved traces yield the same partial order thread model.

Acknowledgement. This work was partially supported by the NSF of U.S. under award HRD-0833093.

References

1. Poulsen, K.: Software bug contributed to blackout (2004), http://www.securityfocus.com/news/8016 (Online accessed July 16, 2011)
2. Lu, S., Tucek, J., Qin, F., Zhou, Y.: AVIO: detecting atomicity violations via access interleaving invariants. In: Proceedings of the 12th International Conference on Architectural Support for Programming Languages and Operating Systems, ASPLOS 2006, San Jose, CA, USA, pp. 37–48 (2006)
3. Luk, C., Cohn, R., Muth, R., Patil, H., Klauser, A., Lowney, G., Wallace, S., Reddi, V.J., Hazelwood, K.: Pin: building customized program analysis tools with dynamic instrumentation. In: The 2005 ACM Conference on Programming Language Design and Implementation, PLDI 2005, Chicago, IL, USA, pp. 190–200 (2005)
4. Holzmann, G.: The Spin Model Checker: Primer and Reference Manual. Addison-Wesley Professional (2003)

5. Lu, S., Park, S., Zhou, Y.: Finding Atomicity-Violation bugs through unserializable interleaving testing. IEEE Transactions on Software Engineering PP(99), 1 (2011)
6. Wang, C., Limaye, R., Ganai, M., Gupta, A.: Trace-Based Symbolic Analysis for Atomicity Violations. In: Esparza, J., Majumdar, R. (eds.) TACAS 2010. LNCS, vol. 6015, pp. 328–342. Springer, Heidelberg (2010)
7. Lamport, L.: Time, clocks, and the ordering of events in a distributed system. Communications of the ACM 21(7), 558–565 (1978)
8. Bernstein, P.A., Hadzilacos, V., Goodman, N.: Concurrency control and recovery in database systems, vol. 5. Addison-Wesley, New York (1987)
9. Yu, J., Narayanasamy, S.: A case for an interleaving constrained shared-memory multi-processor. In: Proceedings of the 36th International Symposium on Computer Architecture, ISCA 2009, Austin, TX, USA, pp. 325–336 (2009)
10. Woo, S.C., Ohara, M., Torrie, E., Singh, J.P., Gupta, A.: The SPLASH-2 programs: characterization and methodological considerations. In: Proceedings of the 22nd International Symposium on Computer Architecture, ISCA 1995, Madison, WI, USA, pp. 24–36 (1995)
11. Musuvathi, M., Qadeer, S., Ball, T., Basler, G., Nainar, P.A., Neamtiu, I.: Finding and reproducing heisenbugs in concurrent programs. In: Proceedings of the 8th USENIX Conference on Operating Systems Design and Implementation, OSDI 2008, San Diego, CA, USA, pp. 267–280 (2008)
12. Flanagan, C., Freund, S.N., Yi, J.: Velodrome: a sound and complete dynamic atomicity checker for multithreaded programs. In: Proceedings of the 2008 ACM SIGPLAN Conference on Programming Language Design and Implementation, PLDI 2008, Tucson, AZ, USA, pp. 293–303 (2008)
13. Wang, L., Stoller, S.D.: Runtime analysis of atomicity for multithreaded programs. IEEE Transactions on Software Engineering 32, 93–110 (2006)
14. Sorrentino, F., Farzan, A., Madhusudan, P.: Penelope: weaving threads to expose atomicity violations. In: Proceedings of the 18th ACM SIGSOFT International Symposium on Foundations of Software Engineering, FSE 2010, Santa Fe, NM, USA, pp. 37–46 (2010)
15. Farzan, A., Madhusudan, P.: The Complexity of Predicting Atomicity Violations. In: Kowalewski, S., Philippou, A. (eds.) TACAS 2009. LNCS, vol. 5505, pp. 155–169. Springer, Heidelberg (2009)
16. Chen, F., Serbanuta, T.F., Rosu, G.: jPredictor: a predictive runtime analysis tool for java. In: Proceedings of the 30th International Conference on Software Engineering, ICSE 2008, Leipzig, Germany, pp. 221–230 (2008)

Parameterized Model Checking of Fine Grained Concurrency

Divjyot Sethi[1], Muralidhar Talupur[2],
Daniel Schwartz-Narbonne[1], and Sharad Malik[1]

[1] Princeton University
[2] Strategic CAD Labs,
Intel Corporation

Abstract. Concurrent data structures are provided in libraries such as Intel Thread Building Blocks and Java.util.concurrent to enable efficient implementation of multi-threaded programs. Their efficiency is achieved by using fine grained synchronization which creates less constrained interaction between the threads. This leads to a large number of possible interleavings and makes concurrent data structures hard to verify. In this paper, we describe our key insights from Murphi based parameterized model checking of these data structures. In particular, we describe the first model checking based framework to handle an unbounded number of threads for these data structures. This framework uses the CMP (CoMPositional) method which has been used in verifying cache coherence protocols. The CMP method requires the user to supply lemmas for abstraction refinement. A further contribution of our work is to show how a significant subset of these lemmas can be generated automatically.

1 Introduction

Concurrent data structures are provided in libraries such as Intel Thread Building Blocks [18] and Java.util.concurrent (JSR-166 [12]) to enable efficient implementation of multi-threaded programs. The efficiency of these data structures is achieved by either making them lock free or by using fine grained synchronization between the threads, i.e., by locking parts of the data structure instead of locking the entire data structure while making updates. This results in less constrained interaction between the threads and thus increases the number of possible interleavings. The large number of possible interleavings make these data structures highly error prone, as exemplified by bugs witnessed in published algorithms [16].

Given the large number of possible interleavings, model checking these data structures is non-trivial. Consequently, existing model checking based efforts [3, 23–25] address the verification of concurrent data structures for only a small number of threads. This motivated our work on model checking these data structures for an unbounded number of threads by applying parameterized model checking techniques. In particular, we leverage the CMP (CoMPositional) method [4], a parameterized verification technique which enables verifying correctness of a system with unbounded number of threads by constructing an abstract model

A. Donaldson and D. Parker (Eds.): SPIN 2012, LNCS 7385, pp. 208–226, 2012.

which consists of only a small number of threads and an environment thread. This technique has been successfully used in verifying message passing systems like cache coherence protocols [17, 19]. The CMP method is discussed below:

1.1 The CMP Method

The CMP method is used to verify symmetric parameterized systems. A symmetric parameterized system, $P(N)$, consists of N identical threads with ids $1..N$. The properties which we verify on these systems using the CMP method are candidate invariants of the form $\forall i \in [1..N].\Phi(i)$, where $\Phi(i)$ is a propositional logic formula on the variables of thread i and shared variables. The CMP method first constructs an abstract model which consists of one thread from the original system (say thread 1 since the system is symmetric) and an abstract thread (named *Other*) that over-approximates the remaining threads (the environment). Then, if the property $\Phi(1)$ holds on thread 1 in the abstract model, $\forall i \in [1..N].\Phi(i)$ holds for $P(N)$ by symmetry. The verification of the abstract model is done by using a model checker (in our case Murphi).

Since the constructed abstract model is an over approximation, the model checker may report spurious counterexamples. In order to remove these counterexamples, the user needs to refine the model by coming up with candidate lemmas which constrain the abstraction.

While the CMP method requires human guidance in the form of supplying candidate lemmas, it essentially uses a model checker as an assistant and transfers most of the proof burden to it. The key difference between the CMP method and theorem proving based techniques then is that the former leverages a model checker. Thus, the lemmas supplied to the CMP method need not be inductive. Theorem proving techniques on the other hand require that all the invariants together with the properties under check be inductive. Further, in practice far fewer lemmas have to be supplied while using the CMP method [19]. The CMP method has been successfully used to verify large scale industrial cache coherence protocols which are significantly larger than the distributed protocols handled by pure theorem proving methods [17].

Mining Candidate Lemmas. To reduce the manual effort of supplying candidate lemmas on the user and to accelerate the proof convergence, we show how several of the candidate lemmas required to refine the abstract model can be mined from the execution trace of a single thread. We use Daikon [6] for this purpose. Daikon takes in program execution traces and infers a collection of candidate invariants for the program that are based on invariant templates. Note that while the candidate lemmas generated using Daikon might be false, the CMP method also checks the lemmas used. Any false candidates are eliminated without affecting the soundness of the proof [11]. It is this feature of the CMP method that allows us to use an off-the-shelf invariant generator without compromising soundness.

1.2   Framework Description

The experimental framework which we use is shown in Figure 1. The input data structure encoded in Murphi (discussed in Section 2) is first augmented by Daikon generated candidate lemmas. These candidate lemmas are generated by analyzing the trace of a single thread (discussed in Section 4). The augmented model then enters the CMP loop (discussed in Section 3). In the CMP loop, the model is automatically abstracted by using the tool *Abster* [19]. Then, in case a proof of correctness or a real counterexample is found, the loop finishes. In case a spurious counterexample is found, the model is updated by either adding more lemmas to or by removing previously added (incorrect) lemmas from the original program, and then re-abstracting the program. This approach is shown in Figure 1 and detailed in Section 3. While lemmas are added to refine the model, the CMP method does not provide any formal guarantees for the eventual termination of the loop. In practice the number of extra lemmas required to be added were reduced due to the initial addition of Daikon generated lemmas (detailed in Section 5).

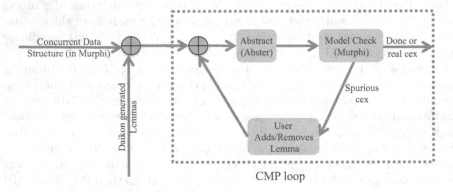

Fig. 1. The Experimental Framework

1.3   Main Contributions

Through this case study of applying the CMP method to verify concurrent data structures, we make the following contributions:

- *Unbounded threads*: We show how concurrent list based set data structures with an unbounded number of threads accessing them can be model checked by the CMP method. Further, these data structures allocate memory dynamically which leads to subtle issues causing a memory usage blowup as the number of threads accessing the data structure increase. We show how the CMP method addresses this.
- *Mining candidate lemmas*: We show how the burden of supplying candidate lemmas to the CMP method can be reduced by mining a significant subset of these lemmas automatically by analyzing the execution trace of a single thread. We use the invariant generator Daikon for this.

- *Experiments*: We describe our insights in verifying several well known concurrent data structures: *Fine-grained, Lock Free* [7,15], *Optimistic* and *Lazy* [8] list based sets. We were also able to find the error in a known buggy version of the *Lock Free* list based set algorithm. Finally, we also describe the particular candidate lemmas we added in detail.

Limitations (1)We assume that the size of the data structure is fixed. We believe that this CMP method based approach, which handles unbounded number of threads, can be extended to handle unbounded sized data structures as well, by using an appropriate finite abstraction for the data structure. (2) Daikon generates invariants by using invariant templates to determine the structure of the invariant. These templates are provided by the user. While user-supplied, these templates were the same for the class of algorithms we verified, thus reducing the burden of creating them.

1.4   Related Work

Verification of concurrent data structures has received significant attention lately [1–3,5,20,21,23–25]. These verification efforts can be broadly classified as manual, model checking based and separation logic based, as detailed below:

Manual: Vafeiadis et al. [21] verified concurrent data structures using a mechanical proof assistant. They specified the interference between concurrent threads using rely and guarantee conditions. They were not able to handle the *Lazy* algorithm. In [5] Colvin et al. proposed using a forward-backward simulation based approach for the *Lazy* algorithm. These approaches allow both an arbitrary number of accessing threads and an arbitrary number of elements but they are manual effort intensive. Our approach, on the other hand, aims for increased automation by leveraging model checkers. Our framework is also able to handle the *Lazy* algorithm.

Model checking based: Vechev et al. [23] describe their experience with verifying Linearizability using the SPIN model checker. While this approach handles algorithms with unknown linearization points, they do not scale to more than a small number of threads and a small list size. Similarly, Zhang et al. [24,25] and Liu et al. [13] used model checking to verify concurrent data structures. They used a naive refinement based approach which does not scale to more than a small number of threads and list size. A different approach is taken by Alur et al. [3]: they treat a list as a string and the thread as an automaton and then derive conditions on the automaton to prove decidability of Linearizability for lists of arbitrary length. The key focus of their work is on decidability instead of scalability; hence they too do not scale to more than 2-3 threads. In contrast, our method is able to handle an unbounded number of threads.

Separation logic based: Verification approaches have been developed for programs specified in RGSep, a logic which combines separation logic with rely-guarantee reasoning [2,20,22]. While their approach is automatic for a subset of

RGSep, the designer still needs to specify concurrent actions which model the inter-thread interference, just like in rely-guarantee reasoning, for proving assertions. Further, this approach requires the designer to have an understanding of RGSep. In contrast, our tool requires the user to specify candidate lemmas, which are propositional logic formulas. Further, the CMP method automatically checks the candidate lemmas as well, so any false lemmas will be weeded out.

2   Encoding Concurrent Data Structures as Parameterized Systems

In this section, we describe how to encode a concurrent data structure as a Murphi model.

We model a concurrent data structure as a program P with N identical threads with ids $1..N$, where N is arbitrary but fixed. Each thread i has a set of l finite local variables L_i. There is also a set of s finite shared variables S. The domain of these variables is independent of N, with the exception of the locks, which also store the thread id information, as discussed in Section 2.2.

The action (in this paper we assume that every line in the pseudocode corresponds to an action) of each thread i is modeled as a *rule* of the form $\rho \Rightarrow a$, where ρ is the guard over variables in $L_i \cup S$ and the action a is a set of assignments to variables in $L_i \cup S$. Further, instead of writing out rules that are identical modulo thread ids or list node ids, we use quantified rules (called *Rulesets* in Murphi language). For instance, we can write

> **Ruleset** $i : Thread$; $p : node$
>   **Rule** $(\rho) \Rightarrow$ **Begin**
> a;
>   **End**; to represent the set of rules obtained by plugging in all possible values

of i and p in the rule $\rho \Rightarrow a$.

The semantics of this guarded-command format are straight-forward: at every time step, the guards of all the rules are checked to see which of the rules are enabled. The Murphi model checker then non-deterministically picks an enabled rule and fires it. Since each thread i has a separate set of rules, the multi-threaded execution follows interleaving semantics.

2.1   Running Example: *Lazy* List Based Concurrent Set

We demonstrate our approach on a concurrent data structure implementing a standard set interface, with *Add*, *Remove* and *Contains* methods. These methods have semantics expected of a standard sequential set *SeqSet* (Figure 2).

Our example follows the *Lazy* list based concurrent set data structure (or *Lazy* set for brevity) defined in [21]. The underlying representation of the *Lazy* set is a linked list, which stores the elements of the set in a (strictly) increasing order with each *node* of the linked list having the following fields: 1) a *key* holding the element's value, 2) a *next* pointer for accessing the next node in the list 3) a

$$SeqContains(e): \quad \{SeqResult := e \in SeqSet;$$
$$return\ SeqResult;\}$$
$$SeqAdd(e): \qquad \{SeqResult := e \notin SeqSet;$$
$$SeqSet := SeqSet \cup e;$$
$$return\ SeqResult;\}$$
$$SeqRemove(e): \quad \{SeqResult := e \in SeqSet;$$
$$SeqSet := SeqSet \setminus e;$$
$$return\ SeqResult;\}$$

Fig. 2. Methods of the sequential set *SeqSet*

marked bit to indicate if the node is a part of the set or not, and 4) a *lock* field representing whether that node is currently locked. In addition, there are two special nodes, the first node *Head* and the last node *Tail*, that can neither be added nor be removed. All the nodes that are reachable from *Head* and do not have the *marked* bit set are considered part of the set, denoted by *ConcSet*.

As shown in Figure 3, the methods of this data structure traverse the linked list using pointers *curr* and *pred* which are local to the methods. For the *Add* method, the local pointer *entry* is used to store the address of the newly allocated node being added to the list. For the *Remove* method, this pointer is used to store the value of the *next* field of the *curr* pointer while removing the node pointed by *curr*. Note that in this work, we assume that each numbered line of the pseudocode shown in Figure 3 executes atomically.

Verifying Correctness. *Linearizability* [10] is the widely accepted correctness criterion for concurrent data structures. Intuitively, Linearizability implies that the execution of every access method for the concurrent data structure appears to occur at some point, the *linearization point*, between the invocation and the response of the method. The linearization points for the *Lazy* set are marked with a ∗ in Figure 3.

As described in [21], Linearizability can be proved by using a refinement based approach. Thus, the Linearizability of the algorithm is established by comparing the results of the concurrent access methods against the results of the access methods of the sequential set, *SeqSet*, with access methods shown in Figure 2. This comparison is done by embedding the calls to *SeqSet* in the implementation at the linearization point. For instance, the linearization point for *Remove* in case the call is successful is marked with [*SeqRemove(key)] on Line 3 in Figure 3d. Similarly, [*SeqRemove(key)] on Line 8 denotes the linearization point in the failing case. If the results returned by concurrent methods and the embedded sequential methods match, the concurrent data structure is Linearizable. Formally, for each $Method \in \{Add, Remove, Contains\}$, we check that $Method(key) \Leftrightarrow SeqMethod(key)$.

Further, to check if *ConcSet* refines *SeqSet*, we also check if their contents match; i.e. $\forall v.v \in SeqSet \Leftrightarrow v \in ConcSet$ holds at all times.

The *Contains* method needs special treatment, because its linearization point depends on the return value of the method. If the element is found in the set, the *Contains* method is linearized at Line 5 in Figure 3a. If the item is not in

```
Contains (key)
 1: node curr := Head;
 2: while (curr.key < key)
 3:     curr := curr.next;
 4: if (curr.key = key &
 5:     !curr.marked) then
              [*SeqContains(key)]
 6:     return true;
 7: else
 8:     return false;
                (a)
```

```
Add (key)
 1: node pred, curr := Locate (key);
 2: if (curr.key ≠ key) then
 3:     entry := new node();
 4:     entry.key := key;
 5:     entry.next := curr;
 6:     pred.next := entry;
              [*SeqAdd(key)]
 7:     result := true;
 8: else
 9:     result := false;
              [*SeqAdd(key)]
10: pred.unlock();
11: curr.unlock();
12: return result;
                (b)
```

```
Locate (key)
 1: while (true)
 2:     pred := Head;
 3:     curr := pred.next;
 4:     while (curr.key < key)
 5:         pred := curr;
 6:         curr := curr.next;
 7:     pred.lock();
 8:     curr.lock();
 9:     if (!pred.marked &
10:        !curr.marked &
11:        pred.next = curr) then
12:         return pred, curr;
13:     else
14:         pred.unlock();
15:         curr.unlock();
                (c)
```

```
Remove (key)
 1: node pred, curr := Locate (key);
 2: if (curr.key = key) then
 3:     curr.marked := true;
              [*SeqRemove(key)]
 4:     entry := curr.next;
 5:     pred.next := entry;
 6:     result := true;
 7: else
 8:     result := false;
              [*SeqRemove(key)]
 9: pred.unlock();
10: curr.unlock();
11: return result;
                (d)
```

Fig. 3. Pseudo-code for linked list based *Lazy* set algorithm. The linearization points are marked with a *.

the set, however, the linearization point is dependent on the history and cannot be statically determined. To prove Linearizability for this case, we proceed as follows: for every invocation of *Contains* such that it returns *false*, we need to determine a point between the invocation and response points such that a call to *SeqContains* also returns *false*. In other words, find a point where the abstract set *SeqSet* does not contain the element sought, say v. If for some invocation, no such point is found then the *Contains* method is not Linearizable.

To check if such a point exists is simple: we keep a history variable aux_v that is set to *false* initially when *Contains(v)* is invoked. If at any point the *SeqSet* does not contain v then aux_v is updated to *true*. Then, when *Contains(v)* returns *false* we just have to check if aux_v is *true* or not. Thus, by checking the candidate invariant $(Contains(v) = false) \Rightarrow aux_v$, we can determine the Linearizability of *Contains*.

2.2   Encoding the *Lazy* Set in Murphi

The state space of the *Lazy* set can be encoded in Murphi as follows. The shared state consists of the linked list and the *SeqSet* which can be encoded as the shared variables S. In particular, the linked list is stored as an array *list* of *nodes* (which are essentially structs). Each *node* holds records with fields *next, marked, key* and *lock*, which correspond to the fields of the *node* discussed in Section 2.1. We encode locks such that they store both their state (locked/unlocked) as well as the thread id of the lock owner.

The local state of each thread which needs to be encoded consists of the variables *curr*, *pred* and *entry*, as shown in Figure 3. We encode these local variables as arrays with domain as thread id, $[1..N]$ and range from 0 to an upper fixed value T. (T corresponds to memory size and is chosen by the user.) Thus, $curr[i]$, $pred[i]$ and $entry[i]$ store the corresponding local variables for thread i. Then, $list[curr[i]].key$ (or $curr[i].key$ for brevity) is the value of the *key* of the node pointed by the *curr* pointer in thread i. Further, in order to do the refinement proof, we need a mechanism to store the result of the call to the access method of *SeqSet* embedded at the linearization point. We store this in *Seqresult[i]* for thread i, as shown in Figure 4.

Figure 4 shows the Murphi encoding of the *Remove* method for thread i. (Due to space restrictions, we do not show the encoding of the entire algorithm.) Each rule in the figure corresponds to a statement of the *Remove* method in Figure 3d. In order to enforce the sequential order of the statements, we added the local variable $pc[i]$. This variable serves as a local program counter and is used in the guards of the rules. The code executes in sequential order starting from top left rule ($pc = 1$) to the bottom right rule ($pc = 11$).

Since the concurrent algorithm needs to be proved correct for an arbitrary set of calls to its interface functions, we encode the threads accessing the data structure such that it non-determinstically selects a *key*, and a method (*Add, Remove* or *Contains*) for execution. It then executes the method on the *key* and then restarts after finishing execution.

```
Ruleset i : Thread
Rule (pc[i] = 1) ⇒ Begin
    pred[i], curr[i] :=
    Locate(key); ¹
    pc[i] + +;
End;

Ruleset i : Thread
Rule (pc[i] = 2) ⇒ Begin
    if (curr[i].key = key)
    then pc[i] + +;
    else pc[i] = 7;
End;

Ruleset i : Thread; Ncurr : node;
Rule (pc[i] = 3
  & Ncurr = curr[i]) ⇒ Begin
    Ncurr.marked := true;
    pc[i] + +;
    Seqresult[i] :=
    SeqRemove(key);
End;

Ruleset i : Thread; Ncurr : node
Rule (pc[i] = 4) ⇒ Begin
    entry[i] := curr[i].next; pc[i] + +;
End;

Ruleset i : Thread; Npred : node
Rule (pc[i] = 5 & Npred = pred[i]
    & Nentry = entry[i]) ⇒ Begin
    Npred.next := Nentry; pc[i] + +;
End;
```

```
Ruleset i : Thread
Rule (pc[i] = 6) ⇒ Begin
    result[i] := true;
    pc[i] := pc[i] + 2;
End;

Ruleset i : Thread
Rule (pc[i] = 7) ⇒ Begin
    [else] pc[i] + +;
End;

Ruleset i : Thread
Rule (pc[i] = 8) ⇒ Begin
    result[i] := false; pc[i] + +;
End;

Ruleset i : Thread; Npred : node;
Rule (pc[i] = 9 &
Npred = pred[i]) ⇒ Begin
    Npred.unlock(i); pc[i] + +;
End;

Ruleset i : Thread; Ncurr : node
Rule (pc[i] = 10 &
Ncurr = curr[i]) ⇒ Begin
    Ncurr.unlock(i); pc[i] + +;
End;

Ruleset i : Thread
Rule (pc[i] = 11) ⇒ Begin
    return result[i];
End;
```

Fig. 4. Murphi model for method *Remove* for thread i: each rule corresponds to a line in the *Remove* method shown in Figure 3.

---

[1] The method *Locate* is shown in pseudocode format in Figure 3.

Memory Allocation/Garbage Collection. The *Lazy* set allocates new nodes when it adds elements and removes references when it removes elements. This requires allocation and potential deallocation of memory.

We encode the memory as an array of size T of shared variables (i.e. list nodes) in the Murphi model. This memory size T is chosen by the user. For a given number of set elements, we can check if the memory of size T is sufficient to model the algorithm or not: if memory is insufficient, a memory allocation error will occur when the *Add* method tries to allocate a new node.

It is non-trivial to manually manage the memory for this algorithm by deleting nodes which are removed. This is because another thread might be accessing the node removed by the *Remove* method, making deletion of the node at the time of removal incorrect [23]. This makes the implementation of a garbage collector essential.

Since Murphi does not provide support for dynamic memory management, we implemented the garbage collector as a function which is called when a new list node is allocated. The function returns *true* if it finds a list node in the memory array which has no references to it. This function can count the references since it has global access to the pointers of all the threads in the model.

Specifying Linearizability. As discussed in Section 2.1, we need to check $Method(key) \Leftrightarrow SeqMethod(key)$, where *Method* is *Add*, *Remove* or *Contains*. Then, the condition (i.e. candidate invariant) to check Linearizability in the Murphi encoding is:

$$\forall i \in [1..N].Seqresult[i] = result[i].$$

The above condition involves variables of a single thread i, universally quantified over all threads. Similarly, the other properties which need to be checked can be specified either as a formula of the above form or as a propositional logic formula on the shared state. As discussed in Section 3, this structure is essential for constructing the CMP abstraction.

3 Parameterized Model Checking Using the CMP Method

In this section we describe the CMP method and then show how it applies to the *Lazy* set.

Given a symmetric parameterized system $P(N)$ with threads $1..N$ and a property involving a small constant number c of threads, the CMP method first constructs a finite abstract model that can be checked using a model checker. The abstraction typically used, called *data type reduction* [14], keeps c threads unchanged and creates one abstract thread *Other* representing threads $[c+1..N]$. The abstraction operation involved in constructing *Other* is syntactic and fast: it essentially involves throwing away all the state variables of threads $[c+1..N]$ and over-approximating expressions involving them. To do the abstraction syntactically, the first step is to reduce the domains of all state variables holding array indices from $[1..N]$ to $[1..c]$. Next, in the Murphi program, thread indices $c+1..N$ are replaced with o (which is the id we use for the *Other* thread) wherever they appear. For instance an expression $pc[i] = 8$ for $i \in [c+1..N]$ reduces to $pc[o] = 8$. Consequently, since the *Other* thread has no state, $pc[o]$ becomes meaningless and so $pc[o] = 8$ is replaced by *true* or *false* (depending on which replacement leads to an over-abstraction). This syntactic abstraction operation is implemented in *Abster* [19].

Since the abstract thread *Other* is completely unconstrained, model checking the abstract model may lead to spurious counterexamples. If this happens, the user refines the system by adding candidate lemmas which are conjoined to the guards of the rules. Formally, suppose that the candidate lemma L is used. Now consider a rule r of the program P defined as: $\rho \Rightarrow a$. Then, refining P with L involves changing this rule to $\rho \wedge L \Rightarrow a$ and then re-abstracting the new program with the new rule obtained. Observe that in this refinement approach, no extra state gets added to the abstract model. This is important for the efficiency of the CMP method based verification. The abstraction refinement procedure is also explained through an example in Section 3.1.

If this refined system passes the model checker, the property is proven. If, on the other hand, there is another counterexample for the refined system, the user must distinguish between three possible cases by examining the counterexample. 1) The counterexample is valid. 2) The counterexample is not valid and the candidate lemma is correct, in which case further refinement is required. 3) The counterexample is not valid and a candidate lemma is incorrect, in which case the incorrect candidate lemma must be removed or modified.

A useful heuristic for determining if the counterexample is due to an incorrect candidate lemma is that it fails for the (concrete) system with a small number of threads (one or two for the data structures we verified). This can either be detected by manual examination of the system (for concurrent data structures we verified, manual examination was sufficient due to relatively short counterexamples). Or, this may also be done by model checking the candidate lemma on the system for a small number of threads. (Before manual examination, we model checked all the lemmas for a model with a single thread.)

One key advantage of the CMP method is that the candidate lemmas used for strengthening are also checked during the process and any false candidate lemma that is added will be detected by the model checker [11]. This guarantees that the refinement step does not affect the soundness of the proof.

3.1   Verifying the *Lazy* Set Algorithm

Linearizability for the *Lazy* set can be specified as a propositional formula over a single thread (and so has $c = 1$), as discussed in Section 2.2. The abstracted system therefore contains the rules from the concrete thread shown in Figure 4 as well as the rules from the abstract thread as shown in Figure 5.

To understand the abstraction in detail, consider the rule from the concrete thread i for $pc = 5$:

% For pc = 3
Ruleset *Ncurr* : *node*
Rule (*true*) ⇒ Begin
  Ncurr.marked := *true*;
    SeqRemove(key);
End;

% For pc = 5
Ruleset *Npred* : *node*;
  Nentry : *node*
Rule (*true*) ⇒ Begin
  Npred.next := *Nentry*;
End;

% For pc = 9
Ruleset *Npred* : *node*
Rule (*true*) ⇒ Begin
  Npred.unlock(o);
End;

% For pc = 10
Ruleset *Ncurr* : *node*
Rule (*true*) ⇒ Begin
  Ncurr.unlock(o);
End;

% For pc = 1,2,4,6,7,8,11
Ruleset
Rule (*true*) ⇒ Begin
  no-op
End;

Fig. 5. Abstracted thread for *Remove* method

Ruleset *i* : *Thread*; *Npred, Nentry* : *node*;
  Rule (*pc*[*i*] = 5 & *NPred* = *pred*[*i*] & *Nentry* = *entry*[*i*]) ⇒ Begin
    Npred.next := *Nentry*; *pc*[*i*] + +;
  End;

For thread 1 this ruleset will be preserved as it is. But for the *Other* thread
the ruleset will be abstracted to

Ruleset *Npred, Nentry* : *node*;
  Rule (*true*) ⇒ Begin
    Npred.next := *Nentry*;
  End;

This is because expressions $pc[i] = 5$, $Npred = pred[i].next$ and $Nentry = entry[i]$ will be conservatively over-approximated to *true*. Similarly, the assignment $pc[i] + +$ becomes a *no-op*. Since i no longer appears in the body of the ruleset, it can be dropped from the ruleset quantifiers as well. A model constructed in this way is an abstraction of the original system.

The above abstract rule is highly unconstrained and so may lead to spurious counterexamples. It can, for example, pick an arbitrary node in the linked list and set its *next* field to another arbitrary node. The next step in the CMP method is refinement of the abstract model using lemmas. One lemma that the user can add is that $entry[i]$ is the successor of $curr[i]$ which is the successor of $pred[i]$. This lemma can be expressed as $pred[i].next = curr[i]$ & $curr[i].next = entry[i]$, or in terms of ruleset $Npred.next = Ncurr$ & $Ncurr.next = Nentry$. Thus, the *strengthened* ruleset is now:

Ruleset $i : Thread$; $Npred, Nentry, Ncurr : node$
    Rule $(pc[i] = 5$ & $Npred = pred[i]$ & $Nentry = entry[i]$ & $Ncurr = curr[i]$
& $Npred.next = Ncurr$ & $Ncurr.next = Nentry)$ $\Rightarrow$ Begin
       $Npred.next := Nentry$; $pc[i] + +$;
    End;

Re-abstracting this strengthened rule leads to the abstract rule below which is more constrained than before, thus ruling out some spurious behaviors.

Ruleset $Npred, Nentry, Ncurr : node$
    Rule $(true$ & $Npred.next = Ncurr$ & $Ncurr.next = Nentry)$ $\Rightarrow$ Begin
       $Npred.next := Nentry$;
    End;

Observe that the above candidate lemma reflects the sequential behavior of the *Remove* method: it expresses the relationship between *pred*, *curr* and *entry* variables which is easily inferred if the sequential behavior of the thread is analyzed.

Finally, note that in the above rules, $Ncurr.next$ is used instead of using $curr[i].next$. This is because using $curr[i].next$ hides the fact that it is a shared variable (accessed by local pointer $curr[i]$) and not a local variable. This can cause the abstraction tool *Abster* to go astray as it operates purely syntactically.

Bounding Memory Usage Blowup. In the concrete model, as the number of threads increase, the number of memory nodes which may have been removed by some *Remove* method but are still referenced by some other *Contains* method may also increase rapidly. These nodes cannot be garbage collected as they are not unreferenced. This is a challenge for model checking since the system state for such algorithms can grow quickly with increasing number of threads. A model with only 2 threads accessing set with at most 2 elements can require as many as 10 nodes [23].

In the CMP abstraction, since the local pointers of the abstract thread are thrown away, a node in the abstract model can only have references from the concrete thread. This naturally bounds the number of nodes which may have been removed from the list and cannot be garbage collected to three (one potentially for *curr*, one for *pred* and one for *entry*), solving the memory usage blowup problem.

4   Automatic Generation of Candidate Lemmas

As discussed in Section 3, a parameterized model may initially be too abstract to prove the desired properties. In this case, candidate lemmas must be added to constrain the model. This step often requires human effort and expertise.

However, since the CMP method is sound and checks candidate lemmas for correctness, candidate lemmas can be mined from the execution traces. We used Daikon [6] for this purpose. Daikon learns invariants from execution traces, which we generated by sequentially executing one thread. The form of the lemmas learnt by Daikon depends on the templates it uses. For example, we discovered that templates which compared variables with constants tended to produce false candidate lemmas. This is because these lemmas are learnt from a single trace and did not generalize to other traces that well. On the other hand, templates which included comparison of integer variables and checking for equality, tended to produce good candidate lemmas, and were therefore used in all following experiments. The templates can be tuned to infer additional lemmas which had to be manually added. *Tuning of templates is a way of adding domain knowledge and thus speeding up verification of similar algorithms.*

Since the front end of Daikon does not accept Murphi, we used Java implementations of the code available at the accompanying website of [9]. While this adds to the mechanical burden of running a tool on a different front end, this does not affect the soundness of our approach: if Daikon finds wrong lemmas or we make a mistake while translating them back to Murphi, the CMP method will still catch this. We plan to automate this step in the future.

5   Experiments

We verified the *Fine-grained*, *Optimistic*, *Lazy* and *Lock Free* algorithms presented in [9] using our framework. These algorithms are briefly described below:

***Fine-grained* Set:** The *Fine-grained* set uses hand-in-hand locking for traversing the list: the thread traversing the list releases the lock on a node only when it has locked the successor. Finally, during addition or removal of a node to the list, the thread keeps the two successive vertices locked.

***Optimistic* Set:** Since hand-in-hand locking uses locks to traverse the list, it creates contention between threads. The *Optimistic* algorithm reduces this contention by traversing the list without locking. For correctness, on finding the location to add or remove a node, the thread locks the nodes and then validates that the node it locked is reachable from the *Head* node by re-traversing the list.

***Lazy* Set:** The *Optimistic* algorithm re-traverses the list to validate the node it locked: the *Lazy* implementation eliminates this overhead by maintaining a *marked* field in each node. The algorithm maintains the invariant that an unmarked node is reachable from *Head*. Another advantage of having the *marked* field is that the *Contains* method no longer needs to acquire a lock.

***Lock Free* Set:** The *Lock Free* implementation eliminates the usage of lock and uses *compare and swap* instead for synchronization. This implementation also uses a *marked* field like the *Lazy* algorithm; we refer the reader to [9] for further details.

The linearization points for most of the methods considered in this paper are known. When they are not known, we use the *aux* variable approach described in Section 2.1. Further, the *ConcSet* for all these algorithms is the set of nodes reachable from *Head*, except for *Lazy* and *Lock Free* where the nodes have to be unmarked as well.

Performance. For our experiments, we used a 4-core, 2.4 GHz Intel processor with 3.7 GB RAM. Figure 6 shows the model checking results. In the figure, the number of items represent the number of elements in the set and the number of list nodes represent the list size in the implementation. We model checked the correctness (Linearizability) of the implementation for a maximum of two items in the set. Note that the number of items does not include the *Head*, *Tail* and memory leak nodes. For example, for the *Lock Free* algorithm, even for two items in the list, the total number of list nodes can go up to 10. In order to cut down the state space and speedup the verification of *Lazy* and *Lock Free* algorithms, we canonicalized the linked list in their implementation: all marked nodes were shifted to the end.

Algorithm	#Items	#List Nodes Required	Time(s)
Fine-grained	1	3	0.11
Fine-grained	2	4	3.73
Optimistic	1	3	0.83
Optimistic	2	4	114.39
Lazy	1	5	18
Lazy	2	8	29554
Lock Free	1	7	1.62
Lock Free	2	10	401.14
Lock Free (Buggy)	1	7	0.63

Fig. 6. Model Checking Results

We were initially surprised by the better performance for *Lock Free* algorithm, especially since it is known to be the hardest for verification. We think that this is probably due to the fact that the *Other* thread of *Lock Free* algorithm does not have lock() and unlock() calls (which we observed significantly slowed down the *Lazy* algorithm); the abstract model then has only 5 statements. This leads to fewer interleavings and thus a speedup despite the 10 nodes in the list.

The *Lazy* algorithm was the slowest among all. We believe that this is because it uses a large number of list nodes (8 for the two item case) and also has significant interference from the *Other* thread due to locks.

5.1   Verification Experience: Candidate Lemmas

We now describe our experience in verifying these algorithms using Daikon generated candidate lemmas. Since Daikon learns candidate lemmas as clauses for each program location (each candidate lemma then is a conjunction of clauses), we compare the number of clauses in the manually added candidate lemmas with the number of clauses inferred automatically. Further, in what follows, we will consider only those clauses which are left after an initial pruning by model checking for a single thread.

Fine-grained **Set.** For the *Fine-grained* algorithm, 15 clauses were inferred by Daikon, 9 of which were correct. We manually had to add an additional 9 clauses. These 9 clauses were added as 4 candidate lemmas: of these 2 restrained the abstract statements from accessing the shared state when it was not locked by *Other* and one constrained that modifications be done to shared state only if the nodes pointed by the local pointers *curr* and *pred* are reachable from *Head*.

Optimistic **Set.** For the *Optimistic* set, 15 clauses were generated by Daikon, of which 2 were spurious. 13 clauses were added manually; these were added as 5 candidate lemmas. Similar to the *Fine-grained* algorithm case, two of these constrained accesses to happen only in locked region and two constrained the local pointers to be reachable from *Head*.

Lazy **Set.** For the *Lazy* set, Daikon generated 39 clauses out of which 1 was spurious. We manually added 9 clauses as 5 candidate lemmas. Three of these constrained accesses to happen only in the locked region and one constrained the local pointers to be reachable from *Head*.

Lock Free **Set.** In the *Lock Free* case, our candidate lemma generation scheme had limited success: we had a large number of spurious clauses. The total number of generated clauses which model check for single thread case is 29. Out of these, only 7 carried through and thus are of help in the proof. The rest of the clauses were falsified. The total number of manually added clauses was 23, from 5 manually added candidate lemmas.

Specific Candidate Lemmas for *Lazy Remove*: We now describe the specific lemmas which we added for the *Remove* method of the *Lazy* set algorithm shown in Figure 3d. As can be seen from the pseudocode, the *Remove* method modifies the shared state (list nodes) in lines 3 and 5. Since the CMP method discards all the local updates in constructing the environment abstraction (shown in Figure 5), lemmas are needed only for the rules corresponding to these lines for refinement.

The first set of candidate lemmas are the ones which describe the relationships between the thread variables while making updates. As discussed in the previous section, such lemmas are learned by using Daikon. For example, an important lemma in this category is that when the rule corresponding to line 3 of the *Remove* method is fired, the node pointed by *curr* is next to that pointed by *pred* and that by *entry* is next to *curr*. Other examples include lemmas which compare the values of the *key* fields of nodes pointed by *pred*, *curr* and *entry* variables.

The second set of candidate lemmas are concerned with synchronization. For the rules corresponding to line number 3 and 5, the variables *pred* and *curr* must be locked by the calling thread at the time of execution of the rules. While these lemmas had to be added manually, they can potentially be added automatically since the only information required is whether the variables should be locked or not. For concurrent data structures, the lock scopes are known statically.

Finally, the last candidate lemma which we had to manually add was for the rule corresponding to line 5. This lemma stated that when the node pointed by *curr* is being removed from the list, it should be marked.

Discussion. We observed that the manually added candidate lemmas, particularly for *Fine-grained*, *Lazy* and *Lock Free* algorithms, had a very similar structure, and had information which could be inferred from a single thread. This strongly motivates further research on exploring even better techniques for inferring lemmas from a single thread.

6   Conclusion and Future Work

In this paper we presented a case study of parameterized model checking of concurrent data structures. In particular, we have shown how concurrent list based set data structures can be model checked for an unbounded number of threads by leveraging an important parameterized model checking based technique. We have also shown how the manual effort involved in the parameterized model checking using the CMP method can be reduced by mining invariants from the execution trace of a single thread.

Our work opens up interesting future research directions. First, it suggests experimental exploration for better invariant generation approaches which can capture most of the lemmas required by the CMP method based verification loop. In particular, we believe that better candidate lemmas can be generated by leveraging higher level specifications like those used for program sketching. Second, it highlights the need for generic data structure abstractions, which can be integrated with the CMP method to model check the data structures for an unbounded size and with an unbounded number of threads accessing them. This is essential for full formal verification.

References

1. Berdine, J., Lev-Ami, T., Manevich, R., Ramalingam, G., Sagiv, M.: Thread Quantification for Concurrent Shape Analysis. In: Gupta, A., Malik, S. (eds.) CAV 2008. LNCS, vol. 5123, pp. 399–413. Springer, Heidelberg (2008)
2. Calcagno, C., Parkinson, M., Vafeiadis, V.: Modular Safety Checking for Fine-Grained Concurrency. In: Riis Nielson, H., Filé, G. (eds.) SAS 2007. LNCS, vol. 4634, pp. 233–248. Springer, Heidelberg (2007)
3. Černý, P., Radhakrishna, A., Zufferey, D., Chaudhuri, S., Alur, R.: Model checking of linearizability of concurrent list implementations. In: Touili, T., Cook, B., Jackson, P. (eds.) CAV 2010. LNCS, vol. 6174, pp. 465–479. Springer, Heidelberg (2010)
4. Chou, C.-T., Mannava, P.K., Park, S.: A Simple Method for Parameterized Verification of Cache Coherence Protocols. In: Hu, A.J., Martin, A.K. (eds.) FMCAD 2004. LNCS, vol. 3312, pp. 382–398. Springer, Heidelberg (2004)

5. Colvin, R., Groves, L., Luchangco, V., Moir, M.: Formal Verification of a Lazy Concurrent List-Based Set Algorithm. In: Ball, T., Jones, R.B. (eds.) CAV 2006. LNCS, vol. 4144, pp. 475–488. Springer, Heidelberg (2006)
6. Ernst, M.D., Perkins, J.H., Guo, P.J., McCamant, S., Pacheco, C., Tschantz, M.S., Xiao, C.: The Daikon system for dynamic detection of likely invariants. Science of Computer Programming 69(1-3), 35–45 (2007)
7. Harris, T.L.: A Pragmatic Implementation of Non-blocking Linked-Lists. In: Welch, J.L. (ed.) DISC 2001. LNCS, vol. 2180, pp. 300–314. Springer, Heidelberg (2001), http://dl.acm.org/citation.cfm?id=645958.676105
8. Heller, S., Herlihy, M., Luchangco, V., Moir, M., Scherer III, W.N., Shavit, N.: A Lazy Concurrent List-Based Set Algorithm. In: Anderson, J.H., Prencipe, G., Wattenhofer, R. (eds.) OPODIS 2005. LNCS, vol. 3974, pp. 3–16. Springer, Heidelberg (2006)
9. Herlihy, M., Shavit, N.: The Art of Multiprocessor Programming. Morgan Kaufmann Publishers Inc., San Francisco (2008)
10. Herlihy, M.P., Wing, J.M.: Linearizability: a correctness condition for concurrent objects. ACM Trans. Program. Lang. Syst. 12, 463–492 (1990)
11. Kristic, S.: Parameterized system verification with guard strengthening and parameter abstraction. In: 4th Int. Workshop on Automatic Verification of Finite State Systems (2005)
12. Lea, D.: The java.util.concurrent synchronizer framework. Sci. Comput. Program. 58, 293–309 (2005), http://dl.acm.org/citation.cfm?id=1127037.1127039
13. Liu, Y., Chen, W., Liu, Y.A., Sun, J.: Model Checking Linearizability via Refinement. In: Cavalcanti, A., Dams, D.R. (eds.) FM 2009. LNCS, vol. 5850, pp. 321–337. Springer, Heidelberg (2009)
14. McMillan, K.L.: Verification of Infinite State Systems by Compositional Model Checking. In: Pierre, L., Kropf, T. (eds.) CHARME 1999. LNCS, vol. 1703, pp. 219–237. Springer, Heidelberg (1999)
15. Michael, M.M.: High performance dynamic lock-free hash tables and list-based sets. In: Proceedings of the Fourteenth Annual ACM Symposium on Parallel Algorithms and Architectures, SPAA 2002, pp. 73–82. ACM, New York (2002), http://doi.acm.org/10.1145/564870.564881
16. Michael, M.M., Scott, M.L.: Correction of a memory management method for lock-free data structures. Tech. rep., Rochester, NY, USA (1995)
17. O'Leary, J., Talupur, M., Tuttle, M.R.: Protocol verification using flows: An industrial experience. In: Formal Methods in Computer-Aided Design, FMCAD 2009, pp. 172–179 (November 2009)
18. Reinders, J.: Intel threading building blocks, 1st edn. O'Reilly & Associates, Inc., Sebastopol (2007)
19. Talupur, M., Tuttle, M.R.: Going with the flow: Parameterized verification using message flows. In: Formal Methods in Computer-Aided Design, FMCAD 2008, pp. 1–8 (November 2008)
20. Vafeiadis, V.: Shape-Value Abstraction for Verifying Linearizability. In: Jones, N.D., Müller-Olm, M. (eds.) VMCAI 2009. LNCS, vol. 5403, pp. 335–348. Springer, Heidelberg (2009)
21. Vafeiadis, V., Herlihy, M., Hoare, T., Shapiro, M.: Proving correctness of highly-concurrent linearisable objects. In: Proceedings of the Eleventh ACM SIGPLAN Symposium on Principles and Practice of Parallel Programming, PPoPP 2006, pp. 129–136. ACM, New York (2006), http://doi.acm.org/10.1145/1122971.1122992

22. Vafeiadis, V., Parkinson, M.: A Marriage of Rely/Guarantee and Separation Logic. In: Caires, L., Vasconcelos, V.T. (eds.) CONCUR 2007. LNCS, vol. 4703, pp. 256–271. Springer, Heidelberg (2007)
23. Vechev, M., Yahav, E., Yorsh, G.: Experience with Model Checking Linearizability. In: Păsăreanu, C.S. (ed.) Model Checking Software. LNCS, vol. 5578, pp. 261–278. Springer, Heidelberg (2009)
24. Zhang, S.J.: Scalable automatic linearizability checking. In: Proceeding of the 33rd International Conference on Software Engineering, ICSE 2011, pp. 1185–1187. ACM, New York (2011), http://doi.acm.org/10.1145/1985793.1986037
25. Zhang, S.J., Liu, Y.: Model checking a lazy concurrent list-based set algorithm. In: Proceedings of the 2010 Fourth International Conference on Secure Software Integration and Reliability Improvement, SSIRI 2010, pp. 43–52. IEEE Computer Society, Washington, DC (2010), http://dx.doi.org/10.1109/SSIRI.2010.37

mctau: Bridging the Gap between Modest and UPPAAL*

Jonathan Bogdoll[2], Alexandre David[1],
Arnd Hartmanns[2], and Holger Hermanns[2]

[1] Aalborg University, Department of Computer Science, Aalborg, Denmark
[2] Saarland University – Computer Science, Saarbrücken, Germany

Abstract. MODEST is a high-level compositional modelling language for stochastic timed systems with a formal semantics in terms of stochastic timed automata, an overarching formalism of which several well-studied models are special cases. The emphasis of MODEST is to make use of existing analysis techniques and tools in a single-formalism, multiple-solution approach. In this paper, we focus on networks of timed automata as supported by UPPAAL. We report on extensions made to MODEST and UPPAAL that allow the transformation of a rich subset of MODEST models to UPPAAL timed automata and enable connections to further tools and formalisms. We present our MODEST-to-UPPAAL tool chain mctau, which allows both a fully automated analysis as well as model transformation, and we compare its performance with the existing mcpta tool.

1 Introduction

MODEST, the "modelling and description language for stochastic timed systems" [6], is a compositional modelling language that combines expressive and powerful syntax-level features—such as recursive process definitions, loops, arrays, exception handling and user-defined data structures—with a formal semantics in terms of stochastic timed automata (STA). STA span a very rich spectrum of semantic models, supporting continuous and discrete probability distributions as well as nondeterminism. Well-known and extensively studied submodels of STA are probabilistic timed automata (PTA) [15], timed automata (TA) [1], and generalised semi-Markov processes (GSMP) [11]. Most of the submodels are easily identifiable on the syntactic level.

MODEST has been used in a wide variety of application studies, ranging from wireless sensor networks [2,18] and communication protocols [13] to architectural dependability models [5], industrial production scheduling [16] and electric power grid management [4]. The principle idea behind the formalism and its supporting tools is to provide a *single-formalism, multiple-solution* approach to modelling and analysis, using existing analysis engines and algorithms where available to avoid unnecessary reimplementations.

* This work has been supported by the European Union FP7-ICT projects Quasimodo, contract no. 214755, and MEALS, contract no. 295261, by the DFG as part of SFB/TR 14 AVACS, and by the DFG/NWO Bilateral Research Program ROCKS.

A. Donaldson and D. Parker (Eds.): SPIN 2012, LNCS 7385, pp. 227–233, 2012.

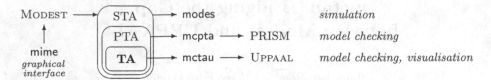

Fig. 1. How the new mctau tool fits in the MODEST TOOLSET

Started in 2008, the MODEST TOOLSET constitutes the second generation [7] of tools with this philosophy, currently including (i) mcpta [12,13], which enables model checking of networks of PTA using the PRISM [14] probabilistic model checker in the background, (ii) modes [5,12], a discrete-event simulator that primarily targets GSMP models but in fact is enhanced to handle certain nondeterministic models in a sound way, and (iii) mime as a graphical user interface that seamlessly integrates the analysis tools into a MODEST source code editor with syntax and error highlighting. The tools are usable and robust.

In this paper, we present a new member of the MODEST TOOLSET family: mctau, providing visualisation and analysis of networks of timed automata. It does so by connecting to the real-time model checker UPPAAL [3]. Although mcpta already includes support for TA as a special case of PTA, we will see that mctau allows a more efficient analysis; in addition to this, the way we bridge several semantic gaps between MODEST and UPPAAL will be of practical use beyond just the mctau tool. Figure 1 provides a toolset overview.

2   Bridging the Gap

A connection between MODEST and UPPAAL had been planned for a long time [7], but several fundamental differences between the two modelling languages have prevented this up to now:

Time Constraints. Constraints on the flow of time are specified as location *invariants* in UPPAAL, while MODEST uses *deadlines* (or *urgency constraints* [8]). As an example, if location l has invariant $c \leq 3$ (where c is a clock variable), time can pass while in l as long as $c \leq 3$ holds. Deadlines, on the other hand, are associated to edges in an automaton, and specify that *some* edge must be taken out of a location once the deadline of *one* outgoing edge becomes satisfied. Invariant $c \leq 3$ can thus be expressed as deadline $c \geq 3$ on some edge leaving l.

Deadlines are more flexible in parallel composition and synchronisation, easily allowing, for example, a synchronising edge to be taken *as soon as possible* in all components. While there are deadlines that cannot be transformed into a single invariant (mainly equality comparison deadlines like $c = 3$ and equivalents) and vice-versa, we have recently shown how to transform all practically relevant deadlines into invariants [12], and this transformation is implemented in mctau.

Assignments. The assignments associated to an edge in UPPAAL are performed sequentially: $x := y, y := x$ will result in x and y both having the same value.

In MODEST, variables are assigned new values in function of their previous ones atomically. $x := y, y := x$ will thus result in swapping x and y. UPPAAL 4.1.5 now implements this semantics as an option (-M at the command line and the Modest checkbox in the option menu of the graphical interface).

Synchronisation. Both UPPAAL and MODEST support the notion of *parallel composition*, where a number of independent processes run in parallel. However, the synchronisation mechanisms differ fundamentally: MODEST supports a CSP/LOTOS-style *multi-way* synchronisation where processes synchronise on edges with the same action label that is part of the intersection of the action alphabets α of the processes. For example, if $\alpha(P_1) = \{a, b\}$ and $\alpha(P_2) = \{b, c\}$ then P_1 (P_2) is free to take action a (c), but P_1 and P_2 must synchronise to take action b. UPPAAL, on the other hand, provides CCS-style *binary* synchronisation where exactly two processes synchronise on a matching pair of actions (e.g. a! and a?) and I/O-automata inspired *broadcast* synchronisation where all processes able to perform an a? action synchronise with one sender performing a!.

Although it is possible, with some effort, to encode binary using only multi-way synchronisation [17], we are not aware of any way to do the opposite in a semantically sound way and without introducing additional intermediate states in ways that would make the state-space explosion problem significantly worse. We thus resolved this discrepancy in a practical manner by adding multi-way synchronisation to UPPAAL 4.1.5 and extending MODEST with broadcast and binary synchronisation. These extensions also open UPPAAL and MODEST for a large number of further tool connections that were previously infeasible such as connecting UPPAAL with CSP-style tools, notably CADP [10] or PRISM.

3   The mctau Tool

mctau is our new addition to the MODEST TOOLSET that, at its core, performs the translation of MODEST models to the XML-based input language of UPPAAL, including advanced features of MODEST such as user-defined functions and data types. It supports all types of properties that are already supported by UPPAAL. mctau is available as a command-line executable and as a fully-integrated analysis engine inside mime. It has two modes of operation:

Export Mode: A .modest input file is transformed into a .xml file with the automata and a .q file with the properties to be analysed. These can be opened in the UPPAAL graphical interface for analysis or further modification.

Analysis Mode: UPPAAL is completely hidden from the user: The model transformation as well as the analysis of the properties, using UPPAAL's command-line verifyta executable, is performed by mctau in a fully automated way. This is also the way that mctau is used from within mime.

Since MODEST is a text-based formalism while UPPAAL is based on a graphical automata notation, mctau incorporates a set of graph layout algorithms, based on

```
action put, get;
process Channel() {
    clock c;
    put {= c = 0 =};
    invariant(c <= TD) alt {
        :: get
        :: tau
    }; Channel() }
```
⇒

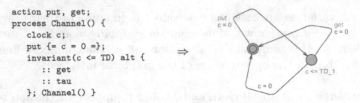

Fig. 2. A MODEST process and its UPPAAL automaton

the Graph# library[1] and adapted for timed automata with all their location and edge labels, to generate easily useable UPPAAL models. Figure 2 shows a simple communication channel in MODEST and the UPPAAL automaton generated by mctau based on the *LinLog* layout algorithm.

Aside from TA, mctau can also cope with networks of PTA: When given a model with probabilistic branching, mctau generates (and analyses) an overapproximation that is obtained by replacing all probabilistic with nondeterministic branching (making sure to discard branches with probability zero). This neither adds nor removes paths through the model, but all probabilities are lost. Still, it is useful for a fast qualitative analysis. mctau then also replaces probabilistic properties by a set of purely timed ones to determine whether the probability is exactly zero or one. For example, property $P_{\max}(\Diamond e)$ to determine the maximum probability (over all schedulers) of eventually reaching a state satisfying expression e is replaced by $\forall \Box \neg e$ and $\forall \Diamond e$: If the first property is satisfied, the original probability must be zero; if the second property is satisfied, it must be one; otherwise, it may be any number in the *closed* interval $[0, 1]$.

This handling of PTA models greatly improves the usability and applicability of mctau since it allows the user to write a single model to subsequently use three different tools—mctau, mcpta and modes—with vastly different background technologies, all of that optionally within the graphical interface of mime.

Tool availability. The MODEST TOOLSET, which includes mctau, and UPPAAL are both freely available for academic users at www.modestchecker.net and www.uppaal.org, respectively.

4   Evaluation

mctau is able to analyse (the nondeterministic overapproximations of) the three original mcpta PTA case studies [13], without requiring any changes to the models. In all cases where mctau reports probability 0 or 1, mcpta does so as well. For the BRP model in particular, we see that whenever mctau reports $[0, 1]$, the actual probability as reported by mcpta is in $]0, 1[$, as shown in Table 1 (model parameters (N, MAX, TD) and property names are as in [13]). This shows how mctau can be of great help in model debugging and for sanity checking of probabilistic models.

---

[1] http://graphsharp.codeplex.com/

Table 1. Results of mctau and mcpta for the probabilistic BRP model $(16, 2, 1)$

property	T_{A1}	T_{A2}	P_A	P_B	P_1	P_2	D_{max}
mctau	*true*	*true*	0	0	$[0, 1]$	$[0, 1]$	$[0, 1]$
mcpta	*true*	*true*	0	0	$4.233 \cdot 10^{-4}$	$2.645 \cdot 10^{-5}$	$9.996 \cdot 10^{-1}$

Table 2. Performance of mctau and mcpta on the nonprobabilistic BRP model

tool	model	standard properties			time-bounded properties		
		states	time	memory	states	time	memory
mctau	$(16, 2, 1)$	880	1 s	27 MB	831	1 s	19 MB
(using UPPAAL)	$(64, 5, 4)$	8 317	2 s	30 MB	8 091	1 s	21 MB
mcpta	$(16, 2, 1)$	3 972	2 s	167 MB	170 371	20 s	253 MB
(using PRISM)	$(64, 5, 4)$	304 785	13 s	187 MB	4 914 666	284 s	686 MB

The BRP model has also been studied as a pure TA model before [9] with some properties that had not been transferred to the PTA model. We were able to reconstruct that TA model in MODEST and check all properties with mctau. The corresponding model file is included in the MODEST TOOLSET download. We also compared the performance of mctau and mcpta (using the digital clocks engine[2]) on a nonprobabilistic version of the original MODEST BRP model. Table 2 summarises the results[3]; as expected (since mcpta/PRISM are not designed for nonprobabilistic models), the more specialised tool shows significantly improved performance.

5   Conclusion

We have presented mctau, a tool providing a link between the MODEST and UPPAAL modelling formalisms. The newly established connection opens the door to a powerful tool chain that gives MODEST modellers access to the editor and simulator of UPPAAL and reinforces the single-formalism, multiple-solution approach of MODEST. This approach might one day provide a possible solution to one of the obstacles that, in our experience, new users seeking to apply model-checking in their subject area face: the daunting number of different modelling languages which makes for low flexibility and a steep learning curve.

mctau was only possible because of recent results and implementation efforts that allowed the semantic gap between the two formalisms to be overcome. The implemented bridge spans a practically disturbing gap between CCS and I/O automata on the one side and CSP and LOTOS on the other. The inclusion of multi-way synchronisation in UPPAAL 4.1.5 is a key enabler for further connections with prominent verification tools such as PRISM or CADP.

---

[2] Use of PRISM's game-based engine was not possible due to its restrictions concerning the use of global variables and the access to other modules' local variables.

[3] Linux VM on Intel Core i5, /usr/bin/time -v for time and memory measurement; "states" is the number of zones explored by UPPAAL for mctau and the number of reachable discrete states (including discretised clock valuations) for mcpta.

UPPAAL nowadays also contains an efficient statistical model checking engine, which we currently do not make use of since it relies on an entirely new and different semantics for timed automata. An investigation of the relationship between this "stochastic" semantics and MODEST is planned as future work.

References

1. Alur, R., Dill, D.L.: A theory of timed automata. TCS 126(2), 183–235 (1994)
2. Baró Graf, H., Hermanns, H., Kulshrestha, J., Peter, J., Vahldiek, A., Vasudevan, A.: A verified wireless safety critical hard real-time design. In: WoWMoM. IEEE (2011)
3. Behrmann, G., David, A., Larsen, K.G.: A Tutorial on UPPAAL. In: Bernardo, M., Corradini, F. (eds.) SFM-RT 2004. LNCS, vol. 3185, pp. 200–236. Springer, Heidelberg (2004)
4. Berrang, P., Bogdoll, J., Hahn, E.M., Hartmanns, A., Hermanns, H.: Dependability results for power grids with decentralized stabilization strategies. Reports of SFB/TR 14 AVACS 83 (2012) ISSN: 1860-9821, www.avacs.org
5. Bogdoll, J., Ferrer Fioriti, L.M., Hartmanns, A., Hermanns, H.: Partial Order Methods for Statistical Model Checking and Simulation. In: Bruni, R., Dingel, J. (eds.) FORTE 2011 and FMOODS 2011. LNCS, vol. 6722, pp. 59–74. Springer, Heidelberg (2011)
6. Bohnenkamp, H.C., D'Argenio, P.R., Hermanns, H., Katoen, J.-P.: MoDeST: A compositional modeling formalism for hard and softly timed systems. IEEE Transactions on Software Engineering 32(10), 812–830 (2006)
7. Bohnenkamp, H.C., Hermanns, H., Katoen, J.-P.: MOTOR: The MODEST Tool Environment. In: Grumberg, O., Huth, M. (eds.) TACAS 2007. LNCS, vol. 4424, pp. 500–504. Springer, Heidelberg (2007)
8. Bornot, S., Sifakis, J.: An algebraic framework for urgency. Inf. Comput. 163(1), 172–202 (2000)
9. D'Argenio, P.R., Katoen, J.-P., Ruys, T.C., Tretmans, J.: The Bounded Retransmission Protocol Must be on Time! In: Brinksma, E. (ed.) TACAS 1997. LNCS, vol. 1217, pp. 416–431. Springer, Heidelberg (1997)
10. Garavel, H., Lang, F., Mateescu, R., Serwe, W.: CADP 2010: A Toolbox for the Construction and Analysis of Distributed Processes. In: Abdulla, P.A., Leino, K.R.M. (eds.) TACAS 2011. LNCS, vol. 6605, pp. 372–387. Springer, Heidelberg (2011)
11. Haas, P.J., Shedler, G.S.: Regenerative generalized semi-Markov processes. Communications in Statistics. Stochastic Models 3(3), 409–438 (1987)
12. Hartmanns, A.: Model-Checking and Simulation for Stochastic Timed Systems. In: Aichernig, B.K., de Boer, F.S., Bonsangue, M.M. (eds.) FMCO. LNCS, vol. 6957, pp. 372–391. Springer, Heidelberg (2011)
13. Hartmanns, A., Hermanns, H.: A Modest approach to checking probabilistic timed automata. In: QEST, pp. 187–196. IEEE Computer Society (2009)
14. Kwiatkowska, M., Norman, G., Parker, D.: PRISM 4.0: Verification of Probabilistic Real-Time Systems. In: Gopalakrishnan, G., Qadeer, S. (eds.) CAV 2011. LNCS, vol. 6806, pp. 585–591. Springer, Heidelberg (2011)
15. Kwiatkowska, M., Norman, G., Segala, R., Sproston, J.: Automatic verification of real-time systems with discrete probability distributions. TCS 282(1), 101–150 (2002)

16. Mader, A., Bohnenkamp, H.C., Usenko, Y.S., Jansen, D.N., Hurink, J., Hermanns, H.: Synthesis and stochastic assessment of cost-optimal schedules. STTT 12(5), 305–318 (2010)
17. Norman, G., Palamidessi, C., Parker, D., Wu, P.: Model checking the probabilistic pi-calculus. In: QEST, pp. 169–178. IEEE Computer Society (2007)
18. Yue, H., Bohnenkamp, H., Kampschulte, M., Katoen, J.-P.: Analysing and Improving Energy Efficiency of Distributed Slotted Aloha. In: Balandin, S., Koucheryavy, Y., Hu, H. (eds.) NEW2AN 2011 and ruSMART 2011. LNCS, vol. 6869, pp. 197–208. Springer, Heidelberg (2011)

FAuST: A Framework for Formal Verification, Automated Debugging, and Software Test Generation*

Heinz Riener[1] and Görschwin Fey[1,2]

[1] Institute of Computer Science, University Bremen, Germany
{hriener,fey}@informatik.uni-bremen.de
http://www.informatik.uni-bremen.de/agra/
[2] Institute of Space Systems, German Aerospace Center, Germany
goerschwin.fey@dlr.de
http://www.dlr.de/irs/

Abstract. We present FAuST, an extensible framework for Formal verification, Automated debugging, and Software Test generation. Our framework uses a highly customizeable *Bounded Model Checking* (BMC) algorithm for formal reasoning about software programs and provides different applications, e.g., property checking, functional equivalence checking, test case generation, and fault localization. FAuST supports dynamic execution and parallel symbolic reasoning using the LLVM compiler infrastructure and an abstraction layer for decision procedures.

Keywords: Formal verification, Debugging, SAT.

1 Introduction

Bounded Model Checking (BMC) [3,7] is a technique to check whether finite-state systems conform to their specifications. BMC searches for counterexamples of bounded length and successively increases the bound until either a counterexample is found or the system's correctness can be guaranteed. The BMC problem is represented symbolically as multiple instances of the *Satisfiability* (SAT) problem. In practice BMC serves as a refutation technique because BMC problems often exhaust a resource limit before the system is proven correct. The instances are then solved using a corresponding *Decision Procedures* (DP), called *Satisfiability Modulo Theories* (SMT) solver.

More recently, BMC is used in software verification [6,12]: the behavior of a program is extracted from its source code and modeled using logic formulae. Today, flexible compilers like the *Low Level Virtual Machine* (LLVM) [14] compiler allow for program analysis and verification directly on the compiler's intermediate representation.

We present FAuST, an extensible framework for Formal verification, Automated debugging, and Software Test generation. FAuST offers a tool bench for different

---

* This work was supported by the German Research Foundation (DFG, grant no. FE 797/6-1).

A. Donaldson and D. Parker (Eds.): SPIN 2012, LNCS 7385, pp. 234–240, 2012.

verification and debugging applications exploiting their similarities. The input of each FAuST tool is a software program. The output depends on its application. For instance, in fault-based test generation [22] the output is a test suite and in fault localization [23] the output is a set of potentially faulty program locations. The core engine of each tool is a highly customizable BMC algorithm.

The conceptual architecture of FAuST is built in three layers: (1) in the *program layer* FAuST deals with analyzing and transforming the input program. (2) In the *application layer* FAuST chooses a suitable background theory and builds a SAT problem from the transformed program depends on the application. (3) In the *logic layer* the SAT problem is simplified and solved using SAT and SMT solvers.

Figure 1 shows the flow of the BMC tool in the FAuST framework for property checking. Dashed boxes denote objects and solid boxes denote transformations on those objects. In the program layer we leverage the LLVM compiler to lower the input program to LLVM's intermediate representation, LLVM-IR. In the application layer we instantiate an encoder with respect to the application, i.e., a customized BMC algorithm which generates a SAT instance from the transformed program. In the logic layer we use metaSMT [10] as a generic API interface to different SAT and SMT solvers. Other FAuST tools operate similarly.

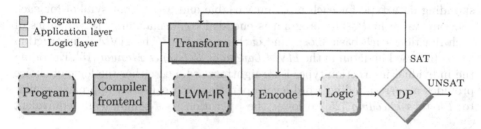

Fig. 1. Flow of the BMC tool within the FAuST framework for property checking

FAuST is the first tool bench which integrates formal verification, automatic debugging, and test generation into a unified framework. The main features are: (1) state-of-the-art compiler technology built on the LLVM compiler infrastructure, (2) dynamic execution using Just-In-Time (JIT) compilation, (3) an abstraction layer for decision procedures leveraging metaSMT, and (4) parallel solving using multiple SAT and SMT solvers simultaneously.

The remainder of the paper is structured as follows: In Section 2 we describe the BMC-based approach to formalize LLVM-IR into logic. In Section 3 we discuss the applications currently integrated into FAuST. In Section 4 we present related work. In Section 5 concludes the paper.

2   Formalizing LLVM-IR into Logic Using BMC

We use a BMC approach to formalize LLVM-IR into logic: given an imperative, non-concurrent program P and an unrolling bound k, we unroll loops and recursive functions in the program with respect to k and transform the unrolled program into *Static Single Assignment* (SSA) [24] form. The transformations for loop unrolling and to establish SSA form are provided by the LLVM compiler infrastructure.

The resulting program consists of global program variables and a set of functions with one entry function. A function f defines a *Control Flow Graph* (CFG) $\mathsf{CFG}(f) := (V_f, E_f)$ with nodes V_f and edges E_f. The nodes $v \in V_f$ correspond to basic blocks and the edges $e \in E_f$ correspond to possible control flow transfers between basic blocks. Each basic block is a sequence of instructions over program variables and constant values and has a unique label. We write $\mathsf{Pred}(v)$ and $\mathsf{Inst}(v)$ to denote the set of predecessors and the set of instructions of the basic block v.

Suppose P is a program consisting of functions f_i, $0 \leq i \leq n$, with the entry function f_0 we encode the program into a logic formula,

$$p := \bigwedge_{i=0}^{n} \bigwedge_{b \in V_{f_i}} \left[\bigvee_{b' \in \mathsf{Pred}(b)} e_{b',b} \leftrightarrow \bigwedge_{s \in \mathsf{Inst}(b)} \mathsf{Encode}(s) \right] \wedge e_{f_0},$$

i.e., an instance of the SAT problem. We introduce a logic variable with corresponding data type for each program variable and a constant symbol for each constant value in P. The program is encoded by formalizing the semantics of each function, each basic block, and each instruction. The LLVM-IR instruction set is discussed in detail in the *LLVM Language Reference Manual* [15]. Encoding the individual instruction types is straightforward, i.e,. either the logic of choice provides a corresponding word-level operation or we use an approach similar to *Tseitin's encoding* [25] to lower the operation to a semantically equivalent

```
0. ;<label>:1
1.  %2 = icmp slt i32 %a, %b
2.  br i1 %2, label %3, label %4
3.
4. ;<label>:3
5.  br label %5
6.
7. ;<label>:4
8.  br label %5
9.
10. ;<label>:5
11. %c = phi i32 [%a, %3], [%b, %4]
```

```
0. (set-logic QF_BV)
1. (declare-fun |%a| () (_ BitVec 32))
2. (declare-fun |%b| () (_ BitVec 32))
3. (declare-fun |%c| () (_ BitVec 32))
4. (declare-fun |%2| () Bool)
5. (declare-fun |-->%1| () Bool)
6. (declare-fun |%1-->%3| () Bool)
7. (declare-fun |%1-->%4| () Bool)
8. (declare-fun |%3-->%5| () Bool)
9. (declare-fun |%4-->%5| () Bool)
10. (assert (=> |-->%1|
11.              (= |%2| (bvslt |%a| |%b|))))
12. (assert (=> |-->%1|
13.     (and (=> |%2| |%1-->%3|)
14.          (=> (not |%2|) |%1-->%4|))))
15. (assert (= |%1-->%3| |%3-->%5|))
16. (assert (= |%1-->%4| |%4-->%5|))
17. (assert (=> (or |%3-->%5| |%4-->%5|)
18.     (= |%c| (ite |%3-->%5| |%a| |%b|))))
```

Fig. 2. A fragment of an LLVM program (on the left) and the corresponding logic formula in SMT-LIB version 2 format (on the right)

logic formula using Boolean connectives. We write $\mathsf{Encode}(s)$ to denote the logic formula obtained from encoding instruction s.

In order to encode the control flow of a program, we introduce one Boolean variable for each edge in a $\mathsf{CFG}(f_i)$, $0 \leq i \leq n$, and additional Boolean variables for each function call and return from a function to the callers site. The value of a Boolean variable corresponds to a control flow transfer in the program, i.e., the value is true if the control flow transfers when the program is executed and false otherwise. We write $e_{b',b}$ to denote the Boolean variable which corresponds to the control flow transfer from basic block b' to basic block b and we write e_{f_i} to denote the Boolean variable which corresponds to the entry of function f_i.

Each satisfying assignment of the resulting logic formula p corresponds to a possible assignment to the program variables in P and determines an execution of the program. Figure 2 shows a fragment of an LLVM program and the logic formula in SMT-LIB version 2 [1] format. The program stores the minimum of two given program variables a and b in program variable c.

3   Applications

In this section we outline the applications currently implemented as FAuST tools and list their runtimes for the ANSI-C program TCAS from the *Software-Artifact Infrastructure Repository* (SIR) using specific SMT solvers. However, FAuST supports a large set of different SAT and SMT solvers via API calls and can pass formulae to any interactive SMT solver supporting SMT-LIB version 2 format. We mainly use FAuST to deal with C and C++ programs. However, FAuSTcan be used for other programming language if an LLVM compiler front-end is available which transforms programs into LLVM-IR. In order to use any tool from FAuST, a user has to mark the program's input variables with special function calls _FAuST_input. The program variables are then treated as open variables with non-deterministic values when encoded. Moreover, the user has to pass the name of the entry function to be checked to a tool.

3.1   Formal Verification

FAuST provides a standard BMC tool for formal verification which supports *property checking* and *functional equivalence checking*. In the former case the user has to provide local assertions in the program's source code. In the latter case a reference implementation serves as the formal specification. Then, the user has to mark corresponding pairs of program variables in the two implementations to be compared with a special function call _FAuST_output. Counterexamples can either be viewed on LLVM-IR or mapped back to the source code passed to the LLVM compiler front-end utilizing LLVM metadata. Optionally, FAuST allows for validation of counterexamples on the real program using LLVM's JIT compiler and execution engine, i.e., a test driver with the values of the counterexample is automatically synthesized, compiled, and executed. Functional equivalence checking of TCAS takes 0.18 seconds using Z3 as SMT solver which is comparable to state-of-the-art BMC tools.

3.2 Automatic Debugging

FAuST provides an extension of the BMC tool for automatic debugging. Given a program that does not conform to its formal specification, the tool computes statements which are potentially faulty. Basically, two strategies are supported: *Model-Based Diagnosis* (MBD) [21,8] and *Error Explanation* (EE) [9]. The MBD strategy computes program variables which when replaced with open variables in the SAT instance correct the program. The EE strategy selects a counterexample and compares the values assigned to the program variables to the values assigned in the most similar execution trace which does not refute the formal specification. Different values indicate potentially faulty statements. In contrast to the Explain [9] tool, FAuST does not use a *Pseudo Boolean* (PB) solver but solves the optimization problem as a binary search over logic variables utilizing incremental SAT. For 41 mutants of TCAS, we computed potentially faulty program locations using both strategies [23]: on average the computation takes 4.37 seconds with strategy MBD and 39.29 seconds with strategy EE using Boolector as SMT solver.

3.3 Test Generation

FAuST provides a mutation-based test generator [22]: a given LLVM-IR program is seeded with artificial faults. The fault seeding is implemented as an LLVM compiler pass. The resulting program, called meta-mutant, contains all faults each guarded with a condition. FAuST instantiates the BMC tool to generate a counterexample for each fault by successively asserting a single guard condition to be true, respectively. From each counterexample a test case is extracted.

Other recent test generators are FShell [11], KLEE [4], and KLOVER [16]. KLEE and KLOVER use a symbolic execution procedure. FShell is a front-end to CBMC and provides a query engine for formulating testing goals. All three tools focus on test case generation subject to traditional coverage criteria. In contrast, our test generator is fault-based, i.e., it imposes constraints that a fault has to be reached, the program state has to be infected, and the infected program state has to propagated to an observable program output. The strength of mutation-based testing criteria was investigated by Offutt and Voes [19]. They outlined that mutation-based criteria subsume several other coverage criteria including *Modified Condition/Decision Coverage* (MC/DC) when a certain set of standard mutations is used.

4 Related Work

Today, BMC is a well established technique for searching bugs in hardware and software. Clarke et al. [6] introduced the *C Bounded Model Checker* (CBMC) which implements BMC considering finite-state systems given as ANSI-C programs. However, CBMC uses its own ANSI-C language parser and relies on a custom-made intermediate representation, called *GOTO programs*. Our BMC core engine is similar to CBMC but uses LLVM-IR as intermediate representation. A program in LLVM-IR is similar to a GOTO program which makes tools based on LLVM-IR neither less efficient nor more abstract than CBMC. However, LLVM-IR is the compiler's intermediate representation which is finally translated into the target code which makes it more suitable for verification and debugging. For instance, it provides the additional capability to detect bugs after certain optimizing transformations are applied to the source code. Also, the LLVM compiler provides a rich tool support for LLVM-IR including a compiler, linker, optimizer, disassembler, and debugger.

Researchers proposed prototype tools based on LLVM [4,17,20,5,16,13,18] for applications like symbolic execution, test generation, and BMC. The most recent BMC tool is LLBMC [18] which focuses entirely on detecting bugs in C/C++ programs either checking for assertions provided by the user or built-in checks, e.g., for overflow detection or memory consistency. However, FAuST is a framework for different applications additionally allowing for test case generation and automatic debugging.

CPAChecker [2] is a configuration software verification platform and follows the idea of having a unified framework for different, formal applications. Programs written in the C and C++ programming language are parsed and transformed into Control Flow Automata (CFA) utilizing Eclipse's CDT plugin. However, the existing procedures implemented for CPAChecker target software verification similar to CBMC.

5 Conclusions

We have presented FAuST, an extensible framework for Formal verification, Automated debugging, and Software Test generation. The framework offers a tool bench for different verification and debugging applications. FAuST utilizes the LLVM compiler infrastructure for analyzing and transforming programs and metaSMT as a generic API interface to different SAT and SMT solvers.

References

1. Barrett, C., Stump, A., Tinelli, C.: The SMT-LIB standard version 2.0 (2010)
2. Beyer, D., Keremoglu, M.E.: CPACHECKER: A Tool for Configurable Software Verification. In: Gopalakrishnan, G., Qadeer, S. (eds.) CAV 2011. LNCS, vol. 6806, pp. 184–190. Springer, Heidelberg (2011)
3. Biere, A., Cimatti, A., Clarke, E., Zhu, Y.: Symbolic Model Checking without BDDs. In: Cleaveland, W.R. (ed.) TACAS 1999. LNCS, vol. 1579, pp. 193–207. Springer, Heidelberg (1999)
4. Cadar, C., Dunbar, D., Engler, D.: KLEE: Unassisted and automatic generation of high-coverage tests for complex systems programs. In: Symposium on Operating Systems Design and Implementation, pp. 209–224 (2008)
5. Chipounov, V., Kuznetsov, V., Candea, G.: S2E: A platform for in-vivo multi-path analysis of software systems. In: Conference on Architectural Support for Programming Languages and Operating Systems, pp. 265–278 (2011)
6. Clarke, E., Kröning, D., Lerda, F.: A Tool for Checking ANSI-C Programs. In: Jensen, K., Podelski, A. (eds.) TACAS 2004. LNCS, vol. 2988, pp. 168–176. Springer, Heidelberg (2004)

7. Clarke, E.M., Biere, A., Raimi, R., Zhu, Y.: Bounded model checking using satisfiability solving. Formal Methods in System Design 19(1), 7–34 (2001)
8. de Kleer, J., Williams, B.C.: Diagnosing multiple faults. Artificial Intelligence 32(1), 97–130 (1987)
9. Groce, A., Chaki, S., Kröning, D., Strichman, O.: Error explanation with distance metrics. International Journal on Software Tools for Technology Transfer 8(3), 229–247 (2006)
10. Haedicke, F., Frehse, S., Fey, G., Große, D., Drechsler, R.: metaSMT: Focus on your application not on solver integration. In: International Workshop on Design and Implementation of Formal Tools and Systems, pp. 22–29 (2011)
11. Holzer, A., Schallhart, C., Tautschnig, M., Veith, H.: FSHELL: Systematic Test Case Generation for Dynamic Analysis and Measurement. In: Gupta, A., Malik, S. (eds.) CAV 2008. LNCS, vol. 5123, pp. 209–213. Springer, Heidelberg (2008)
12. Kröning, D.: Software verification. In: Biere, A., Heule, M., van Maaren, H., Walsh, T. (eds.) Handbook of Satisfiability, pp. 505–532. IOS Press (2009)
13. Vujošević-Janičić, M., Kuncak, V.: Development and evaluation of LAV: An SMT-based error finding platform. In: International Conference on Verified Software: Theories, Tools and Experiments, pp. 98–113 (2012)
14. Lattner, C., Adve, V.: LLVM: A compilation framework for lifelong program analysis & transformation. In: International Symposium on Code Generation and Optimization, pp. 75–88 (2004)
15. Lattner, C., Adve, V.: LLVM language reference manual (2012) (last visit on March 27, 2012)
16. Li, G., Ghosh, I., Rajan, S.P.: KLOVER: A Symbolic Execution and Automatic Test Generation Tool for C++ Programs. In: Gopalakrishnan, G., Qadeer, S. (eds.) CAV 2011. LNCS, vol. 6806, pp. 609–615. Springer, Heidelberg (2011)
17. McMillan, K.L.: Lazy Annotation for Program Testing and Verification. In: Touili, T., Cook, B., Jackson, P. (eds.) CAV 2010. LNCS, vol. 6174, pp. 104–118. Springer, Heidelberg (2010)
18. Merz, F., Falke, S., Sinz, C.: LLBMC: Bounded model checking of C and C++ programs using a compiler IR. In: International Conference on Verified Software: Theories, Tools and Experiments, pp. 146–161 (2012)
19. Offutt, J., Voas, J.M.: Subsumption of condition coverage techniques by mutation testing. Technical Report ISSE-TR-96-01, George Mason University (1996)
20. Ramos, D.A., Engler, D.R.: Practical, Low-Effort Equivalence Verification of Real Code. In: Gopalakrishnan, G., Qadeer, S. (eds.) CAV 2011. LNCS, vol. 6806, pp. 669–685. Springer, Heidelberg (2011)
21. Reiter, R.: A theory of diagnosis from first principles. Artificial Intelligence 32(1), 57–95 (1987)
22. Riener, H., Bloem, R., Fey, G.: Test case generation from mutants using model checking techniques. In: IEEE International Conference on Software Testing, Verification, and Validation Workshops, pp. 388–397 (2011)
23. Riener, H., Fey, G.: Model-based diagnosis versus error explanation. In: International Conference on Formal Methods and Models for Codesign (to appear, 2012)
24. Rosen, B.K., Wegman, M.N., Zadeck, F.K.: Global value numbers and redundant computations. In: Symposium on Princples of Programming Languages, pp. 12–27 (1988)
25. Tseitin, G.S.: On the complexity of derivation in propotional calculus. In: Automation and Reasoning: Classical Papers in Computational Logic 1967-1970 (1983); Originally published in 1970

Model Checking DSL-Generated C Source Code

Martin Sulzmann and Axel Zechner

Informatik Consulting Systems AG, Germany
{martin.sulzmann,axel.zechner}@ics-ag.de

Abstract. We report on the application of SPIN for model-checking C source code which is generated out of a textual domain-specific language (DSL). We have built a tool which automatically generates the necessary SPIN wrapper code using (meta-)information available at the DSL level. The approach is part of a larger tool-chain for developing mission critical applications. The main purpose of SPIN is for bug-finding where error traces resulting from SPIN can be automatically replayed at the DSL level and yield concise explanations in terms of a temporal specification DSL. The tool-chain is applied in some large scale industrial applications.

1 Introduction

The SPIN model checker [4] supports the embedding of native C source code for verification purposes. This has the advantage that there is no need to re-model the application in the PROMELA modeling language and the potentially error-prone model-to-model transformation step from a source model to PROMELA can be avoided entirely. As discussed in [5], the method is the easiest to apply in the verification of single-threaded code, with well-defined input and output streams. Our interest here is in the verification of synchronously executed C source code which perfectly matches these criteria.

The C source code we intend to model check is generated out of a textual domain-specific language (DSL) which is part of a DSL-based tool-chain for software development of mission critical systems. Figure 1 provides a summary. Our focus so far was on implementation and testing. What has been missing is static verification. To close this gap, we have integrated SPIN in our tool chain to guarantee a smooth integration between SPIN for model-checking and our DSL-based software development approach. See Figure 2.

The important point is that all testing and verification steps are performed at the C source code level where the C source code is generated out of the DSL. Hence, there is no need to validate the transformation step from DSL to C source code. The purpose of the DSL is to support 'higher-level' application/domain abstractions which in our experience has significant advantages compared to 'low-level' programming at the C source code level.

In this paper, we provide an overview of the purpose of the DSLs and their integration with SPIN. The particular contribution is the SPINRunner tool which effectively represents the SPIN-DSL integration described in Figure 2. Further details of the SPINRunner tool, e.g. the implementation (DSLs and tools) as well as some example from the Automotive area, are freely available via

http://ww2.cs.mu.oz.au/~sulzmann/spin-dsls.html

A. Donaldson and D. Parker (Eds.): SPIN 2012, LNCS 7385, pp. 241–247, 2012.
© Springer-Verlag Berlin Heidelberg 2012

2   DSL Tool-Chain Overview

First, we review the various DSLs and their interaction in terms of implementation and testing. See Figure 1. For implementation we use a rule-based DSL in spirit of the Atom DSL [3] where in each cycle every rule is tried sequentially. Our DSL code generator translates each rule into straight-forward C code, in essence, simple if-then statements. Similar to SCADE [8], we generate a function `rules_init()` to initialize state variables and a periodically executed function `rules_process()`. All DSL variable declarations, e.g. input, output, state and local, are declared as global C variable declarations. Thus, we can ensure predictable memory consumption.

For testing, we use a DSL to specify use cases to stimulate the application. The stimulation is weaved together with the C code of the application and yields a test executable. Running the test executable yields a finite program trace which is then matched against a property DSL which describes linear temporal logic (LTL) [7] specifications. LTL trace matching yields a detailed test report based on the method described in [9].

The DSLs have been applied with success in some large scale industrial applications in the Aerospace& Defense area. An important feature is the ability to customize the DSLs to specific application needs. For example, we have built

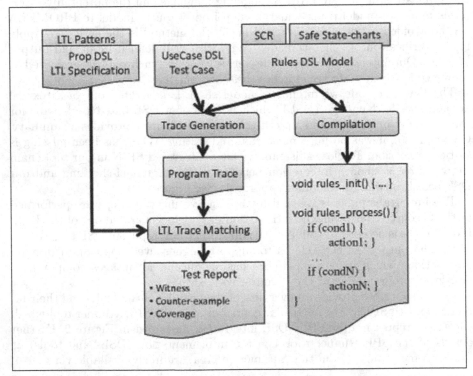

Fig. 1. DSL Tool-Chain Overview – Implementation and Testing

numerous extensions such as Software Cost Reduction (SCR) [2] style mode
and output tables, safe state-charts a la SCADE and new forms of LTL pattern
abstractions [1] etc. Such extensions can be fairly quickly integrated in our approach thanks to our use of *internal* DSLs. The advantage of an internal DSL is
that we can make use of the host language, in our case Haskell, to specify new
constructs as 'library' extensions. That is, at the Haskell level, new constructs
are mapped to existing constructs without having to implement new parsers,
code generators etc.

3   SPIN-DSL Integration

Figure 2 gives an overview of the SPIN-DSL integration. The C source code generated out of the rule-based DSL is literally embedded into a PROMELA model
which includes the LTL specification and a closed world model of the environment specified at the DSL level. The environment is represented by the input
variables of the DSL model. To obtain a closed world model, we must set these
inputs. For example, we can define equivalence classes among the set of input
variables to reduce the state space. We also provide for a number of optional
automatic optimizations by for example reducing the set of input variables to
those used in the currently checked LTL property. The entire process of generating the PROMELA model out of the DSLs and performing the model checking
is done automatically by the SPINRunner tool. That is, the user is freed from

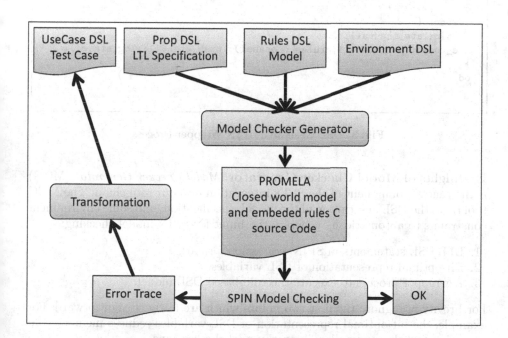

Fig. 2. SPIN-DSL Integration for Verification

any low-level model checker interaction and can focus on the high-level DSL modeling part.

In our experience, this approach works fairly well for medium-sized examples. For example, we can fully model check a realistic example taken from the Automotive domain. For many real-world applications, the state space is simply too big such that model checking would yield an answer within some reasonable amount of time. For us this is not a serious issue. Our main use of SPIN is for bug-finding rather than fully static verification. In our experience, model checking often reveals many simple but tedious to spot coding errors by producing error traces.

The error trace can then be used to reach the point in the application where the violation occurs. Additionally, we can provide explanations in terms of the LTL specification which has been violated. Our tool automatically transforms the SPIN error trace into a test case of the UseCase DSL. Thus, we stimulate the application to obtain a program trace which is then matched against the LTL specification. Our constructive LTL matching algorithm provides a detailed test report which includes explanations which parts of the LTL specification have been violated.

```
active process ModelWrapper(){
  atomic{
    c_code { rules_init(); push_state(); }
  }
  do
  ::atomic{
    stimulate_inputs();
    c_code { pop_state(); rules_process(); push_state(); log_state(); }
  }
  od
}
```

Fig. 3. DSL-Generated SPIN Wrapper Process

Highlights of Model Checker Generator. *Model Checker Generator* (MCG) is the central component of the SPIN integration into our tool-chain. The MCG tool takes the DSL description of the model, specification, and some environment constraints to automatically generate the input for SPIN model checking:

1. LTL DSL statements in SPIN expression format.
2. Bit-optimal representation of DSL variables.
3. A wrapper process to execute the rule-based DSL model.

For brevity, we ignore the first two points which are fairly straightforward. For example, the bit-optimal representation of DSL variables reduces memory consumption and thus may allow 'longer' model-checker runs.

Figure 3 shows the central components of the SPIN wrapper code to execute the DSL model (i.e. its C code representation). We first atomically initialize the DSL model by executing `rules_init()` followed by repeated non-deterministic atomic execution of `rules_process()`.

Functions `push_state()` and `pop_state()` exchange state information between SPIN and the C interface of our DSL model. We only need to keep track of DSL variables which represent state and global input and output. Any locally declared DSL variable can be ignored because such variables are functionally defined by the surrounding context.

Function `stimulate_inputs()` represents the environment model for closed-loop verification. We non-deterministically select global input values. To reduce the set of input combinations, and thus the state-space of model-checking, we build equivalence classes of input values (as discussed in [6]). The definition of equivalence classes can be specified at the DSL level and has the consequence that model-checking is potentially incomplete. That is, depending on the representative of the equivalence class, an actual violation of an LTL specification might remain undetected. As already mentioned, our main motivation for the integration of DSL is for bug-finding and the ability to replay error traces at the DSL level. Hence, the incompleteness issue is not of major concern for us.

The trace logger function `log_state()` is activated during simulation of SPIN error trails. This function transforms the internal representation of valuations of input, output and state variables to a format readable for the subsequent steps of our tool chain.

4   Industrial Case Study: Motor-Start Stop (MSA)

MSA is application is an example from the Automotive area whose purpose is depending on the state of the vehicle to either switch on or switch off the engine (e.g. to save fuel, if the vehicle is not moving).

MSA consists of nine input variables, e.g. measuring the speed, brake pressure etc. There are three output variables to indicate the status of the MSA (on/off), engine recommendation (on/off) and MSA LED status (on/off).

The entire application is formalized by nine LTL statements. Here is a fairly simple statement which states that the LED shall be set if the MSA is active.

```
always $
  (valueOut msaStatus .==. constE MSA_Active)
  .=>.
    (valueOut msaLed .==. constE On)
```

Our DSLs are implemented as *internal* DSLs which come come with a bit of syntactic overhead because we re-use the syntax of the host language. Extra combinators such as `valueOut` and `constE` are required to embed the DSL into Haskell. The significant advantage of internal DSLs is that we quickly build new DSL extensions as libraries.

The implementation of the MSA application makes use of SCR [2] style mode and output tables. These extensions are mapped to the simple `rule`'s construct

Table 1. Time / memory usage for different properties

List of SPIN options used for benchmark:
Option 1: depth first search   -DSFH -DBFS -DSAFETY
Option 2: safety with optimizations -DSAFETY -DSFH
Option 3: safety   -DSAFETY
Option 4: acceptance

	Option 1		Option 2		Option 3		Option 4	
	time [s]	[kbytes]	time [s]	[kbytes]	time [s]	[kbytes]	time [s]	[kbytes]
Engine_Off	34.900	1,690,020	24.400	345,713	27.200	345,713	60.300	689,036
Engine_On1	41.000	1,690,117	-	-	-	-	-	-
Engine_On1b	7.030	402,840	1.830	345,518	1.780	345,518	1.960	688,841
Engine_On2	3.370	116,062	0.340	345,518	0.420	345,518	1.400	688,841
LED_Off	1.940	116,062	0.340	345,518	0.617	345,518	0.895	688,841
LED_On	2.400	116,062	0.605	345,518	0.315	345,518	1.620	688,841
MSA_Active	43.200	1,690,117	22.100	345,616	30.500	345,616	41.300	688,939
MSA_Inactive1	42.900	1,690,117	13.000	345,518	10.800	345,518	25.200	688,841
MSA_Inactive2	1.900	116,062	0.245	345,518	0.240	345,518	0.615	688,841

which provides the basis of the Rules DSL. The entire MSA application boils down to about 67 primitive rules.

Table 1 shows some benchmark results for our MSA example. The Tables show model-checking time / memory usage for different LTL properties. We have applied the optimizations mentioned in the previous sections. The results are obtained on a Dell Latitude E5510, Intel Core i5 CPU 2.67 GHz, 4GB Main Memory running with Windows 7 32-Bit. To get comparable results SPIN was run in single CPU mode only.

Acknowledgments. We thank the reviewers for their comments.

References

1. Dwyer, M.B., Avrunin, G.S., Corbett, J.C.: Patterns in property specifications for finite-state verification. In: Proceedings of the 21st International Conference on Software Engineering, ICSE 1999, pp. 411–420. ACM, New York (1999)
2. Faulk, S.R., Heitmeyer, C.L.: The SCR approach to requirements specification and analysis. In: Proc. of Requirements Engineering (RE 1997), p. 263. IEEE Computer Society (1997)
3. Hawkins, T.: Atom DSL, http://hackage.haskell.org/package/atom/
4. Holzmann, G.: Spin model checker, the: primer and reference manual, 1st edn. Addison-Wesley Professional (2003)
5. Holzmann, G.J., Joshi, R.: Model-Driven Software Verification. In: Graf, S., Mounier, L. (eds.) SPIN 2004. LNCS, vol. 2989, pp. 76–91. Springer, Heidelberg (2004)
6. Richard Kuhn, D., Okun, V.: Pseudo-exhaustive testing for software. In: Proc. of 30th Annual IEEE / NASA Software Engineering Workshop (SEW-30 2006), pp. 153–158. IEEE (2006)

7. Pnueli, A.: The temporal logic of programs. In: 18th Annual Symposium on Foundations of Computer Science, pp. 46–57. IEEE (1977)
8. Scade suite, http://www.esterel-technologies.com/products/scade-suite/
9. Sulzmann, M., Zechner, A.: Constructive Finite Trace Analysis with Linear Temporal Logic. In: Brucker, A.D., Julliand, J. (eds.) TAP 2012. LNCS, vol. 7305, pp. 132–148. Springer, Heidelberg (2012)

SMTInterpol: An Interpolating SMT Solver

Jürgen Christ, Jochen Hoenicke, and Alexander Nutz*

Department of Computer Science,
University of Freiburg
{christj,hoenicke,nutz}@informatik.uni-freiburg.de

Abstract. Craig interpolation is an active research topic and has become a powerful technique in verification. We present SMTInterpol, an interpolating SMT solver for the quantifier-free fragment of the combination of the theory of uninterpreted functions and the theory of linear arithmetic over integers and reals. SMTInterpol is SMTLIB 2 compliant and available under an open source software license (LGPL v3).

1 Introduction

For many years, satisfiability modulo theories (SMT) solvers have been used by verification tools. Recently, many verification tools use Craig interpolants to create abstractions from state spaces or derive loop invariants. We present SMTInterpol, an SMT solver able to produce Craig interpolants for the quantifier-free fragment of the (combination of the) theories of uninterpreted functions, and linear arithmetic over integers and reals, i.e., the SMTLIB logics QF_UF, QF_LIA, QF_LRA, QF_UFLIA, and QF_UFLRA. It is SMTLIB 2 compliant, implemented in Java, and available under an open source license (LGPL v3) from its website http://ultimate.informatik.uni-freiburg.de/smtinterpol/. The solver is proof producing and can extract an unsatisfiable core, or inductive sequences of Craig interpolants [16] from its resolution proofs. Furthermore, interpolants for different partitions can be generated as needed for model checking of recursive programs [14].

SMTInterpol participated in the main and in the application track of the SMT-COMP 2011 [1], the annual competition for SMT solvers. In the logics QF_UFLIA and QF_UFLRA, SMTInterpol could solve as many problems as the winning solver. This shows that, while not (yet) as fast as other solvers, SMTInterpol provides decent performance.

Related Work. Other interpolating solvers that read SMTLIB are MathSAT [13], Princess [4], OpenSMT [5], and the interpolating version of Z3 [17]. OpenSMT does not support linear integer arithmetic. MathSAT, Princess, and interpolating Z3 (iZ3) are evaluated in Section 5.

---

* This work is supported by the German Research Council (DFG) as part of the Transregional Collaborative Research Center "Automatic Verification and Analysis of Complex Systems" (SFB/TR14 AVACS).

A. Donaldson and D. Parker (Eds.): SPIN 2012, LNCS 7385, pp. 248–254, 2012.
© Springer-Verlag Berlin Heidelberg 2012

Besides the tools mentioned above, there are other tools that do not read SMTLIB but are able to produce interpolants. Foci [15] can produce interpolants for the combination of uninterpreted functions (EUF) with linear real arithmetic (LRA) or integer difference logic, CSISat [3] supports the combination of EUF and LRA but is unsound for linear integer arithmetic (LIA). CLPProver [20] only supports the conjunctive fragment of EUF and LRA. In contrast to these three solvers, SMTInterpol supports the combination of EUF and LIA.

2   Architecture of SMTInterpol

In this section, we will shortly explain the different components of SMTInterpol and the techniques implemented by these components.

User Interaction. SMTInterpol supports the SMTLIB [2] script language and provides a Java API modeled after the commands of this language through its `Script` interface. Users can either give commands via an SMTLIB file or the standard input channel of the solver, or use the API.

CNF Conversion. Every asserted formula gets converted into *Conjunctive Normal Form* (CNF), which is a conjunction of disjunctions of literals. SMTInterpol uses a variant of the encoding proposed by Plaisted and Greenbaum [19] to convert a formula into CNF.

DPLL Core. SMTInterpol follows the DPLL($\mathcal{T}$) [12] paradigm. The DPLL engine serves as a truth enumerator and communicates with a set of satellite theories.

Satellite Theories. SMTInterpol currently contains two satellite solvers: one for uninterpreted functions and one for linear arithmetic. The solver for the theory of uninterpreted functions is based on congruence closure [9]. The solver for linear arithmetic implements a variant of simplex [11]. Additionally, it uses the "cuts from proofs" [10] technique to deal with integer or mixed integer problems. Theories are combined using model-based theory combination [18].

Models and Proofs. SMTInterpol can produce models for satisfiable formulas and resolution proofs for unsatisfiable formulas. From these proofs, SMTInterpol can extract unsatisfiable cores or Craig interpolants.

Interpolants. The architecture of the interpolation engine follows roughly the DPLL($\mathcal{T}$) paradigm: A *core interpolator* produces *partial interpolants* for the resolution steps while theory specific interpolators [15,6] produce partial interpolants for $\mathcal{T}$-lemmas. In the presence of *mixed literals*, i.e., literals that do not occur in any block of the interpolation problem, special *mixed literal interpolators* combine partial interpolants.

3   How to Use SMTInterpol

SMTInterpol is written in Java and runs on any computer with a recent Java installation. After downloading, it can be started from the command line with `java -jar smtinterpol.jar` and reads input in the SMTLIB [2] format. We refer to the SMTLIB tutorial [7] for more information on the standard and the logical foundations.

SMTInterpol also provides a Java API[1], which allows it to be integrated as a library inside other tools. The API reflects the commands provided by the SMTLIB standard, and it includes a minimal interface for the construction of terms and sorts. During term construction SMTInterpol checks for well-typedness and reports type errors.

4   Interpolation for SMTLIB Logics

Given a pair (ϕ_1, ϕ_2) of formulas such that $\phi_1 \wedge \phi_2$ is unsatisfiable, a *Craig interpolant* [8] is a formula ψ that (1) is implied by ϕ_1, (2) is inconsistent with ϕ_2, and (3) only contains symbols shared between ϕ_1 and ϕ_2. Given a sequence of formulas $\phi_1, \ldots, \phi_n$, an *inductive sequence of interpolants* (in the sense of McMillan [16]) is a sequence of formulas $\psi_0, \ldots, \psi_n$ such that (1) $\psi_0 \equiv \top$, (2) $\psi_n \equiv \bot$, (3) $\psi_{i-1} \wedge \phi_i$ implies ψ_i for $0 < i \leq n$, and (4) ψ_i for $0 < i < n$ contains only symbols shared between the first i formulas and the remaining $n - i$ formulas.

SMTInterpol produces inductive sequences of interpolants for the SMTLIB logics QF_UF, QF_LRA, QF_UFLRA, QF_LIA, and QF_UFLIA. Since the integer logics defined in the SMTLIB standard are not closed under interpolation, SMTInterpol extends these logics with the division and modulo operators with constant divisor. With these two additional operators it is possible to express the floor and ceil operators used in other interpolation algorithms [13].

To support interpolation, SMTInterpol extends the SMTLIB standard with the `get-interpolants` command. This command expects as parameters at least two names of named top-level formulas, i.e., formulas that were asserted using the command `(assert (! formula :named Name))`, or the conjunction of such names. If more than two parameters are supplied, an inductive sequence of interpolants is computed. The command can be used after a satisfiability check returned *unsat* and before a `pop` command changed the assertion stack of the solver. Interpolant computation can be redone with a different partition by calling `get-interpolants` again with different arguments. This is needed, e.g., to compute nested interpolants for recursive programs [14]. Since SMTInterpol extracts interpolants from proofs, users have to set the option `:produce-proofs` to *true* to enable interpolant computation.

Figure 1 shows how to compute interpolants with SMTInterpol. The left-hand side of the figure shows the API usage and the right-hand side shows the corresponding SMTLIB 2 commands. The example asserts the formula $x > y \wedge x = 0 \wedge y > 0$, checks satisfiability, computes an inductive sequence of interpolants between the individual conjuncts, and an interpolant between $x = 0$ and $x > y \wedge y > 0$.

---

[1] The documentation for the Java API is available at the website.

```
Script s = new SMTInterpol(Logger.getRootLogger(), true);
s.setOption(":produce-proofs", true);                          (set-option :produce-proofs true)
s.setLogic(Logics.QF_LIA);                                     (set-logic QF_LIA)
s.declareFun("x", new Sort[0], s.sort("Int"));                 (declare-fun x () Int)
s.declareFun("y", new Sort[0], s.sort("Int"));                 (declare-fun y () Int)
s.assertTerm(s.annotate(                                       (assert (!
  s.term(">",s.term("x"), s.term("y")),                          (> x y)
  new Annotation(":named", "phi_1")));                           :named phi_1))
s.assertTerm(s.annotate(                                       (assert (!
  s.term("=", s.term("x"), s.numeral("0")),                      (= x 0)
    new Annotation(":named", "phi_2")));                         :named phi_2))
s.assertTerm(s.annotate(                                       (assert (!
  s.term(">", s.term("y"), s.numeral("0")),                      (> y 0)
    new Annotation(":named", "phi_3")));                         :named phi_3))
if (s.checkSat() == UNSAT) {                                   (check-sat)
  Term[] interpolants;
  interpolants = s.getInterpolants(new Term[] {                (get-interpolants
    s.term("phi_1"),                                             phi_1
    s.term("phi_2"),                                             phi_2
    s.term("phi_3") } );                                         phi_3)
  ... /* Do something ... */
  interpolants = s.getInterpolants(new Term[] {                (get-interpolants
    s.term("phi_2"),                                             phi_2
    s.term("and", s.term("phi_1"), s.term("phi_3"))             (and phi_1 phi_3))
    } );
  ... /* Do something ... */
}
```

Fig. 1. Two different ways to compute Craig interpolants using SMTInterpol. The left-hand side shows the Java code using the `Script` interface. The right-hand side shows the corresponding SMTLIB script.

The interpolation procedure for mixed literals (literals containing symbols of more than one interpolation block) is loosely based on the method of Yorsh et al [21]. The basic idea of the approach used in SMTInterpol is to virtually purify each mixed literal using an auxiliary variable, to restrict the places where the variable may occur in partial interpolants, and to use special resolution rules to eliminate the variable when the mixed literal is used as a pivot. In essence, for convex theories, this approach can be seen as a lazy version of the method of Yorsh et al. The approach also works for non-convex theories using disjunctions in the interpolants. The technical details are yet to be published and out of the scope of this paper.

5   Experiments

SMTInterpol participated in the SMT-COMP [1] 2011, the annual competition for SMT solvers. While SMTInterpol is not yet as good as the state-of-the-art solvers Z3 and MathSAT, it can still solve most of the problems in the competition. We compared the interpolation engine in SMTInterpol to MathSAT [13] and interpolating Z3 on a set of benchmarks provided by McMillan [17]. The original benchmark set was converted to SMTLIB 2 format. We did not consider non-SMTLIB solvers. Table 1 compares the runtime of SMTInterpol, MathSAT, and iZ3 on a standard laptop[2]. We restricted the comparison to these solvers

---

[2] Running a 64-bit Linux on an Intel Core2 Duo 2.4GHz with 4 GB of RAM.

Table 1. Comparison between SMTInterpol, MathSAT, and interpolating Z3 (iZ3) on the benchmark suite from McMillan [17], and some small benchmarks. (ok) denotes that the solver produced a quantified interpolant, NA denotes that the solver does not support the logic used in this benchmark.

	SMTInterpol		MathSAT	iZ3
	Solving	Interpol.		
fdc_1	28.61 s	0.13 s	17.53 s	4.79 s
fdc_2	34.26 s	0.11 s	14.01 s	3.72 s
fdc_3	34.87 s	0.10 s	15.53 s	4.28 s
mouserA_1	2.63 s	0.04 s	0.54 s	0.16 s
mouserA_2	2.97 s	0.02 s	0.92 s	0.27 s
mouserA_3	4.89 s	0.02 s	0.79 s	0.28 s
mouserB_1	105.33 s	0.15 s	104.58 s	12.20 s
mouserB_2	92.28 s	0.08 s	59.41 s	16.63 s
mouserB_3	103.32 s	0.20 s	64.35 s	17.68 s
ndisprot_1	5.75 s	0.20 s	1.34 s	0.50 s
ndisprot_2	29.84 s	2.72 s	error	6.68 s
serial_1	32.03 s	0.01 s	7.41 s	3.72 s
serial_2	27.23 s	0.02 s	6.41 s	2.47 s
wmm_1	1.45 s	0.03 s	0.26 s	0.21 s

	SMT-Interpol	Math-SAT	iZ3	Princess
uf001	ok	ok	ok	ok
uf002	ok	ok	ok	(ok)
lia001	ok	NA	ok	(ok)
uflia001	ok	NA	ok	(ok)
uflia002	ok	NA	ok	(ok)
uflia003	ok	NA	ok	(ok)
uflia004	ok	NA	ok	(ok)
uflra001	ok	NA	NA	NA
uflra002	ok	NA	NA	NA
uflra003	ok	NA	NA	NA

since they were used in the original paper, and are, to our knowledge, the only solvers that can handle these benchmarks. While Princess supports QF_UFLIA, it crashes with a stack overflow on these benchmarks. For SMTInterpol we distinguish between the time for solving and the time for interpolation. While SMTInterpol is not as fast as the other two solvers, it can produce interpolants for all these problems while MathSAT produces an error on ndisprot_2. The example also shows that computing interpolants is usually much faster than solving, which is consistent with McMillan's observation [17].

Additionally, some small benchmarks for the interpolation of reals, integers, and uninterpreted functions are published at the website of SMTInterpol. OpenSMT, FOCI, CLPProver, and CSISat do not support most of the theories used in these benchmarks, MathSAT does not fully support interpolation for linear arithmetic, interpolating Z3 and Princess do not support linear real arithmetic benchmarks, while SMTInterpol is able to produce interpolants for all of them.

6 Future Work

We plan to extend the solver to more expressive logics containing quantifiers and arrays. Additionally, the computation of nested interpolants [14] should be directly supported by a modified version of the `get-interpolants` command.

7 Conclusion

We have presented SMTInterpol, an interpolating SMT solver that is complete for the combination of the theories of uninterpreted functions and linear arithmetic. Thus, SMTInterpol can produce interpolants in some theory combinations not supported by any other solver. Since SMTInterpol is shipped under LGPL v3 and is written in a platform independent language, it is ideal to be integrated into model checkers.

References

1. Barrett, C.W., de Moura, L., Stump, A.: SMT-COMP: Satisfiability Modulo Theories Competition. In: Etessami, K., Rajamani, S.K. (eds.) CAV 2005. LNCS, vol. 3576, pp. 20–23. Springer, Heidelberg (2005)
2. Barrett, C., Stump, A., Tinelli, C.: The SMT-LIB Standard: 2.0. In: SMT (2010)
3. Beyer, D., Zufferey, D., Majumdar, R.: cSIsat: Interpolation for LA+EUF. In: Gupta, A., Malik, S. (eds.) CAV 2008. LNCS, vol. 5123, pp. 304–308. Springer, Heidelberg (2008)
4. Brillout, A., Kroening, D., Rümmer, P., Wahl, T.: An Interpolating Sequent Calculus for Quantifier-Free Presburger Arithmetic. In: Giesl, J., Hähnle, R. (eds.) IJCAR 2010. LNCS, vol. 6173, pp. 384–399. Springer, Heidelberg (2010)
5. Bruttomesso, R., Pek, E., Sharygina, N., Tsitovich, A.: The OpenSMT Solver. In: Esparza, J., Majumdar, R. (eds.) TACAS 2010. LNCS, vol. 6015, pp. 150–153. Springer, Heidelberg (2010)
6. Cimatti, A., Griggio, A., Sebastiani, R.: Efficient Interpolant Generation in Satisfiability Modulo Theories. In: Ramakrishnan, C.R., Rehof, J. (eds.) TACAS 2008. LNCS, vol. 4963, pp. 397–412. Springer, Heidelberg (2008)
7. Cok, D.R.: jSMTLIB: Tutorial, validation and adapter tools for SMT-LIBv2. In: NASA Formal Methods, pp. 480–486 (2011)
8. Craig, W.: Three uses of the Herbrand-Gentzen theorem in relating model theory and proof theory. J. Symb. Log. 22(3), 269–285 (1957)
9. Detlefs, D., Nelson, G., Saxe, J.B.: Simplify: a theorem prover for program checking. J. ACM 52(3), 365–473 (2005)
10. Dillig, I., Dillig, T., Aiken, A.: Cuts from Proofs: A Complete and Practical Technique for Solving Linear Inequalities over Integers. In: Bouajjani, A., Maler, O. (eds.) CAV 2009. LNCS, vol. 5643, pp. 233–247. Springer, Heidelberg (2009)
11. Dutertre, B., de Moura, L.: A Fast Linear-Arithmetic Solver for DPLL(T). In: Ball, T., Jones, R.B. (eds.) CAV 2006. LNCS, vol. 4144, pp. 81–94. Springer, Heidelberg (2006)
12. Ganzinger, H., Hagen, G., Nieuwenhuis, R., Oliveras, A., Tinelli, C.: DPLL(T): Fast Decision Procedures. In: Alur, R., Peled, D.A. (eds.) CAV 2004. LNCS, vol. 3114, pp. 175–188. Springer, Heidelberg (2004)
13. Griggio, A., Le, T.T.H., Sebastiani, R.: Efficient Interpolant Generation in Satisfiability Modulo Linear Integer Arithmetic. In: Abdulla, P.A., Leino, K.R.M. (eds.) TACAS 2011. LNCS, vol. 6605, pp. 143–157. Springer, Heidelberg (2011)
14. Heizmann, M., Hoenicke, J., Podelski, A.: Nested interpolants. In: POPL (2010)
15. McMillan, K.L.: An Interpolating Theorem Prover. In: Jensen, K., Podelski, A. (eds.) TACAS 2004. LNCS, vol. 2988, pp. 16–30. Springer, Heidelberg (2004)

16. McMillan, K.L.: Lazy Abstraction with Interpolants. In: Ball, T., Jones, R.B. (eds.) CAV 2006. LNCS, vol. 4144, pp. 123–136. Springer, Heidelberg (2006)
17. McMillan, K.L.: Interpolants from Z3 proofs. In: FMCAD (2012)
18. de Moura, L., Bjørner, N.: Model-based theory combination. Electr. Notes Theor. Comput. Sci. 198(2), 37–49 (2008)
19. Plaisted, D.A., Greenbaum, S.: A structure-preserving clause form translation. J. Symb. Comput. 2(3), 293–304 (1986)
20. Rybalchenko, A., Sofronie-Stokkermans, V.: Constraint Solving for Interpolation. In: Cook, B., Podelski, A. (eds.) VMCAI 2007. LNCS, vol. 4349, pp. 346–362. Springer, Heidelberg (2007)
21. Yorsh, G., Musuvathi, M.: A Combination Method for Generating Interpolants. In: Nieuwenhuis, R. (ed.) CADE 2005. LNCS (LNAI), vol. 3632, pp. 353–368. Springer, Heidelberg (2005)

S2N: Model Transformation from SPIN to NuSMV*
(Tool Paper)

Yong Jiang and Zongyan Qiu

School of Mathematical Sciences, Peking University, Beijing 100871, China
yongjiang043@gmail.com, qzy@math.pku.edu.cn

Abstract. SPIN and NuSMV are the two most widely-used model checkers. Because they have different characters, it makes sense to have a translator from SPIN models to NuSMV models. In this paper we describe a tool named S2N which builds a bridge from SPIN to NuSMV. With S2N users could choose the appropriate ways as needed to build and check their models. This work can also be thought as a study on the model transformation.

Keywords: Model checking, SPIN, NuSMV, S2N.

1 Introduction

Model checking [1] is an important verification method. People have developed many model checkers, including the widely-used SPIN and NuSMV. SPIN [2] provides a higher-level modeling language Promela with C-like syntax, that makes the models easy to build and read. NuSMV [3] provides a relative lower language for describing state transition systems. On the other hand, SPIN supports only LTL to describe properties, while NuSMV can check LTL properties, as well as CTL properties.

SPIN and NuSMV are impressive and successful in their respective fields. Making their advantage merged would be helpful for modeling to some extent. Here we present a tool S2N which can translate models in Promela to the language of NuSMV. In this case we get various benefits. On one side, modeling complicated systems in NuSMV is hard and error-prone, but with S2N we could have a higher-level language for the work. On the other side, S2N works as it extends SPIN system with the ability to check CTL and other properties NuSMV supports. [4] reported a similar idea, but the project seems abandoned without producing a workable tool. Now we have a preliminary version of S2N whose homepage is located at http://code.google.com/p/s2n. With S2N, SPIN 6.1.0 and NuSMV 2.5.4, we have carried out some experiments, which indicate that for some problems SPIN is more efficient, but sometimes NuSMV works better. The link between the two checkers appears meaningful. Due to the space, we leave more details in a report on the S2N's homepage.

2 Translation Techniques

Assume the Promela program being translated is S. S2N generates from S a program N which should be acceptable as the input of NuSMV. In Promela, processes are the

* Supported by NNSFC grand no. 90718002,61100061.

A. Donaldson and D. Parker (Eds.): SPIN 2012, LNCS 7385, pp. 255–260, 2012.

running instances of proctypes; on the other hand, in the input language of NuSMV, a process is an instance of a module generated with the keyword 'process'. When S2N translates S to N, it translates a proctype in S to a module in N.

In some detail, for each proctype in S, we use distinct integers to mark each of the statements. In the corresponding module in N, we introduce a variable pc and let its value run over these mark integers. Other variables in the module will be modified according to the current value of pc. The key is to guarantee that the changing history of pc is consistent with the flow of S. Moreover, S2N generates some extra modules to simulate channels in Promela. For each channel type in S, S2N generates a module, and the channel IO will be made as the state transition of the instances of these channel modules.

As a result, what S2N produces is a set of nested modules, one of which is the main module. Each module consists of three parts sequentially: the variable declarations, the initialization and transition, and the constraint expression:

```
MODULE name
  VAR
    ...            -- variable declarations of this module
    pc : ...       -- program counter of associated process
  ASSIGN
    init(...) := ...
    ...            -- initialization of variables in this module
    next(...) := ...
    ...            -- transition of variables
  TRANS
    ...            -- constraints about pc and scheduling
```

2.1 Marking

A process in a Promela program could be thought as an independent state transition system, so we mark each proctype in the program independently. In a proctype, we mark each of the elementary statements, including assignments, expressions, channel IOs, goto statements and break statements. And for the nondeterminism, we also mark if-selection and do-repetition statements.

Here is a simple proctype with marks, in which we use identifiers of the form "M+$mark$" to represent marks and use a '@' sign to separate them from statements.

```
mtype = {p1, p2, p3};
chan queue = [3]of{mtype};
active proctype enqueue ()
{
    mtype ele;
    M1   @ do
          :: M2   @ if
                    :: M3   @ ele = p1;
                    :: M4   @ ele = p2;
                    :: M5   @ ele = p3;
                   fi;
```

```
        M6   @ queue ! ele;
    od;
}
```

The statements will be represented by their marks during the translation. For the example above, given that pc is 3 in the current state, we know that the next statement to execute in this process will be "*ele* = *p1*". According to the type of this statement, S2N knows how to perform the next transition.

2.2 Variable Declaration

We translate all the global variables in the Promela program to variables in the main module of the resulting NuSMV program, and the local variables in Promela proctypes to variables in the corresponding modules. Each NuSMV module produced from a proctype will have its own variable pc.

For the data types, bit and bool in Promela are translated to boolean type in NuSMV; mtype is naturally translated to enumeration type; pid, byte, short, int and unsigned are all translated to signed word type with 32 bits. Channel variables are translated to instances of some module standing for the channel type.

There are some constraints about types in S2N. Boolean and enumeration type are isolated with other types, thus boolean or enumeration variables can be operated only with variables of the same type.

2.3 Initialization and Transition

At the first state all the variables should be initialized. The state transition happens only on the assignments and channel IOs, while the other statements have no effect on variables. Every transition has at least one condition, which says that variable pc should be equal to the mark of the corresponding statement.

As the example above, part of the translation involving variable ele will be

```
init(ele) := p1;
next(ele) := case
                pc = 3 : p1;
                pc = 4 : p2;
                pc = 5 : p3;
                ...
             esac;
```

2.4 Constraint Expression

The constraint expression usually has the form as follows:

```
(  running & (
     pc = ... & ... & next(pc) = ...
   ...
   | pc = ... & ... & next(pc) = ...
```

```
      )
   | !running & next(pc) = pc
   )                        -- constraint of program counter
& (  pc = ... & ...
   |  pc = ... & ...
   ...
   ) -> running
& (  pc = ... & ...
   |  pc = ... & ...
   ...
   ) -> !running           -- constraint of scheduling
```

This expression is a conjunction of three literals. The first branch defines the transition of variable pc while the rest is for scheduling. The transition rules for pc are built based on the flow of the Promela program. When the current module is blocked, the value of pc doesn't change. For atomic sequences in SPIN , the output module should keep running among the sequences as atomic steps. On contrary, modules should not be scheduled to run in some cases, like when the current statement is not executable.

3 Tool and Experiments

In this section, we give some details of the tool, especially the features of SPIN that are currently supported. After that, we discuss some experiments and results.

3.1 Features Supported

Currently S2N has supported large part of the most important features of Promela. It translates one proctype at a time, so the complexity of translation is linear to the number of proctypes in the SPIN model. Features as follows are supported by current version.

Types and Variables. S2N supports all data types in Promela. Channels can be either global or local, but they could not be passed as parameters or message data in other channels. In other words, users of S2N should declare channels with initialization and only use them to send and receive message. S2N supports rendezvous communication.

Expressions. S2N supports the common boolean and arithmetic operations, const, variable reference, and operations about channels including empty, nempty, full, nfull, len. S2N also supports dynamic processes launched by run command.

Statements. S2N supports assignment, standard channel IO, expression, break, goto, skip, as well as flow controlling including selection, repetition, sequence, labeling, atomic, and unless. It also supports weak d_step, which has the same affect with atomic except that it can't escape from the sequence of d_step in unless.

Others. S2N supports C-style macros and init, while typedef, inline and _pid are not supported yet. The array indexes must be numeric constants, which is a severe limitation, and we will try to remove this shortage in the future. S2N does not support translation of the property claims yet, so users should add manually their properties to the NuSMV model.

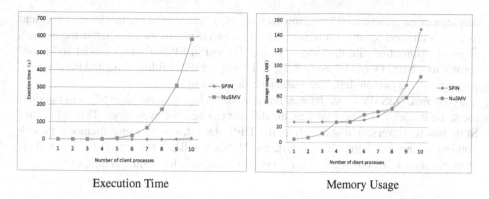

Execution Time   Memory Usage

Fig. 1. Execution with different numbers of clients in Sleep-Wakeup Process Scheduling

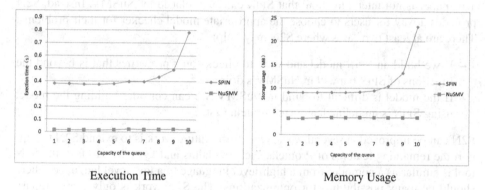

Execution Time   Memory Usage

Fig. 2. Execution with different capacities in Queue

3.2 Experiments

We have done many experiments. Here we give two examples with statistic data to show the usage and features of S2N. We take the examples from existing SPIN work.

Sleep-Wakeup Process Scheduling. This algorithm was proposed by Ruane [5]. In one implementation [6] which we use here, several client processes compete for some resource, and one server takes responsibility for waking up asleep processes when the resource is available. We transform the model written in Premela to a NuSMV model, and check the property that the resource is accessed by at most one process all the time. The statistics are depicted in Fig. 1.

In this example, SPIN model runs faster than NuSMV model from seven clients onwards, and the memory usage of NuSMV increases slower than SPIN from eight clients onwards. This is probably because of SPIN's on-the-fly and partial order reduction strategy, and NuSMV stores states with BDD trading memory use for time. It shows that for small models, NuSMV model transformed from S2N could work as well as SPIN .

Queue. Queue is a widely used data structure. To model a queue with some fixed capacity, it is not easy using NuSMV since we have to consider the move of elements after dequeue or enqueue operations. However, using SPIN to write the model is convenient as SPIN's channel feature. Moreover, with the C-style macro we can change the queue's capacity without rebuild the model. We implement in SPIN a queue model and transform it to a NuSMV model using S2N, and compare the building time and the memory usage for these two models. The results are depicted in Fig. 2.

As shown, NuSMV is much faster and consumes less memory than SPIN in building the same model. For bigger queues, the differences become even large. This is because SPIN has to traverse the states, thus the DFS stack takes up more memory, though nothing is checked here. By contrast, the NuSMV's BDD reduces the storage. This example shows that our strategy for translating channels to module is efficient.

4 Conclusion and Future Work

This paper is not intend to entail that SPIN can be replaced by NuSMV. Instead, S2N provides a way for users to choose the appropriate model checker for their problems. There are at least two cases where S2N may help:

- If we build an SPIN model and want to check some properties that is beyond the functions of SPIN but within NuSMV's domain.
- If the model is difficult to build in NuSMV, we can consider building the model using SPIN 's modeling language Promela first.

S2N can be improved in several ways. One of the future work is to extend S2N to support the remaining features of Promela, such as claims and typedef. In fact, the S2N tool is similar as a compiler from a high-level language to a low-level language. There should be many possibilities for optimizations. The S2N work is only a preliminary attempt in this direction. There is a lot of work to do on exploring the language design and implementation techniques for the formal modeling, because this field is much unmature in comparison with the filed of practical programming.

References

1. Merz, S.: Model Checking: A Tutorial Overview. In: Cassez, F., Jard, C., Rozoy, B., Dermot, M. (eds.) MOVEP 2000. LNCS, vol. 2067, pp. 3–38. Springer, Heidelberg (2001)
2. Holzmann, G.J.: The SPIN model checker: Primer and reference manual. Addison-Wesley (2004)
3. NuSMV tutorial, http://nusmv.fbk.eu/NuSMV/tutorial/index.html
4. Baldamus, M., Schröder-Babo, J.: p2b: A Translation Utility for Linking Promela and Symbolic Model Checking (Tool Paper). In: Dwyer, M.B. (ed.) SPIN 2001. LNCS, vol. 2057, pp. 183–191. Springer, Heidelberg (2001)
5. Ruane, L.M.: Process synchronization in the UTS kernel. Computing systems 3(3), 387–421 (1990)
6. Bang, K.-S., Choi, J.-Y., Yoo, C.: Comments on "The model checker SPIN". IEEE Transactions on Software Engineering 27(6), 573–576 (2001)

Author Index